Karl Marx and Contemporary Philosophy

Also by Andrew Chitty

HAS HISTORY ENDED? FUKUYAMA, MARX, MODERNITY
(*co-editor with Christopher Bertram, 1994*)

Karl Marx and
Contemporary Philosophy

Edited by

Andrew Chitty
University of Sussex

Martin McIvor

palgrave
macmillan

2009

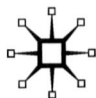

First published 2009 by
PALGRAVE MACMILLAN

Palgrave Macmillan in the UK is an imprint of Macmillan Publishers Limited,
registered in England, company number 785998, of Houndmills, Basingstoke,
Hampshire RG21 6XS.

Palgrave Macmillan in the US is a division of St Martin's Press LLC,
175 Fifth Avenue, New York, NY 10010.

Palgrave Macmillan is the global academic imprint of the above companies
and has companies and representatives throughout the world.

Palgrave® and Macmillan® are registered trademarks in the United States,
the United Kingdom, Europe and other countries.

ISBN-13: 978-0-230-22237-3   hardback
ISBN-10: 0-230-22237-4   hardback

This book is printed on paper suitable for recycling and made from fully
managed and sustained forest sources. Logging, pulping and manufacturing
processes are expected to conform to the environmental regulations of the
country of origin.

A catalogue record for this book is available from the British Library.

A catalog record for this book is available from the Library of Congress.

10 9 8 7 6 5 4 3 2 1
18 17 16 15 14 13 12 11 10 09

Printed and bound in Great Britain by
CPI Antony Rowe, Chippenham and Eastbourne

This book is dedicated to the memory of
Joe McCarney, 1941–2007

Table of Contents

Notes on Contributors

Christopher J. Arthur formerly taught philosophy in the School of Social Sciences at the University of Sussex, England. He is the author of *Dialectics of Labour* (Basil Blackwell, 1986) and *The New Dialectic and Marx's 'Capital'* (Brill, 2002). He has published also the following books: edited and introduced *The German Ideology* by Marx and Engels (Lawrence & Wishart, 1970), edited and introduced *Law and Marxism* by E. B. Pashukanis (Inklinks, 1978), abridged and introduced *Marx's Capital: A Student Edition* (Lawrence & Wishart, 1992), edited and introduced *Engels Today: A Centenary Appreciation* (Macmillan, 1996), edited and introduced (with G. Reuten) *The Circulation of Capital: Essays on Volume Two of Marx's 'Capital'* (Macmillan, 1998).

Terrell Carver is Professor of Political Theory at the University of Bristol. He has published extensively on Marx and Engels and their relationship to contemporary social theory. His most recent book in this area is *The Postmodern Marx* (Manchester University Press, 1998). Currently he is working on a new translation of the 'main manuscript' from which the opening chapter of *The German Ideology* was constructed.

Andrew Chitty is a Lecturer in Philosophy at the University of Sussex, where he teaches the UK's only Masters course in Marx's philosophy. He is co-editor of *Has History Ended? Fukuyama, Marx, Modernity* (Avebury Press, 1994) and has written widely on Hegel and Marx. He was a founding organiser of the Marx and Philosophy Society.

Andrew Collier is a Professor of Philosophy at Southampton University, where he has lectured for 18 years. He is also a founder member and trustee of the Centre for Critical Realism. His recently published books include *Christianity and Marxism* (Routledge, 2001), *In Defence of Objectivity* (Routledge, 2003) and *Marx* (Oneworld, 2004).

Georgios Daremas is a Senior Lecturer in the Communications Department of the University of Indianapolis, Athens campus. He has published articles on Marx, Hegel, the Frankfurt school, communication theory and the epistemology of social sciences.

Robert Fine is Professor of Sociology at the University of Warwick. His most recent work is *Cosmopolitanism* (Routledge, 2007). His other books include *Political Investigations: Hegel, Marx, Arendt* (Routledge, 2001) and *Democracy and the Rule of Law: Marx's Critique of the Legal Form* (Blackburn, 2003). He has been doing research on *Humanitarian military intervention* (ESRC) and currently on *Antisemitism in France and the UK* (Ford Foundation). His ongoing and somewhat esoteric concern is with the relation of critical social theory to the natural law tradition.

John Grant has a Ph.D. in political theory from Queen Mary, University of London. He has a number of journal articles forthcoming, including 'Foucault and the Logic of Dialectics' (*Contemporary Political Theory*) and 'Marcuse Remade? Theory and Explanation in Hardt and Negri' (*Science & Society*). His research interests include critical theory, conceptual frameworks of political criticism, with specific emphasis on the dialectical tradition, and the role of citizen engagement in policy making.

Gillian Howie is a Senior Lecturer in Philosophy at the University of Liverpool. Her recent publications include *Aura of Expressionism* (Palgrave Macmillan, 2002) and 'Natural Kinds in Feminist Theory: Essentialism Revisited' (*Contemporary Political Theory*, 2006). She is founding director of the Institute for Feminist Theory and as part of the IFTR series has co-edited *Gender, Teaching and Research in Higher Education* (Ashgate, 2001), *Third Wave Feminism* (2nd edn Palgrave Macmillan, 2007), *Menstruation* (Palgrave Macmillan, 2005), *Women and the Divine: Feminism and Transcendence* (Palgrave Macmillan, 2008). She is currently working on *Essentialism Revisited: Feminism, Materialism and Marxism* (Palgrave Macmillan, 2009).

Joseph McCarney taught Philosophy at London South Bank University from 1969 to 2000. He was the author of numerous articles on Marx and Marxist thought, and of three books: *The Real World of Ideology* (Harvester, 1980); *Social Theory and the Crisis of Marxism* (Verso, 1990) and *Hegel on History* (Routledge, 2000). He was working on the Hegel–Marx relationship when he died tragically in a car accident in August 2007.

Martin McIvor has a Ph.D. in political theory from the London School of Economics, where he taught history of political thought. He is an organiser of the Marx and Philosophy Society and a longstanding editor of the journal *Historical Materialism: Research in Critical Marxist Theory*. He writes on a range of topics in philosophy, politics and public policy including work published or forthcoming in the *Journal of the History of Philosophy, Imprints, Soundings* and *The Lancet*. He is currently working as a trade union researcher.

Scott Meikle is Senior Research Fellow in Philosophy in the University of Glasgow. He was educated at Salesian College, London, and at Bristol and Oxford Universities. He is the author of *Essentialism in the Thought of Karl Marx* (Duckworth, 1985) and *Aristotle's Economic Thought* (Clarendon Press, 1995) and the editor of *Marx*, International Library of Critical Essays in the History of Philosophy (Ashgate, 2000).

Patrick Murray is Professor of Philosophy at Creighton University in Omaha, Nebraska, USA. He is the author of Marx's *Theory of Scientific Knowledge* (Humanities Press, 1988) and editor of *Reflections on Commercial Life: Classic*

Texts from Plato to the Present (Routledge, 1997). He is a member of the International Symposium on Marxian Theory (ISMT) and has contributed to all the ISMT books. He is a member of the editorial advisory boards of *Historical Materialism* and *Critique of Political Economy*.

Moishe Postone is Professor of History at the University of Chicago. His publications include *Time, Labor and Social Domination: A Reinterpretation of Marx's Critical Theory* (Cambridge University Press, 1993); *Marx est-il devenu muet face à la mondialisation?* (Les Éditions de l'Aube, 2003); and *Marx Reloaded: Repensar la teoria critica del capitalismo*, edited by Alberto Riesco and Jorge Garcia Lopez (Traficantes de Suenos, 2007); and 'Critique and historical transformation', *Historical Materialism* 12 (3), 2004.

William Clare Roberts teaches philosophy and political science at McGill University. His research focuses on the intersections between the history of political economy and the history of political and ethical philosophy, with special attention to Marx and Aristotle. He is author of 'The Origin of Political Economy and the Descent of Marx', in *Marx, Critical Theory, and Religion: A Critique of Rational Choice*, edited by Warren S. Goldstein (Brill, 2006), and 'Marx Contra the Democrats: The Force of *The Eighteenth Brumaire*', *Strategies: Journal of Theory, Culture & Politics*, 2003.

Sean Sayers is Professor of Philosophy at the University of Kent, Canterbury. He has written extensively on topics of Hegelian and Marxist philosophy from a Hegelian-Marxist perspective. His books *include Plato's Republic: An Introduction* (Edinburgh University Press, 1999); *Marxism and Human Nature* (Routledge, 1998); *Reality and Reason: Dialectic and the Theory of Knowledge* (Blackwell, 1985); and *Hegel, Marx and Dialectic: A Debate* (1980, reprinted Gregg 1994). He has also co-edited *Socialism, Feminism and Philosophy: A Radical Philosophy Reader* (Routledge, 1991); *Socialism and Democracy* (Macmillan, 1991); and *Socialism and Morality* (Macmillan, 1990). He was one of the founding editors of *Radical Philosophy*, and a founder of the Marx and Philosophy Society.

Roberto Veneziani is a lecturer in Economics at Queen Mary, University of London. He has published numerous articles on Marxism and analytical Marxism in various economics and philosophy journals including in the *Journal of Economic Theory, Philosophy of the Social Sciences, Metroeconomica*, and the *Review of Radical Political Economics*. He has also published a number of contributions on justice and equality of opportunity including in the *Journal of Public Economic Theory* and *Social Choice and Welfare*. He is one of the founders and organisers of the Analytical Political Economy Workshops.

Introduction

Andrew Chitty and Martin McIvor

Around the turn of the twenty-first century, ten years after the fall of Soviet communism and what many viewed as a conclusive intellectual and historical victory for liberal democratic capitalism, observers in various quarters began to register a new wave of popular interest in the ideas and arguments of Karl Marx. New questions were being asked about the atomised and anomic experience of living amid the consumer culture of advanced 'market societies', and about the deeper social conflicts and increasingly global systemic risks that they were generating. Liberated from the factional and institutional interests that had hitherto decisively shaped the dissemination and reception of his writings, Marx began to stand out as a thinker who had sought to confront and interrogate the emerging social transformations of his time – transformations that had decisively shaped subsequent social and economic history, and that some suggested were now repeating themselves on an extended scale and with even deeper cultural effects.

In 1997 the *New Yorker* magazine seemed to touch a nerve in declaring Marx 'the Next Big Thinker': 'Globalisation is the buzzword of the late 20th century, on the lips of everybody from Jiang Zemin to Tony Blair, but Marx predicted its ramifications 150 years ago' (Cassidy, 1997). Meanwhile a new generation of young political activists mobilising around issues of global economic justice, environmental sustainability and opposition to Western militarism became increasingly curious about a thinker whose radical critique of capitalist society and its iniquitous and destructive effects had inspired such a diverse variety of movements for change. In 2005 the BBC ran a popular poll in which members of the public were invited to vote for 'the greatest philosopher of all time'. To the evident surprise and even embarrassment of the organisers, Marx came out top by a dramatic margin, with more than twice as many votes as the second-ranked David Hume and many more than Socrates, Plato, Aristotle, Kant or Wittgenstein.

Part of the paradox was that Marx's relationship to philosophy as an academic discipline has always been contested and problematic. Although

Marx devoted the bulk of his time at university in Berlin to the study of philosophy and seemed for a time to uphold the view, propounded by Hegel and his intellectual followers, of philosophy as the critical key or unifying foundation for all other fields of inquiry, Marx soon changed course, famously renouncing philosophy on the grounds that, rather than merely understanding the world, he wanted to change it. Nevertheless the philosophical enthusiasms of his youth remained a constant reference point for Marx, and his later writings on history, politics and particularly economics were seen by contemporaries to be curiously, often bafflingly, entangled with the complexities of logic or metaphysics. Yet Marx never set forth in any clear or unambiguous form the role such questions had played in his mature thought; the few explicitly methodological remarks scattered through his later texts raise more questions than they answer, while a promise 'to make accessible to the ordinary human intelligence, in two or three printers' sheets', his use of the Hegelian 'dialectic', was never delivered (Marx, 1965). And so Marx's readers have consistently felt compelled to try to understand the relationship between his arguments and those of mainstream philosophy as a means of approaching his methodology as a social scientist, and of better understanding the impetus of a political project which, by his own account, aimed to translate his generation's original philosophical aspirations into a transformative historical practice.

The Marx and Philosophy Society was established in the UK in 2003 to provide a forum in which those interested in such questions could come together, share and debate ideas and perspectives. Founded with the aim of encouraging 'scholarly engagement with, and creative development of, the philosophical and foundational aspects of Marx's work', the Society has always emphasised that it 'welcomes contributions from any philosophical or political position'. Though dependent on volunteer organisers with many other demands on their time, and with hardly any material resources of its own to draw on,[1] the Society has survived and grown far beyond its founders' original expectations. Our seminars and conferences have been able to draw upon an impressive range of high-quality contributions from writers and academics working throughout and beyond the English-speaking world, and have consistently attracted large audiences, often largely made up of younger scholars and students, making for discussions that have broken new ground while remaining accessible to those less immersed in the terminology and lore of Marxism and Marxology. Never a solely academic exercise, a particularly gratifying aspect of these meetings has been the way they have made for lively and engaging discussions of the practical and political implications of Marx's thought, with many participants bringing experiences and perspectives drawn from their own involvement in various forms of social activism, while rarely descending to sectarian recitations of dry doctrines and fixed positions that can so easily mar such debates.

This collection brings together finished versions of a selection of the most significant papers that were presented in their original form at meetings of the Society during the first five years of its existence. Most have been revised since their initial presentation, often in light of questions and points raised during the Society's discussions. They represent, then, some of the most groundbreaking and sophisticated work on Marx and philosophy currently being pursued and also reflect, we think, the open, plural and inquiring spirit that has characterised the Society's activities.

Predecessors

The first section of the book examines aspects of Marx's relationship with the philosophical traditions he was shaped by and engaged with. We open the collection with a chapter by Joseph McCarney, one of the founder members of the Society, who lost his life in a tragic car accident in 2007. McCarney focuses his attention on Marx's first explicit articulation, in 1843, of the nature of his intellectual break with Hegelianism, a pivotal moment in his attempt to develop a radical alternative to the philosophical paradigm which had framed his earliest inquiries. From the start, Marx is concerned with avoiding the conservative political implications that Hegel drew from his thought, but insists that these must be understood not as a merely superficial or pragmatic 'accommodation' on Hegel's part but as the result of a tendency rooted in the inadequacy of his philosophical 'principle'. McCarney argues that Marx's 1843 *Critique of Hegel's Doctrine of the State* entertains a number of conflicting readings of Hegel's metaphysics – as a 'pantheism' which views all existence as divine or rational; as a personalised theism which upholds transcendent divinity and sovereign monarchy in parallel terms; and as a mystical 'acosmism' which entails indifference or disdain for the world and the practicalities of trying to change it. On all three readings Hegel's metaphysics leads to conservative or quietist political conclusions. But for McCarney, Marx's true achievement as a critic of Hegel lies in his recognition in Hegel of 'a logic of non-accommodation, a logic to which [Hegel] himself is unfaithful'. This is his valorisation of social reason – 'Spirit' or *Geist* – over the blind necessity of nature. Marx's rejection as a 'zoology' of the contemporary Prussian political and social order that Hegel endorses thus extends Hegel's own logic in order to draw from it political conclusions quite opposed to Hegel's.

Martin McIvor makes a case for reading Marx as a 'post-Kantian' thinker – one whose analyses build upon a distinctively 'modern' and specifically Kantian conception of subjectivity and agency. Drawing on the work of scholars such as Robert Pippin who have emphasised the foundational role of the idea of self-determination in Kant's critique of traditional morality and metaphysics and the importance of this idea for later German Idealist philosophy, McIvor highlights Marx's deployment of concepts and arguments that suggest that, in important respects, he means to carry forward this philosophical revolution at the same time as radicalising and, in some senses, displacing it. When much of today's moral and political theory is avowedly neo-Kantian, and the drift of some of the most creative 'post-analytic' philosophy has seemed to many to be increasingly Hegelian, such an approach to Marx's project may reveal new and unexpected points of contact with contemporary concerns and debates.

Scott Meikle digs deeper into the philosophical past to gain a vantage point from which Marx's critical engagement with modern economic thinking can be fully appreciated. For Meikle, Marx's early commentaries on the writings of James Mill and other political economists of his time must be seen as the product of a confrontation with the post-Humean utilitarianism and empiricism of nineteenth-century English radicalism from the point of view of a civic humanism and metaphysical realism formed by the Aristotelian tradition still dominant in German-speaking academic culture. An awareness of this tradition, argues Meikle, helps us see the force of Marx's critique of the new capitalist culture that sought to deny or suppress not only the true social conditions of human flourishing but even the intrinsic nature and value of the things of our world, reducing everything to empty instrumentality or abstract tradeability. This non-contemporaneity in Marx's thought, Meikle suggests, should be recognised as politically productive, enabling insights into the fundamental character of capitalist modernity inaccessible to those who take its categories and practices for granted.

Political philosophy

The chapters in our next section raise further questions about the relation of Marx's thought to mainstream currents of contemporary political thought. It is another paradox of Marx's position that a thinker who might seem to be the most 'political' of philosophers – too political, perhaps, to be counted a true philosopher – also seems to stand somewhere outside the mainstream of 'political philosophy' as normally conceived. Georgios Daremas argues that Marx's early critique of politics and the 'political state', even of a formally democratic one, is rooted in a far more demanding conception of democracy or popular sovereignty that would annul the distinction between a public, political realm and a separate 'civil society' made up of competing private interests. This 'real societal democracy', in Daremas's terms, would make good the promise of modern democratic politics at the same time as dissolving its erstwhile constitutive terms and categories.

Andrew Collier advances the provocative thesis that Marx's political thinking has more in common with conservatism than with liberalism. Although Marx frequently allied himself with liberals in the positions he took on practical political issues, Collier insists that he is philosophically much closer to conservatives in his refusal to base his positions upon abstract concepts such as utility or rights, freedom or equality, instead proceeding from an organic model of society which 'survives and develops by solving its problems as they arise'. But this highlights the critical importance of Marx's notion of *contradiction* in marrying this particularist, immanent political methodology with a revolutionary conclusion. For Collier, Marx's critique of contemporary society is based not on external ideals, but on the development of institutions and values within capitalism which are antagonistic to the system and generate the possibility of its replacement – trade unions being the classic case in point. Paradoxically, Collier argues for a recognition of *tradition* as a driving force of class struggle, against a capitalist 'progress' and 'modernisation' that is hostile to human and environmental values.

Robert Fine offers a link from Marx's political thinking to the 'economic' analyses of *Capital*, by reading the latter as an implicit response to Hegel's *Philosophy of Right*. Fine argues that while Hegel addresses the *ideal* 'forms' of modernity – analysing and interrelating key categories such as abstract right, personality, ownership, contract, guilt, morality, family, civil society and the state – Marx's 'critique of political economy' addresses its *material* forms: value, exchange value, money, capital, profit, rent and interest. Both deploy a parallel methodology, turning philosophical analysis into the objective and 'scientific' treatment of actually existing social forms and both, argues Fine, adopt an ironic or ambivalent attitude to modernity and its constitutive forms. For Fine, we should not read Marx's account as one that contradicts or undermines Hegel's; rather, read side by side the two accounts offer mutually complementary pictures of modern society that testify to the dichotomy or tension it generates between persons and things, free will and determination, and to the abstract domination and destructive violence that can arise from the fetishisation of either side.

Labour, money and capital

The central section of the collection takes us to the heart of Marx's distinctive achievement – his efforts to develop a philosophical account of the fundamental forms of the modern economy: abstract labour, value, money and capital.

Andrew Chitty argues that 'capital' first appears in Marx's early writings as an abstract, alienated and therefore inadequate realisation of humanity's 'species-being'. Central to this conception is an account, originating with Rousseau and developed by Hegel, of human beings as essentially free and 'universal', although dependent for the realisation of this essential nature upon a certain structure of social relations. Marx goes beyond Rousseau and Hegel in locating the realisation of this 'species-being' not at a purely moral or political level but in the very process of social labour and mutual production, at the same time as diagnosing its 'alienation' in the shape of capital. Capital is thus conceived not simply as an accumulation of wealth used by its owner to generate more wealth (as in Adam Smith) but more fundamentally as the alienated realisation of the human essence. Attention to these movements in the early development of Marx's thought raises questions about the relation of his 'mature' economic analyses to a philosophical anthropology of freedom and universality.

Sean Sayers considers the charge, raised in different forms by thinkers such as Jürgen Habermas, Ted Benton, Hannah Arendt and most recently Michael Hardt and Toni Negri, that Marx's social analyses depend on universalising and absolutising a particular paradigm of labour and production that gains its applicability from conditions specific to nineteenth-century industrialisation. Sayers offers a philosophical analysis of Marx's concept of labour that reveals it to be far more supple and sophisticated than such characterisations recognise. For Sayers, Marx develops a concept of labour as reflective, self-conscious, formative activity that transforms the material world into an objectification of the subject's needs and intentions. It can help us think about the activities of the hunter-gatherer and about agricultural or craft-based forms of productive activity as well as about the increasingly socialised or 'universal' labour processes of industrial and 'post-industrial' societies. In fact, Sayers suggests, Marx's account anticipates Habermas's notion of 'communicative action', Arendt's notion of work as 'world-making' and Hardt and Negri's analyses of 'immaterial' or 'bio-political' labour. For Marx, human labour is always already communicative and world-making, transforming not only its immediate raw material but also subjectivity and social relations.

Chris Arthur offers a detailed reconstruction of Marx's argument in *Capital* that the social practice of exchange effects a 'practical abstraction' that identifies heterogeneous commodities as the bearers of equivalent 'value'. This new 'social form' of value is made actual through the institution of money, which is the condition of the possibility of the commensurable valuation of commodities. The complex relationship posited in the activity of sale and purchase between money as the 'universal equivalent' and the world of commodities alongside which it sits as another particular commodity can be analysed by means of analogy with the activity of judgement and conceptualisation examined by Hegel in his *Science of Logic*. Marx's philosophical analysis of money, Arthur argues, is the starting point for his account of capitalism as a world in which monetary relations have become hegemonic, and money has become the aim, rather than just the means, of circulation, thus constituting a new form of value, capital, which depends on the exploitation of useful labour for its expansion.

Patrick Murray focuses on this pivotal transition from money to capital as the key to Marx's theoretical revolution. Murray starts from what he takes to be a symptomatic failure by Hegel to notice and explore the far-reaching implications of money's self-expansion through the capital/wage-labour relationship. It is Marx's greatest insight, Murray contends, to see that the emergence of this disruptive and divisive dynamic challenges all the claims of bourgeois thought for modern autonomy and the supremacy of legal and political forms based on equal rights of ownership and citizenship. Hegel counts on the ability of the constitutional state to 'buffer' and reconcile the clashes and conflicts of 'civil society' in which capital develops, but in truth, he has no conception of the extraordinary forces it is up against. For Murray this must cast doubt on Hegel's status as an unsurpassed theorist of the modern condition, and secures Marx's standing as an indispensable corrective to his social thought.

William Roberts's essay explores in more depth the ways in which human activities and social practice are restructured and transformed by their subsumption under the cycle of capital accumulation. Capital realises and reproduces an all-encompassing collective productivity that is radically abstracted from concrete or individual intentions or acts. The purposeful production of useful things, what the Greeks called *technê*, is thus displaced by a wholly abstract form of labour that serves only to sustain and further augment the power of this 'animated monster' that has taken the reins of history. Some 'analytical Marxists' have baulked at this suggestion of a 'mysterious speculative construction that cannot be reduced to any set of lower-order mechanisms', but Roberts stresses that it is precisely Marx's project to explain how, 'from the structure of our active interrelations – buying and selling goods, hiring labour, looking to make a profit, etc.' we are led to 'the coming into being of an abstract, spiritual subject, which we embody as its moments, but the logic of which we do not control'.

Twentieth-century developments

During the twentieth century Marx's ideas were applied and extended in myriad and often conflicting ways, often by way of commentary or reconstruction that aimed to clarify their implicit philosophical presuppositions or to reinforce them by combining them with more contemporary methodological frameworks. This section offers fresh assessments of three contrasting twentieth-century attempts to develop Marx's arguments – the Hegelian Marxism of Georg Lukács, the 'structuralist' Marxism of Louis Althusser and the analytical Marxism of G. A. Cohen, Jon Elster and John Roemer.

Moishe Postone recounts how Lukács re-emphasised and reappropriated the Hegelian dimensions of Marx's thought as a way to place subjectivity and praxis at the heart of that thought in opposition to the scientism and determinism of Second International orthodoxy. Lukács recovered the categories of *Capital* from crudely economistic readings to reaffirm them as constitutive of both the objective and subjective dimensions of modern social life. As such they furnished the basis for 'a brilliant social and historical analysis of modern western philosophy' as a series of attempts 'to wrestle with the problems generated by the peculiar abstract forms of life characteristic of its (capitalist) context', attempts which misrecognised such problems as transhistorical and ontological. For Lukács, Marx was the first thinker adequately to address such problems by doing so in social and historical terms. Lukács's theory of 'reification' further enlarges the scope of Marx's critique to take in the range of significant social, economic, political and cultural features of twentieth-century capitalism, in particular marrying it to accounts of rationalisation and bureaucratisation such as Weber's. However, Postone takes issue with Lukács's account of the proletariat as the subjective agent of history, arguing that it depends upon notions of labour, history and totality that should be seen as internal to capital's self-reproduction rather than its external negation. Instead he argues that for Marx it is capital itself that has become the 'subjective agent' of contemporary history.

Louis Althusser is usually remembered as a thinker who set himself against 'Hegelian' Marxism and all Hegelian 'residues' in Marx's thought as distractions from its true 'scientific' achievement. But John Grant points out that Althusser's attempt to construct a truly materialist 'dialectic' stood in a far more complex relation to Hegel's thought than this reputation suggests. Althusser insisted that Marxism must dispense with 'humanist' conceptions of the 'constitutive subject' as unscientific and ideological. But in later writings Althusser pointed to a 'positive heritage' that Marx took up from Hegel, centred on notions of contradiction and negativity which retained the potential to disrupt and reopen the teleological and totalising aspects of Hegel's thought, and providing the basis for a conception of structural antagonism and history as a 'process without a subject'. Grant argues that beyond this, Althusser's work suggests the need for a further, more 'existential', notion of 'subjects in process' to account for lived experience and the possibility of political struggle and revolt.

Analytical Marxism was founded, in contrast to most other tendencies of the twentieth century, on an explicit *renunciation* of any distinctively 'Marxist' method and instead sought to assess and develop Marx's substantive claims on the basis of mainstream social science and analytical philosophy. Roberto Veneziani asks if this results in a 'research programme' that is distinctive and, in Lakatos's sense, progressive. Veneziani argues that the more narrowly defined 'Rational Choice Marxism', with its insistence on methodological individualism and rational choice explanations, encounters serious problems, not least those arising from the social formation of individuals and the demonstrable possibility of collective action. Such action can only be explained with reference to, in Adam Przeworski's terms, 'individuals who are embedded in different types of relations with other individuals within a multidimensionally described social structure', and whose actions cannot be reduced to pure instrumental rationality but rather may be accounted for by 'norms' and 'identity' which 'have an irreducibly social dimension'. However, Veneziani argues that a less reductive and more methodologically sophisticated form of Analytical Marxism may have an important role in a revival of socialist theory in its rigorous reconstruction of a theory of history and class struggle, its account of the state after socialism as 'progressively self-effacing', and its exploration of normative values such as self-realisation, autonomy, community and equality.

Feminist philosophy

The most recent period has seen a number of challenges to Marxism's claim to provide a 'total' account of modern forms of domination and social struggle, or even one that can claim theoretical or explanatory primacy over other key dimensions raised by 'new social movements' and their associated theoretical elaborations. This final section looks at one of the more important of these challenges, that of feminist theory.

Terrell Carver begins with an overview of the 1980s 'marriage' and subsequent divorce of Marxism and feminism and then returns to a text by Marx's close collaborator, Frederick Engels, whose *Origin of the Family, Private Property and the State* offers what is in some ways a surprisingly radical revision of the 'orthodox' Marxism that Engels has been credited with constructing, a revision that has been paid little attention by subsequent commentators on Marx other than those writing from an explicitly feminist perspective. Engels 'adapted Marx's concept of "material" production to include human re-production, and attempted to build on this revision an apparatus of twin-track "determination" in history, involving sex-oppression as well as class-oppression'. Carver suggests that the innovations of this text – in which Engels effectively initiated the so-called dual-systems theory of class and gender oppression – have not been explored as thoroughly by mainstream Marxist thought as they might have been, given their implications for the 'materialist interpretation of history' and the foundational concepts of production and labour. Carver concludes by pointing to the ways in which the categories of both 'class' and 'woman' have been increasingly construed as 'subjective and performative' in the last 20 years, and intimates the possibility on this basis, not so much of a second marriage as of a supersession of the divide between Marxism and feminism.

Gillian Howie argues that feminism has much to gain from a continuing encounter with Marxism, and registers a concern that the exclusion of materialism, associated with socialist feminism, has led to 'a form of "cultural" feminism within which is a particular thread of anti-realism that has left feminism unable to articulate, investigate or analyse its own conditions'. Taking a less sanguine view of the 'postmodern' turn in recent feminism, she sees it as presenting both strategic and theoretical problems: the emphasis on diversity has made collective action more problematic, while the rejection of 'objectivism' or 'realism' has made it more difficult to 'interrogate underlying and generative structures and mechanisms'. Drawing on the work of Catherine MacKinnon, Howie argues that we should return to 'phenomenologically inspired' feminist accounts of sexual objectification and re-glue these not only to Marx's theory of reification but also, more trenchantly, to the labour theory of value. To avoid this falling back into 'old knowledges' and a form of Marxist reductionism, she argues that we need to begin from experience and that a 'dialectical' distinction between subject and object must be maintained. For Howie, feminists 'need to regroup economic analysis and recent sophisticated accounts of subjectivity' if they are to address key questions 'about the nature of developing global capital' – from child poverty and the family to war over the Middle East and the international sex trade.

Conclusion

The essays collected here reflect the diversity of contributions to the Society, covering different themes and coming from different perspectives and often revealing differences of emphasis or outright disagreements of interpretation and evaluation; therefore, it would be wrong to impose any false unity on them. Nevertheless are there any general themes that can be outlined and broad conclusions drawn from this collection?

A first is the continued relevance of 'philosophical anthropology' in discussions of Marx's thought. As highlighted by Chitty, Sayers and Roberts, and developed in different directions by Grant and Veneziani, Marx had a foundational concern with the most basic qualities and categories of human being, such as action, interaction and sociality, and in how these grounds are taken up in a social system. This is apparent not only in his early concept of 'species-being' but in the founding categories of *Das Kapital*.

A second theme that emerges strongly is that of Marx as a theorist deeply engaged with modernity, understood as an epoch dating especially from the eighteenth century and characterised by the repudiation of tradition, a celebration of critique and change and a focus on humans as free and self-determining. Writing as these ideas were beginning to sweep the popular consciousness of Europe for the first time, Marx confronted and questioned the transformations in European society that were behind them in a way more penetrating than perhaps anyone before him or since. But Marx's precise relation to modernity and its ideas is unclear. For Meikle, he was a critic of modernity shaped by classical concerns; for McIvor and Daremas, he was one who sought to push forward and fulfil the promise of modernity; and for McCarney and Collier, he was a thinker who combined conservative and modern concerns in an attempt to write from a standpoint consciously located 'within' a process of progressive historical change, rather than sanctifying or criticising the status quo from a point outside society or history.

In relation to this point, we can see even more clearly the importance of Hegel, himself poised between tradition and modernity, liberalism and organicism, a concern for freedom and a concern for community, as Marx's recurrent philosophical reference point. Marx's writings can be seen as an ongoing engagement and argument, sometimes explicit, sometimes implicit, with Hegel, and it is noticeable how many of the chapters in this collection (among them McCarney, Daremas, Fine, Sayers, Arthur, Murray and Grant) focus on this relation, and devote almost as much time to Hegel as to Marx. Hegel is more than just another important thinker, such as Aristotle, Spinoza or Kant, to whom Marx can be profitably compared – for Hegel's thought is the prism through which Marx encountered and understood all these other writers. If we think, along with contemporary commentators such as Pippin (1991) that Hegel represents the most ambitious and sophisticated attempt until then to define modern subjectivity, make sense of the modern world and make us feel at home in it, then Marx's work represents a sustained challenge to Hegel's account and conclusion. They cannot be directly compared – Marx showed no interest in metaphysical speculation and Hegel wrote comparatively little on the economy – but Marx's work can be seen as a continuous interrogation of Hegel's account of modernity, picking at its weak points, raising unanswered questions, opening up issues that Hegel had closed off.

Central to this discussion is the issue (raised most explicitly in this book by Murray, but implicit also in the contributions of Meikle, Fine, Arthur, Roberts and Postone) of whether Hegel had satisfactory dealt with the extraordinary transformation of European economic life over the previous century, in short the spread of capitalist economic relations across the continent, and the tendencies of the rules of exchange and drives for accumulation inherent in these relations to subvert and upset his system – not least its account of the relationship between economics, politics and culture and its promise of an individual reconciliation with a harmonious social order. Marx's picture of the capitalist economy, as it emerges from these chapters, is one in which the practices of abstraction, formalisation, detachment and universality, ultimately rooted in the very practice of buying and selling, take on a life of their own in a supra-individual system of alienation and abstract domination, one that destroys our sense of community and humanity and renders ridiculous our claims to individual autonomy or political self-determination.

All this raises the troubled and well-known question of whether Marx's own account of the contemporary world is too 'totalising' and of the relation of Marxist thought and politics to other lines of critique and projects of emancipation. The chapters on gender and feminism that conclude the collection explore these questions. They give some sense of the complexity and openness of Marx's own thought, but also of the need for other traditions of critique to make some sense of the power of the economic practices and structures of capitalism to which he devoted so many decades of study.

Finally, in what sense is Marx's thought relevant to contemporary *philosophy*, as opposed to, say, sociology, economics, politics or cultural studies? It is true that Marx wrote little that directly addressed the core topics of contemporary academic philosophy insofar as these are restricted to metaphysics, logic, epistemology, philosophy of mind or aesthetics. But if philosophy today is interested in the relation between the fundamental categories and characteristics of human action and experience on the one hand and social structures and historical change on the other; in the interrelations between contemporary science, politics, culture and economics; in the way in which our own society frustrates and creates possibilities for aspirations to community, democracy and social justice and more fundamentally in the relation between human self-realisation and social form, then these chapters amply demonstrate Marx's continuing philosophical relevance. The questions Marx was asking remain our questions today.

Note

1. Thanks are due to the Lipman-Miliband Trust who provided a small start-up grant that enabled the Society to get going.

Bibliography

Cassidy, John (1997) 'The Return of Karl Marx', *The New Yorker*, 20 October 1997.
Marx, Karl (1965) Letter to Engels, 14 January 1858, in Karl Marx and Friedrich Engels, *Selected Correspondence*, 2nd edn (Moscow: Progress Publishers), p. 100.
Pippin, R. C. (1991) *Modernism as a Philosophical Problem: On the Dissatisfactions of European High Culture* (Oxford: Basil Blackwell).

PART I MARX AND HIS PREDECESSORS

1

'The Entire Mystery': Marx's Understanding of Hegel

Joseph McCarney

> In these paragraphs is contained the entire mystery of
> the *Philosophy of Right* and of the Hegelian philosophy in
> general.
>
> (Marx, 1962, pp. 264–5; 1975, pp. 63–4)[1]

This striking claim appears early in Marx's *Critique of Hegel's Doctrine of the State*, at a point at which he had concluded the discussion of only paragraphs 261 and 262 of the *Philosophy of Right*. It seems clear that it is the second of these paragraphs that he has effectively in view in reaching his verdict, and it is in dealing with that paragraph that the theoretical interest of the preceding discussion lies. The two parts of the verdict should be considered separately. So far as the mystery of the *Philosophy of Right* in particular is concerned, Marx's discussion of paragraph 262 offers only a strong hint, a hint developed later in *Critique*, as to the direction of his thinking. There is a great deal more in that discussion that bears on the mystery of 'the Hegelian philosophy in general', but it is for all that by no means easy to see precisely what this mystery consists in for Marx. What is immediately obvious is that at the heart of it is the question of the nature of the Idea, the central pillar of Hegel's metaphysics, and of its relationship to what Marx calls 'the ordinary empirical world' (Marx, 1962, p. 262; 1975, p. 62). Beyond that, one comes up against the fact that the portion of text in question offers a number of different versions of the answer. Marx does not advert to, or acknowledge, these differences but proceeds as though pursuing a single line of thought. The difficulty is that the line being pursued changes in unheralded and unremarked ways from one place to another in the text. Thus, the various possibilities are laid down side by side without any movement of reconciliation or decision. This is itself somewhat mysterious in the case of a thinker of Marx's reflexive and analytical powers, more mysterious than has generally been recognised in the literature on his understanding of Hegel.

His commentary on paragraph 262 of the *Philosophy of Right* is worthy of, and will repay, close examination.

Marx, in keeping with his practice in *Critique*, prefaces the discussion of the paragraph by quoting it in full. It will provide an indispensable background for this inquiry if his example is followed:

> The actual Idea is the spirit which divides itself up into the two ideal spheres of its concept – the family and civil society – as its finite mode, and thereby emerges from its ideality to become infinite and actual spirit for itself. In so doing, it allocates the material of its finite actuality, i.e., individuals as a *mass*, to these two spheres, and in such a way that, in each individual case, this allocation appears to be *mediated* by circumstances, by the individual's arbitrary will and personal choice of vocation.
>
> (Hegel 1991a, pp. 285–6)

The first line of thought to be found in Marx's commentary depends on some formulations that spring with particular directness from Hegel's text, either simply as quotations or as uncontentious glosses. The most significant of them are to be found in the following passages:

> The so-called 'actual Idea' (spirit as infinite and actual) is represented as though it acted according to a determinate principle and with a determinate intention. It divides itself into finite spheres, and it does this 'in order to return to itself, to be for itself', and indeed does this in such a way that it is just as it actually is.
>
> (Marx, 1962, pp. 261–2; 1975, p. 61)

> [T]he actual Idea has as its way of being [*Dasein*] not an actuality developed out of itself, but rather the ordinary empirical world.
>
> (Marx, 1962, p. 262; 1975, 62)

> The actual becomes phenomenon, but the Idea has no other content than this phenomenon. Moreover, the Idea has no goal other than the logical one, 'to be for itself as infinite actual spirit'.
>
> (Marx, 1962, p. 264; 1975, p. 63)

These passages will surely seem, even at first glance, to fit together harmoniously enough. Before attempting to state the principle of their unity, however, it may be well to confirm that what is in question here is a persistent theme in Marx's dealings with Hegel. To begin with, one should note some indications that its origins go back a long way, indeed to the time when those dealings began. Thus, there are youthful foreshadowings that, though admittedly not of great evidential value in themselves, are at least suggestive in the present context. The first is a verse epigram on Hegel: 'Kant and

Fichte like to soar to the heavens, seeking there a distant land, I but seek to grasp properly that which – in the street I find' (Marx and Engels, 1977, p. 608; 1975a, p. 577). Some six months later Marx was to summarise in a letter to his father his first encounter with the philosophy of the time:

> From the idealism which, by the way, I had compared and nourished with that of Kant and Fichte, I arrived at the point of seeking the Idea in actuality itself. If previously the gods had dwelt above the earth, now they had become its centre.
>
> (Marx and Engels, 1977, p. 8; 1975a, p. 18)

That Marx has Hegel's example in mind at this point is suggested by the fact that he goes on at once to invoke him explicitly, as a great name to set against the others. It seems in any case reasonable to suppose that Hegel provided a significant part of the inspiration for the change in question, a view supported by the congruence between Marx's newfound goal and that ascribed to Hegel in the epigram.

For more substantial evidence of the interpretation of Hegel now being considered, one must, however, look to the period after the writing of *Critique*. In the *Economic and Philosophic Manuscripts* of 1844, Marx asserts on Hegel's behalf that 'the subject comes into being only as a result' and that 'this result, the subject knowing itself as absolute self-consciousness, is therefore *God, absolute spirit, the self-knowing and self-moving Idea*' (Marx and Engels, 1977, p. 584; Marx, 1975, p. 396). A little later, again in the context of expounding Hegel, this passage occurs:

> [T]he abstraction which comprehends itself as abstraction knows itself to be nothing; it, the abstraction, must relinquish itself, and so arrive at an essence which is its exact opposite, at *nature*. Hence the entire logic is the proof that abstract thought is nothing for itself, that the absolute Idea is nothing for itself, that only *nature* is something.
>
> (Marx and Engels, 1977, p. 585; Marx, 1975, p. 397)

These statements from *Critique* and *Manuscripts* may be seen as contributions to the theoretical working out of Marx's youthful vision of Hegel as seeking to grasp what he finds in the street, or indeed of his own Hegelian aspiration to seek the ideal in actuality itself. Their most prominent feature is the spirit of dynamism they exude. What underlies and unites them, one might suggest, is the sense of a vast, indeed cosmic, process of becoming. This is the process in and through which the Idea comes to be 'just as it actually is'. It is entirely consistent with such a view that the Idea should be thought of as initially 'nothing', an abstraction devoid of content. It becomes something by taking on the form of the actual, in particular by 'relinquishing' itself as nature. Since it can achieve fullness of existence only by doing so, it also seems appropriate to think of it as essentially a result. The cosmic process of becoming is a teleological one in so far as it is animated and guided throughout by a specific intention and goal, the self-creation of the Idea. Clearly it is a thoroughly non-heavenly, this-worldly and, it seems natural to say, 'immanent', conception of the Idea that is at work here.

Some further light may be shed on this conception by noting a comment Marx adds to the first of the passages from *Critique* quoted above. Immediately after referring to the 'actual Idea' returning to itself, he remarks: 'At this point the logical, pantheist mysticism appears very clearly' (Marx, 1962, p. 262; 1975, p. 61). To appreciate the force of 'logical', it will be helpful to introduce a refinement of terminology. In Hegel's most discriminating usage, what relinquishes itself as nature, and ultimately as spirit, is said to be not the Idea as such, but rather the Idea as it figures in logic, or simply the 'logical Idea':

> The Idea reveals itself in its purest form in thought, and it is from this angle that logic approaches it. It expresses itself in another form in physical nature, and the third form which it assumes is that of spirit in the absolute sense.
>
> (Hegel, 1975, p. 46)

This scheme provides the structure of the *Encyclopaedia*, Hegel's fullest statement of his system; that is to say, his most systematic attempt at a definition of the Idea. Thus, the three volumes of that work are entitled, successively, *The Science of Logic*, *The Philosophy of Nature*, and *The Philosophy of Spirit*. It is specifically the Idea as it is regarded in logic that may properly be described as 'abstract thought', the abstraction which 'knows itself to be nothing' and 'has no goal other than the logical one' of being for itself as 'infinite actual spirit'. Marx is, of course, familiar with this point of terminology, and makes explicit use of it. Thus, shortly after the section of *Critique* being examined here, he remarks that Hegel's 'sole interest' is in 'rediscovering the Idea simply [*schlechthin*], the logical Idea, in each element, be it that of the state or of nature' (Marx, 1962, p. 268; 1975, p. 67). What underlies this remark, it may be suggested, is the conception of the 'the Idea simply, the logical Idea' as having acquired a content as nature and as the spirit whose highest manifestation is the state, and as being ripe for rediscovery in that content. The position set out in the passages from Marx quoted above may now be said to have a logical character just by virtue of the central significance for it of the logical Idea.

To bring out the appropriateness of 'pantheist', it will be helpful to note another feature of Hegel's usage that is fully acknowledged by Marx. Indeed, it is present in the passage quoted above in which 'God', 'absolute spirit' and 'the self-knowing and self-moving Idea' are treated as equivalent expressions. What is of particular concern here is the equivalence of 'God' and 'the Idea'. It is consistently maintained by Marx in expounding Hegel, as in the comment elsewhere in *Critique* that 'to see a particular empirical being [*Dasein*] posited by the Idea' is 'to encounter at every level an incarnation of God' (Marx, 1962, p. 306; 1975, p. 99). The practice is explicitly warranted by Hegel himself: 'God and the nature of the divine will are one and the same thing; it is what we call in philosophy the *Idea*' (Hegel, 1975, p. 46). Putting this the other way around, the Idea is what in religion is called God. In the light of this equivalence, it becomes clear that Hegel's God, as depicted so far, is essentially the God of pantheism. That the cosmic subject is integrally bound up with 'the ordinary empirical world', being 'nothing' without it, suggests as much of itself. It is true that, as Marx acknowledges, it is, in its fullness of existence, strictly a result, and hence, the empirical world has to figure as an arena of God-making. Thus, it is an inherently dynamic, indeed historical, version of pantheism that is in question. This does not, however, affect the basic point. Pantheism, as usually conceived, is essentially the doctrine that God is, somehow or other, to be identified with the totality of what there is, with the universe considered as a unified whole. Hegel's God, as presented thus far by Marx, meets this condition without difficulty. For in that presentation the content of the divine is exhausted by the two realms of nature and human society, and God is to be conceived as immanently engaged within those realms in the task of self-creation. Admittedly, what is divine cannot be wholly constituted by them in that there is a ghostly residue, a purely formal, but foundational, element, the religious counterpart, so to speak, of the logical Idea.[2] If, however, one now adds this element to what has to be included in the enumeration of what there is, God and the universe may be thought of as being identical and as constituting the totality of existence, in line with the traditional doctrine of pantheism. Thus, 'pantheist' is no less apt and illuminating than 'logical' in characterising Hegel's position as it has emerged so far from Marx's account.

The value of the term is, however, not yet exhausted. For this portion of text also points towards a pantheist reading of Hegel that is undynamic and unhistorical. Thus, it asserts that in Hegel 'empirical actuality [*Wirklichkeit*] is accepted as it is and is also declared to be rational' (Marx, 1962, p. 264; 1975, p. 63). The second part of this assertion has surely to be taken as a reference not to paragraph 262 of the *Philosophy of Right* but rather to what is undoubtedly the best-known thesis of that work, the so-called *Doppelsatz*. The claim in the 'Preface' is that 'What is rational is actual; and what is actual is rational' (Hegel, 1991a, p. 20). In the 'Introduction' to the *Encyclopaedia* Hegel was to observe that 'These simple propositions have seemed shocking to many', but only, he goes on to explain, on the basis of a misunderstanding. For 'what is there is partly *appearance* and only partly actuality', and actuality has to be distinguished from 'contingent existence' and from various other ontological determinations (Hegel, 1991b, pp. 29–30).

The implication Hegel wishes us to draw is that, if we take account of the many-layered character of this ontology, it will be clear that he was not seeking to confer the authority of being rational on everything that, in some sense or other, exists. What is actual is indeed rational, but this, it appears, is a matter of conceptual necessity, of a condition that must be satisfied for anything to count as truly 'actual'.

Whatever the ultimate merits of this explanation, the point to note at present is that Marx has to be accounted, at least in one strand of his thinking, among the readers of the *Philosophy of Right* who have failed, in Hegel's eyes, to understand the message. The blurring of distinctions that signals such failure is already present in the portion of text that is our prime concern. Thus, the reference to 'empirical actuality' is itself somewhat discordant in view of Hegel's desire to distinguish actuality from whatever is merely empirical. It is for him, one might say, a theoretical, not an empirical, concept. Moreover, the formulation that actuality 'is declared to be' rational seems insensitive to the internal, conceptual connection that is involved. Much more decisive, for present purposes, however, is the following assertion later in *Critique*: 'That the rational is actual proves itself to be in *contradiction* with the *irrational actuality* which at every point is the opposite of what it asserts, and asserts the opposite of what it is' (Marx, 1962, p. 339; 1975, p. 127). The specific form of irrationality in question at this point is the role of the Estates in Hegel's doctrine of the state. In the light of his *Encyclopaedia* explanation, however, it appears that the rationality of the actual cannot be contradicted by any such irrationalities of mere existence, and indeed to speak of an 'irrational actuality' is itself a contradiction in Hegelian terms. That Marx seems oblivious to this aspect of the situation suggests that on occasion at least he takes the *Doppelsatz* thesis in just the way Hegel sought to correct. It is an understanding that may fairly be characterised as undynamically pantheist.

In order to bring this out one should note that while 'the Idea' is what in philosophy is called 'God', it also, for Hegel, conveys 'the proper philosophical meaning of "reason"' (Hegel, 1991b, p. 288). This too is a feature of Hegel's terminology of which Marx is aware, as is sufficiently shown by his use of the phrase 'universal reason' where the context would lead one to expect 'the Idea' (Marx, 1962, p. 295; 1975, p. 89). Thus, we are licensed to regard 'reason' and 'God', through their connection with 'the Idea', as being themselves interchangeable terms for many purposes. Hence, to hold that all that exists is rational amounts in religious terms to holding that God is already fully present and realised in all things, without the need of any cosmic process of self-creation. It accords well with this conception that Marx should declare in *The Holy Family* that 'if the Christian religion knows only *one* incarnation of God, speculative philosophy has as many incarnations as there are things' (Marx, 1962, p. 733; Marx and Engels, 1975b, p. 74).[3] This undynamic pantheism of being rather than becoming is particularly significant in the context of his practical grounds for rejecting Hegel's philosophy and will later come up for discussion in that context.

To speak of 'pantheism', however the term is understood, will not suffice to convey fully the character of Marx's account. For in the portion of text that is of immediate concern, there are indications of another view, one that is quite at odds with 'pantheist', and that, it should be added, sits uneasily with 'logical'. These indications have primarily to do with the emphasis placed there on the 'alien' (*fremd*) character, the 'otherness', of the Idea in relation to the empirical world. The main expository remarks in this vein are as follows:

> Actuality is not expressed as itself but as another actuality. The ordinary empirical world does not have its own spirit but rather an alien one as its law.
>
> (Marx, 1962, p. 262; 1975, p. 62)

> Family and civil society [...] owe their being [*Dasein*] to a spirit other than their own; they are determinations posited by a third party, not self determinations.
>
> (Marx, 1962, p. 263; 1975, p. 63)

> [E]mpirical actuality [...] is not rational because of its own reason but because the empirical fact in its empirical existence [*Existenz*] has a meaning other than itself.
>
> (Marx, 1962; p. 264; 1975, p. 63)

This line of thought is sustained elsewhere in *Critique*:

> The various powers [of the state] are not determined through their 'own nature' but through an alien one.
>
> (Marx, 1962, p. 272; 1975, p. 70)

> Hegel wants to write the life history of the abstract substance, the Idea, so that human activity etc. must appear as the activity and result of something other.
>
> (Marx, 1962, pp. 305–6; 1975, p. 98)

The theoretical implications are, however, most fully developed in *Manuscripts*. In the course of commenting on a passage from *The Philosophy of Nature*, Marx writes:

> Externality [*Äußerlichkeit*] is to be taken here in the sense of alienation [*Entäußerung*], an error, a defect, that ought not to be. For what is true is still the Idea. Nature is only the *form* of its *other-being* [*Anderssein*]. And

since abstract thought is the *essence*, what is external to it is in its essence merely *external*.

(Marx and Engels, 1977, p. 588; Marx, 1975, pp. 399–400)

The central concern in these remarks is, as before, the relationship between the Idea and the empirical world. The contrast with the previous interpretation may be marked in a traditional way by saying that what we have now is a 'transcendent', rather than 'immanent', Idea, for the conditions normally associated with transcendence seem clearly to be met here. The Idea is in its substantial existence both utterly distinct from, indeed alien to, the empirical world and utterly superior to it as the source of its being and significance. The label in question is in any case one that Marx is willing to apply quite casually to Hegel's philosophy, as in a reference in *Manuscripts* to 'the old *philosophical* and especially *Hegelian transcendence*' (Marx and Engels, 1977, p. 469; Marx, 1975, p. 282). In truth it may be said to capture his most enduring view of the matter. Thus, it is surely the transcendent reading that is being invoked in what may be thought to be his best considered, indeed valedictory, judgement on it. In the 'Afterword' to the first volume of *Capital* he refers to Hegel's transformation, 'under the name of the Idea', of 'the process of thinking' into an '*independent* subject', the 'creator [*Demiurg*] of the actual world' (Marx, 1969, p. 12; 1976, p. 102). The claim that Hegel's Idea is essentially an independent creator serves quite adequately to capture the strand of thought in *Critique* at present being considered.

It is a claim that takes one to the verge of depicting the situation in religious terms. In those terms it would have to be acknowledged that it is with the God of theism that one has now to deal. For that God is in large part to be defined by just the characteristics that were attributed to the transcendent Idea. Such a God is indeed fully independent of, and infinitely superior to, the created world in all its manifold imperfections. That the theistic God should also be conceived of as 'alien' is a possibility allowed for in at least some versions of the doctrine. A striking presentation of it is given by Hegel himself in his account of the 'unhappy consciousness', a form of religious consciousness he seems to associate in particular with medieval Christianity (Hegel, 1977, pp. 126–38). For Marx too, not surprisingly given his time and place, Christianity provides the primary model of theism. He is, moreover, eager, at least on occasions, to associate this model with Hegel, indeed to treat Hegel in some sense as a Christian philosopher. Thus, in *Critique* the religious equivalent of the Idea is taken at one point to be the first person of the Holy Trinity, God the Father (Marx, 1962, p. 272; 1975, p. 70). After the reference to the Hegelian transcendence in *Manuscripts*, Marx went on to undertake to demonstrate 'on another occasion' the 'historical nemesis' that overcame this transcendence in the realm of theology (Marx and Engels, 1977, pp. 469–70; Marx, 1975, p. 282). A few months later he was to redeem this undertaking in *The Holy Family*, a work in which the relationship between Hegelian philosophy and Christian theology is a key motif. Thus, at one point he remarks that the chief objects of his criticism, 'Bruno Bauer and Company', had arrived at Hegelian idealism, and thereby the *'restoration of the Christian theory of creation in a speculative Hegelian form'* (Marx, 1962, p. 835; Marx and Engels, 1975b, p. 170). It seems fair to conclude that the connection with Christianity is a significant theme of Marx's dealings with Hegel. A question arises rather obviously at this point as to how a body of thought can be at once pantheist and Christian. The issues are best explored, however, by reverting to the language of philosophy so as to consider them in terms of the Idea.

A way forward may be found by considering the implications of the term 'alien'. It is, to begin with, not easy to see how the Idea can be conceived of as alien in relation to the content without which it is 'nothing'. That content might more readily be seen as integrally bound up with its existence in any substantial sense, its existence as 'something'. There scarcely seems enough conceptual room here for the notion of the alien to take root. This impression is enhanced if one assumes, as seems obligatory, that what is alien must count as an independent existence in relation to its other. The independence of the Idea in that sense is hard to square with its crucial dependence on what is empirical in order to become 'just as it actually is'. More generally, one might wonder how the Idea as pure abstraction can conceivably be alien to, and thereby in tension with, a particular content. It might rather be thought of as endlessly accommodating of, and adaptable to content, a point that Marx in effect makes rather frequently himself in complaining of the supposed arbitrariness of Hegel's procedure in relating the Idea to objects in the world.[4] Thus, it might be supposed that the relation of being alien is more naturally conceived of as holding between distinct contents, rather than between a given content and a pure form.

The sense of incongruity here is sharpened if one takes account of the reference in *Manuscripts* to 'externality' as 'alienation' with the implication of error or defect. How, it might be asked, can that through which the Idea achieves its sole aim and goal, the purpose of its existence, be understood in such a way? So far as the Idea is concerned, what Marx calls externality must surely be said, if one is to use evaluative language, to be an unqualified good, indeed the highest good, in that it furnishes the potential for, and ultimately the realisation of, fulfilled existence. Marx's evaluative language has another significant implication. In saying that externality 'ought not to be' he may surely be taken as implying that it might not have been, on the common, and intuitively plausible, assumption that 'ought not' implies 'can refrain from, or avoid'. Now the entire external world comes to figure as mere contingency. This is, however, at odds with the terms in which Marx expounds Hegel elsewhere, as in the passage quoted earlier where he asserts that the Idea 'must' relinquish itself as nature. In doing so he is, one might add, faithfully reflecting Hegel's own practice which notoriously, and to a degree that has seemed excessive even to sympathetic readers, insists on the necessity of all relationships involving the categories of the system.

It seems that what we have to deal with here are opposed metaphysical visions, an opposition expressed most sharply in the relationship they postulate between the Idea and the world. On one side there is a conception of the Idea as essentially emergent, being partly constituted by the things of the world and coming to its truth and fullness of existence only in and through them. On the other, it stands in no such relation of ontological dependence and has no need of involvement in any such cosmic process, being entirely self-subsistent, eternally complete, a starting point rather than a result. It is, one should note, hard to see what could be the point of characterising this conception as 'logical'. For it leaves no room for the distinctive role of the logical Idea as the formal subject that of necessity, out of its own emptiness, initiates the process of self-creation. The language of religion will serve to sharpen the opposition here. On the first, 'pantheist', view, the central truth is that, as Hegel has epigrammatically expressed it elsewhere, 'Without the world God is not God' (Hegel, 1984, p. 308n). On the second, 'theistic', one, the created world is in no way essential to God's being, but is itself the product of a gratuitous act of divine benevolence and freedom, and to that extent is indeed purely contingent. It may provide an arena of divine agency but is by no means to be understood as the indispensable vehicle of divine fulfilment. It is natural to wonder how such incompatible views can be maintained in a short portion of text. Reflections on the subject would, however, be premature in that even taken together these views by no means exhaust its resources. For it contains elements of yet another position that stands in contrast to each of them.

The direction in which to seek this third position is indicated in the remark cited above that, in Hegel's hands, 'the actual becomes phenomenon'. That is to say, it is specifically to the ontological status of the world and its objects that one should look. Elsewhere in our portion of text referred to, Marx had said that the actual relationship between the state and individual 'is expressed by speculative philosophy [der Spekulation] as appearance [Erscheinung], as phenomenon' (Marx, 1962, p. 262; 1975, p. 61). This use of 'appearance' and 'phenomenon' as effectively equivalent is fully in keeping with the tradition of classical German philosophy from which both Hegel and Marx derive.[5] In Hegel's practice at least, neither implies a devaluing in any significant sense of the objects to which they refer. As Marx had noted in a passage quoted earlier, the phenomenon supplies all that the Idea has by way of content, and that is surely a sufficiently estimable role to play. Moreover, 'appearance' is Hegel's standard term for the perceptible forms assumed by essence, its worldly embodiments, and there is nothing derogatory in that usage either. Thus, he insists that essence 'must appear [erscheinen]' and that it is 'not behind or beyond appearance but since the essence is what exists, existence is appearance'. An important distinction emerges, however, when he warns that appearance 'must not be confused with mere semblance [*Schein*]' (Hegel, 1991b, p. 199). Here, as so often in his philosophy, he is seeking to retain a link with ordinary usage, the association of *Schein* with what is superficial and deceptive, a 'shining'. In this respect too his practice is fully in keeping with the philosophical background against which his thought developed.[6]

The important point for present purposes is that Marx by no means confines himself to the language of 'appearance' and 'phenomenon' in expounding Hegel but also, indeed more typically, uses that of 'semblance'. Thus, with reference to the same relationship of state and individual as before, he goes on to say that, in Hegel's account, it is presented as a 'seeming [*scheinbar*] mediation' (Marx, 1962, p. 262; 1975, p. 62). Elsewhere in *Critique* he remarks that the body of the object is, for Hegel, 'really only a semblance' (Marx, 1962, p. 272; 1975, p. 70). In *Manuscripts* the theme is sustained and developed. Thus, the 'product', that which is 'posited', is said to be given the role of 'an independent, actual essence [*Wesen*]' by Hegel, but only 'as a semblance' (Marx and Engels, 1977, p. 577; Marx, 1975, p. 389). Taking the theme further, the object for Hegel is said to be merely 'the *semblance* of an object, a will-o'-the-wisp [*ein vorgemachter Dunst*]' (Marx and Engels, 1977, p. 580; Marx, 1975, p. 392). Still more decisively, in the vein this opens up, one should note the repeated insistence that in Hegel's philosophy the object is a 'nullity' [*Nichtigkeit*] (Marx and Engels, 1977, pp. 576, 579; Marx, 1975, pp. 389, 391). It seems fair to conclude that, at least in one strand of Marx's reading of Hegel, the ontological status of objects in the world is devalued as drastically as might readily be conceived. This makes an obvious contrast with the other strands in it. Neither the view that the empirical world is partly constitutive of God nor the view that it is God's creation have any tendency to imply that it is a nullity, and ordinary pantheists and theists would surely unite in denying such a conclusion. On the other hand, a reader of Hegel might well be reminded at this point of his account of the philosophy of Spinoza: 'The world is determined in the Spinozist system', Hegel declares, 'as a mere phenomenon without genuine reality [*Realität*]', or, to put the point emphatically, '*there is no world*' (Hegel, 1970, pp. 133–4; 1991b, p. 97). Elsewhere he describes Spinoza as maintaining that 'there is no such thing as what is known as the world', and that 'in and for itself it is nothing [*Nichts*]' (Hegel, 1986, p. 195; 1995, p. 281). Hegel proposes that this position should, in virtue of its denial of the world, properly be called 'acosmism' (Hegel, 1991b, p. 97; 1995, p. 281). In the strand of Marx's reading of him being considered, that label, it may be suggested, applies with equal warrant to his own philosophy.

The large issue of Hegelian acosmism, as it arises from Marx's account, is one to which nothing like full justice can be done here. Nevertheless, an attempt should be made to go beyond establishing its presence in that account in order to uncover something of its supposed theoretical motivation, so far as that may be ascertained from Marx. The question to be asked is why should Marx's Hegel wish to deny the world. The answer suggested by the section of *Critique* that is of prime concern has itself a Spinozan cast. This is so in the sense that the underlying metaphysical impulse is assumed there to be essentially that which Hegel attributes to Spinoza in propounding his 'acosmism'. That description is invoked by Hegel in the context of defending Spinoza against charges of atheism and pantheism. 'At the very least', Hegel points out, 'a philosophy that maintains that God, and *only* God, *is* should not be passed off as atheism' (Hegel, 1991b, p. 97). Moreover, he argues:

> If we accept a view that is widely held, and understand pantheism to be the doctrine that considers finite things as such, and the complex of them, to be God, then we shall be forced to acquit Spinoza's philosophy of the charge of pantheism, because no truth at all is ascribed to finite things or to the world is a whole in that philosophy.
>
> (Hegel 1991b, p. 227)

In this portion of text the Hegelian Idea is conceived on a scale sufficiently large, indeed cosmic, as to match that on which the God of Spinoza functions. That much is suggested by the reference to pantheistic mysticism, even if the reference does not otherwise belong with the particular line of thought being pursued at present. It fits with the other indications of this largeness of conception that Marx should describe the Idea as seeking, through its dealings with the finite, to 'enjoy and bring forth its own infinity' (Marx, 1962, p. 264; 1975, p. 63). It should also be noted that the only possible ground of acosmist leanings that is identified in Marx's commentary on paragraph 262 is the Idea's assumption of the role of subject. It is this that leads what he calls the 'actual subjects', such as the family and civil society, to become 'unactual' moments of the Idea (Marx, 1962, p. 262; 1975, p. 62). Thus, the Idea seems to operate here more or less in the manner of Spinoza's God as a monopolist absorbing all existence into itself and thereby draining ontological validity from anything else. Hence, it might be suggested that there is a cosmological inspiration of a broadly Spinozan kind at work. It will bring this suggestion into sharper focus if one considers an alternative basis for acosmism that may also be found in Marx's dealings with Hegel.

To do so is to reintroduce another major figure in the history of philosophy into the picture. Some years before Hegel's defence of Spinoza appeared, Fichte had defended himself against a charge of atheism in just the same terms, by claiming that properly speaking he should rather be called an 'acosmist' (Fichte, 1981, p. 54). The possibility to be considered is that there may be, so to speak, a Fichtean as well as a Spinozan strain of acosmism at work in Marx's thinking about Hegel. The key source will, however, have to be *Manuscripts* rather than *Critique*. Marx sets the scene there with the claim that, for Hegel, 'man is posited as being equivalent to self' and that this self is 'man as an *abstract egoist, egoism* raised to its pure abstraction in thought' (Marx and Engels, 1977, p. 575; Marx, 1975, p. 387). It is a claim that accords rather better with conventional views of Fichte than of Hegel. These are, moreover, views that Marx seems content to fall in with, both earlier in his career, as in a reference to 'Fichte's world-creating ego [*Ich*]', and later, as in one to 'the pure egoism of *Fichte's ego*' (Marx and Engels, 1977, p. 221; 1975a, p. 494; Marx 1962, p. 813; Marx and Engels 1975b, p. 149). The description of Hegel's self as an abstract egoist is not in itself particularly telling in the context of the present inquiry. What is significant is the fact that elsewhere in *Manuscripts* this self assumes precisely a Fichtean world-creating role. For in the course of the discussion the focus of Marx's interest seems to move away from the Hegelian subject as itself a cosmic reality, whether eternally complete or engaged in self-creation. Instead the Idea, 'which has given the Hegelians such terrible headaches', is briskly said to be 'from beginning to end nothing other than *abstraction*, i.e., the abstract thinker'. This abstraction, or abstract thinker, is then depicted as resolving 'to let nature which it concealed within itself only as an abstraction, as a thing of thought [*Gedankending*], to *issue freely from itself*' (Marx and Engels, 1977, pp. 585–6; Marx, 1975, pp. 397–8). Shortly afterwards the theme is restated with a flourish. In Hegel's scheme, nature, Marx declares, 'lay enclosed in the thinker', who, in releasing it, 'believed he was creating essences [*Wesen*] out of nothing, out of pure abstraction, in a divine dialectic' (Marx and Engels, 1977, p. 587; Marx, 1975, pp. 398–9). Marx leaves us in no doubt that in his view this conception is mistaken, and indeed is wholly fantastic. The conception itself is, however, closer to the Fichtean world-creating ego than to the Hegelian Idea, at least in any of its usual interpretations and as it is interpreted by Marx himself elsewhere.

It seems that, in Marx's account of Hegel, two distinct routes to acosmism, the denial of the world, may be discerned. The first goes by way of the assumption that the absolute subject has, so to speak, usurped all the available space, crowding out everything else. The problem is that, as Hegel says of Spinoza, 'there is too much God' (Hegel, 1995, pp. 281–2). By the second route the world turns out to be ontologically deficient just in virtue of being merely a projection of the consciousness of the individual self. Here we are in the domain of what, in the Marxist tradition, has standardly been termed 'subjective idealism', with Fichte as its stock exemplar and object lesson. It should be added that in a general way Marx is fully aware of the value of such a taxonomy of influences for understanding Hegel. Thus, in *The Holy Family* we are told that: 'In *Hegel* there are *three* elements, *Spinozan substance*, *Fichtean self-consciousness* and the *Hegelian* necessarily-contradictory *unity* of the two, the *absolute spirit*' (Marx, 1962, p. 838; Marx and Engels, 1975b,

p. 172). The preceding discussion has tried to show that both the Spinozan and the Fichtean heritage may at any rate be traced in Marx's acosmist version of Hegel's metaphysics. These elements may indeed be said to be necessarily contradictory in that context since they compete for the role of explaining why the world is a nullity, and both cannot be successful. There is, it should be noted, a further question as to the merits of Marx's claim that the unity of Hegelian absolute spirit itself, that is, of the highest stage of the Idea, is necessarily contradictory on account of its dual heritage. This raises however, such large, substantive issues of Hegelian metaphysics that it must fall outside the limits of the present inquiry.

The inquiry has tried to show the diversity of Marx's readings of that metaphysics. It has naturally enough been necessary to draw on different elements of its chosen portion of text to confirm and illustrate this thesis. However, it is also natural to suspect that the various alternatives can scarcely be held so neatly apart in the text as such a procedure might suggest. The suspicion would be correct. The most striking instance of their simultaneous presence in one sentence arises in connection with 'circumstances, arbitrary will and choice of vocation'. Marx comments that these constitute an *'actual mediation'*, which is, however, in Hegel merely 'the *appearance of a mediation* which the actual Idea undertakes with itself and which goes on behind the curtain [*hinter der Gardine*]' (Marx, 1962, p. 262; 1975, pp. 61–2). It is at first sight a puzzling comment. 'Behind the curtain' might be thought to suggest a transcendence which can after all be signalled by 'behind' as well as 'beyond'. Thus, what is in question, it might be supposed, is, to put it in religious terms, the hidden God of theism, working away behind the scenes to manipulate what takes place in front of them. This seems at variance, however, with the insistence that the operations in question are undertaken by the subject solely 'with itself', a difficulty surely so far as their wider efficacy is concerned. Such insistence might be taken rather as a way of characterising the monopolising pantheist subject. Now, however, the imagery of 'behind the curtain' begins to seem inappropriate. For in pantheism there is, so to speak, no dividing curtain, and hence no space behind it, or indeed in front: its unitary vision will not allow such a duality of structure. Hence, if theism or pantheism were the only alternatives, it might have to be concluded that what we have here is a comprehensively mixed metaphor. It is necessary to ask whether the acosmist reading might be able to make better sense of it.

There is an initial awkwardness arising from the fact that the key term Marx uses is 'appearance', where 'semblance' might be thought more appropriate to signal acosmism. This may simply have to be explained, however, in terms of the occasional indifference he shows to the nuances of Hegel's technical vocabulary, an indifference that has already been noted in this particular case and in the still more important one of 'actuality'. Moreover, the acosmist standpoint has no need of, and does not lend itself naturally to, the image of the curtain. Both in its Spinozan and its Fichtean versions it can be expounded satisfactorily without recourse to any such structural device which must rather figure for it as a complication and an encumbrance.[7] By contrast, the device seems to fit perfectly well into a theistic picture of the hidden God and the two realms of the divine and the human. Thus, it may have to be admitted that no reading is possible that will smoothly accommodate every detail of Marx's formulation. If difficulties of detail can be laid aside, however, it may well appear that the acosmist reading has a general advantage over its rivals. This is that it is perfectly adapted to capturing what may reasonably be regarded as the essence of what Marx wishes to convey, the sense that, for Hegel, the ordinary empirical world comprises only misleading outer shows to which reality does not pertain. What it does pertain to are the purely self-regarding operations of the Idea, operations that themselves seem well-suited to being explicated in terms of either the Spinozan absolute or the Fichtean ego. Thus, it appears that while each of the three ways of interpreting Hegel that have been described here can offer some purchase in this case, none is altogether satisfactory. This may itself, however, be taken as testifying to the weight of the diverse interpretative choices that were pressing on Marx. It is hardly surprising that they should on occasion come together to a disharmonious and disconcerting effect at a single point in his work.

It should now be possible to turn fruitfully to the question signalled earlier of how a thinker of Marx's stature could harbour, apparently contentedly, such conflicting views. The question cannot be treated with anything like adequacy here, but something may be said at least to suggest where further inquiry might be rewarding. It should also serve to shed light from a fresh angle on the central theme of this inquiry, the hidden diversity of his dealings with Hegel. To start with, it may help to recall the commonplace that, in the most general terms, the pattern of those dealings is one of critical engagement followed by rejection. It is no doubt true that Hegelian residues remain throughout Marx's career, with some version of the dialectical method the most obvious candidate, and that throughout it also he was to display at different periods a varying sense of indebtedness and appreciation in regard to Hegel. Nevertheless, the overall pattern is clear. It is also clear that an essential dimension of Marx's attitude from the beginning is his awareness of the practical implications of Hegel's philosophy. Thus, it is significant that, even at his most Hegelian, his chief involvement with it takes the form of 'a critique of Hegel's doctrine of the state'. It should, of course, be remembered also that, as Marx was inclined to insist, the practical and theoretical are not to be held rigidly apart here. Thus, he rebukes Hegel's pupils who 'explain one or the other determination of his system by accommodation and the like'. What Marx wishes to stress instead is 'the possibility that this apparent accommodation has its deepest roots in an inadequacy or inadequate formulation of his principle itself' (Marx and Engels 1977,

p. 326; 1975a, p. 84). The present inquiry has sought to show that in truth he formulates Hegel's 'principle' in a number of different ways. What they have in common, it should now be remarked, is that each may, in its own distinctive fashion, serve to root a verdict of accommodation. Hence, the possibility to be considered is that Marx's practical repudiation of Hegel's philosophy is over-determined to an extent he may have found sufficiently congenial and reassuring as to obscure the need for more self-conscious reflection. This situation might at any rate have held for the relatively brief period in which the relationship with Hegel is of vital concern to him, before he turns all his attention to his true lifework beyond philosophy.

The case of pantheism, at least in its undynamic form, seems straightforward enough, and it is this form that is involved whenever Marx touches on the pantheist roots of Hegel's accommodation. If all things are incarnations of God, they are all to be accepted just in virtue of their character as divine. If whatever exists is rational, then whatever exists is to be accepted as having the authority of reason. In this form pantheism is a doctrine of universal accommodation.

Where the theistic reading is concerned, it will simplify matters helpfully to focus on a central feature of the world to which Hegel is accused of having accommodated himself. This is the institution of monarchy, with the Prussian monarchy as the chief case in point. In one aspect the process through which, according to Marx, the institution is legitimated in Hegel's thought is entirely straightforward and, indeed, follows essentially the same lines as in the pantheist reading. 'Hegel is concerned', Marx asserts 'to present the monarch as the actual "God-man", as the actual embodiment of the Idea' (Marx, 1962, p. 285; 1975, p. 81). To have such a status is clearly to be worthy of respect, indeed devotion. Hence, this approach serves to legitimate monarchy just by directly generating a positive evaluation of it. Another, more complex, line of thought may, however, be detected in Marx's account. Indeed, what has been said so far does not do justice to his sense of the metaphysical impulse that underpins Hegel's attitude to monarchy. The character of this impulse is suggested in the general claim, quoted by Marx, that 'subjectivity attains its truth only as a *subject* and personality only as a *person*' (Hegel, 1991a, p. 317; Marx 1962, p. 283; 1975, p. 79). It is in keeping with this claim that the paragraph of the *Philosophy of Right* from which it comes should seek, as Marx puts it, 'to establish the Idea as "*one* individual"' (Marx, 1962, p. 287; 1975, p. 82).

The scene is now set for a kind of structural parallelism of the divine and human realms. It is a conception entirely familiar to Marx since it figured explicitly and prominently in intellectual debates in Germany in his formative decade of the 1830s.[8] Thus, corresponding to the personal subject of the universe in general, the God of theism, there is the personal subject in the human realm, as exemplified above all by the King of Prussia. Here one has to deal not with an incarnation of the divine, but rather with an analogue or mirror image of it. The conception is of a form of homology in which the institutions of the human world are normatively underwritten by being, so to speak, projected on to a cosmic screen. Hence, the legitimacy that pertains to them is that of whatever is in harmony with, indeed re-enacts, the basic character of the universe. The model of structural parallelism is deeply congenial to Marx and he continues to make use of it in his later work. In *Capital*, for example, he traces an 'analogy' between the religious world and the world of commodities. Christianity in particular, with its cult of the abstract man, is said to be the form of religion that 'corresponds best [*ist ... die entsprechendste*]' to a society based on commodity production in which all private labours are brought into relation as homogeneous human labour (Marx, 1969, pp. 52, 58; 1976, pp. 165, 172). It is not at all surprising that the model should play a part in his thinking about the way Hegel's accommodation is rooted in the principle of theism.

The practical significance of acosmism has to be approached somewhat differently since it is scarcely possible in this case to speak in any straight-forward way of legitimating existing institutions. These must suffer, along with all the other elements of nature and society, under the blight of being unreal. Attention should turn rather to the legitimation, or more strictly the de-legitimation, of practices. When this shift is made, it becomes possible to see, with Marx, that acosmist philosophy is, so to speak, objectively conservative. In general terms it seems reasonable to suppose that a belief in the nullity of the world must tend to dry up the springs of action. At the very least it must devitalise and subvert any project of theoretically grounding a programme for radical, not to speak of revolutionary, change. Thus, the existential implications of Spinozan acosmism would seem to lie not in any form of practice but rather in contemplation of the sole, all-encompassing reality and a principled indifference towards the specific character of its semblances. It may be more fruitful at present, however, to pursue the matter in relation to the Fichtean version.

According to that version, nature, as was noted earlier, lay concealed within, and was brought forth by, the thinker as a 'thing of thought'. This view of the ontological status of nature is also applied in *Manuscripts* to the components of the human social world. Thus, for instance, 'wealth and state power' are said to be understood by Hegel as 'thought-essences [*Gedankenwesen*]' (Marx and Engels, 1977, p. 572; Marx, 1975, p. 384). It follows that the entire process of generation of the natural and social worlds, a process of 'alienation' in Marx's terms, takes place entirely within consciousness and that an alteration of consciousness is all that is required to overcome such alienation. Hence what Hegel offers is a 'sublating [*Aufheben*] in thought which leaves its object in existence in the actual world' while believing that 'it has actually overcome it' (Marx and Engels, 1977, pp. 582–3; Marx, 1975, p. 394). It is in this sense that one may speak of his Fichtean acosmism as objectively conservative. It sheds further light on how the topic is pursued by Marx in relation to Hegel's followers, the Young Hegelians. It is pursued all the more vigorously as their pretensions to be revolutionary thinkers need, in Marx's view, to be exposed. Since theirs is, however, at best merely a revolution of consciousness they are, 'in spite of their allegedly 'world shattering' statements' in truth 'the staunchest conservatives' (Marx and Engels, 1962, p. 20; 1976, p. 30). It is true that a more substantial form of change seems called for by the most genuinely Fichtean of these thinkers, Max Stirner, but it amounts at best to a call for self-change: 'I, the actual man, do not have to change actuality, which I can only change together with others, but have to change myself in myself' (Marx and Engels, 1962, p. 193; 1976, p. 212). Hence that is what the rebellion proclaimed by Stirner means in the end: 'anything you like, except action' (Marx and Engels, 1962, p. 366; 1976, p. 382). What is primarily excluded from its meaning, in Marx's view, is collective action for social and political change, action to transform the existing structure of wealth and state power. In treating this structure as merely a projection of individual consciousness, Fichtean acosmism serves to represent any such programme of action as misconceived, beside the point and, thereby, as lacking legitimacy.

A variety of grounds is, it appears, adduced in Marx's writings for holding that accommodation is rooted in a principle of Hegel's philosophy, that this philosophy embodies, so to speak, a logic, or logics, of accommodation. That variety in turn reflects the more fundamental variety of Marx's interpretations of the principle in question. The matter cannot be left, however, without observing that Marx also recognises in Hegel a logic of non-accommodation, a logic to which he is himself unfaithful. Indeed, this recognition belongs at a deeper level of insight, a level at which Marx's true achievement as a critic of Hegel comes into view. The discussion has so far has focused on his dealings with 'Hegelian philosophy in general', in effect with the metaphysics. What has emerged may be said to have itself something of the character of a mystery story with its tantalising fragments, shifting perspectives and hidden, unresolved tensions. The story would be incomplete, however, if it did not take account of Marx's success in getting to the heart of the 'mystery' of the *Philosophy of Right*. Not to do so would, moreover, be to fail to make full use of the portion of text which has been our chief resource. For that offers clear guidance as to where one should turn.

The guidance comes in a sentence near the beginning of the commentary on paragraph 262: 'Family and civil society appear as the dark ground of nature from which the light of the state emerges' (Marx, 1962, p. 261; 1975, p. 61). The principle of the line of criticism that is thereby introduced is that Hegel's doctrine of the state is dominated throughout, to its structural detriment, by this dark ground. The key pressure points are identified by Marx as the hereditary monarchy, the hereditary legislators and the institution of primogeniture, particularly as it concerns landed property. At all of these points a purely natural determinant, that of birth, is allowed to trump the claims of reason, spirit and society. This situation is the subject of incisive criticism by Marx, as exemplified in the following passage:

> Hegel everywhere sinks from his political spiritualism [*Spiritualismus*] down into the crassest *materialism*. At the summit of the political state it is always birth that makes determinant individuals into embodiments of the highest political tasks. The highest activities of the state coincide with individuals through their birth, just as the situation of an animal, its character, mode of life etc. are directly born with it. The state in its highest functions acquires an *animal* actuality.
>
> (Marx, 1962, pp. 395–6; 1975, p. 174)[9]

The force of this criticism lies precisely in its immanent character. For Hegel's preference for spirit (*Geist*) over nature is, as Marx is well aware, built into the very fabric of his thinking. Thus, spirit is a higher stage, embodying a fuller, more concrete, definition, of the Hegelian Idea. Moreover, the success of spirit in emancipating itself from nature is for Hegel the ultimate determinant of progress in history.[10] It is calamitous for his project in political philosophy that he should accept that, as Marx puts it, what rules the state, itself supposedly the 'highest existence [*Dasein*] of freedom', the 'existence of self-conscious reason', and the 'realisation of the free spirit', is 'blind natural necessity' (Marx, 1962, pp. 328–9; Marx 1975, pp. 118–9). Hegel fails here to follow his own best insights, the non-accommodationist logic that should have led him to reject institutions whose 'secret' is 'zoology' (Marx, 1962, p. 397; Marx 1975, p. 175). In drawing attention to this triumph of nature over spirit, Marx strikes at the very foundations of the institutional structure depicted in the *Philosophy of Right*. It is in this sense that he may be said to have revealed the 'mystery' of that work in the form of its fundamental disharmony and lack of organic connection with Hegel's system.

A more deadly strain of criticism could hardly be conceived. It cannot, however, be said to have received its due in the mainstream of Hegel scholarship, a region where Marx's importance as a critic has gone largely unacknowledged. This failure has, no doubt, many causes, but it must in some degree reflect a more general failure, on the part of both admirers and opponents, to pay close attention to the specificity of his account of Hegel, a failure that makes it difficult to bring any particular aspect of it into sharp focus. The present inquiry has attempted to illustrate on a small scale the value of paying such attention. Concentrating on the question of the nature of the Idea and of its relationship to the empirical world, as depicted by Marx, and using a brief portion of text as springboard, it has distinguished three positions. These may be summed up in the propositions that this world is partly constitutive of the Idea, that it is a creation of the Idea and that, by comparison with the Idea, it lacks genuine reality. These positions were labelled pantheism, theism and acosmism respectively. Pantheism, it was shown, is present in Marx's account in two versions, historical and unhistorical, and two distinct streams of thought feed into acosmism, one of Spinozan and the other of Fichtean provenance. These diverse formulations of Hegel's 'principle' yield diverse theoretical grounds for his 'accommodation' and hence, indirectly, for Marx's rejection of the practical dimension of his thought.

A complex picture has now emerged, a complexity which, as was hinted earlier, has not been adequately reflected in the literature on the relationship between Hegel and Marx, as anyone acquainted with that literature could surely testify. It has been possible here to outline it only in the most schematic terms, and much remains to be done by way of exploring in detail the elements of the picture and the connections between them. It is, one might suggest in conclusion, vitally important that commentators sympathetic to Marx and his legacy should participate in such projects. They owe him the respect that consists in submitting his work to the most rigorous critical analysis they can manage. To do so is, moreover, the only way to exhibit decisively the abundance and fertility of his ideas and thereby confirm him in his rightful place as a major, indispensable figure in Western philosophy. There is no cause to fear the outcome of such analysis, whatever its degree of rigour. Marx has no need of being patronised by our excessive tenderness, a tenderness that is particularly misguided where his dealings with Hegel are concerned. It is time to dispense with the disabling irony of treating as a source of clear, univocal, instantly authoritative truths what is in reality one of the richest imbroglios in the history of thought.

Notes

1. All translations from Marx are by the present writer. A reference to the German source is given followed by a standard English translation.
2. For this, and other, reasons some commentators have preferred to call Hegel a 'panentheist' rather than 'pantheist'. Provided the sense in which 'pantheism' is being ascribed to him is sufficiently clear, this is, however, a question of terminology which need not be pursued here. See Whittemore, 1960, pp. 134–64.
3. It is clear from the context that here, as often with Marx, 'speculative' and 'Hegelian' are interchangeable terms.
4. See, e.g. Marx 1975, pp. 67, 73–4, 93, 98, 128.
5. See, e.g. Kant, 1998, p. 347.
6. See, e.g. Kant 1998, p. 384.
7. It is tempting to speculate that Marx, steeped as he was in ancient philosophy, is influenced at some level here by the classic acosmist parable of Plato's *Cave* with its use of similar theatrical imagery.
8. For an illuminating discussion, see Breckman, 1999.
9. Cf. Marx, 1962, pp. 303–4; 1975, pp. 96–7, 328–9, 118–19.
10. See, e.g. Hegel 1975, pp. 152–96.

Bibliography

Breckman, Warren (1999) *Marx, the Young Hegelians, and the Origins of Radical Social Theory: Dethroning the Self* (Cambridge: Cambridge University Press).

Fichte, Johann Gottlieb (1981) *Gesamtausgabe der Bayerischen Akademie der Wissenschaften*, Band 6, (eds) Reinhard Lauth and Hans Gliwitzky (Stuttgart-Bad Cannstatt: Friedrich Fromman Verlag).

Hegel, Georg Wilhelm Friedrich (1970) *Theorie Werkausgabe*, Band 8, (eds) Eva Moldenhauer and Karl Markus Michel (Frankfurt am Main: Suhrkamp).

—— (1975) *Lectures on the Philosophy of World History. Introduction: Reason in History*, trans. H. B. Nisbet (Cambridge: Cambridge University Press).

—— (1977) *Phenomenology of Spirit*, trans. A. V. Miller (Oxford: Oxford University Press).

—— (1984) *Lectures on the Philosophy of Religion*, vol. 1, (ed.) Peter C. Hodgson (Berkeley: University of California Press).

—— (1986) *Theorie Werkausgabe*, Band 20, (eds) Eva Moldenhauer and Karl Markus Michel (Frankfurt am Main: Suhrkamp).

—— (1991a) *Elements of the Philosophy of Right*, trans. H. B. Nisbet (Cambridge: Cambridge University Press).

—— (1991b) *The Encyclopaedia Logic*, trans. T. F. Geraets, W. A. Suchting and H. S. Harris (Indianapolis: Hackett).

—— (1995) *Lectures on the History of Philosophy*, vol. 3, trans. E. S. Haldane and Frances H. Simson (Lincoln: University of Nebraska Press).

Kant, Immanuel (1998) *Critique of Pure Reason*, trans. Paul Guyer and Allen W. Wood (Cambridge: Cambridge University Press).

Marx, Karl (1962) *Frühe Schriften*, Band 1, (eds) Hans- Joachim Lieber and Peter Furth (Stuttgart: Cotta Verlag).

—— (1969) *Das Kapital*, Band 1 (Frankfurt am Main: Ullstein).

—— (1975) *Early Writings*, trans. Rodney Livingstone and Gregor Benton (Harmondsworth: Penguin).

—— (1976) *Capital*, vol. 1, trans. Ben Fowkes (Harmondsworth: Penguin).

Marx, Karl and Engels, Friedrich (1962) *Werke*, Band 3 (Berlin: Dietz Verlag).

—— (1975a) *Collected Works*, vol. 1 (London: Lawrence and Wishart).

—— (1975b) *The Holy Family, or Critique of Critical Criticism*, trans. Richard Dixon and Clemens Dutt, 2nd edn (revised) (Moscow: Progress Publishers).

—— (1976) *Collected Works*, vol. 5 (London: Lawrence and Wishart).

—— (1977) *Werke, Ergänzsungsband*, Erster Teil (Berlin: Dietz Verlag).

Whittemore, Robert C. (1960) 'Hegel as Panentheist', *Tulane Studies in Philosophy*, 9.

2
Marx's Philosophical Modernism: Post-Kantian Foundations of Historical Materialism

Martin McIvor

Recent years have witnessed a remarkable resurgence of interest in the 'German Idealist' movement, one that can arguably be said to have transformed our understanding and appreciation of its key thinkers.[1] Originating in the latest German scholarship, this revival has carried over into Anglo-American philosophical discussion where it has connected with contemporary 'post-analytic' concerns with normativity, discursivity and sociality, and post-Rawlsian debates around contractualism and communitarianism. Attention has focused most obviously upon Immanuel Kant and Georg Hegel – now seen less as (respectively) dry moralist and esoteric metaphysician, and more as powerful and pivotal thinkers of subjectivity, agency and modernity. But it has also extended to take in Johann Fichte, Friedrich Schelling, the early Romantics, even figures who until recently were known only to few historical specialists such as Karl Reinhold or Friedrich Jacobi.

Curiously, however, these inquiries have not yet been followed through into a reconsideration of the ideas of Karl Marx, whose philosophical and political outlook was to a great extent formed through a critical engagement with the legacy of German Idealism. Nor, it must be said, have Marxist philosophers devoted much explicit consideration to what new light might be thrown on Marx's thought by this re-evaluation of the intellectual background against which he first began to define his distinctive project. My aim in what follows is to set out an initial approach to this question – necessarily sketchy and inconclusive, but also, I hope, stimulating and suggestive.

Philosophy after Kant: Freedom and reasons

Any attempt to summarise the insights and implications of a voluminous body of recent commentary that ranges from Christine Korsgaard's reappropriations of Kant to Robert Pippin's re-presentation of Hegel must of necessity be crude and simplistic. I make no claim to do justice to its intricacy and internal diversity, nor to the controversy and debate it has aroused.[2] Nevertheless I think it is possible to identify some broad themes and issues that have motivated contemporary interest in the ideas and debates of the German Idealist period.

At the heart of this new interest, I would suggest, is a cluster of issues that have come to be associated with what we now tend to call the condition and experience of 'modernity' – a condition which, in important respects, is still our own today. Stated very briefly, we can say that for philosophical purposes, the problems of modernity are first and foremost problems of justification – 'traditional' ways of thinking and living no longer seem so self-evidently authoritative, 'given' or determined by external or internal 'nature', so we find ourselves asking why we should sustain them, or what should replace them. This is sometimes designated as the problem of 'normativity' – the realisation that we interpret the world and act in it according to general norms or rules that we ourselves apply to particular impressions or situations, raising the question of the legitimacy and revisability of those rules. In the influential account of Jürgen Habermas: 'Modernity can and will no longer borrow the criteria by which it takes its orientation from the models supplied by another epoch; *it has to create its normativity out of itself*' (Habermas, 1987, p. 7). For Korsgaard, 'there has been a revolution, and [...] the world has been turned inside out. The real is no longer the good [...] the ethics of autonomy is the only one consistent with the metaphysics of the modern world' (Korsgaard, 1996, pp. 4–5). For Pippin, the 'basic issue' of modernity is 'the problem of "autonomy", or genuine self-determination or self-rule' (Pippin, 1999, p. 3).

Kant is now seen by many commentators to be centrally concerned with this problem, and both his critical epistemology and his 'constructivist' morality can be seen as an attempt to answer it. According to Terry Pinkard, Kant 'captured a deep, almost subterranean shift in what his audience was coming to experience as necessary for themselves: from now on, we were called to lead our own lives, to think for ourselves' (Pinkard, 2002, pp. 19–20). And Hegel, though once seen as mounting a retreat from Kant's position to a more traditional form of metaphysics as the foundation of science, and a more traditionalist emphasis upon culture and community as the basis of our morality, can also be read as attempting to follow through Kant's project in a more radical and systematic way.[3] It is because I think this interpretation captures some important aspects of Hegel's thought that I take up the term 'post-Kantian' as the best way of capturing the movement of philosophy that, according to this reading, is inaugurated by Kant but is continued in the more ambitious Idealisms of Fichte, Schelling and Hegel.

Three interrelated themes emerge from this reading of the German Idealist period that I think are worth keeping in mind when we think about Marx's trajectory. I will summarise these as the challenge of self-determination, the critique of 'reflection', and the sociality of normativity. In so far as we are willing to see the movement of German Idealist thought as consistent and coherent, we can see these as three steps in a continuous line of argument.

First, the challenge of self-determination. This is the proposition that human beings, as conscious, rational beings, are in a fundamental sense free to choose and responsible for the ways in which they interpret the world and the ways in which they act in it. We can find variations of this idea expressed by many thinkers in many periods, but it can be argued that Kant was the first European philosopher to think through its implications to the degree of sophistication and systematicity that he did. His seminal *Critique of Pure Reason* is developed from the claim that human 'knowledge' is founded upon an active organisation of sensible 'intuitions' by the self-determining 'understanding':

> [C]ombination does not lie in the objects [...] and cannot as it were be borrowed from them through perception and by that means first taken up into the understanding, but is rather only an operation of the understanding, which is itself nothing other than the faculty of combining *a priori* and bringing the manifold of given representations under unity of apperception.
>
> (Kant, 1997, p. 248)

The 'objectivity' of such knowledge then turns on an argument for the rules (or concepts, or 'categories') employed in this synthesis as binding upon any possible rational subject. As Pippin highlights, Kant stresses the 'spontaneity' of this act of synthesis – in the philosophical sense of 'an uncaused or perhaps self-caused cause [that] cannot be described as empirically grounded' (Pippin, 1989, p. 23).[4] And as Henry Allison makes clear, this 'spontaneity of the understanding' finds its 'practical analogue' in Kant's practical and moral philosophy, in 'the spontaneity of the agent as rational deliberator', that is

> the capacity to determine oneself to act on the basis of objective (intersubjectively valid) rational norms and, in light of these norms, to take (or reject) inclinations or desires as sufficient reasons for action. According to this model, then, the intentional actions of a rational agent are never '*merely*' the causal consequences of the agent's antecedent psychological state [...] but require, as a necessary condition, an act of spontaneity.
>
> (Allison, 1990, p. 170)

The world as it is given to us – even in the form of our awareness of pleasure or happiness – does not, on its own, tell us how to act. As autonomous beings we must act on rules that we give ourselves. The Categorical Imperative is one of Kant's ways of characterising the way in which our actions must be tested and justified if we are to rise to this challenge.

Kant himself stressed that 'the concept of freedom [...] constitutes the *keystone* of the whole structure of a system of pure reason, even of specula- tive reason' (Kant, 1996, p. 3). This notion of radical self-determination became the governing idea of Fichte's development of Kant's philosophy, in his absolutisation of the '*Ich*' or 'I' or 'Ego' of self-consciousness (Fichte, 2008), and was upheld by Schelling and Hegel as the definitive insight of modern philosophy. Thus Hegel affirmed in 1801, in a text that endorsed Schelling's early philosophy as a positive and necessary development of Fichte's, 'the determinate and express principle of Idealism' that 'the world is a product of the freedom of intelligence' (Hegel, 1977a, p. 130).

The second theme which I wish to highlight is the critique of 'reflection' or 'the understanding' which was developed most fully by Schelling and Hegel as, in their eyes, a necessary radicalisation and completion of Kant's principle of self-determination. In their early criticisms of Kant, Schelling and Hegel argued that in order to fully live up to the challenge of freedom that Kant had outlined, we must reject any point of view that regards our experience or agency as being determined or limited by something outside it, something 'beyond' our comprehension or control. In their view, Kant himself had fallen victim to this illusion by retaining an incoherent place in his system for a supersensible 'thing-in-itself', the ultimate object of knowledge which we could never know anything about, and in the practi- cal domain with his assumption that the 'kingdom of ends' – the ultimate goal of moral action in which all rational beings find harmony with one another – could never be realised in the here and now. As Schelling put it in his 1800 *System of Transcendental Idealism*:

By the thing-in-itself, which he introduced into philosophy, Kant at least provided the first impulse which would carry philosophy beyond ordinary consciousness [...] but he never even considered clearly, let alone explained, that this ground of explanation lying beyond [*jenseits*] consciousness is in the end no more than our own ideal activity, merely hypostatised into the thing-in-itself.

(Schelling, 1978, p. 99)

This immanent critique of Kantian epistemology was generalised by Schelling and Hegel into a broader cultural diagnosis of reason's self-abnegation: 'Reason [...] acknowledges its own nothingness by placing that which is better than it in a *faith outside and above* itself, as a *beyond*' wrote Hegel in *Faith and Knowledge* (Hegel, 1977b, p. 56).[5] In his later independent work, this theme was developed by Hegel as a critique of 'the understanding', a faculty or mode of thought which performed the necessary task of defining the world as a system of identities and oppositions, but which was mis- taken or misleading in so far as these distinctions were taken to have their foundations in an external order of 'essences' rather than being its own active

creation. The overcoming of this 'inversion' is the pivotal climax of the early
section on 'the understanding's' projection of a supersensible 'thing-in-itself'
in Hegel's *Phenomenology of Spirit*:

> The inner world is, for consciousness, still a *pure beyond*, because con-
> sciousness does not as yet find itself in it. It is *empty*, for it is merely the
> nothingness of appearance, and positively the *simple* or *unitary* universal.
>
> From the idea, then, of inversion, which constitutes the essential nature
> of one aspect of the supersensible world, we must eliminate the sensuous
> idea of fixing the differences in a different sustaining element; and this
> absolute concept of the difference must be represented and understood
> purely as inner difference. ...
>
> This curtain [of appearance] hanging before the inner world is therefore
> drawn away, and we have the inner being [the 'I'] gazing into the inner
> world [...] *self-consciousness*.
>
> (Hegel, 1977c, pp. 88, 98–9, 103)

The conclusion to this argument in the *Phenomenology*, as Pippin and Pinkard
interpret it, is the assertion of what I will here summarise as 'the sociality of
normativity' – the realisation that our cognitive and practical ordering of the
world must refer not to some ground or authority beyond our activity nor
to a purely individual act of self-determination, but instead to the social and
historical practices of communication and recognition which emerge out
of the struggle to reconcile such individual acts. 'We usually suppose that
the Absolute must lie far beyond [*jenseits*]; but it is precisely what is wholly
present, what we, as thinkers, always carry with us and employ, even though
we have no express consciousness of it', writes Hegel (1975, p. 59). Here is the
point at which Hegel's system can sound like a strange religion of rationalist
metaphysics ('reason is the soul of the world, inhabits it, and is immanent in
it, as its own, innermost nature, its universal'; Hegel, 1975, p. 56), in which
everything is a mere moment of the all-embracing Idea. But it is important
to understand the route by which Hegel arrives at such grand formulations
as one which is aiming to give proper recognition to the extent to which our
world is shaped by an ongoing and dynamic process of reasoned inquiry and
argument in which we, as rational subjects and agents, are fully conscious
and autonomous participants. Most importantly, for Hegel, this immanence
of reason is to be located not only in the advance of empirical experience
and scientific investigation which delivers the 'natural' world we inhabit, but
also in the cultural history and social practices through which we come to
recognise and engage one another as fellow subjects and reasoners.

Thus, despite the sometimes exotic terms in which it was expressed,
Hegel's 'Absolute Idealism' has been read by recent commentators as a move

to recast and resituate the moral and epistemological problems of philosophy as internal to the development of self-authorising linguistic practices and social institutions that remains highly suggestive today, dovetailing with the work of 'post-analytic' philosophers such as Richard Rorty, John McDowell or Robert Brandom. In Pinkard's account, Hegel

> intended his 'Doctrine of the Concept' [...] as the theory of normativity that would cash out his overall claim that our ascriptions of knowledge are not *comparisons* of any kind of subjective state with something non-subjective; they are *moves within* a social space structured by responsibilities, entitlements, attributions, and the undertakings of commitments.
> (Pinkard, 2002, p. 257)

This philosophical perspective in turn implies a cultural or political project that would render this self-legislation fully self-conscious and autonomous, following through the implications of this transformed understanding of subjectivity and agency for the legitimacy and authority of our social practices and institutions. Hence Pippin's claim for the epochal significance of German Idealism as a philosophical movement:

> As understood by Kant, the early Fichte and Schelling, and Hegel and the left Hegelians, the modern enterprise is [...] tied to an essentially practical goal, what one might call a kind of 'metaphysical politics': working out, articulating, helping to defend and so to realize, the possibility of free self-determination, agency, spontaneity, activity, a self-directed 'purposive life', eventually (in Hegel) a necessarily collective agency.
> (Pippin, 1997, p. 8)

In sum, then, there are three interrelated strands to this account of post-Kantian idealism that I wish to draw upon in what follows: (1) an emphasis on, and commitment to exploring the implications of, Kant's account of the 'self-determining' character of self-conscious knowledge and action; (2) a critique of any 'reflective' standpoint that absolutises a given order of things or relations by reference to an underlying reality or system of essences 'beyond' our comprehension or control; and (3) an account of 'Reason', the ongoing normative activity of conceptualisation and reconceptualisation, as encompassing and permeating all our social experiences and interactions, suggesting a socio-historically immanent self-determination that can be read as a more comprehensive and thoroughgoing realisation of the ideal of self-determination proclaimed by Kant. In the remainder of this chapter I want to suggest that, if plausible, this reading of post-Kantian philosophy throws new light upon Marx's thought that may prove to be highly revealing. For, as I will attempt to indicate, if we look again at Marx's texts, we can see him picking up these themes explicitly, and, I will argue, using them to structure his philosophical anthropology, his critique of capitalist modernity, and his projection of a communist future.

Marx on self-determination

It is well known that Marx's earliest philosophical outlook was formed by his participation in an intellectual milieu that has become known as the 'Young Hegelian' or 'Left Hegelian' movement. In the 1830s and 1840s intellectual life in Germany was dominated by debates among, and reactions to, the work of writers and thinkers who sought to revive the radical impetus which they took to be the basis of Hegel's philosophy. I want to stress at this point the extent to which these thinkers were interested in recovering the ideal of self-determination which recent commentators have identified as a central concern of post-Kantian philosophy. I will illustrate this with examples of two philosphers who were especially (and successively) influential upon the young Marx – Bruno Bauer and Ludwig Feuerbach.

Bauer achieved notoriety in the late 1830s as a coruscating critic of official religious ideology in the name of 'self-consciousness', which he describes as 'the all-powerful magician, who creates the world and all its differences', and so 'the sole force of the world and history' (quoted in Rosen, 1977, pp. 73, 77). I think it is clear that if we look at Bauer's claims for 'self-consciousness', he is drawing upon and developing the fundamental Kantian idea of self-consciousness as spontaneous, outside and unrestricted by the empirical world we experience and, at the same time, the ground or organising principle of that world. Similarly, though less transparently, we can detect the same idea at work in Feuerbach's critique of religious belief in the *Essence of Christianity*. As is well known, Feuerbach's argument is that religion is nothing other than humanity's misrecognition of its own 'nature' as an alienated other, but what is often overlooked is that for Feuerbach, '[t]his nature is nothing else than the intelligence – the understanding' (Feuerbach, 1989, p. 33). All the philosophical definitions of God are attributes of 'the understanding': 'that which conditions and coordinates all things', the 'criterion of all reality', the 'self-standing and independent essence', which 'comprehends all things in itself, because it is itself not a thing, because it is free from all things' (Feuerbach, 1989, pp. 33–43).

Marx's earliest piece of substantial writing, his doctoral thesis on the ancient Greek atomists Democritus and Epicurus, is permeated by appeals to this principle of 'self-consciousness' (Marx, 1975b; for a full exploration of this text see McIvor, 2008). Philosophy, Marx stridently affirms, stands in irreconcilable opposition to 'all heavenly and earthly gods who do not acknowledge human self-consciousness as the highest divinity'. In an important long footnote to the dissertation Marx argues that the so-called ontological proofs for the existence of God amounts only to '*proofs of the existence of essential human self-consciousness*' (Marx, 1975b, p. 104). And tellingly, I think, he appeals at this point to an early essay by Schelling 'On the "I" as a principle of philosophy' (Schelling, 1980) against the later Schelling's reversion to what in Marx's eyes amounted to a reactionary legitimation of religious and political orthodoxy (Marx, 1975b, p. 103).

Soon afterwards, under the influence of Feuerbach, Marx begins to articulate this radical principle in more naturalist or anthropological terms.[6] But I think we can still detect a clear echo of this post-Kantian theme of radical self-determination as the fundamental ordering principle of the world, even as Marx seeks a new language with which to express this radical humanism.[7] If we are serious about uncovering the mysterious origin or ground of our world, we need look only to ourselves. 'To be radical is to grasp things by the root', Marx writes in late 1843, 'but for man the root is man himself' (Marx, 1975f, p. 251). Increasingly Marx feels that to grasp this root, we must take human beings not merely as constructed by the then emerging ideology of constitutional liberalism, as a free citizens participating in a legal and public domain of formal equality, but also in their most everyday productive interactions with each other and with their material environment. In the famous *Economic and Philosophical Manuscripts* of 1844 Marx applies this principle to the field of political economy, and grounds his critique of the system of private property in a notion of humanity's 'species-being'. This concept is sometimes read in pseudo-Aristotelian terms, as if Marx aimed to identify the *telos* of human nature which we are cosmically ordained to fulfil. But I think we get closer to the radicalism of Marx's conception if we notice how his account builds upon the post-Kantian account of human activity as conceptually mediated and, therefore, implicitly reflexive or self-conscious, and for that reason, radically free or 'spontaneous'.

> The animal is immediately one with its life activity. It is not distinct from that activity, it *is* that activity. Man makes his life activity itself an object of his will and consciousness. He has conscious life activity. It is not a determination with which he directly merges [...] he is a conscious being, i.e. his own life is an object for him, only because he is a species-being. Only because of that is his activity free activity [*freie Tätigkeit*].
>
> (Marx, 1975h, p. 328)

On this reading, our nature is precisely to have no nature, to be free to create or develop it according to our own rules and standards.[8]

Moving forward to Marx's 'mature' writings on political economy in the *Grundrisse* and *Capital*, I think we can see the same presumptions at work. This can perhaps be brought out most forcefully by noticing how close Marx's account of the distinctive character of human labour is to one that had already been offered by Kant in the *Critique of Judgement*. Kant is seeking to offer a definition of human 'art' (by which intends the general activity of making things, 'fine art' being a special case):

> By right we should not call anything art except a production through freedom, i.e., through a power of choice that bases its acts on reason. For though we like to call the product that bees make (the regularly constructed honeycombs) a work of art, we do so only by virtue of an analogy with art; for as soon as we recall that their labour is not based on any rational deliberation on their part, we say at once that the product is a product of their nature (namely, of instinct), and it is only to their creator that we ascribe it as art.
>
> (Kant, 1997, p. 170)

Marx's famous account of the 'exclusively human' form of labour in *Capital* is strikingly continuous with this account:

> [W]hat distinguishes the worst architect from the best of bees is that the architect builds the cell in his mind before he constructs it in wax. At the end of every labour process, a result emerges which has already been conceived by the worker at the beginning, hence already existed ideally. Man not only effects a change of form in the materials of nature; he also realizes his own purpose in those materials. And this is a purpose he is conscious of, it determines the mode of his activity with the rigidity of a law, and he must subordinate his will to it.
>
> (Marx, 1976, pp. 283–4)

Both Kant and Marx stress that, unlike animals' unconscious or instinctive interactions with their natural environment, human engagements with the material world are necessarily mediated by intentional or purposive concepts of the 'objects' they aim to produce; both writers argue on this account that human beings' consciously purposive activity is by that token a kind of *self-legislation*, giving a law to oneself. Of course, we are not used to thinking of Kantian autonomy in this way, since we are accustomed to discussing it in the context of Kant's writing about how we might resolve moral or political problems. But I think it is clear that, even on Kant's terms, as a philosophical description of human activity, this ideal of self-legislation should be equally applicable to 'material' or 'economic' activities that we are not used to bringing into such discussions. But of course this is precisely what Marx is concerned to do. For Marx, all our activities are conceptually mediated, and so free from brute empirical determination and subject to a conscious rational ordering or normative integration.

My first claim, then, is that Marx's early philosophical outlook is clearly governed by a concern with the principle of self-determination that is implicit in Kant's original account of the spontaneity of human self-consciousness.

And while his later writings seek to materially situate and to some extent 'naturalise' this capacity through notions such as 'species-being' or 'the labour process', he has clearly held onto the intrinsic connection, articulated and developed by post-Kantian philosophy, between conceptuality and autonomy, onto the idea of free activity as action under a rule that I give myself. Thus it would appear that, to an extent that has perhaps not been adequately recognised, a post-Kantian ideal of free self-determination remains fundamental to Marx's social thought and, by his own account, at the heart of his political, historical and economic analyses.[9]

Marx against 'the beyond'

My second claim will be that what I have summarised as the critique of 'reflection' or 'the understanding' in post-Kantian thought can also be traced as a recurrent motif throughout Marx's writings, and, indeed, that it plays an important role in structuring his critique of bourgeois society and the categories of political economy.

Again, this can be shown to be a central trope in the writings of the Young Hegelians among whom Marx first developed his own ideas in the 1830s and 1840s. Repeatedly we find that the central target of their critique is the erection of some higher truth or moral authority 'beyond' human comprehension or control. Any such notion, the Young Hegelians always insist, can be nothing other than humanity's own misrecognised creation, problematically insulated from rational critique. Thus Douglas Moggach has recently written that for Bauer, 'in religion, self-consciousness is alienated, and appears to be passive, though it is never truly so. Rather, thought deceives itself about its own activities, attributing them to another, transcendent source, which it has unknowingly generated' (Moggach, 2003, p. 34). And, as already indicated, I think it is important that we recognise the extent to which Feuerbach's critique of religious belief draws upon a post-Kantian critique of 'the understanding' that mistakenly looks beyond itself for something that is in truth nothing other than its own free act.

In his youthful writings Marx often invokes the terms of this critique of 'the beyond'. In an early letter written to his father which records his first conversion to the Hegelian school, Marx renounces his romantic poetry on the grounds that 'it was purely idealistic. My heaven, my art, became a world beyond [*Jenseits*], as remote as my love' (Marx, 1975a, p. 11). A section of his dissertation criticising conventional religious support for moral action through the sanction of punishment in the afterlife is titled 'Fear and the Being Beyond [*das jenseitige Wesen*]' (Marx, 1975b). Marx's familiarity with the Hegelian critique of Kant's practical philosophy is clear from the *German Ideology*, where it is asserted that Kant 'transferred the *realisation* of [the] good will, the harmony between it and the needs and impulses of individuals, to *the world beyond*' (Marx and Engels, 1970, p. 97). But from an early stage Marx (following Feuerbach's lead) begins to turn this critique back against Hegel himself, arguing that his own mature system is ultimately guilty of the same formalism and mystificatory orientation to 'the beyond' of which Hegel had accused his predecessors. In 1843 Marx describes Hegel's *Philosophy of Right* as 'abstract extravagant *thinking* on the modern state, the reality of which remains a thing of the beyond', and announces that it is 'the *task of history*, once the *beyond* [*Jenseits*] *of truth* has vanished, to establish the *truth of this world*' (Marx, 1975f, p. 244). Finally, in the 1844 manuscripts the link is made between this critique of religious and political alienation and the account of alienated labour that is at the root of his early critique of political economy:

> Just as in religion the spontaneous activity of the human imagination, the human brain and the human heart detaches itself from the individual and reappears as the alien activity of a god or of a devil, so the activity of the worker is not his own spontaneous activity. It belongs to another, it is a loss of his self.
>
> (Marx, 1975h, pp. 326–7)

There has been much debate among readers of Marx about whether his account of alienation persists in his later writings on the capitalist mode of production in *Capital*. I want to take a somewhat different tack and argue that Marx's developed critique of the categories of political economy, and the fetishism of capitalist social relations that they reproduce, takes the form of the critique of reflection or 'the understanding' developed by Schelling and Hegel.[10] We have seen that Schelling and Hegel criticised the notion of a fixed essence or 'thing-in-itself' behind sensible appearance as the misrecognised proxy for our own active role in organising experience; and related such epistemological tangles to a broader failure to appreciate and bring to full self-consciousness the foundational role of social reason in shaping and ordering the world we inhabit.[11] Marx applies a similar critique to the 'metaphysical subtleties and theological niceties' of the commodity itself, which we first encounter as having a strange, two-tiered structure: an outward, concrete existence and an inner, 'supersensible' social meaning or market 'value' (Marx, 1976, p. 163).[12] In time, says Marx, 'men try to decipher the hieroglyphic, to get behind the secret of their own social product' – and Marx credits the classical political economy of Smith and Ricardo with the 'belated scientific discovery that the products of labour, in so far as they are values, are merely the material expressions of the human labour expended to produce them' (Marx, 1976, p. 167). Thus we see that the commodity embodies an 'inversion' [*Verkehrung*] of 'the relation between value and the force that creates value' (Marx, 1976, p. 425). But this theoretical recognition cannot by itself take us out of the 'inverted world' in which 'the sensibly-concrete counts only as the form of appearance of the abstractly general' (Marx, 1978, p. 140). For this 'bewitching' metaphysic is implicit in the practical relations of a society in which 'private labours [are] carried on independently of each other' and their 'social character' is realised and validated only in the act of exchange and the concept of an abstract, commensurable 'value' which such a practice entails (Marx, 1976, p. 167). The very idea of an object having a 'value' distinct from and 'beyond' its sensible concrete properties is then a consequence of our own theoretical and practical separation from the collective labour process in which we are unconsciously or unpurposively playing a part – 'a social formation in which the process of production has mastery over man, instead of the opposite' (Marx, 1976, p. 175).

The critique of 'the understanding', then, reappears in Marx's mature analysis of political economy as a critique of the value form itself. For it is precisely through the rules of the market and the 'law of value' that the capitalist economy dominates and exploits us, despite being nothing other than our own collective activity of mutual reproduction. Marx's response to this predicament is radical and simple. Since it is the collective or social aspect of our activity that is mystified in this way – that part of our labour which meets the needs of others and those objects of need which we depend upon others to produce – we can only raise it to the level of self-conscious activity by constituting a collective subjectivity and agency that can bring these processes under conscious collective control.[13] The practical and historical parallel to Hegel's tearing away of the 'curtain of appearance' to reveal the active role of self-consciousness in constituting the world of experience is a collective realisation and recovery of the role of our own social labour in producing the world of use-values we find before us. This is the meaning, and necessity, of communism for Marx.

The self-conscious normativity of communism

Notoriously, Marx says very little about what communism would actually be like – he viewed this as the task of history, and working class struggle, to determine. But if we study the hints that he does offer, and consider the intellectual sources of his commitment, I think that we can suggest at least a philosophical account of Marx's communist ideal, even if not a political or economic one. The germ of this idea is, I would argue, already present in Kant's thought, as is brought out by Korsgaard:

> When we interact with each other what we do is deliberate together, to arrive at a shared decision. Since the conclusion of a practical syllogism is an action, the result is an action that we perform together, governed by a law we freely choose together. The free choice of this law is an act that constitutes our unified will and makes shared action possible. That, in Kant's view, is what interaction is.

[T]he conditions for successful interaction are the joint conditions of respect for the other's humanity, and the treatment of her reasons as considerations with public normative standing: when we interact, we legislate together, and act together, for the good of the whole we in this way create.

(Korsgaard, 2002, pp. 15–16, 25)[14]

On my reading, communism recommends itself to Marx as the most thoroughgoing possible achievement of this Kantian ideal of free and self-conscious collective self-legislation – the final 'working out' of the 'metaphysical politics' of social self-determination that Pippin identifies at the heart of the Idealist enterprise (Pippin, 1997, p. 8). It would mean that this necessity of justification, of giving reasons to ourselves and others for the norms under which we act, would be felt and responded to throughout our activities and relationships, including those areas of 'economic' life where such a requirement is currently suspended or blocked by the abstract rules of market exchange. Communism means that social normativity 'goes all the way down'.

We can find evidence of Marx's early allegiance to this ideal of collective self-legislation in his earliest political writings. In his early journalism for the *Rheinische Zeitung*, Marx is explicitly committed to what he calls the 'ideal and thorough view of recent philosophy' which 'considers the state as the great organism, in which rightful, ethical and political freedom has to be actualised, and in which the individual citizen in obeying the laws of the state obeys only the natural laws of his own reason, of human reason' (Marx, 1975c, p. 202; translation modified). At the same time Marx develops a critical approach towards modern constitutional and bureaucratic politics that condemns it as an empty and mechanical attempt to unify and organise society from the outside, instead of allowing the various elements of society to develop and express their own inherent universality and interconnection by actively unifying and organising themselves. And he defends the necessity of the public sphere created by a free press in terms that recall Kant's characterisation of the public use of reason as an activity of collective self-criticism and Hegel's account of speculative reason as that which can dissolve and transcend the abstract oppositions and aporias of 'the understanding'.[15]

In his 1843 critique of Hegel, Marx counterposes to the abstract structures of the modern state a conception of radical or 'true' democracy which abolishes the distinction between the political state and civil society and in which society's collective self-determination is raised to full collective self-consciousness. Thus conceived, Marx writes:

Democracy is the solution to the *riddle* of every constitution. In it we find the constitution founded on its actual ground: *actual human beings* and the *actual people*; not merely *implicitly* and in essence, but in *existence* and actuality. The constitution is posited as the people's *own* work. The constitution is in appearance what it is in reality: the free product of human beings.

(Marx, 1975e, p. 87)

The effect of this politicisation of civil society, Marx writes, is that 'the *legislature* entirely ceases to be important as the *representative* body' because it is now understood that '*every* function is representative. For example, a cobbler is my representative in so far as he satisfies a social need' (Marx, 1975e, pp. 189–90). My suggestion, here, is that Marx's notion of a society in which 'every man is representative of other men' is intended as a more complete actualisation of the post-Kantian conception of the social space of normativity in which we feel accountable for acting on reasons that all could accept.

Shortly afterwards Marx begins to suggest that this epochal shift in which we refer not to some external order nor to our individual acts of self-determination but to each other for the orientation and justification of our activity is immanent in the historical experience of the proletariat – 'that class which no longer realizes social freedom by assuming certain conditions external to man and yet created by human society, but rather by organizing all the conditions on the basis of social freedom' (Marx, 1975f, pp. 255–6). And in the manuscripts of 1844 Marx begins to focus more insistently upon material production and economic relationships, and to couch this in a naturalistic vocabulary taken from Feuerbach. But I think what Marx is doing here is trying to implant a post-Kantian ideal of mutual recognition, or the Hegelian ideal of a fully self-conscious social normativity, more deeply into the very fabric of our most everyday activities and social relationships – such that we see our own production and consumption of material goods as a socially situated and normatively structured activity in a way that bourgeois society relegates to explicitly moral or public domains. In his notes on James Mill, Marx counterposes to the system of antagonistic exchange an explicitly communal productive life in which 'the ideal relation to the mutual objects of our production' is 'given by our mutual needs', so that 'each of us would have *doubly affirmed* himself and his neighbour in his production', each producer would feel 'recognised' by their neighbours as extensions of one another's 'nature' or agency, and 'our productions would be as many mirrors from which our natures would shine forth' (Marx, 1975g, pp. 277–8).[16]

Finally, I think we can see this idea at work at those moments in Marx's mature writings where he tries to say something about the quality of post-capitalist society. This is a society in which 'the practical relations of everyday life between man and man, and man and nature, generally present themselves to him in a transparent and rational form' and the 'social life-process, i.e. the process of material production' becomes 'production by freely associated men, and stands under their conscious and planned control' (Marx, 1976, p. 173). I think it is clear from these words that Marx views communist production as explicitly normative, that is, a self-conscious carrying through of purposes and projects that have been (or, perhaps, could have been) freely deliberated and agreed upon by all concerned, and so can be seen by every individual as rationally justified. Communism is even described in contractualist, Rousseauian terms as 'an association of free men, working with the means of production held in common, and expending their many different forms of labour-power in full self-awareness as one single social labour force' (Marx, 1976, p. 171). Marx is sometimes criticised at this point for supposing that social relations in a modern complex society could ever be 'transparent in their simplicity'. But it seems to me that, read against the background of Marx's philosophical inheritance, comments like this should be taken not to imply that everyone could at all times know everything about what everyone else was doing, but rather that our ongoing efforts to harmonise our needs and capacities were conducted within the context of an explicit collective commitment to mutual reproduction and development. In such a society every act of production would be seen for what it always is; that is, a contribution to a process of social production, and so consciously judged and directed on that basis.

Conclusion

The foregoing discussion has necessarily been selective and partial. In highlighting the moments at which Marx appears to make use of ideas and arguments taken up from post-Kantian philosophy, I in no way mean to suggest that this amounts to a complete or definitive account of his philosophical presuppositions and orientations. As I have been able to indicate only in passing, Marx's entire project is premised upon a rejection of this philosophical tradition's one-sided 'idealism' and its associated underestimation of the forces at work in the capitalist economy.

But the very moves by which Marx struggles to break out his inherited philosophical frameworks suggest that he sees the political and material struggles of nineteenth-century Europe as a translation and transposition of the post-Kantian project: while in Germany the 'supersession of estrangement' is based in the recognition of '*Ich = Ich*' or '*man as universal self-consciousness*', in France it is based in political equality and in England in 'real, material, *practical* need'. In this way 'the solution of theoretical problems is a function of practice and is mediated through practice' (Marx 1975h, p. 364). And as Marx stressed as he came to his own 'settling of philosophical accounts', the 'materialism' upon which he founds his subsequent investigations is *not* materialism as we know it – in which 'the thing, reality, sensibility, is conceived only in the form of the *object*' – but a materialism totally transformed by a notion of 'human activity [*Tätigkeit*]' that he says has been 'developed abstractly by Idealism' (Marx, 1975i, p. 421; see also Carver, 1998, p. 27). Indeed, it is clear that the incorporation of this notion of activity is what makes Marx's materialism *historical*.[17]

A recent review of the attempt by 'analytical' Marxists to effect a clean separation of Marx's ideas from their Hegelian philosophical ancestry concluded ruefully that 'a necessary, but not sufficient, condition of any future salvation of Marxism (or, at least, of central Marxist insights), may be to make sense of Hegel' (Roberts, 1996, pp. 222–3). At the same time Pinkard was arguing that recent developments in Anglo-American philosophy may mean that only now are we 'finally in a position to begin assimilating what Hegel has to say to us' (Pinkard, 1994, p. 3). My argument is that until we have fully taken the measure of the post-Kantian legacy, and the ways in which Marx sought to redeploy many of its key concepts and lines of critique upon the new terrain of society's material self-reproduction, we will not be able to fully appreciate or evaluate Marx's distinctive theoretical and political project.

Notes

1. Earlier versions of this chapter were given as part of the Royal Institute of Philosophy Public Lecture series at Roehampton University on 31 October 2006 and at a special panel organised by the Marx and Philosophy Society at the Historical Materialism Annual Conference at SOAS on 10 December 2006. For helpful comments at those events, I am grateful to Milton Fisk, Meade McCloughan, Nina Power, Jonathan Rée and Raj Seghal. I am also indebted to Terrell Carver, Bob Cannon, John Charvet, Andrew Chitty, Philip Cook, Nicholas Gray, Will Roberts and Michael Rosen for feedback and discussions which have helped me develop the ideas contained in it, and to Andrew Chitty again for helping me finalise the text for publication. Of course all responsibility for errors and weaknesses remains my own.
2. To gain a sense of the richness and depth of this scholarship and debate see Ameriks, 2000, Sedgwick, 2000, or the special August 1999 issue of the *European Journal of Philosophy* (vol. 7, no. 2) on 'Hegel and His Legacy'.
3. For the now classic advancement of this reading see Pippin, 1989.
4. See also Pinkard, 2002, p. 35.
5. This self-abnegation, under the heading of 'positivity', is a central theme of Georg Lukács's account of Hegel's early development (Lukács, 1975). I am grateful to Andrew Chitty for highlighting this.
6. There is some reason for supposing that the turn from pure conceptuality and abstract self-consciousness towards a more immanent notion of 'Being', and accompanying rejection of Hegel's formalism and 'panlogicism', which Marx picked up from Feuerbach, was influenced by the critique of Hegel's 'negative philosophy' developed by Schelling in his later years. See Breckman, 2006, pp. 81–2.
7. According to David McLellan (1969, p. 75) the original manuscript of Marx's 1843 critique of Hegel's political theory shows that he 'in several places crosses out the term "self-consciousness" which he had originally written and substitutes another term more evocative of practical realities'.

8. For similar readings of the 'philosophical anthropology' of 1844 see Margolis, 1992, pp. 333–4, 340; and Dyer-Witheford, 2004, pp. 5–7.
9. Robert Cannon argues that Marx's 'modernism' goes awry when he bases his critique of capitalism upon 'a transhistorical premise concerning the "ontological" properties of labour' rather than 'the modern norm of self-constitution (and the struggles of agents to redeem it)' (Cannon, 2005, pp. 147, 156). Though I am sympathetic with much in Cannon's argument I am not persuaded that this charge can be pinned to Marx, not least because this 'modern norm of self-constitution' is so integral to Marx's very concept of labour.
10. I am especially indebted here to the argument of Patrick Murray (1993) that Marx's critique of political economy is rooted in Hegel's critique of 'the logic of essence'.
11. Merold Westphal's (1979, p. 110) gloss on the *Phenomenology*'s section on 'Force and the Understanding' is worth keeping in mind here: 'Lacking self-consciousness, Understanding is snared by what Whitehead calls the fallacy of misplaced concreteness. That is to say, when it finds certain conceptual devices useful for some purpose it immediately and without further ado takes these for the definitive expression of the real. Understanding [...] is still consciousness, focused on its object, not self-consciousness, aware of itself [...] Not recognizing its own creative activity in its own products, it becomes enslaved to them as if they were independently and eternally given'.
12. For a brilliant exploration of this strange metaphysic see Arthur, 2001.
13. One way of putting this would be to say that the 'social synthesis' or 'coherence' of our actions which Alfred Sohn-Rethel described as 'the precondition for the survival of every kind of society' becomes fully conscious and collectively self-determined rather than enforced by the law of value or some other mystified social or political order (Sohn-Rethel, 1978, p. 5).
14. For further illuminating contemporary philosophical discussion of the foundations of collective agency, see Gilbert, 1992.
15. See, e.g. Marx 1975d, p. 349: 'In the realm of the press, rulers and ruled alike have an opportunity of criticising their principles and demands, and no longer in a relation of subordination, but on terms of equality as *citizens of the state*; no longer as *persons*, but as *intellectual forces*' (translation modified).
16. Contrast the world of commodities described in *Capital* in which 'our productions' appear not as direct expressions or clear mirrors of 'our natures', but as mysterious 'hieroglyphs' or inessential bearers of a mysterious and abstract 'value'.
17. See Osborne, 2005. Indeed in the *German Ideology* Marx and Engels refer to themselves as 'practical materialists', suggesting that this is how they would name the 'new materialism' of the tenth of the Theses on Feuerbach (Marx and Engels, 1970, pp. 32, 123). I am grateful to Andrew Chitty for drawing my attention to this.

Bibliography

Allison, Henry E. (1990) *Kant's Theory of Freedom* (Cambridge: Cambridge University Press).

Ameriks, Karl (ed.) (2000) *The Cambridge Companion to German Idealism* (Cambridge: Cambridge University Press).

Arthur, Chris (2001) 'The Spectral Ontology of Value', *Radical Philosophy*, 107, pp. 32–42.

Breckman, Warren (2006) 'The Symbolic Dimension and the Politics of Left Hegelianism', in Douglas Moggach (ed.) *The New Hegelians: Politics and Philosophy in the Hegelian School* (Cambridge: Cambridge University Press).

Cannon, Bob (2005) 'Retrieving the Normative Content of Marxism', *Historical Materialism* 13(3), 135–62.

Carver, Terrell (1998) *The Postmodern Marx* (Manchester: Manchester University Press).

Dyer-Witheford, Nick (2004) '1844/2004/2044: The Return of Species-Being', *Historical Materialism*, 12(4), 1–23.

Feuerbach, Ludwig (1989) *The Essence of Christianity*, trans. G. Eliot (New York: Prometheus Books).

Fichte, J. G. (2008) *The Science of Knowledge*, trans. P. Heath and J. Lachs (Cambridge: Cambridge University Press).

Gilbert, Margaret (1992) *On Social Facts* (Princeton, NJ: Princeton University Press).

Habermas, Jürgen (1987) *The Philosophical Discourse of Modernity* (Cambridge: Polity Press).

Hegel, G. W .F. (1975) *The Encyclopaedia Logic: Part I of the Encyclopaedia of Philosophical Sciences with the Zusätze*, trans. T. F. Geraets, W. A. Suchting and H. S. Harris, (Indianapolis, IN/Cambridge: Hackett).

—— (1977a) *The Difference Between Fichte's and Schelling's System of Philosophy*, trans. H. S. Harris and W. Cerf (Albany, NY: State University of New York Press).

—— (1977b) *Faith and Knowledge*, trans. W. Cerf and H. S. Harris (Albany, NY: State University of New York Press).

—— (1977c) *Phenomenology of Spirit*, trans. A. V. Miller (Oxford: Oxford University Press).

—— (1989) *Science of Logic*, trans. A. V. Miller (Atlantic Highlands, NJ: Humanities Press International).

Kant, Immanuel (1987) *Critique of Judgement*, trans. W. S. Pluhar (Indianapolis, IN: Hackett Publishing Company).

—— (1996) *Critique of Practical Reason*, trans. Mary McGregor in *Practical Philosophy* (Cambridge: Cambridge University Press).

—— (1997) *Critique of Pure Reason*, trans. P. Guyer and A. W. Wood (Cambridge: Cambridge University Press).

Korsgaard, Christine (1996) *The Sources of Normativity* (Cambridge: Cambridge University Press).

—— (2002) *Self-Constitution: Agency, Identity and Integrity*, The Locke Lectures, Lecture Six: Integrity and Interaction, available at http://www.people.fas.harvard.edu/~korsgaar/Korsgaard.LL6.pdf

Lukács, Georg (1975) *The Young Hegel: Studies in the Relations between Dialectics and Economics*, trans. Rodney Livingstone (London: Merlin Press).

Margolis, Joseph (1992) 'Praxis and Meaning: Marx's Species Being and Aristotle's Political Animal', in G. E. McCarty (ed.) *Marx and Aristotle: Nineteenth Century German Social Theory and Classical Antiquity* (Savage, MD: Rowman and Littlefield).

Marx, Karl (1975a) 'Letter from Marx to his Father in Trier', in Karl Marx and Friedrich Engels, *Collected Works*, vol. 1 (London: Lawrence and Wishart).

—— (1875b) 'Difference Between the Democritean and Epicurean Philosophy of Nature', in Karl Marx and Friedrich Engels, *Collected Works*, vol. 1 (London: Lawrence and Wishart).

—— (1975c) 'The Leading Article in No. 179 of the *Kölnische Zeitung*', in Karl Marx and Friedrich Engels, *Collected Works*, vol. 1 (London: Lawrence and Wishart).

—— (1975d) 'Justification of the Correspondent from the Mosel', in Karl Marx and Friedrich Engels, *Collected Works*, vol. 1 (London: Lawrence and Wishart).

—— (1975e) 'Critique of Hegel's Doctrine of the State', in L. Colletti (ed.) *Karl Marx: Early Writings* (Harmondsworth: Penguin).

—— (1975f) 'A Contribution to the Critique of Hegel's *Philosophy of Right*. Introduction', in L. Colletti (ed.) *Karl Marx: Early Writings* (Harmondsworth: Penguin).

—— (1975g) 'Excerpts from James Mill's *Elements of Political Economy*', in L. Colletti (ed.) *Karl Marx: Early Writings* (Harmondsworth: Penguin).

—— (1975h) 'Economic and Philosophical Manuscripts', in L. Colletti (ed.) *Karl Marx: Early Writings* (Harmondsworth: Penguin).

—— (1975i) 'Concerning Feuerbach', in L. Colletti (ed.) *Karl Marx: Early Writings* (Harmondsworth: Penguin).

—— (1976) *Capital Volume 1*, trans. B. Fowkes (Harmondsworth: Penguin).

—— (1978) 'The Value-Form', trans. M. Roth and W. Suchting, *Capital and Class*, 4, 130–50.

Marx, Karl and Engels, Frederick (1970) C. J. Arthur (ed.) *The German Ideology* (London: Lawrence and Wishart).

McIvor, Martin (2008) 'The Young Marx and German Idealism: Revisiting the Doctoral Dissertation', *Journal of the History of Philosophy*, 46 (3), 395–419.

McLellan, David (1969) *The Young Hegelians and Karl Marx* (Basingstoke: Macmillan).

Moggach, Douglas (2003) *The Philosophy and Politics of Bruno Bauer* (Cambridge: Cambridge University Press).

Murray, Patrick (1993) 'The Necessity of Money: How Hegel Helped Marx Surpass Ricardo's Theory of Money', in Fred Moseley (ed.) *Marx's Method in Capital: A Reexamination* (New Jersey: Humanities Press).

Osborne, Peter (2005) *How To Read Marx* (London: Granta).

Pinkard, Terry (1994) *Hegel's Phenomenology: The Sociality of Reason* (Cambridge: Cambridge University Press).

—— (2002) *German Philosophy 1760–1860: The Legacy of Idealism* (Cambridge: Cambridge University Press).

Pippin, Robert (1989) *Hegel's Idealism: The Satisfactions of Self-Consciousness* (Cambridge: Cambridge University Press).

—— (1997) *Idealism as Modernism: Hegelian Variations* (Cambridge: Cambridge University Press).

—— (1999) *Modernism as a Philosophical Problem: On the Dissatisfactions of European High Culture* (Oxford: Blackwell).

Roberts, Marcus (1996) *Analytical Marxism: A Critique* (London: Verso.)

Rosen, Zvi (1977) *Bruno Bauer and Karl Marx: The Influence of Bruno Bauer on Marx's Thought* (The Hague: Martinus Nijhoff).

Schelling, F. W. J. (1978) *The System of Transcendental Idealism*, trans. P. Heath (Charlottesville, VA: University Press of Virginia).

—— (1980) 'Of the I as a Principle of Philosophy', in *The Unconditional in Human Knowledge: Four Early Essays*, trans. F. Marti (Lewisburg, PA/London: Bucknell University Press/Associated University Press).

Sedgwick, Sally (ed.) (2000) *The Reception of Kant's Critical Philosophy* (Cambridge: Cambridge University Press).

Sohn-Rethel, Alfred (1978) *Intellectual and Manual Labour: A Critique of Epistemology* (London and Basingstoke: Macmillan).

Westphal, Merold (1979) *History and Truth in Hegel's Phenomenology* (New Jersey and London: Humanities Press).

3
Marx, the European Tradition, and the Philosophic Radicals

Scott Meikle

'The burghers' golden boy'

In 1843, at the age of 25, Marx was appointed editor and then editor-in-chief of a progressive liberal newspaper, the *Rheinische Zeitung*, with what was for the time an impressive circulation of over 3000.[1] The paper was influential; the Czar of Russia had complained in person to the Prussian ambassador about some of Marx's articles in it. (It is easy to forget how small the ruling stratum in Europe was in the early nineteenth century.) It was financed and directed by senior businessmen of the Ruhr, the leading industrial region of Germany, and among its directors were two future prime ministers of Prussia. Their aim was to advance the cause of business and democracy in the highly traditional kingdom of Prussia, which was not very business-friendly or democratic. They also wanted to advance the good of humanity, having more elevated notions than most of their Manchester equivalents. They were looking for a revolution to sweep away the remaining restraints imposed by traditional European monarchy, and 1848 was only five years into the future. Marx wrote to Ruge in May of that year, in characteristic vein, of

> the self-confidence of the human being [...] only this feeling, which vanished from the world with the Greeks [...] can again transform society into a community of human beings united for their highest aims, into a democratic state.

(Marx, 1975a, p. 137)

Only a few months earlier Marx had counselled the publisher, Renard, to reassure the president of the Rhineland that the paper would moderate its tone, especially on religious subjects. He had publicly repudiated communist ideas in the columns of the paper. This is the company Marx was keeping, and this was where he stood in 1843: an important and admired figure in the rising political establishment of German business and progressive politics. Yet within a year Marx had turned his back on the entire movement of the democratic and forward-looking burgers and had joined the sparser ranks of those opposed in principle to market economy, its system of money, and its culture of economics.

This was an epic *volte-face*, and we have to ask what could have produced it? What changes of thought, interacting with what underlying attitudes, could have led Marx to change the course of his life so completely – to abandon his ambitions to enjoy a leading and rewarding part in the political future of his country, and to jeopardize his and his wife Jenny's chances of a secure and prosperous family life? Let us look at the changes of thought first, and then at the underlying attitudes those changes reacted with.

The shock of reading economics

The changes of thought have been covered in the biographies. They resulted from his efforts to assess for the *Rheinische Zeitung* proposed laws restricting the customary right of poor people to gather firewood in the forests, which was coming under threat from commercial interests, and with the difficulties the winegrowers of the Mosel were suffering at the time. Facing these issues caused Marx to think about the material or economic interests of people in different parts of the society.[2] This in turn led him into reading up for the first time the new economic thought coming in partly from France, but mainly from England and Scotland. We can see in the *Marx Engels Gesamtausgabe* that in late 1843 he was reading and making excerpts from Jean-Baptiste Say, Frederic Skarbek, Adam Smith, Xenophon, Ricardo, James Mill, and McCulloch (Marx and Engels, 1981).

What he read stopped him in his tracks. The notes and excerpts he took at the time show him to have been shaken morally and intellectually. It revealed to him just exactly what sort of world of life and relationships, culture and ethics, he and his associates on the *Rheinische Zeitung* were campaigning to bring into Germany. Mevissen, a leading industrialist and board member of the *Rheinische Zeitung*, recalling the year 1843 in his memoirs, records that Marx 'was already then, by his concentrated study of economics, preparing his conversion to communism' (cited in McLellan, 1973, pp. 42–3).

The intensity and emotion of Marx's reaction suggest some potent prior inoculation against the sort of thing he met with in economic thought, and this brings us to the underlying attitudes. These are less familiar grounds, and they may be approached by looking at the record Marx left of this first serious encounter with economic thinking in his little-known *Comments on James Mill's Elemens de l'Economie Politique*, written in the first part of 1844, before or along with the start of the much better known *Economic and Philosophical Manuscripts*. The *Comments on James Mill* differ from the *Manuscripts*, as McLellan notes, in focusing more on economic thought and its concepts.[3]

Many of these underlying attitudes have to do with Marx's familiarity with the ancient world, its history, its languages, Greek and Latin, and its literature, drama, and philosophy. Classical learning was common among educated people in all parts of Europe in Marx's day. In our own day it has almost entirely gone, and this is now a gulf separating Marx from his modern reader. It is a major obstacle to the comprehension of his work today. Allusions and turns of phrase that were enough to convey entire perspectives and value systems to his contemporaries, convey little or nothing to most modern readers, who are parochially modern in comparison. These things are not just a matter of literary effect; they can make all the difference in understanding what Marx was really going on about and what had been moving him. Germany had a particularly strong tradition of classical scholarship, and Marx's knowledge was outstanding even by German standards. Greek and Latin were second nature to him, and throughout his life he would read ancient authors in the original languages as relaxation after a day's work. His knowledge of the Greek philosophers, particularly of Aristotle whom he greatly admired, was very detailed, and he read and studied all of Aristotle's scientific works for his doctoral dissertation on Epicurus.[4] Much of this philosophical inheritance was still part of the educational system, in the form of the Scholastic tradition, the official philosophy of the Catholic countries of Europe, and it infused the teaching in schools and universities. Furthermore, many ethical values and social attitudes found in the Greek authors were still to be found not greatly changed all over Continental Europe in Marx's time, especially the Rhineland which was so staunch that successive French and Prussian occupying armies were warned by their political masters in Paris and Berlin against interfering with the Catholic Church there (Nicolaievsky and Maenchen-Helfen, 1936, pp. 2–3). The values and attitudes to be found in economic thought, however, were very different, and though they had made great cultural inroads in Britain, especially in the early decades of the century through the quasi-religious movement of Utilitarianism well described by Halévy (1928), in other parts of Europe their influence was still largely a thing of the future, and it is quite clear that they came as a surprise to Marx.

The economic and the human

Marx's discussion of exchange in the *Comments on James Mill* expresses the traditional view, going back to the Greeks, that exchange should be an act aimed at helping someone else as well as yourself, a 'human, social act', as Marx puts it here, 'by which man's products mutually complement one another' (Marx 1975c, p. 212). The spirit in which it should be done should be one of friendship, what the Greeks called *philia*, and the act should serve to help your neighbour meet his needs as well as to help you meet yours, and to reinforce the social bond by showing grace and generosity to your neighbour, in the hope and expectation that when you need something your neighbours will show grace to you. This was a traditional sensibility, established philosophically by the Greeks and passed on in the Scholastic tradition of Europe, which people were brought up with in places like the Rhineland. So it comes as a shock to Marx to realize that, in the market system portrayed in economic thought, exchange has lost this human, friendly, and ethical dimension altogether. This is the first expression of what is a strong and pervasive feeling in the *Comments on James Mill* that the focus of market relationships is all wrong, that their spirit is too indifferent to others, that they are anti-social and destructive of proper sentiments of empathy, support and *philia*. He notes, for instance, that in conditions of the market 'I have produced for myself and not for you, just as you have produced for yourself and not for me [...] it is not *social* production' (Marx, 1975b, p. 225). The same sentiment appears much later in the *Critique of the Gotha Programme* in the suggestion that in post-market society work will be properly social and hence 'life's prime want' (Marx, 1974). (This is one of many indications that Marx's ethical sentiments changed little throughout his life.) Even 'our complementing each other is likewise a mere semblance, the basis of which is mutual plundering'. 'What gives your need of my article its value, worth and effect for me is solely your object, the equivalent of my object' (Marx, 1975b, p. 226). His point is that there is insufficient human content to this sort of exchange relationship, which has become abstract and dehumanized, in which the parties relate not as people but as formal and impersonal administrators of a portion of value or money. He feels that we should not live like this, measuring equivalents, acting in a spirit of calculation for private advantage, using the needs of those around us as occasions for advancing our own interests, concerned only with what at around this time he calls 'filthy self-interest' (Marx, 1975c, p. 267). He seems to find it particularly bitter to reflect that sociable acts like lending and exchanging should have been twisted into something base and self-regarding.

Such objections today might seem romantic, sentimental, and over-refined. If so, this might be thought a symptom of how much more, since Marx's day, living under markets has eroded the humanity of our culture and sensibility. Such a reaction would suggest a degree of individualism that shows little understanding of what it is to live in an ethical community – a community that has an ethics and runs by it and knows what solidarity and humanity are and does not leave its major ethical decisions to market forces. This is really Marx's point. He says that the more developed the 'social power' of the market

the more *egotistical*, asocial and estranged from his own nature does man become [...] [and] turns man as far as possible into an abstract being [...] and transforms him into a spiritual and physical monster.

(Marx, 1975b, p. 220)

It shocks him even more to realize what is behind this emptying out of the ethics from exchange, namely, that the act of exchange has ceased to be a personal act and has become something of quite a different kind, a technical element in an entire system of prices and impersonal exchanges, which has completely detached from the needs, capacities, and personalities of those engaged in performing the acts. This is just what Kolakowski means by the 'dehumanization' caused by the system of money and markets. The relation of exchange has ceased to be a human relationship, and has become what Marx calls here for the first time an 'abstract relationship' (Marx, 1975b, p. 213). He means that it is a rule-governed relationship between two bits of money or commodity value, in which the role of the human participants is limited to that of the momentary legal owners and administrators of the quantities of money, in which capacity they are expected to behave in a 'businesslike' manner, that is, to conserve the value without in principle acknowledging any personal obligation such as consideration and generosity. 'We mutually regard our products as the *power* of each of us over the other and over himself', he says, 'our product has risen up against us; it seemed to be our property, but in fact we are its property' (Marx, 1975b, p. 226). Here Marx is already clearly conceiving the market system as an objective set of abstract (i.e. 'economic') relationships that overrides human relationships and displaces humans from the centre of human affairs and puts capital at the centre instead. In this first brief work on economic thought, Marx has already put together the deepest and most distinctive insights that his later critique of economic thought or political economy is built on.

The economic and the natural

Marx is taken aback to find that in economic thought the individual being of the thing as an entity in the world, its real nature, its properties, and the kind it belongs to, are thought unimportant enough to be ignored, or even, as he complains on one occasion, 'extinguished' (Marx, 1975c, pp. 285–6), in the face of the economic identities that are imposed on them as commodities on the market. In the early writings he often refers to the particularity and peculiar character that items in the world have as 'the real content'. The practice of disregarding these 'real contents' in the course of forcing a false homogeneity onto things that are in nature heterogeneous, that is required in economic thought in order that things might bear what he calls the 'economic abstraction', he finds philosophically crass and, in a sense, morally objectionable too.

It is not immediately clear perhaps why this undiscriminating attitude to things should disconcert Marx so much. Such sensitivity is uncommon today (at least in the Anglophone countries – it may be different elsewhere) and people are usually quite ready to accept the practice of referring to things belonging to different kinds indiscriminately as 'commodities' or 'utilities'. Marxian writers sometimes grumble about it, and they usually got the sensitivity from reading Marx. But to get an idea of where Marx got his sensitivity from and what its significance is, it is necessary to bring in fundamental differences that have grown up between the philosophical traditions of Britain and the rest of Europe.

In most of Continental Europe the tradition of Scholastic Aristotelianism remained an important influence in one form or another, and this was not limited only to countries that remained Catholic during the Reformation, because the same was true in some of the regions that went Protestant (see for example Dickey, 1987, pp. 227–30). But in England and Scotland, where the Protestantism was more militant, Aristotelian philosophy was perceived as a corrupt thing of Rome, and it was eradicated root and branch. This led to a deep and fundamental division of philosophical tradition that is still plainly visible today, and which has in some ways grown deeper with time.

Scholasticism has traditionally focused mainly on questions about being, and the Empiricist tradition of the English-speaking countries more on questions about knowledge. Where Scholasticism has tended to start with questions like 'what kinds of thing are there?' and 'what kind of thing is this?', Empiricism has tended to start with questions like 'what do I really know?' and 'what kinds of knowledge are there?' So greater weight is given to logic and metaphysics in the Scholastic tradition than in the Empiricist tradition, which has generally tended to give greater weight to epistemology or theory of knowledge at the expense of metaphysics. One effect of this is that in the treatment of things in Scholastic philosophy, there has been a greater emphasis on kind, and conditions of identity and difference, or of what it takes for a thing to belong to a kind or not to belong to it – things that the Empiricist tradition has tended comparatively to neglect. Marx's sensitivity to the propensity of economic thought to lump things together indiscriminately, and even to imply a certain homogeneity among them, is partly due to this greater theoretical awareness of the reality of heterogeneity.

But it is also partly due to another deep difference between the two traditions in their attitudes to the concepts of ordinary language and to the logic or metaphysics of those concepts. The Aristotelian attitude is that these concepts, together with the criteria associated with their use, and the logical connections that link them together in the network of language, is the proper object of philosophical analysis. Identity is a primitive notion, primitive in the sense that it cannot be analysed or dismantled into more basic ideas, because there are no ideas more basic than it (see the discussion in Wiggins, 1980, pp. 49–55). Since it is not analysable, the best we can do is to uncover and describe the actual practices and criteria that are used everyday in individuating and re-identifying things of the different kinds that there are, in order to enhance the understanding we already have of the sameness and difference as ascribed to things. These practices and criteria vary; those for one kind of living entity differ from those of another, and from those for non-living entities, and from those for such a thing as a republic. These criteria are built into the language we all use everyday, without our usually reflecting on the rules and criteria involved in this use, but they can be brought out into the open for our conscious scrutiny by studying how people speak when using a term for things and kinds, and identifying the conditions that hold when they decide to apply a term, or are absent when they decide not to use it.

This is the conception of the task and competence of philosophy Strawson called 'descriptive metaphysics'. He contrasted it with the conception of 'revisionary metaphysics', more popular with the Empiricist tradition, according to which the metaphysics of natural language is a fit subject for reform and not just for analysis. This reforming or Whiggish view was nicely expressed by Bertrand Russell who once said that the metaphysics of natural language is the metaphysics of the Stone Age. The Utilitarian movement, in perhaps an excess of reforming zeal, was prepared to reform the metaphysics of human action by abolishing all ends of action except one, utility. Marx was brought up with the Aristotelian view, and so he sees the casual disregard economic thought shows towards the metaphysics of natural language as not only false but also as coarse, presumptuous, and, in a sense, even disrespectful. Wittgenstein was brought up in the same tradition, and in his second philosophy takes just this Aristotelian attitude to the metaphysics of ordinary language.

The notion of kind is fundamental in Aristotelian thought, and it is not something that it is appropriate to treat casually. Our ordinary idea of a thing includes the idea that things fall into kinds. When thought about systematically, it is normal to distinguish organic things and inorganic ones, and each of these fall into other kinds, and each into yet others. Things are subject to change, but their identities persist through change, and these identities are bound up with the continuity of the path they trace through space and time, with their membership of natural kinds, which they fall into in virtue of their composition, properties, structure, origin, typical or nomological behaviour, and so forth. These are natural identities, and to Marx's sensibility, neglecting them in favour of commercial identities that we have made up and imposed is crude and unsavoury.

Someone of Marx's intellectual and ethical sensibility was bound to find the treatment of things in economic thought obnoxious. It was easier for these conceptual practices, essential to economic thought, to develop in England and Scotland, because the subjects of logic and metaphysics, together with the study of Aristotle's works as a whole, disappeared from the curriculum of the English-speaking philosophical tradition from the seventeenth century onwards. Hobbes and Locke still knew something about it, but by Hume's time, as is quite clear from his *Treatise*, all knowledge of it had gone (Hume, 1969). Its disappearance removed an important obstacle in the path of the formation of modern commercial language and economic thought.

Economics – a disturbed vision

In contrasting so starkly the things of the natural realm as they are grasped philosophically with the way they are represented in economic thought, Marx is beginning to form the view that runs through all his later work that economic thought represents a distorted view of the world, and of the place of humans in it. He is identifying a phantom world of what he calls 'economic abstractions', the abstract man, abstract labour, and the abstract thing or commodity. This is a world painfully familiar to us today, where the useful thing has become the 'utility' or the 'product', and the useful activity has become the 'service'. But perhaps the most telling economic neologism is denominating the active man or woman the 'human resource', thus projecting the human person as an aspect of capital, one of two kinds of resources that capital has, human and non-human. This is a sequel so grotesque that it is difficult to think that even Marx's sardonic insight into capitalist cynicism could have imagined it coming to pass. Marx has identified a world in which the natural being of everything is recast to make it into a projection of capital. A realm of abstractions has come to exist alongside the elements of the natural world, and its abstract elements have attached themselves to their corresponding equivalents in the natural world and are forcing them through the operations of markets to adopt unnatural identities, to follow out unnatural patterns, and to lead unnatural lives.

It is worth noting in passing that the notion of 'abstract labour', so important in a later interpretation of Marx's work, makes its first appearance in 1844 in the *Economic and Philosophical Manuscripts*. But it does so in the philosophical context of the realm of economic abstraction, where man is abstract as an economic entity supplying labour capacity, the useful thing is abstract as the utility, and activity is abstract as labour. It does not appear here in the role, given later in the labour theory of value, of the 'substance' of value, or embodied quantities of labour-time. Marx here draws a contrast between labour 'in its generality and *abstraction*' and labour 'still bound to a *particular natural* element [...] a *particular* mode of existence determined by nature' (Marx, 1975c, p. 292). What he seems to be getting at is a distinction between *actions*, which naturally fall into different kinds, and *labour*, the economic concept, which denotes whatever is covered by the wage bill, that is, whatever is done by those in receipt of wages, which in economic contexts does not necessarily fall into kinds, but is simply 'disutility', the opposite of pleasure or utility.

This idea of economic thought as a set of weird, sinister, and unnatural abstractions, foisted onto the natural world and masking and perverting the real nature of things, crops up in Marx's work throughout his life, in the *Communist Manifesto*, in the *Contribution*, and in Volume 1 of *Capital*. With it goes a conviction that the economic realm, or the natural realm as seen through economic concepts, is a deeply disturbed vision of reality, one that is false, mercenary, profane, antisocial, and inhuman. In *Capital* he calls it 'the fetishism of commodities'; in the *Manifesto* he says that it brings it about that 'all that is solid melts into air; all that is holy is profaned'.

This insight becomes the theory of fetishism and abstraction in *Capital*, and here in the *Comments on James Mill* and the *Economic and Philosophical Manuscripts*, it is already the main element of his first reaction to economic thought. Such a reaction can be formed and expressed only by someone with a firm and articulated grasp of the natural state of the things in the world, and this is just what knowledge of the Aristotelian metaphysics of substance and attribute gave him. It is only against such a view that it is possible to come to recognize the state of things and activities as described in the 'abstract' terms of economic thinking for what it is, and articulate what is amiss in it. Marx does recognize it, though it cannot be said that he is especially articulate about what is wrong with it. Nevertheless, it is the most distinctive insight of Marx's career. (There are other candidates for that role, of course, foremost among them the not-very-political view that money prices may be derived from embodied abstract labour-times.) To have arrived at the idea of economic thought as a realm of abstraction, Marx first needed a firm grasp of what economic thinking is abstracting from. He never explicitly elaborates on this or explains his meaning. He states the position in the baldest terms, referring, insistently but without amplification, to 'the real content' and the 'specific', 'particular', and 'natural' characteristics of things and actions that economic thinking ignores or abstracts from. He simply takes the Aristotelian view of the natural world for granted, quite naturally since he was brought up to think in those terms, like everyone he knew, and it came entirely naturally to him. It would not have occurred to him that it might be something that needed explaining.

But to people of Anglophone culture it often does need explaining. When the position Marx holds is put as baldly as he puts it, then for readers without some grasp of the philosophical background, and especially for readers with an uncomplicated Empiricist cultural background, his point is not likely to be particularly obvious. Today matters are made even worse by the fact that common thought and language are now so penetrated by economic and utilitarian ideas that we are probably a good deal less sensitive than an educated German of the 1840s to the kind of thing that Marx notices about economic thinking and the concepts it uses. It shows in the literature, where for the most part little has been made of Marx's complaints about 'abstraction' in economics, despite the fact that they are so repeated and emphatic, and are really the main thrust of his objection to economic thinking.[5] This is to be expected when the grasp of any philosophical contrast with the world as seen through economic abstractions is so atrophied. Without an articulate grasp of the unfetishized world, the theory of fetishism itself is hard to articulate or even conceive. The theory of fetishism is essentially a contrast between the world as grasped using the concepts of natural language, and as grasped using the economic neologisms of Modernity. It is precisely the unfetishized grasp of the world that has been so undermined by generations of exposure to market thought and language, and to the largely market-inspired philosophy that in Britain replaced Scholastic Aristotelian philosophy.

Indeed, the long neglect of philosophy in the Marxist tradition allowed it to become significantly infiltrated by economic thinking, while the things in economic thinking that Marx complained about got worse without much serious Marxist comment or resistance. Smith was still in touch with the natural world of things and people through the notion of use-value, but it all got much worse in the latter part of the nineteenth century, especially with the systematic attempt to increase quantification in economics sponsored by Jevons. Marx was sensitive to this sort of thing before the worst of it had happened, and when the worst did happen, the Marxist tradition was not in good enough shape to grasp much of what it meant or what was wrong with it.

Marx is equally dismayed that in economic thinking the natural world of things and people, the 'world of creation' as people used to say, should come to be portrayed as secondary to an artificial tissue of money relations of our own making. Even worse is the fact that sometimes the real natures of those things, people, and actions actually seem to be subverted by this *ersatz* realm of reflections of money so that it 'melts into air'. The way he expresses himself carries the suggestion that he feels this is a disrespectful and presumptuous attitude and that it has something of the quality of blasphemy about it. He says that

> the essence of money is [...] that the human, social act by which man's products mutually complement one another, is estranged from man and becomes the attribute of money, a material thing outside man [...] this mediator [*sc.* money] now becomes a real God [...] Its cult becomes an end in itself [...] objects separated from this mediator have lost their value. Hence the objects only have value insofar as they represent the mediator, whereas originally it seemed that the mediator had value only insofar as it represented them.
>
> (Marx, 1975b, p. 212)

J. G. A. Pocock describes the feelings that many had in Augustan England about the replacement of real property in land as the basis of civic personality with mobile property in pensions, office, credit, and funds. It was felt that, compared with land, money had a quality of fiction, depending as

Locke had said, on 'fancy and agreement', and this had the effect of making them feel that they were 'doomed to inhabit a world more unstable in its epistemological foundations than Plato's cave' (Pocock, 1975, pp. 450–1). Marxist writers have been much given in the past to making claims that identify philosophical ideas as no more than 'reflections' of social, institutional, or economic arrangements. Such claims are notoriously difficult to substantiate to the satisfaction of anyone who isn't already disposed to believe them, and the reductionist spirit in which those claims were often made invited scepticism and earned such claims a poor reputation. This is a shame, because in this case one should probably not shrink from observing how nicely Hume's undermining of the substantiality of things, their kinds, and their natures fits with the attitude to things that comes to the fore in market culture, where the natural being of a thing is secondary to, or confused with, its being a depository of money or exchange-value, a 'commodity'. The nature of the thing C is of little interest in the circuit of capital M–C–M´, because any C will do when the overriding point is the difference between M and M´. The Humean conception of a thing, the nebulous 'bundle of qualities', without a nature and without the derided Grecian 'chimera' of substance, is fairly amenable to the economic view of the things in the world. But the Scholastic view that Marx held is quite impossible to reconcile with the economic view because it is not vague and epistemologically deconstructed, but is realistic, material, and ontological; it is also worked out in logical and metaphysical detail, so that kinds and heterogeneity are not so easily set aside.

The thing exchanged in such a system, Marx suggests, begins to lose its specific nature as a particular thing, and even its character as a personal possession: 'since men engaged in exchange do not relate to each other as men, things lose their significance as human personal property' (Marx, 1975b, p. 213). As the thing's natural properties retreat into the background and the thing itself becomes more abstract (the 'commodity'), so money seems to become part of the thing in a confused sort of way. To the economic mind, Marx suggests, money does not exist only as metal, but rather it exists 'under all forms of commodities', and it 'is present in [...] all activities'. The natural world of things and activities comes, in economic thinking, to be pervaded by money as by an aether. Money becomes their true content, while the natural being withdraws into an incidental role. Marx suggests with heavy irony that the economists have penetrated to a great truth: in attaining the insight that the 'essence of money' is its 'abstract universality', they have seen through the 'crude superstition' of the metallists who identified money as metal, and have arrived instead at the 'refined superstition' that sees money in everything, and regards everything as a representation of money, rather than as the natural thing that it is (Marx, 1975b, p. 213).

The confusion is then compounded in the economic mind by unreflectively supposing that the thing's being a representation of money is a *natural* fact about the thing. Things come to be seen as being *by nature* objects of buying and selling with a price. In this way convention is read back into nature. But things are not by nature expressions of money, their status as such expressions being historical and social not natural. In economic thinking, the natural character and the social character of things are not properly distinguished, and the result is that nature and convention become hopelessly muddled. In Greek philosophy, as Marx knew well, nature and convention, *nomos* and *phusis*, were always distinguished with great care. The distinction was a prominent theme in ancient philosophy, in marked contrast to economic thought from which it is almost entirely absent. The confusion in economic thought that arises from this absence was the principal focus of Marx's reaction to economic thinking in the *Comments on James Mill*, and it remained so throughout his life. Again we find the theory of the fetishism of commodities, as the ideology of the epoch of market economy, already present. So the *Comments on James Mill* together with the *Economic and Philosophical Manuscripts* may be said to be, in an apt phrase of Kolakowski's, 'the first draft of the book that Marx went on writing all his life' (Kolakowski, 1978, p. 132).[6]

The dehumanization of society by capitalism

Credit looks like a human sort of relationship, but Marx thinks that in reality it is even more 'dehumanized' than exchange, and even more '*infamous and extreme*, because its element is no longer commodity, metal, paper, but man's *moral* existence, man's *social* existence, the *innermost depths* of his heart, and because under the appearance of man's *trust* in man it is the height of distrust and complete estrangement'. The one who gives his trust in advancing the credit, shows his trust that the recipient is a 'good' man, that is, a man who is 'able to pay' (Marx, 1975b, p. 214).

Marx's feelings about credit are deep and his expression impassioned: '[O]ne ought to consider how vile it is to *estimate* the value of a man in *money*, as happens in the credit relationship,' he says.

> Credit is the *economic* judgment on the *morality* of a man [...] In credit, the *man* himself [...] has become [...] the *mode of existence of capital* [...] *Human individuality*, human *morality* itself, has become both an object of commerce and the material in which money exists (Marx, 1975b, p. 215).

It is 'a false system', and these arrangements are 'an extreme consequence of vileness'. He speaks of 'the immoral vileness of this morality' (Marx, 1975b, p. 215).

Credit is a familiar part of life to us, and people these days usually do not have strong negative feelings about it as long as it is done reasonably honestly. So we have to ask just where such disgust with credit, such an intense sense of its cynical depravity, is coming from. Part of the answer is that Marx feels that the credit relationship is not a human one, because the human person, the 'borrower', has become merely a phase in an M–C–M´ operation; he or she is the C term in the middle. The point of the operation is to expand M into M´, and the borrower is a means to this, and so the borrower is in principle no different from the machinery and raw materials that are the means for any business to expand its capital outlay M to become M´. To the creditor the borrower is simply a means, and if he is exploitable the creditor will have dealings with him otherwise not regardless of considerations of any other kind. This is a very different thing from charitable lending, and in comparison it is unedifying. This sentiment is not readily entertained today in the Western world. But it was common enough in Marx's day in Europe because people then were familiar with the system of reciprocity lending in ancient Greece. Commercial lending, so far as it existed in Athens, was used only by visiting traders and resident aliens. A citizen would not need to resort to it unless he had a reputation as a welsher so that he could not rely on the friendship and trust of his friends and neighbours. Everyone else relied on friendly or *eranos* lending. When a citizen was in need, he expected to be able to call upon help from his friends, and they had the same expectation. It was a matter of honour not only to repay such debts but also to incur them. Aristotle records that a temple of the Graces was put up in a prominent place in the city to remind citizens that grace required that 'we should serve in return one who has shown grace to us, and should another time take the initiative in showing it' (Aristotle, 1985, 5, 1133a3ff). Just this sort of sentiment remained in the official teaching of the Catholic Church on the subject of usurious lending. Not very long before Marx's time the encyclical *Vix Pervenit* of 1745 reaffirmed the age-long prohibition of usury in firm and detailed terms. It was recognized that it was sometimes and in some circumstances right to ask for a consideration beyond the return of the principal, but it was added that this did not include the mere making of the loan itself, and that anyone who convinced himself that it was always right to demand a consideration just for the making of a loan was convincing himself of a 'grievous error'. The point behind the teaching was that lending is supposed to be a charitable, friendly, or neighbourly act, done out of the generosity of the one in view of the need of the other, not an act for enriching oneself from the need of another. The latter act, in the moral atmosphere Marx was brought up in, was simply sordid, impersonal, and a perversion of a human relationship. An earlier generation of followers of Marx might have preferred not to acknowledge that Marx entertained such convictions, seeing them as expressions of feudalism. If they are feudal then perhaps one should conclude that not everything feudal is bad, anymore than everything modern is good.

But there is something more fundamental behind Marx's deep revulsion from credit. We get a clue near the beginning of the *Comments on James Mill*, right in the middle of this treatment of credit, in a passage dealing with man and community:

> [H]uman nature is the true community of men, by manifesting their nature men create, produce, the human community [...] the social entity, which is no abstract universal power opposed to the single individual, but is the essential nature of each individual. [...] Men, not as abstractions, but as real, living, particular individuals, *are* this entity.
>
> (Marx, 1975b, p. 217)

This might be taken for an effusive bit of nineteenth-century high-mindedness, but it is a highly significant passage, and when it is unravelled it tells us most of what we need to know in order to comprehend the intensity of feeling in Marx's reaction to economic thought. But the significance of the passage is not apparent on the face of it, unless one knows as much about Greek social thought as Marx and many of his contemporaries did, in which case the significance will be obvious immediately. The references are to Aristotle's theory about the nature of a human being, the nature of human society, the purpose of the state, and the connections between them. Human nature and human society are not fully separable things in Aristotelian thought, and the sort of relationship Aristotle thinks holds between individual and society is what Marx is getting at, in this passage, by identifying human nature with the community – an identification that might well seem puzzling if one does not know where it comes from.

According to Aristotle, human society is a natural growth, a *suntheton* or 'compound whole constituted by nature', not an artificial 'association', as it becomes in the modern liberal or economic tradition stemming from Hobbes and Locke. It is a natural growth because it is produced by the natural exercise of the capacity that humans have for social living. That capacity is part of the nature of humans, and it distinguishes them from the other five sorts of creatures Aristotle distinguishes in the *De Anima*. So the natural condition befitting a creature with this capacity is one which results from the capacity having been able to operate so as to produce its natural result, that is, a condition of living in a society or community, the *politikon bion* or polis life. For man is by nature one who lives in a polis, he is a polis animal or *zoon politikon* (an expression Marx uses in the letter to Ruge cited in the first paragraph above). Members of the human species have a capacity for language and living together in a social life, and they attain developed human natures when that capacity has been successfully exercised, so that they do have a language and do live a social life in a community. The community makes possible the full attainment of human nature, and human nature, in having the capacity for living in society, makes possible the emergence and existence of community; each is a condition for the existence of the other. Man has by nature a capacity for society, and society is the result of that capacity operating. This is what lies behind Marx's identifying human nature with community, and it is also what he means by the phrase cited in the previous paragraph that 'by manifesting their nature men create, produce, the human community'. The point is made again in the *Economic and Philosophical Manuscripts*, where Marx notes that 'we must avoid postulating "society" again as an abstraction vis-à-vis the individual. The individual *is the social being*' (Marx, 1975c, p. 299).

This is a very different conception of individual and society from the one most familiar in modernity, namely, that society is a voluntary association arrived at by individual parties contracting together for private advantage. Marx consciously contrasts his own Scholastic view to this modern market one when he writes in the passage above that 'the social entity, which is no abstract universal power opposed to the single individual, but is the essential nature of each individual'. It is just this difference between the Aristotelian view and the modern view that he is getting at. His feeling that market relations like credit embody 'extreme vileness' arises from his sense of its being a self-interested use of others, and therefore the complete opposite of grace, generosity, and *philia*, which is the cement of the social bond. Such an arrangement as credit cannot exist without community, yet in its nature, credit irresponsibly and cynically serves to undermine community for the sake of private monetary enrichment, so that it is a leaching and parasitical thing. The very idea evidently disgusts him, as it would anybody brought up in the Scholastic tradition with the sort of knowledge of and sympathy for the ancient world and its literature that Marx had. Commercial values were not admired in the ancient world, and the sentiment pervades ancient literature. Plato, no less than Aristotle, criticizes commerce as a force unstitching the sorts of relationships of trust, *philia*, generosity, and the spirit of the Graces that ought to exist between citizens, and he says that it 'fills the land with buying and selling, breeds shifty and deceitful habits in a man's soul, and makes the citizens distrustful and hostile' (Plato, 2005, 705a).

Once Marx gets to grips with the economic literature in 1843, the whole weight of this tradition of thought and sensibility is brought to bear, through him, on all the buying and selling, the credit system, the system of wage labour, and the whole capitalist bag of tricks. As he reads about these arrangements in the work of Mill and the others, he comes to see that they contradict what he understands to be the very nature and point of humans living in community at all. Once he realized this, the tissue of capitalist life and institutions become profoundly disturbing. They come to be seen as a cynical perversion of what human life and community should be. 'Hence', as he says,

> *as* they are, so is this entity itself [...] the society of this estranged man is a caricature of his *real community* [...] his activity therefore appears to him as a torment, his own creation as an alien power, his wealth as

poverty, the essential bond linking him with other men as an inessential bond, and separation from his fellow man as his true mode of existence, his life as a sacrifice of his life [...] his production as the production of a nullity.

(Marx, 1975b, p. 217)

These insights become the moving principle of Marx's life's work, and in *Capital* he sets out to expose just how this law-governed alien power, which we have produced out of our own life activity, dominates us, controls our activity, and perverts our communities.

The point of the community, Aristotle famously says, is not just 'life', the abundance of its physical necessities, but the 'good life' (Aristotle, 1981, 1, 1252b30–1). The good life is life as lived by a person who has been formed properly in character and intellect, whose capacities have been educated and given room for their free exercise in a life of setting one's own goals and pursuing them and has acquired the sense and taste to know which goals are worth something. This is what Marx is evoking in the letter to Ruge cited at the beginning, where he speaks of 'a community of human beings united for their highest aims'. The point of the state is to provide conditions in which everyone can do well and lead a flourishing life, the good life, and not a life of consuming, which Aristotle was perfectly familiar with and likens to the life of grazing cattle – oddly the very simile often used today to describe the shallow pleasure-seeking of the yuppies.[7] Hobbes, writing at the beginning of the liberal or economic tradition, thinks the point of the state is to establish a monopoly of force with the purpose of ensuring that contracts are kept, that is, to provide law and order so that commerce can flourish (Hobbes, 2007). Such an idea is explicitly rejected in the Aristotelian tradition, and Aristotle writes that even if a large population of people come together and lived near each other, and had laws to prevent cheating in exchange, still 'if they associated in nothing more than military alliance and the exchange of goods, this will not be a *polis*', because a *polis* exists for the sake of the good life; it is partnership in living well, not just in living (Aristotle, 1981, 3, 1280b, 17–35).

Aristotelianism has not been well regarded either by Marx's friends or by his critics. Progress Publishers of Moscow used to list Aristotle in the glossary at the back of their books as 'Aristotle – ancient Greek philosopher, vacillated between idealism and materialism'. Schumpeter, in best Progress Publishers' style, saw in Aristotle's analysis of money and trade nothing more than 'the ideological preconceptions to be expected of a man who lived in, and wrote for, a cultivated leisure class' (Schumpeter, 1954, p. 60). Philosophers like Ross and Mulgan pursue the same reductionist line. They are both defensive in the face of criticism of trade and money lending, and they both casually dismiss Aristotle as a snobbish hanger-on of the aristocracy (Ross, 1949, p. 243; Mulgan, 1977, p. 49). The left too, equally superficially, tends to see the Greek authors in general, and Aristotle in particular, as expressing an aristocratic landowners' 'ideology' that despised work and thought slavery natural. But this was not how Marx viewed the Aristotelian tradition. Of course he recognized the ideology when it cropped up, as who could fail to, but he did not think that that was all there was to it. He did not take a *histmatiker*'s reductive view of it as being nothing more than ideology. He shared Aristotelian metaphysics, and the Aristotelian view of individual and community, of human nature, and of the point of the polis. It is clear in all his work from the period around 1844 that this tradition provides the foundation and much of the detail of his reaction to economic thought, and it remained the foundation of his thought and sensibility throughout his life.

Throughout the pages of the *Comments on James Mill* and the *Economic and Philosophical Manuscripts* there is an emotional revulsion from market relationships and values, a feeling that this is not the spirit in which to live, not the way to see things, and not the way to feel and act. He speaks later of Ricardo's 'cynicism' and 'indifference towards men'; he complains about the 'filthy self-interest' that pervades the market system. Contemptuous references to 'huckstering' big and small, and to the 'huckstering spirit', are to be found on every other page of the *Comments*, and he complains of 'the devaluation of men' that comes with 'this whole estrangement connected with the *money* system' (Marx, 1975c, pp. 256–72). What Marx had in the back of his mind was the spirit of life in classical Greece. To act selfishly was thought shameful. To take advantage of your neighbour and gain an advantage for yourself at his expense, was not thought smart, it was thought a disgrace. And it didn't pay either, because a reputation for behaving like that would lose you the trust of those around you, and they would no longer feel bound by *philia* and the duties of community to help you. The professional buyer and seller was not admired because it was felt that he made a living by taking things from people, and the usurer was despised as a predator.

Against a background of social feelings of this sort, the relationships of the market, impersonal, uncharitable, stinting, calculating, and self-interested are not going to seem very admirable. In economic thought these relationships are portrayed as the natural state of man, and Marx observes:

> Society, says Adam Smith, is a commercial society. Each of its members is a merchant. It is seen that political economy defines the estranged form of social intercourse as the essential and original form corresponding to man's nature.
>
> (Marx, 1975b, p. 217)

The contrasting society he has in mind, the non-estranged form of social intercourse is classical Greek society. Greece, and especially Athens, is the yardstick that Marx measures modernity against, and we can see him do it again and again throughout his life, in the *Economic and Philosophical Manuscripts*, the *Contribution*, the *Grundrisse*, and in *Capital*. Marx is not alone in this of course. Generations of Europeans have used classical Greece as a kind of looking glass in which to get some detachment and perspective on what they have made of themselves so far. The Greeks have represented an ideal, and they have been held in affection and admiration. Marx later wrote that the works of the Greeks 'are in certain respects regarded as a standard and unattainable ideal', and he asked himself why this was so. He answered that the Greeks represent the fascination of 'the historical childhood of humanity where it attained its most beautiful form and it exerts an eternal charm because it is a stage that will never return' (Marx, 1970, pp. 150–1).

Classical education gave thinkers like Hegel, Marx, and Nietzsche, a detailed grasp of life in a non-market society run according to a social ethic, and this gave them a strong contrast with modernity, an exchange-based society run by market forces. It gave them a chance of detachment and perspective that was invaluable for assessing the present. The loss of it is politically significant.

Marx and the tradition

Can we draw any conclusions from all this? The influence of Aristotelian metaphysics is operating at a fundamental philosophical level in the *Comments on James Mill*. We are not talking only about political and social philosophy, subjects at a much less fundamental level. We are talking about the most general and fundamental area in philosophy, metaphysics; the theory of the nature of things, of what it is to be, or to exist, for things of different kinds; for ordinary material objects, for animals, for human individuals, and for societies of human individuals. Thought of this depth and generality was purged in England and Scotland in the course of the social, moral, and intellectual upheavals that produced market economy and economic thought, from the sixteenth and seventeenth centuries onwards. But it was not wiped out on the Continent. Marx's response to economic thought is unique; there is nothing else in literature with the same penetration. And its profundity arises from the depth and sophistication of the metaphysical resources he is able to call upon.

To get a sense of the depth imparted by Scholastic metaphysics, and of the contrasting superficiality of economic thought, one has only to compare Marx's analysis of economic value, commodities, and money, in Chapter 1 of *Capital*, with the inarticulate struggles to be found in Smith and Ricardo on that subject. Whether or not Marx's analysis of value is ultimately defensible is not the point at present. The point is that it does attain the dimensions of an analysis, extended, subtle, penetrating, and sophisticated. Smith and Ricardo cannot get an analysis started and they come to a grinding halt after only a couple of sentences directly on the subject.[8] Neither of them can get a purchase on saying something about the nature of a property (in this case exchange-value), because they are entirely without the resources needed for this sort of task, namely, the logic of categories of predicate: quality, quantity, relation and so forth. And the same goes for Samuel Bailey's work on value a few years later. Marx's treatment consists in a systematic deployment of the logic of the categories together with the distinction between nature and convention. If we look at the Anglophone tradition in philosophy, which was all that was available to Smith and Ricardo, we find that in Hume there is no treatment of categories of predicate, and Hume is not an exceptional case. A glance at the index entries under 'quantity' yields only witty paradoxes about mathematicians. There is no logic in the *Treatise*. Logic and metaphysics had simply been done away with in the purge of Aristotelianism. This is historically the philosophical culture that produced much of economic thought, so it is not especially surprising that Marx, coming at it from his own quite different philosophical culture, should be scandalized to find that in economic thought it is considered acceptable to ride roughshod over distinctions between kinds and over the distinction between nature and convention.

The unavailability of Aristotelian logic and metaphysics contributed to the capacity of the English and Scottish writers to beget the economic view of the things in the world, because it made the logical obstacles in their path invisible to them. And equally the retention of that logic and metaphysics on the Continent contributed to Marx's capacity to stand back from economic writing, when he encountered it, and to identify the philosophical coarseness and inadequacy of the view it takes of things. His Scholastic training also gives him the sensitivity, probably already lost to many Anglophone readers of economic thought at the time, to spot the crude and mercenary character of the view it takes of people and their activities and the cynical view it takes of the point of life in the community.

This gives us a sense of the seriousness of what is going on in Marx's confrontation with economic thought. Marx is not being particularly original, or brilliantly deploying some groundbreaking innovation in nineteenth-century German philosophy, contrary to most of the usual hagiographic pictures. Instead, the revolutionary novelty of his reaction lies in the fact that he represents, in a modern form, the philosophical tradition that had evolved over two thousand years in Europe, when it was free from the pressures generated by life under markets that led us to inform the material and social worlds with the fetishism of the commodity. Scholastic Aristotelianism itself might, in earlier times, have been subject to other unattractive cultural pressures, but that is not the point. The point is that those pressures, whatever they may have been, were not the peculiar commodity fetishizing pressures from the market that the thought of modernity has had to accommodate and express. What we are looking at in the *Comments on James Mill* is a fundamental confrontation between philosophical traditions, the ancient pre-market one and the revolutionarily new market one which is fully fet-ishized, economic thought. In this fundamental respect, Marx is a thinker fully in the two thousand year old mainstream European philosophical tradition. It is just because of this that he has the resources behind him and ready to hand to be able to resist being taken in by economic thought, to see what is going on in it, and to part company so precisely and thoroughly with it.

Notes

1. A version of this paper was presented to the Marx and Philosophy Society annual conference on 10 September 2005.
2. His considerations here had nothing at all to do with Hegel, as Heinz Lubasz (1976) has shown.
3. McLellan suggests that in the *Comments on James Mill* Marx 'dealt with the categories of classical economics he had planned to discuss in the unfinished part of his manuscript on alienated labour' (McLellan, 1973, p. 112). The editors of the *Collected Works* think it is possible that the *Comments on James Mill* might have 'anticipated the thoughts expounded in the missing pages of the second manuscript of this work', i.e. the *Economic and Philosophical Manuscripts* (Marx 1975b, p. 596, n. 48).
4. The Doctoral Dissertation itself much later earned the appreciation of Cyril Bailey, the eminent classicist and authority on Epicurus, who regarded it as original especially for its time.
5. A notable exception in the literature is Kay and Mott, 1982.
6. Kolakowski is speaking of the *Economic and Philosophical Manuscripts*, rather than the *Comments on James Mill*, which he does not consider.
7. 'The many, the most vulgar, would seem to conceive the good and happiness as pleasure, and hence they also like the life of gratification. Here they appear completely slavish, since the life they decide on is a life for grazing animals; and yet they have some argument in their defence, since many in positions of power feel the same way as Sardanapallus [and also chose this life]' (Aristotle, 1985, 1095b16ff).
8. Ricardo only manages to cite Smith's couple of lines: 'It has been observed by Adam Smith, that "the word Value has two different meanings, and sometimes expresses the utility of some particular object, and sometimes the power of purchasing other goods which the possession of that object conveys. The one may be called *value in use*; the other *value in exchange*"' (Ricardo, 1951, p. 11).

Bibliography

Aristotle (1981) *The Politics* (Harmondsworth: Penguin).
Aristotle (1985) *Nichomachean Ethics*, trans. T. Irwin (Indianapolis: Hackett).
Dickey, Laurence (1987) *Hegel: Religion, Economics, and the Politics of Spirit 1770–1807* (Cambridge: Cambridge University Press).
Halévy, Elie (1928) *The Growth of Philosophical Radicalism*, trans. Mary Morris (London: Faber and Gwyer).

Hobbes, Thomas (2007) *Leviathan* (Harmondsworth: Penguin).

Hume, David (1969) *A Treatise of Human Nature* (Harmondsworth: Penguin).

Kay, Geoffrey and Mott, James (1982) *Political Order and the Law of Labour* (London: Macmillan).

Kolakowski, Lezek (1978) *Main Currents of Marxism: Volume 1* (Oxford: Oxford University Press).

Lubasz, Heinz (1976) 'Marx's Initial Problematic: The Problem of Property', *Political Studies* 24 (1) pp. 24–42.

Marx, Karl (1970) *The German Ideology: Part One*, (ed.) C. J. Arthur (London: Lawrence and Wishart).

—— (1974) 'Critique of the Gotha Programme' in *The First International and After: Political Writings: Volume 3* (Harmondsworth: Penguin).

—— (1975a) 'Letters from the Deutsch-Französische Jahrbücher', in Karl Marx and Friedrich Engels, *Collected Works*, vol. 3 (London: Lawrence and Wishart).

—— (1975b) 'Comments on James Mill', in Karl Marx and Friedrich Engels, *Collected Works*, vol. 3 (London: Lawrence and Wishart).

—— (1975c) 'Economics and Philosophical Manuscripts', in Karl Marx and Friedrich Engels, *Collected Works*, vol. 3 (London: Lawrence and Wishart).

Marx, Karl and Engels, Friedrich (1981) *Karl Marx – Friedrich Engels Gesamtausgabe* (MEGA), IV/2 Text: Excerpte und Notizen 1843 bis Januar 1845.

McLellan, David (1973) *Karl Marx: A Biography* (London: Macmillan).

Mulgan, R. G. (1977) *Aristotle's Political Theory* (Oxford: Oxford University Press).

Nicolaievsky, Boris and Maenchen-Helfen, Otto (1936) *Karl Marx: Man and Fighter* (London: Methuen).

Plato (2005) *The Laws* (Harmondsworth: Penguin).

Pocock, J. G. A. (1975) *The Machiavellian Moment* (Princeton: Princeton University Press).

Ricardo, David (1951) *The Works and Correspondence of David Ricardo*, vol. 1, (eds) P. Sraffa and M. H. Dobb (Cambridge: Cambridge University Press).

Ross, William David (1949) *Aristotle* (London: Methuen)

Schumpeter, Joseph (1954) *A History of Economic Analysis* (London: Routledge).

Wiggins, David (1980) *Sameness and Substance* (Oxford: WileyBlackwell).

PART II   MARX AND POLITICAL PHILOSOPHY

4
Marx's Theory of Democracy in His Critique of Hegel's Philosophy of the State

Georgios Daremas

Marx's theory of democracy is a critique of the 'political state' in political philosophy, tied to his conception of the *good society*. Marx's discussion of 'democracy' is faced with two difficulties. Firstly, the notion of 'democracy' is a 'contested terrain' revealing clashing political worldviews underneath its theory. Because of its hegemonic role in the existing 'general consciousness', even authoritarian politics masks itself as 'democratic', as in the recent Imperial promulgation of the *export* of democracy as a packaged set of political conditions *imposed* on the ruled by a dominant alien ruler. In such neo-colonialism disguised as 'democracy' there is a grand inversion of form and content, where *democracy* as the *self-determination of the societal whole by itself for itself* is presented as being the product of the will of One *over* the communal self of an heteronomous many.

The second difficulty concerns the historical absence of any *democratic* institutional life in the early nineteenth century. Universal enfranchisement, political parties, public trials and an independent judiciary, parliaments as representation of the *general will*, publicity of assembly proceedings (Marx, 1975b, pp. 145, 147), and other political institutions associated with representative democracy were non-existent (Sperber, 1991). Even demands for a democratic state based on *popular sovereignty* were officially censored.

In such political context dominated by centralised absolutisms and an anaemic civil society, Marx's 1843 critique of the principles of the modern constitutional state through a detailed critical examination of Hegel's *Philosophy of Right* is highly original. He had already criticised the exclusionary forms of political representation of the monarchical state arriving at his core idea that if there is to be true political representation, it 'must be conceived only as the people's *self-representation* [*Selbstvertretung*]' (Marx, 1975c, p. 306). 'Universal enfranchisement' emerges as a necessary political precondition in order to overcome the 'abstract political state' itself as a *separate* realm from civil life so as to *restore* to society, its real human form as a unified societal community of all.[1]

I will explore the socio-political relationship against which Marx erects his theory of democracy. This is the relationship between civil (bourgeois) society and the political state,[2] and its mode of conditioning the relation between state sovereignty and the people in a way it ought not to do. Also, in the *Critique of Hegel's Doctrine of the State* (Marx, 1975a) even though Marx has not yet developed any notion of social class determination of individual existence, his challenge to the contours of Hegel's state will awaken him to the existence of supra-individual structures of relation that determine individual will formation. Furthermore, Marx concurs with basic conceptual presuppositions made by Hegel but he also negates major Hegelian theoretical consequences through logical inversions and by his use of a *social materialist* perspective that supersedes the Hegelian primacy of the Idea as state-spirit with the notion of *society* as the essence of the human species-being, its 'species-life itself, society' (Marx, 1975d, p.164). Lastly, I employ the prism of *presentism*,[3] of focusing on the issues under discussion having in mind their significance for us today, that is, 'our criticism centres on the very questions of which the present age says: *that is the question*' (Marx, 1994, p. 62). Hence I highlight the contemporary relevance of Marx's critical remarks on the constitutional republic.

The political state against civil society

Marx engages with the hard core of the *Philosophy of Right* (Hegel, 1991) which deals with the constitution of the 'inner sovereignty' of the state, the political state proper. Hegel's state (*der Staat*) is an ethico-political organism that realises as its universal end the unity of 'subjective and objective freedom' (Hegel, 1991, §258, p. 276). The 'political state' (*politische Staat*) is the plexus of political institutions (the three powers of monarchy, the executive and the legislative) which in espousing the universal aims of the state-community secures objective freedom as the highest end and as a prerequisite for the exercise of the subjective freedom of the particular individuals who constitute the members of civil society.

Marx in unfolding his critique follows Hegel's exposition which is structured as a movement from the general to the concrete, from the most abstract to the most specific, and this obliges Marx to face on from the very start the essential blueprint of Hegel's conception of the 'modern' state (Hegel, 1991, §§261–2, pp. 283–6). Marx immediately identifies 'an unresolved *antinomy*' in the organic connection that Hegel posits between 'family and civil society' and the political state in §261. 'On the one hand, the state stands opposed to the sphere of the family and civil society as an "*external* necessity"' to which family/civil society 'are subordinate [...] and [...] dependent'. On the other hand, Hegel counterpoises to the relation of 'external necessity' that 'other relationship in which the family and civil society are related to the state as their "*immanent* end"' (Marx, 1975a, p. 59).

To talk of the state as the organic unity of civil society with the political state and at the same time to see it as composed by a dual relationship of 'external necessity' and 'immanent end' is to posit an unsurpassable conflict in the conceptual articulation of the state. And since 'Hegel makes no mention of empirical conflicts', this clash must concern 'the *essential relationship* between these spheres themselves' (Marx, 1975a, p. 59). So, it is not only a logical *contradiction* that lurks in Hegel's theorisation of the state but also an *antinomy* in the very essence of the modern state that Hegel 'describes' speculatively. It becomes evident that Marx, methodologically, employs the mode of *immanent* or internal critique that rests on holding accountable the theorist under criticism for logical contradictions and inconsistencies which derive from his/her *own* premises.[4] These are self-contradictions that result in the self-destructive negation of the coherence of the system in the eyes of critical Reason. This is a mode of critique that works via *determinate negation* of the opponent's premises and presuppositions and of socio-historical reality itself (Marx, 1994, p. 58).

The philosophical crux of Marx's rebuttal is that no organic unity can exist as such if it is internally divided in such a way that its *membra disjecta* are perennially in conflict, unified through an opposition that continually tends to explode 'the internal essence of the thing' (Marx, 1975a, p. 60), to disintegrate it into its component member parts. Hegel's concept of the *divided identity* of the state has unduly privileged 'one side' of the identity, 'the aspect of estrangement within the unity' (Marx, 1975a, p. 60) and this estrangement as *separation* has turned the political state into a despot over civil society, 'a merely external compulsion exerted by the ruling power upon private life' (Marx, 1975a, pp. 78–9) instead of providing a 'rational system' that harmoniously resolves their mode of imbrication.

Hegel's idea of the rational state as an 'ethical organism' is premised on two conditions. Firstly, that the state is actually ethical and does not just pretend to be so. This means that the citizens of the state have self-consciously accepted and internalised as 'second nature' the institution-alised political constitution and thus they recognise the necessity of the existence of a *political authority* that takes care of the universal interest since they themselves in their particularity are mainly engaged with their private concerns. This *political authority* also recognises and guarantees their rights and ensures their free exercise. Thus, they ought to respect and be committed to the *duties* they owe to the state whose 'strength consists in the unity of its universal and ultimate end with the particular interest of individuals' (Hegel, 1991, §261, p. 283). The very *strength* of the (political) state itself rests on the degree of acceptance of the universal aims it pursues by the particular interests of the individuals. The more consonant they are with each other, the greater the *strength* of the state, the more they diverge, the less its strength and the greater the loss of its ethical character. On this basis, Marx's critique of the state's *executive power* as a bureaucracy which follows its own particular interests and treats the state as its private property (Draper, 1977, p. 82) under the pretext of promoting the universal end may be absolutely right as far as empirical state policies are concerned, but it cannot invalidate *per se* this Hegelian presupposition of the rational state. But if the ethical bond of *duty* which *grounds* the legitimacy of the political state as a universalistic agency *over* the particular interests of individuals *in their own consciousness* is not to remain an empty ideal, introduced *externally*, then it has to face up to the presence of its absence in the actual civil society. For such an ethical bond to subsist which unifies the particular with the universal *after their divorce*, the members of civil society themselves must not be inherently divided into private selves and public personae in their empirical social existence. They should not be intrinsically split into self-seeking egoists and other-directed human beings opposed to their 'communal essence' (*Gemeinwesen*) as an adversarial *sociality* which at the same time is the social precondition of their formation as individuals and the absolute structure of social interdependency through which *only* they can 'satisfy' their human needs and personal interests. But it is precisely the dissolution of *this* ethical bond that we see as being realised in contemporary liberal democracies, encapsulated in the 'image' of the *schizophrenic citizen*. In his/her *political/public* identity as member of the state s/he understands that *taxation* is necessary to provide for social welfare and the other collective functions (education, public health, pension, defence, material infrastructures) needed to maintain the *social integration* of the whole society intact. But in his/her *private/egoistic* identity s/he does not *want* to pay any taxes (or the less the better) 'feeling' taxation as an 'oppressive' burden on his/her 'free' individuality. Instead, in a self-contradictory fashion s/he *desires* everyone else to pay his/her taxes[5] (the 'free rider' strategy) or in the form of a spurious universality no-one to pay any taxes in blatant opposition to his/her status as a citizen and its concomitant political and ethical obligations.

The second condition of the ethical/rational state is the universality of laws. Laws in their generality must not discriminate against citizens nor privilege any special interests (Hegel, 1999, p. 177). Of course, equal treatment via universal laws of socially unequal citizens results in the reproduction of inequality not equality, as Marx with acuity would argue later in life (Marx, 1996, p. 214). In spite of 'formal rationality' the principle of universalistic law is *in itself* defective within the context of bourgeois civil society. The *modern constitutional state* which operates on the principle of the 'rule of law' and thus *prima facie* treats its citizens universalistically still suffers from the 'absolute' contradiction that it reduces human beings to 'legal persons' in order *afterwards* to recognise their 'essential human rights' as supposedly intrinsic in their very individuality. Within bourgeois social life 'juridical personality' is divorced from and thus opposed to the actual existence of human beings with the consequence that 'legal existence' becomes the *absolute* presupposition of being *human* rather than the inverse. This general condition is seen starkly in the predicament of refugees, of *stateless* persons who in not having their human existence recognised 'legally' by a state are reduced to a sub-human existence.

The presuppositions of the constitutional state have been 'cogently analysed' by Hegel but he has not 'demonstrated their validity' (Marx, 1975a, p. 96). Against the constitutional, law-based *political republic*, '[i]n democracy [*Demokratie*], man does not exist for the sake of law, but the law exists for the sake of man, it is *human existence*, whereas in other political systems man is a *legal existence*. This is the fundamental distinguishing feature of democracy' (Marx, 1975a, p. 88). The 'abstract' existence of law in bourgeois modernity is further accentuated not only by the problem of the 'implementation deficit'[6] but even more by the actual implementation. There is not only lack of accountability and of popular control of the state's administrative action but also no protection against its use of legal power as abuse, whenever the 'bureaucratic hierarchy' itself 'sins' through the *official* action of its civil servants (Marx, 1975a, p. 114).

In 'true' democracy, law-making and the political state *tout court* must manifest the self-rule of the people as a social whole and be its 'determinate content' as an expression of the 'self-determination of the people' (Marx, 1975a, p. 89). Law itself must be the 'incarnation of reason', of the people's will as 'species-will' [*Gattungswillen*] (Marx, 1975a, p. 120), and not a political product issuing as if by the 'blind necessity of nature' (Marx, 1975a, p. 118). In democracy, the executive power of the state 'is the property of the whole people' (Marx, 1975a, p. 116). Thus, inclusive, participatory involvement of the whole in the executive functioning of the democratic community becomes its ethical norm.

In Hegel, the evolution of state forms exhibits the secularisation of the 'principle of freedom' in an historical process that leads increasingly to the universalisation of individual human freedom (Hegel, 1980, pp. 54, 55), and the *modern* state emerges as the incarnation of generalised freedom. Its *differentia specifica* vis-à-vis all previous state forms is the *differentiation* of civil society as an autonomous complex of socio-economic relations from the political state *within* the state. In Hegel's conception this *differentiation* is a worthy achievement since it permits the expression of the subjective freedom of the particular wills. The *autonomy* of civil society from its political tutelage under feudalism or from its subservience to the political power of *res publica* in classical state forms raises vexing questions. What keeps political society together, how does it secure its *social integration*? Which institutional complex can *reconcile* the centrifugal tendencies of a particularistic, self-centered civil society with a system of political organisation that caters to the universal concerns of the societal community?

Marx responds to this constitutive dilemma of political modernity proffering the solution of the *de-differentiation* of the political state from civil/bourgeois society into a novel societal configuration where 'political power' is absorbed into 'social power' with the resultant transcendence of both prior abstract forms of the *political* and the *civil*. This is the democratic polity which realises *human emancipation* and the organisation of wo/man's or man's '*social* forces' (Marx, 1975d, p. 168). Democracy as state or the state of democracy supersedes the divided essence of communal social life rent into the private, egoistic individual, the 'self-enclosed monad' on the one hand and the universalistic, 'abstract' political existence of the citizen on the other. 'Democracy' ceases to be one species of political constitution among other alternative and opposing species of political constitutions, and it is elevated to the *genus* of political constitution per se.[7]

Hegel's 'political state' consists of the 'inner differentiation' of the developed state-spirit into the three powers of the *legislative*, the *executive*, and the *sovereign* who embodies the decisionism of supreme will, all powers being dialectically interlocked in the unitary form of the constitutional monarchy (Hegel, 1991, §273, p. 308). Marx attacks all three powers as fundamentally incapable of furnishing the *mediating links* which could make civil society cohere with the political state in an organic whole. The brunt of the criticism is received by the institution of the monarchy, presented by Hegel as the apex of the state's power system. The major defect of the monarchical principle concerns the issue of incumbency. Hegel wants to support *hereditary monarchy* and this commits him to an *anacolouthon*, an illegitimate logical jump from the *natural* (biological) to the *social*. The institution of the sovereign is an invention of society. In no way can the sovereignty of a state incarnated in a person ever be derived *immediately* from an *accident* of natural birth. To reduce the personification of state sovereignty to the natural features of the incumbent naturalises political domination and makes the actual people who form the state appear as an attachment of his 'naturally' held sovereignty. The people instead of being the actual basis of constituted sovereignty appear to be constituted by the sovereign's person. The fundamental relation of *representation* in the constitutional state by which the sovereign is bound to 'his' people and not the people to their sovereign, has been inverted. If 'he is sovereign only as the representative of the united people, then he is himself only a representative and symbol of the sovereignty of the people. The sovereignty of the people is not based on him, but he on it' (Marx, 1975a, p. 85).

Another flaw involves the attribution of the state's will, its supreme decision-making expressive of the state's 'self-determination', to the monarch as a *private* person. Such unconditional prerogative is irrational because the 'affairs of the state' concern 'the modes of action and existence of the social qualities of men' (Marx, 1975a, p. 78), their communal existence as social beings engaged in webs of social relations out of which spring the collective functions and aims of the state. To abstract from the 'species-forms' (*Gattungsgestaltungen*) of social life, family, community, society in order to endow a social locus like monarchy or 'a head of state' with a non-social 'self-determining' arbitrary will only turns state sovereignty into a private affair of the single, all-encompassing 'representative' of state sovereignty; it makes the state appear to be the monarch's *private property* and thus reveals the state in its 'higher authority' as an imposition over society rather than as its particular political domain that promotes its common non-private affairs.

In the history of political philosophy, 'sovereignty' has always been conceived as *indivisible*, for otherwise the conflict of power is interminable and destructive of the state. This is a position accepted by both Hegel and Marx. Hence, '[s]overeignty of the monarch or of the people – that is the question' (Marx, 1975a, p. 86). Since we cannot have two sovereignties in one but only two 'opposed conceptions' of it, of which only one can be true, and since sovereignty must express the *'demos* as a whole' and not be embodied in a part superimposed on the whole, then all forms of government which are *separated*, functioning independently of the social whole even if they claim to 'represent it', are illegitimate polities. Only democracy satisfies the rational condition of being the *identity* of 'both form and content' (Marx, 1975a, p. 87), of establishing as the universal end the common affairs of the society and in being actually 'the free creation' of the social co-participation of all members of society in its self-determination, a recognition and realisation of our human essence as a universalistic social species-being.

The realisation of democracy does not necessarily lead to the *elimination* of the political state. This is one of the options left to the democratic community. We could have alternatively the presence of political functions and agencies which implement *particular* purposes with the proviso that such a 'political state' reflects a *particular* form of existence of the people and it does not 'assume the significance of the *universal'* (Marx, 1975a, p. 88), hiding its particularity. It thus loses its superordinate position and becomes subordinated to the democratic rule of society. Marx recognises that the political state in its developed form as a *political republic* is a 'form of universal reason' albeit in abstractness and hence in opposition to, transcendent to and in 'remoteness' from the other spheres of society. As an expression of 'the life of the people' it was 'the hardest to evolve' in an historical process that can be called the *labour of democratising politics*.[8] Democracy is not a ready-made constitutional blueprint to be adopted when people desire to do so but a protracted socio-historical process of humanity reclaiming its rational, communal existence as its own collective freedom. The people *labour* to give *birth* to novel forms of political existence that bring democracy closer to its essential character and they also *labour* through struggles and revolutions to *produce* the contents of democracy. 'The sphere of politics has been the only state-sphere in the state, the only sphere in which both form and content was that of the species [*Gattungsinhalt*], i.e. truly universal' (Marx, 1975a, p. 89).

Civil society against the state

The bifurcation of the state into the political state and civil society is at the same time the separation of civil society from the state. This separate, *independent* existence of civil society is the principal condition of the modern political world (Marx, 1975a, p. 137). It is the other pole of the antinomy that vitiates modern society. Hegel senses this crucial contradiction, as Marx says glibly. Hegel is aware that if the *mediating links*, the ethical duty of citizenship, patriotism, civic trust, regulative and welfare agencies, overseeing authorities, corporate associations as intermediary bodies, parliaments as representative assemblies of the 'many', and the civil service as a 'universal class' serving the universal end and a meritocratic institution open to *all* that integrate civil society with the political state are de-legitimated and lose their organic character, then the state as an *ethical organism* does not have any chances of self-preservation (Daremas, 2006, pp. 337ff). In such a case the state becomes an arena of conflicting particular interests that fight over its 'universal and permanent resources' (Hegel, 1991, §199, p. 233) or it gradually disappears and the political community reverts to a 'state of nature' with its contingent atrocities. So Hegel is cognizant of the disastrous consequences that follow if the political state is *uncoupled* from civil society. His theoretical flaws result from his attempt to construct the rational state as a hybrid 'mixture' of pre-modern (prior to the French revolution) obsolete political institutions *and* the modern constitutional state so that its 'syncretism'[9] can vouchsafe the state-spirit's continuity and trivialise the revolutionary genesis of the political republic, and from his prioritisation of the Idea of the state's spirit as the *source of determination* of the modern civil society.

Hegel expresses the primacy of the actual Idea in determining the contours of civil society in §262. Marx considers that this paragraph condenses 'the whole mystery of the *Philosophy of Right* and of Hegel's philosophy in general' (Marx, 1975a, p. 64). Both conceptual axes of the Marxian critique originate from the *inversion* of its two central theses. Firstly, on the socio-historical terrain, Marx *inverts* the source of determination in the state–civil society relationship and proclaims that civil society is the *real* source of determination of the state rather than the reverse. Secondly, on the logical terrain, Marx *inverts* the subject–predicate relation as speculated by Hegel since in his philosophy '[t]he Idea is subjectivized and the *real* relationship of the family and civil society to the state is conceived as their *inner, imaginary* activity. The family and civil society are the preconditions of the state; they are the true agents; but in speculative philosophy it is the reverse' (Marx, 1975a, p. 62).

Influenced by Feuerbachian premises, Marx counterposes to Hegel's bifurcated reality 'the ordinary empirical world' governed by its own mind and not by a mind alien to it. The existence which *corresponds* to Hegel's

Idea is not a self-generated reality but 'just the ordinary empirical world' (Marx, 1975a, p. 62). With this socio-ontological primacy of the 'ordinary empirical world' as the real basis of the spirituality of the state, Marx sides with classical liberalism's social contractarian origination of political society from natural society and he stresses that it is 'the course of their own life that joins them together to comprise the state' and not the life of the Idea as state (Marx, 1975a, p. 63).

In place of Hegel's internal division of the state into civil society and political state, Marx acknowledges the division of civil society into a 'social order' of community life forms and the realm of an *individualising* political sphere. The private citizen, if s/he wants to attain 'the status of *citizen of the state*' so as to obtain political significance and efficacy, must withdraw from all 'available forms of community' in civil life into a 'pure unadorned *individuality*' (Marx, 1975a, p. 143). This is analogous to the present-day constitutional 'representative' republic where the political status of the private citizen premised on the individualistic principle of formal political equality of 'one man one vote' leads individual political will formation to be 'unencumbered' by social embedment and consideration of 'universal concerns'. In tandem with a shrinking political domain, under growing de-politicisation and the crisis of party politics, the citizen is eclipsed by the consumer and political activity is transfigured into political market behaviour. Marx sees modern civil (bourgeois) society as the 'logical conclusion of the principle of *individualism*' where individualistic existence is the *ultimate goal* and social activity, work, recreation, spiritual aims, cultivation of personality and solidaristic ties with others have turned into mere *means* (Marx, 1975a, p. 147). Hence, the absoluteness of the principle of individualism dissolves all the erstwhile social bonds that united actual women and men in an interdependent communal co-existence. The individual is *abstracted* from his/her *sociality* and is posited as a one-sided formal existence apart and in opposition to it. This is isomorphic to the one-sided formal abstraction of the public citizen as separate from his/her social being effected by the political state. The 'atomism of society' reflects itself in an inverted form as the *political universalism* of the political state with its duty to promote the universal end while it only universalises the individualisation of the abstract political citizen. The duplication of atomised civil society into a separate universalising political state constitutes the latter as 'practical illusions' in the forms of bureaucracy and legislature. All in all, 'the *political state is an abstraction* from civil society' (Marx, 1975a, p. 145).

The emergence of bourgeois society is the result of an historical process of the dissolution of the estates as fixed, politically constituted classes into 'mere *social* differences in private life of no significance in political life'. This process was completed by the French Revolution which thus 'accomplished the separation of political life and civil society' (Marx, 1975a, p. 146). Marx's presentation of the *social organisation* of bourgeois society hints at the formation of an 'underclass' of propertyless labourers and focuses on the non-class determinability of the social position of the individual with which he opposes Hegel's argument of a 'hidden' unperceived empirically, supra-individual structure of determination of the social allocation of individuals in society.

In pre-modern civil society, the class distinctions, the division of individuals into estates, were distinctions 'between autonomous groups distinguished by their *needs* and their *work*.' In contradistinction, within modern society 'distinctions are variable and fluid and their principle is that of *arbitrariness*. The chief criteria are those of *money* and *education* [...] The principle underlying civil society is neither need, a natural moment, nor politics. It is a fluid division of masses whose various formations are arbitrary and *without* organization. The only noteworthy feature is that the *absence of property* and the *class of immediate labour*, of concrete labour, do not so much constitute a class of civil society as provide the ground on which the circles of civil society move and have their being' (Marx, 1975a, pp. 146–7).

Hegel in §262 had asserted that the actual Idea as spirit *assigns* 'human beings as a *mass*' into families and civil society, that it allocates them into definite social functions and that this distribution is *mediated in appearance* by the individual's 'circumstances, his caprice and his personal choice of his station in life.' Marx fulminates against Hegel on two counts. Firstly, against the idea that the mediation of the place of individuals in social life by 'circumstances, caprice and personal choice' is described as an apparent one and not as a *real mediation* that truly determines their station in life. Secondly, that Hegel presents the 'ordinary empirical world' of individual circumstances, caprice and personal choice as a phenomenal world *behind* which 'mysterious forces' are active and like an 'invisible hand' organise the distribution of individuals into social positions. The real Idea performs an inversion where the 'self-determining' individuals of caprice and personal choice appear to be determined by a process 'that takes place behind the scenes'. These immediate, perceptible, sensuous conditions of 'caprice and personal choice' are 'not regarded as true, necessary, and intrinsically self-justified; they are not as *such* deemed to be rational [by Hegel]' (Marx, 1975a, p. 62). Thus an essence, a hidden, true reality is posited by Hegel that does not correspond to its appearance, though it is itself expressed through appearance. This dual Hegelian reality of a reality behind reality explains also Marx's insistent labelling of Hegel's philosophy as 'dualism'. It is true that Hegel distinguishes between the 'reality' of transient and contingent phenomena and events manifested in the world and the essential core of the same actual reality that he calls 'Reason in the world', the immanent universal principle expressing itself as the logical articulation of the *objective* organisation of the world (Hegel, 1975, §24, p. 37).

What may such *assignment* by the Idea mean in non-speculative language? In any nation-state, all individual members of society either belong to a family union or live as single persons. Whether they form families or wish to maintain a celibate existence certainly appears to be a matter of capricious choice. This is the element of mediation that Hegel speaks about. But what is seen from the viewpoint of the particular individual as contingent, if seen from the vantage point of the social whole, the state, emerges as otherwise to contingency. It emerges as a universal necessity that a definite proportion of individuals must form families (and since this is a societal *ratio*) and that some will remain childless. Without such ratio or *measure* of distribution of the 'mass of individuals' no society can ever be physically reproduced. So a *social law* exists unbeknownst to the individuals (which operates behind their backs so to speak), unaffected by their personal preferences but *apparently* expressed through their personal choices. Furthermore, individuals seem to decide on their own their vocations, their professions, and their participation in the 'economically active population' of a country. But no society can ever be reproduced if its *active population* is nil. Thus there is a necessary *total social division of labour* (regardless of the distorted and alienated features it assumes in the historically specific capitalist division of labour) that *assigns* or *allocates* individuals to certain types of employment in certain changing proportions necessary for any state to maintain itself. So the contingent choices of employment of individuals are revealed from the *perspective of totality* to be *choices under the determination of invisible constraints* that assign individuals to their stations in life partly not only through their personal will but also in spite of it.

No principles that reflect the *overall existence* of the state or modern society as a whole are recognised by Marx to exist as *determinants* of individual social trajectories. Thus far Marx's is a standard liberal view that the *empirical social order* is constituted by the actions of individuals ('caprice and personal choice') existing as *aggregates* ('fluid division of masses whose formations are arbitrary'), and their 'station in life' is the personal decision of each one in isolation ('the principle of *individualism*').

Marx's view nonetheless, retains a certain distance from the individualist liberal outlook. He does not argue that the social situation of societal members is purely decided by personal whim and arbitrariness. They are actually involved in relations of co-determination due to the social interdependence of needs that they have as material creatures, and thus they are dependent on social others and through the others to the whole of society. But he still conceives the relations of social determination to which individuals are subjected as *contingent* and *accidental* and not as *structural* ones, clusters of relations which they experience directly as empirical, sensuous persons and to which they can respond whenever they choose to as free, self-determining wills. He has not conceived yet that the *patterns* of social determination which affect and shape individuals in social life are not immediately perceivable in experience as they would be were they outcomes of chance encounters and random circumstances, and that instead they are *consequences* of a *deeper* structural organisation of class relations (and that a social class as a *real* abstraction is never *directly* experienced by any class subject), of an essential/historical reality behind empirical reality which is uncovered by scientific reason when it examines society as a whole.

In contrast to his rejection of the Hegelian Idea as an essential supra-individual process of determination of phenomenal existence and his stress on the personalistic character of empirical existence in atomised bourgeois life, Marx will soon adopt a version of *involuted reality*. Discussing social class formation based on the formation of the bourgeoisie, he emphatically proclaims that 'the class in its turn assumes an *independent* existence as against the individuals, so that the latter *find* their conditions of life *predetermined,* and have *their position in life and hence their personal development assigned to them* by their class' (Marx and Engels, 1998, pp. 85–6; my emphasis). The changed perspective on the trajectory of individuals determined by their class positions and the sum-total of the socio-historical determinations is reiterated even in reference to the capitalist division of labour, the distribution structure generated by the production sphere where the individual '[f]rom his birth he is assigned to wage-labour by the social process of distribution' (Marx, 1998, p. 12).

The bestowal of a permanent *political* role to private property in the system of political representation compels Marx to grapple with the salience of private property in the constitution of the political state. Hegel assigns permanent political representation to the landed gentry via the institution of primogeniture which bequeaths the whole land to the first born male and thus keeps the property intact and ensures 'independence of means', a prerequisite for Hegel for the growth of a political orientation 'beyond' any particularistic interests, and thus conducive to an 'unharnessed' service of the common affairs. Since in primogeniture landed property is transferred from generation to generation, its existence transcends the life span of its successive owners. And since Hegel had tied the possession of land property to its possessor's 'independent' will formation, it follows that the real determination of individual will is private property itself rather than the free volition of the owner himself. Private property itself emerges as 'the *subject* of *will*; the will survives only as the *predicate* of private property' (Marx, 1975a, p. 168). A real inversion takes place. Private property emerges as the *substantive* characteristic of the human personality and human will as the quintessence of freedom turns into a 'property of property'. Given that all the contemporary forms of political representation in the state's legislature presupposed property qualifications, it becomes plausible to claim, as Marx does, that the abstract political state in the *semblance* of its independence from private property is actually 'the power of private property itself' and what remains to the state is 'the *illusion* that it determines where it is in fact determined' (Marx, 1975a, p. 168).

Even for us today, when *formal* property qualifications have been abolished and candidacies for legislative assemblies are formally open to the entirety of the state's members, electoral processes are so drastically mediated by the media of mass/public communication, political advertising and political marketing campaigning that a considerable financial threshold has been established that *informally* excludes the majority of citizens from even considering such *abstract* possibility. Participation in legislative activity has turned into a neo-feudal prerogative of the propertied class and its 'representatives'.[10]

Marx in connection to property makes an association that underpins his later mature writings. Since society is the necessary socio-material substratum of private property vouched by 'the will of society', private property is directly or indirectly 'conditioned by its connections with the wealth of the whole society, with property conceived as social property' and thus there 'is *no true private property*' (Marx, 1975a, p. 166). Private property is in a sense a practical *illusion* albeit with very *real* effects. It is a legally recognised and secured *expropriation* of the communal resources of our societies and, in the present circumstances of globalising capitalism, of humanity's 'social powers' as a whole. Marxian democracy is incompatible with such a *state* of affairs.

Any theory of democracy must conceptualise a rational state within which people's sovereignty is or can be self-consciously actualised. Marx's critique of both Hegel's state and the modern constitutional state castigates the disembodied character of existing 'democracy' as pure formalism where the 'democratic element' participates only 'in abstraction' in an 'abstract political state' divorced from the 'universal affairs' of the actual society. The first step to remedy this schism is the actualisation of political democracy via the consolidation of genuine popular representation (Psychopedis, 1999, pp. 463–4). For only '[i]n his political role the member of civil society breaks away from his class, his real private position; only then does he come into his own as a *human being*, only then does his determination as the member of a state, as a social being, appear as his human determination' (Marx, 1975a, p. 147). If political democracy secures the manifestation of a will of the people that is knowledgeable and bound to 'the laws of reason' (Marx, 1975a, p. 120) then the preconditions have been set to overcome political democracy itself, to annul the separation between political state and civil society by eliminating both simultaneously and 'elevating' the essence divided between political and private existence to its true identity as a non-fragmented communal social existence of humanity where 'differences in unity' prevail rather than 'different unities'.

Notes

1. That is, to restore in novel form, the destroyed communal nature of the species-being as 'was originally' manifested in pre-modern religion (Marx, 1975d, p. 155), and to restitute the sentiment of collective freedom that 'vanished from the world with the Greeks' (Marx, 1975e, p. 137).

2. 'the universal secular contradiction between the political state and civil society' (Marx, 1975d, pp. 159–60).
3. I owe the term and concept to Andrew Chitty.
4. This critical method is completely ignored in Teeple's otherwise penetrating reconstruction of Marx's 'method' in his *Critique* (Teeple, 1984, pp. 86–90).
5. 'The attitude of the bourgeois to the institutions of his regime ... he evades them whenever it is possible to do so in each individual case, but he wants everyone else to observe them' (Marx and Engels, 1998, p. 194).
6. '[T]he movement of this world within its framework of laws is bound to be a continual suspension of law' (Marx, 1975d, p. 173).
7. 'Democracy is the *essence of all political constitutions*, socialized man as a *particular* political constitution; it is related to other forms of constitution as a genus to its various species, only here the genus itself comes into existence and hence manifests itself as a *particular* species in relation to the other species whose existence does not correspond to the generic essence' (Marx, 1975a, p. 88). That the *genus*, the universal, is (can be) realised in a *species*, as a particular, is none other than Hegel's 'concrete universal', the ultimate synthesis of universality in particularity as individuality.
8. '[T]he *political state* is a register of the practical struggles of mankind' (Marx, 1975f, p. 143). Also, see Kouvelakis, 2003, pp. 305, 310.
9. Like the conflation of the 'medieval estates-system' with the modern 'legislature' (Marx, 1975a, p. 163).
10. '[I]n actual fact politics has become the serf of financial power' (Marx, 1975d, p. 171).

Bibliography

Daremas, G. (2006) 'The "Lebenswelt" of the State in Hegel's Philosophy of Right', in A. Arndt, P. Cruysberghs and A. Przylebski (eds) *Das Leben denken*, vol. 1 (Berlin: Akademie Verlag).

Draper, H. (1977) *Karl Marx's Theory of Revolution: State and Bureaucracy* (New York: Monthly Review Press).

Hegel, G. W. F. (1975) *Logic: Part One of the Encyclopedia of the Philosophical Sciences* (Oxford: Clarendon Press).

—— (1980) *Lectures on the Philosophy of World History. Introduction: Reason in History*, (ed.) J. Hoffmeister (Cambridge: Cambridge University Press).

—— (1991) *Elements of the Philosophy of Right*, (ed.) A. W. Wood (Cambridge: Cambridge University Press).

—— (1999) 'On the Scientific Ways of Treating Natural Law', in Dickey and Nisbet (eds) *Hegel: Political Writings* (Cambridge: Cambridge University Press).

Kouvelakis, S. (2003) *Philosophy and Revolution: From Kant to Marx* (London: Verso).

Marx, Karl (1975a) 'Critique of Hegel's Doctrine of the State', in *Early Writings*, (ed.) L. Colletti (Harmondsworth: Penguin).

—— (1975b) 'Debates on Freedom of the Press', in K. Marx and F. Engels, *Collected Works*, vol. 1 (New York: International Publishers).

—— (1975c) 'On the Commissions of the Estates in Prussia', in K. Marx and F. Engels, *Collected Works*, vol. 1 (New York: International Publishers).

—— (1975d) 'On the Jewish Question', in K. Marx and F. Engels, *Collected Works*, vol. 3 (New York: International Publishers).

—— (1975e) 'Letter to Ruge, May 1843', in K. Marx and F. Engels, *Collected Works*, vol. 3 (New York: International Publishers).

—— (1975f) 'Letter to Ruge, Sept. 1843', in K. Marx and F. Engels, *Collected Works*, vol. 3 (New York: International Publishers).

—— (1994) 'A Contribution to the Critique of Hegel's Philosophy of Right: Introduction', in J. O'Malley (ed.) *Marx: Early Political Writings* (Cambridge: Cambridge University Press).

—— (1996) 'Critique of the Gotha Programme', in T. Carver (ed.) *Marx: Later Political Writings* (Cambridge: Cambridge University Press).

—— (1998) 'Introduction to the Critique of Political Economy', in K. Marx with F. Engels, *The German Ideology* including the *Theses on Feuerbach* and the *Introduction to the Critique of Political Economy* (New York: Prometheus Books).

Marx, Karl and Friedrich Engels (1998) *The German Ideology* including the *Theses on Feuerbach* and the *Introduction to the Critique of Political Economy* (New York: Prometheus Books).

Psychopedis, K. (1999) *Norms and Antinomies in Politics* (Athens: Polis).

Sperber, J. (1991) *Rhineland Radicals: The Democratic Movement and the Revolution of 1848–1849* (Princeton: Princeton University Press).

Teeple, G. (1984) *Marx's Critique of Politics, 1842–1847* (Toronto: Toronto University Press).

5
Marx and Conservatism

Andrew Collier

I want to argue that one reason for some of the common misunderstandings of Marx's political philosophy is that he is compared and contrasted with liberal political philosophy rather than with conservative political philosophy.[1] It is thought that he is asking the same questions as liberals and giving different answers, whereas I will argue that it is closer to the truth to say that he is asking the same questions as conservatives and giving different answers. It is easy to make this mistake, since Marx was quite obviously closer politically to liberals than to conservatives: he was himself active in liberal politics before he became a socialist, and during the German revolution of 1848, when he was already a socialist, the journal he edited was not a socialist journal, but represented a coalition of socialists and liberals, united around the proposal of a democratic republic. Later in his life, part of what separated him and Engels from both Lassalle among the German socialists and Hyndman among the English socialists was that Lassalle and Hyndman favoured a deal with the conservatives against the liberals, while Marx would doubtless have preferred that, if a deal was going to be made at all, it be one with the liberals to defeat the conservatives. But the political distance between two positions and the philosophical distance are two different things.

Perhaps a word is necessary here to clarify what I mean by conservatives and liberals. I mean two related things: first, the two tendencies in the politics of capitalist society, conservatism tending to preserve surviving pre-capitalist institutions, particularly hereditary offices, regulation of trade and an official religion, while liberalism tends to seek to abolish pre-capitalist institutions, and in particular favours representative government, a free market and a secular state. The second meaning is the two sorts of argument by which these tendencies typically defend themselves. It is the latter that I am mainly concerned with in this paper. Neither meaning maps with complete accuracy onto the parties calling themselves 'Liberal' and 'Conservative', though there is a loose fit, particularly in the nineteenth century. The British Conservative Party since Margaret Thatcher for instance has been mainly liberal both in its aims and in its arguments to defend them, although modern theoretical defences of conservatism such as Lord Hailsham's or Roger Scruton's are conservative in both senses (Hailsham, 1947; Scruton, 2007).

Philosophically speaking, liberalism typically defends particular policies in terms of certain abstract concepts: utility, property, freedom, equality, justice and human rights. In much analytical philosophy it is assumed that political philosophy just is the discussion of the definitions of these ideas, and that political differences are those about which of these ideas take priority. However, with the qualified exception of Plato, no political philosopher before Locke thought in this way. They thought rather: we have a certain kind of state; what is the best way to run that kind of state? Sometimes, different kinds of states are recognised, and the question asked is which policies are appropriate to each kind. Thus for Spinoza there are three kinds of state – monarchy, aristocracy and democracy. Different laws are appropriate to each of these kinds – different land ownership laws, a different kind of army, and so on. Spinoza thinks that democracy is best; he is in fact the first philosopher to think that (Spinoza, 2005). But that does not mean that, in a monarchy, one ought to be asking the question 'how can we change this monarchy into a democracy?' Rather, one should be asking 'what is the best way to run this monarchy?' For this reason Spinoza thought that the English people were wrong to overthrow Charles I, and this was shown by the fact that they ended by making Cromwell king in all but name. I don't know what Spinoza's teacher Menasseh ben Israel would have thought of this, since he took the trouble to visit Cromwell and negotiate the return of Jews to England – the one achievement of the Puritan Revolution that has survived. However this shows that Spinoza's style of political philosophy is a conservative one, despite his liberal and democratic preferences. It is, so to speak, a problem-solving approach to politics, taking the existing constitution as given.

Now people who compare Marx to liberalism feel that he ought to be committing himself to one or other of the abstract ideals in terms of which liberal political philosophy defines itself. They find that he seems sceptical, and they suspect cynical, about all these ideals. They jump forthwith to the conclusion that he has a Machiavellian or totalitarian contempt for the things that they defend under these headings, for example, freedom of speech or freedom from arbitrary arrest. Thus Lewis Feuer, in one of his abominable notes to his Fontana selection of Marx's and Engels' works, says, 'The amoral component in Marx's thinking emerges in his references to the "nonsensical phraseology" about "rights"' (Feuer, 1969, p. 153). He seems unaware that John Stuart Mill was equally sceptical about the concept of human rights, as indeed have most political philosophers been. Since President Jimmy Carter made human rights a popular issue, the philosophical problems about the concept seem to have been largely forgotten. I have recently seen a confrontation on TV between Rowan Williams and Imran Khan, the lawyer famous for his involvement in the Stephen Lawrence case. The Archbishop was criticising views which base everything on human rights, and Khan obviously felt that this took away any basis for oppressed groups' resistance, as in the Lawrence case. Yet it is quite unclear what work the concept of human rights would do in criticising the Metropolitan Police over this appalling case. All we need is the principle that murderers should be punished.

Of all the abstract ideals that liberalism has used to defend itself, human rights is probably the one most popular today, but in Marx's time it was regarded as old hat and freedom and equality were the leading ideals. I shall discuss Marx's scepticism about liberal ideal-based politics with reference to these concepts. If one were trying to make out a case for Marx being a political philosopher of the liberal type prioritising some ideal, freedom would be the most plausible candidate: he treats it as in a sense *the* political ideal, which no one can admit to being against. Nevertheless, he does not *use* the concept in his political arguments, though he defends particular freedoms like freedom of the press – one of the few issues on which I believe Marx's views are outmoded. He does not explicitly demystify the concept of freedom, so when I shall do so shortly, I am to a degree putting words into his mouth. But he does explicitly demystify the concept of equality as a political ideal, so I shall turn to this concept first.

The Gotha Programme, the founding programme of the German Social Democratic Party (SPD), included the phrase: 'the proceeds of labour belong, with equal right, to all members of society'. Marx's critique of this phrase, which he objects to, is based on the idea that equality is always equality in some respect, not absolute equality:

A right can by its nature only consist in the application of an equal standard, but unequal individuals (and they would not be different individuals if they were not unequal) can only be measured by the same standard if they are looked at from the same aspect, if they are grasped from one *particular* side, e.g., if in the present case they are regarded *only as workers* and nothing else is seen in them, everything else is ignored. Further: one worker is married, another is not; one has more children than another, etc., etc. Thus, with the same work performance and hence the same share of the social consumption fund, one will in fact be receiving more than another, one will be richer than another, etc. If all these defects were to be avoided rights would have to be unequal rather than equal.

(Marx, 1974, p. 347)

That is, one must choose which equality one wants: equal pay for equal work, or equal satisfaction of needs, or indeed, in a hierarchical society, equal remuneration of equal social status. The concept of equality cannot by itself tell you which equalities to favour.

Likewise, the concept of freedom cannot tell you by itself which freedoms to favour. In Marx's own time, this is clearly shown in the argument about factory legislation limiting the hours of work. Many Liberals, for instance John Bright (generally regarded as on the left of the Liberal Party since he favoured democracy), opposed factory legislation, which deprived the employer of the freedom to work his workers 18 hours a day and of course deprived the worker of the freedom to work 18 hours a day. But such laws were the only way of establishing freedom to have some hours of waking leisure in each day, and hence the freedom to socialise, to educate oneself, to participate in politics, and so on. Today we have disputes between the 'right to roam' and the right to keep ramblers off one's property, between the freedom to play loud music late at night and the freedom to get some sleep. Underlying the views of the contestants in these conflicts is some idea of what constitutes a good life. I have heard that when the footpaths across the English countryside were being closed in their hundreds, a Tory cabinet minister questioned about this said that no one wanted to go for walks in the country. I suppose most Tories either live in the country, or live in suburbs which they never leave except closeted in their car.

But this does not mean that the correct method in political philosophy is to construct an ideal of human life and then work out what political arrangements would be most conducive to it. What people want to do, and what they therefore resent restraint on doing, is largely a function of their traditions. It is possible that Americans, like Tories, do not feel their lack of freedom to ramble over agricultural land, though a country where you cannot do so would feel to me like a prison. Likewise, Muslims presumably do not feel the lack of freedom to take alcoholic drinks in countries where this is not allowed, and most English people, it seems, do not feel their lack of freedom to spend time with their children. Whether a law is perceived as a limit to freedom or a facilitation of freedom depends entirely on whether people feel the need to do what it forbids, or to do what it makes possible. One can conceive of a people for whom compulsory education would be the biggest restraint on their freedom imaginable. This means that freedoms are relative to traditions, and the goal of having many freedoms for all presupposes either shared traditions, or at least traditions which do not generate incompatible requirements. Thus there will usually have to be more constraints on freedoms in a multicultural society, though there are compensating freedoms which a multicultural society enables. In conclusion of the discussion of freedom: there can be no ideal of freedom in general, only of certain freedoms, and which are appropriate will depend largely on local traditions.

So much by way of a case for the impossibility of a coherent political philosophy of the liberal type. What then is the correct method? Let us start by looking closer at the conservative method. It consists in asking: what is the best policy for the state we've got? This need not mean 'state' in the narrow sense of governmental apparatus. Underlying most conservative thought is the idea of society as an organism. Modern writers usually call this a metaphor drawn from biology, but this is not strictly correct. The notion stems from Aristotle, for whom there are various kinds of organisms, the *polis* being one, the animal being another. A state, like an animal, has needs, and can have problems. It survives and develops by solving its problems as they arise. These are not problems only relative to some ideal like freedom or equality. They are problems relative to the organism's need to flourish. They would not be problems for some other kinds of organisms: a feudal society does not need new markets, any more than a giraffe needs meat.

What happens if a society encounters problems that it cannot solve? This can happen by virtue of accidents, for instance the destruction of its resources by an earthquake or an inundation. But interestingly, it can also happen by virtue of its own developmental tendencies. This too is paralleled by events in the life of biological organisms. There comes a point where a caterpillar can do nothing unless it develops into a butterfly; a grain of wheat must fall into the ground and die if it is to bring forth fruit. Engels uses these examples to illustrate dialectical progression (Engels, 1968). There may be times in the life of a society when in order to flourish it has to change into something else. This does presuppose, as in the case of the butterfly, some sort of identity between the society before and after the change. This identity partly consists in the identity of most of the people of the society through the change. But it also involves the identity of a great many of the values held by those people. People do not make a revolution in order to realise completely new values. They do so in order to defend the values they already had in the old society. To give two examples: the English puritans who overthrew Charles I believed that they were defending traditional English liberties against the innovations of the king, and Lenin in his writings of 1917 said, in reply to Zinoviev and Kamenev, who thought that the revolution was premature, that it was not the intention of the soviets to 'introduce' socialism or anything else by decree: they had to take over because it was the only way of organising food supplies and other arrangements necessary to the continued existence of civilised society (Lenin, 1964).

Now despite this it is quite common for revolutionaries to have what might be called a Noah Complex, to want to clear away everything and start from scratch. The most sinister example of this is the Pol Pot regime in Cambodia, which wanted to kill all with whom the revolutionaries were not perfectly satisfied as human material for a totally new society. It is curious that they used exactly the same metaphor as Descartes, the apple barrel, with people replacing ideas as the apples: tip the whole lot out and only put back what you are completely satisfied with. But the French Revolutionaries were also, I think, influenced by Descartes, though by twentieth-century standards even the Jacobin terror was relatively sparing in bloodshed. But the Noah Complex was there, as illustrated by the Revolutionary Calendar. Curiously, although the calendar was presumably expected to spread world-wide as other French Revolutionary innovations like the metric system and driving on the right did, its months are named after features of the weather and the agricultural year which are specific to France, if not to particular regions of the country. For example, Thermidor is not a hot month in Australia.

Marx, though obviously influenced by the French Revolution, which had brought great benefits to his native Rhineland, was also influenced by Hegel's critique of it. He is free from the Noah Complex, and starts from recognised problems of existing society, which he argues are insoluble within that society. I think this approach of Marx has had good historical effects, even on the Russian Revolution. For instance with respect to art: Lenin and Trotsky insisted that the first duty of the new state was to preserve the artworks of the old regime and make them accessible to the whole people, rather than fostering consciously revolutionary art. Oddly enough, even Lunacharsky, Lenin's opponent on this issue and a patron of 'prolecult' (proletarian culture), resigned as people's commissar for culture when he heard that St Basil's Cathedral had been shelled in the revolutionary takeover, though he resumed his post when the story turned out to be a false alarm.

Marx reaches revolutionary conclusions from the usually conservative premises that society is an organism and that the task of politics is to serve the good of the organism, not to realise certain ideals.

At this point it might be asked: is all that I am saying that Marx's political philosophy was what we would now call 'communitarian'? I think not. I have various objections to communitarianism which I have spelt out elsewhere and do not need to repeat here (Collier, 1999, pp. 60–2). Communitarianism is absolutely right in its criticisms of people like Rawls and Nozick, just as Hegel was right in making much the same criticisms against Rousseau and Kant. But communitarianism – lacking a dialectical conception of change – uses a conservative methodology to arrive, not at either conservative or revolutionary conclusions, but at liberal conclusions. That is only possible because there exist liberal communities. And there are only liberal communities because our ancestors led revolutions against Charles I and James II and George III and Louis XVI and Kaiser Bill, and so on. If communitarianism cannot find a way of justifying revolutions, it can only endorse liberalism after the fact.

Marx is saved from this problem by his notion of contradictions, which is why I have always argued that whatever you think of dialectic as a general theory, it – as a theory of specific contradictions – is the centre of his political philosophy. What he shares with conservatism is his belief in starting from where we are rather than from an idea of where we want to go, and asking what can be done, not for the good of people in general, but for the good of *these* people, with *these* traditions, *these* needs, *these* skills, *these* resources. What divides him from conservatism is his belief that the existing society involves contradictions, which prevent it from flourishing, and which can only be eliminated by changing the system. It is definitive of contradictions that they are both essential to the society of which they are part, and destructive of it. So Marx's critique of capitalism is essentially an immanent critique, not a critique in terms of ideals not shared by that society.

This last statement may seem surprising: are not capitalist values those of commercialism which socialists are bound to reject? But capitalist society is not just the capitalist economy. The institutions of capitalist societies which generate values in their participants include families and circles of friends, trade unions and co-operative societies, churches and mosques, allotment associations and babysitting circles and so on, and these generate values of mutual help and solidarity and other non-commercial virtues. Let us take trade unions as a case in point. They are clearly part of capitalist society, arising spontaneously in every capitalist society where they are not suppressed by a dictatorship, and co-determining the character of the societies in which they arise. They may be antagonistic to capitalist corporations in that they fight them over wages and working conditions, but they are opponents within the system. But on Marx's assumptions, this does not mean that they have an interest in defending capitalist society; they are precisely that element of capitalist society which is potentially the core of a possible replacement of that society, and the values which they generate in their members – values which are never merely monetary, except in the Association of University Teachers – are the values for which people will fight against capitalism. Capitalism creates, not just a class which could overthrow it, but values in the name of which it might be overthrown.

For though an immanent critique, Marx's critique of capitalism is certainly a revolutionary one. This combination of views seems implausible to many people, because they have a model of a social organism as a contradiction-free agent, the needs and values of which cannot generate the demand for its own abolition. Hence there are people who will argue that because trade unions are part of capitalism, they cannot contain the seeds of a new system. Yet for Marx no new system could grow unless it had seeds in the old one. Precisely what is unique about dialectic is its conception of organisms which, *pace* Spinoza, have a conatus to their own destruction and replacement, alongside their more regular conatus to their perpetuation. Now of course it is an empirical question whether any organism has this self-destructive conatus or not. But all the evidence today seems to point to the current organism of global capitalism having a tendency to destroy not just itself but life on earth.

Now suppose it is true, as I have maintained, that Marx builds a revolutionary politics on a methodology which comprises conservatism plus a theory of contradictions. Is this just a curious fact about Marx's political philosophy, at an entirely 'meta' level, or does it make any difference to his politics? We have already seen one difference it might have made: the civilised attitude of the Bolsheviks towards art, when all pre-Marxist Russian leftists had despised any art that did not serve their propaganda purposes. We have also seen the effect of the opposite conception of revolution, the Noah Complex, in Cambodia, in generating atrocities. But I think quite a lot of attitudes on the western left would be quite different if we learnt from Marx on this matter.

This comes from a re-evaluation in Marxist terms of two concepts, which are traditionally opposed, and one of which is commonly associated with conservatism, the other with liberalism: the concepts of *tradition* and *progress*.

First of all, tradition. This has a place in conservative ideology, though less unambiguously in conservative politics. For as G. K. Chesterton says:

> All conservatism is based upon the idea that if you leave things alone you leave them as they are. But you do not. If you leave a thing alone you leave it to a torrent of change.
>
> (Chesterton, 2004, p. 86)

But the appeal of conservatism, not just to those who benefit economically from it such as property speculators, but to ordinary men and women, is partly down to its reputation as the preserver of traditions. And people's affection for traditions is not always irrational. Traditions are actually a very democratic thing compared with fashion, which is always the tool of the plutocracy.

However, I want to look at the place of tradition in Marx's thought. It actually has a very important place, and as a scientific concept, not an ideological one. Consider Marx's argument against Citizen Weston in *Value, Price and Profit* (Marx, 1935). Marx is defending the idea that real wages can be increased for the whole working class even under capitalism, by trade union action. He is out to disprove the 'wage fund theory' or 'iron law of wages', which would make this impossible. But his argument leads him to the conclusion that wages are the value of labour-power, and what gives labour-power its value is the amount of labour necessary to produce the worker's means of subsistence. If subsistence were defined in medical terms as what keeps the worker alive and fit to work, we would not have escaped the 'iron law of wages'. But for Marx it is not: it is defined by a traditional standard of living which can be different at different times and places, and can be raised in the long term by continued trade union pressure. According to Louis Althusser, Marx says 'English workers need beer and French workers need wine' (Althusser, 2008). I have never been able to find this quote, but it is consistent with his general account of subsistence as tradition-determined.

English workers will not accept an income so low that it precludes consumption of beer, even though they could arguably be just as healthy without it. What is tradition doing here? It is providing a point of resistance to the needs of capital, with benefit to the workers. The different class nature of tradition and fashion is brought out here: fashion serves the needs of capital, tradition resists them.

Since I shall be criticising my comrades on the left in this section, I should perhaps start by giving credit where it is due, namely to the late leader and founder of the Socialist Workers' Party, Tony Cliff, who liked to define the role of the Marxist party as 'the memory of the working class'. This contrasts with the political amnesia fostered by the media. To give two examples: I recently saw a celebrity on TV state that Tony Blair was the first Labour Prime Minister to be elected for a second term; no one challenged this statement, and within a few days I had heard it repeated by a Labour MP. Yet it is within living memory – my memory in fact – that Clem Attlee was elected for a second term in 1950 and Harold Wilson was in 1966. The other example is of changed value-judgements rather than facts: at the time of Iain Duncan Smith's ejection, much was made of the fact that he had been elected by the whole Tory Party not just the MPs, and this was presented as admirably democratic. Was I the only one to remember what a violation of the British constitution and a crisis for parliamentary democracy it was supposed to be when Labour allowed ordinary party members to have a say in the election of the leader in the 1980s? Both these examples are cases in which amnesia helps the reputation of present leaders, and memory would have led to questioning it.

Now to the concept of progress. This is often thought to be as much part of the armoury of Marxist values as of liberal ones. But its application in Marxism is strictly circumscribed. Two related things progress: technology and the experimental sciences. As a consequence of technological advancement, progress in the reduction of the working day becomes *possible*, though not inevitable (during the Industrial Revolution the working day increased, as Marx documents in *Capital*). If the working day is reduced, progress in democracy becomes *possible* (again not inevitable), since workers come to have time to participate in education, politics and management. And that is it. There is no progress in the arts, as Marx's fragment on Greek art confirms (Marx, 1970, pp. 150–1). There is no progress in other areas of intellectual life. And there is not necessarily any progress in morality. To take two examples of moral decline: the Renaissance period started burning witches, which, despite popular belief, had not happened in the Middle Ages, and the twentieth century re-introduced torture, which the nineteenth had largely abolished.

Now it is quite widely believed, and I suspect more on the left of centre than on the right, that there is progress in other areas too. This is due to the confusion of progress with fashion. In areas where fashion is relatively innocent, like dress, nobody over the age of sixteen confuses fashion with progress. But in politics and academic life, practically everyone does. You have probably all had referees of your publications complaining that you discuss an article written in June 2003, and unaccountably neglect one written in September 2003, which naturally, being later, supersedes it. In my view academic publications would be much improved if there were a law forbidding the discussion of other people's work until they had been dead long enough for it to go out of copyright.

To take a political example, Tony Blair is on record as saying (in connection with Clause 4 of the Labour Party constitution): 'Those who seriously believe we cannot improve on words written for the world of 1918 when we are now in 1995 are not learning from our history but living it'. The curious thing about these words is that I suspect that even many of those who had no time for the gibberish that Blair was foisting on his party would find that argument difficult to answer. Yet why on earth should something written in 1918 become out of date just by the passage of time? If it were something about the internal combustion engine or the Treaty of Versailles, that would be different. But when it is about an economic system that we have had since the sixteenth century and still have, it is nonsense. Hats and pots of meat paste may become out of date just by the passage of time, but scientific theories only become out of date when they are refuted by a better theory, and nothing else in the intellectual world gets out of date at all.

Now I want to suggest three reasons why this cult of progress, which always confuses fashion with progress, is harmful.

(1) It transforms political defeats, which the left like any other movement must suffer from time to time, into surrender. When we are defeated, instead of thinking 'how do we regroup our forces and recover lost ground?' we are led to think 'we can't put the clock back, we'd better adapt to the new situation'. If the left had thought like that in the 1930s, we would never have put the clock back on fascism.

(2) Within capitalism, institutional progress always means replacing non-commercial institutions by commercial institutions. 'Modernisation' means moving towards totalitarian commercialism, by which I mean, not capitalism combined with a totalitarian state, but the intrusion of commercialism into every aspect of life, which can quite well happen in a liberal democracy, and is happening, to the degradation of all human and environmental values.

(3) The idolisation of progress brings with it a psychological ideal: that of the totally adaptable person, changing identity with every new day like Ruby Tuesday in the Rolling Stones' song. This means that the loyalty and integrity necessary, not only for changing the world for the better, but even for ordinary decency in personal life, become unthinkable. This situation is normalised by postmodernist thought, as is the rest of totalitarian commercialism.

I conclude that we should at least be more sympathetic to tradition, and more sceptical about progress, than has been usual on the left.

Note

1. This chapter was presented to the Marx and Philosophy Society on 29 May 2004.

Bibliography

Althusser, Louis (2008) *On Ideology* (London: Verso).
Chesterton, G. K. (2004) *Orthodoxy* (Whitefish, Montana: Kessinger Publishing).
Collier, Andrew (1999) *Being and Worth* (London: Routledge).
Engels, Friedrich (1968) *Dialectics of Nature* (London: Lawrence and Wishart).
Feuer, Lewis (1969) (ed.) *Karl Marx and Friedrich Engels: Basic Writings on Politics and Philosophy* (London: Collins).
Hailsham, Viscount (1947) *The Case for Conservatism* (Harmondsworth: Penguin).
Lenin, V. I. (1964) 'The Tasks of the Proletariat in the Present Revolution', in *Collected Works*, vol. 24 (Moscow: Progress Publishers).
Marx, Karl (1935) *Value, Price and Profit* (New York: International Publishers).
—— (1970) *The German Ideology: Part One*, (ed.) C. J. Arthur (London: Lawrence and Wishart).
—— (1974) 'Critique of the Gotha Programme', in *The First International and After: Political Writings: Volume 3* (Harmondsworth: Penguin).
Scruton, Roger (2007) *Arguments for Conservatism* (New York: Continuum).
Spinoza, Benedict de (2005) *A Theologico-Political Treatise and a Political Treatise* (New York: Dover).

6
An Unfinished Project: Marx's Critique of Hegel's *Philosophy of Right*

Robert Fine

This chapter seeks briefly to reconstruct Marx's critique of Hegel's *Philosophy of Right* and develop the intuition that the equivocations evident in Marx's reading of this text were prematurely resolved in the promise of Marx's inversion of Hegel's 'mystical dialectic'. I suggest that this reading of the *Philosophy of Right* and this conception of how to respond to it posed an unnecessary obstacle to the fulfilment of Marx and Engels' own lifelong project: that of complementing their critique of political economy with a critique of the moral, legal and political forms of capitalist society. Not only does it blunt the edges of Hegel's critique but in so doing it also deprives Marx and Engels of a much needed resource for overcoming pre-critical and naturalistic approaches to these 'ideal' elements of capitalist society. Instead of reading the Hegel–Marx relation through Marx's own formulation of it, I suggest that a more productive alternative is to read the *Philosophy of Right* and *Capital* alongside one another as complementary critiques of the 'ideal' and 'material' elements of capitalist society: the one addressing the fetishism of the subject and the other addressing the fetishism of the object. It is not by reading what Marx says about Hegel but by reading what he does in *Capital* that we learn most about his relation to the *Philosophy of Right*.

The chapter begins with two sections on Marx's critique of Hegel's *Philosophy of Right*: first, the young Marx's critique of Hegel's so-called doctrine of the state and second, Marx's 'inversion' of Hegel's dialectic. In each case I raise questions concerning the validity of the reading of Hegel contained in Marx's response. In the following two sections I reconstruct aspects of Hegel's *Philosophy of Right* read, as it were, through Marx rather than in opposition to Marx. The first of these sections addresses the central issue raised by Marx in his critique of the 'doctrine of the state', the role of representation in the state. The second addresses more broadly the scientific and critical nature of Hegel's project in the *Philosophy of Right*. The last section makes the case for reconstructing the unity of Hegel and Marx and reading the *Philosophy of Right* and *Capital* alongside rather than in opposition to one another.

The young Marx's critique of Hegel's 'doctrine of the state'

The young Marx's guilty verdict on Hegel's 'doctrine of the state' has long overshadowed access to the text within Marxist social and political thought. Marx maintained that Hegel concealed the forms of domination and unreason characteristic of the modern state beneath a speculative veneer of freedom and reason. According to Marx, Hegel reified the predicate of the modern state, the idea of the universal, before deducing from this idea the mundane institutional forms of the state – the constitution, monarchy, legislature and executive (Marx, 1992, p. 80). Once Hegel converted universality into a subject and the actual state into a mere moment of this 'mystical substance', the dogmatic character of the *Philosophy of Right* seemed set: Hegel's concern was simply to rediscover "the idea" in every sphere of the state that he depicted, to 'fasten on what lies nearest at hand and prove that it is an *actual* moment of the idea' (Marx, 1992, p. 98).

Marx argued that Hegel gave a roughly accurate empirical account of the operations of the modern state but that the contribution of speculative philosophy was merely to convert empirical facts into the actualisation of the 'Idea'. The resemblance Marx saw between Hegel's conception of a 'rational state' and the actual nineteenth century Prussian state led him to despair of finding any critical edge in the substance of Hegel's politics. 'God help us all!' was his final, exasperated comment after citing a passage in which Hegel seemed to deduce ministerial authority and two houses of parliament, Commons and Lords, from the Idea of the Universal (Marx, 1992, p. 198).

The value of reading Hegel's *Philosophy of Right* for Marx lay in the mirror of reality it offered – not just in Hegel's description of the institutions of the modern state but also in Hegel's inversion of subject and predicate which mirrored the actual inversion of subject and predicate in bourgeois society: '*uncritical mysticism* is the key both to the riddle of modern constitutions [...] and also to the mystery of the Hegelian philosophy, above all the *Philosophy of Right*' (Marx, 1992, p. 149). In a society in which human beings are transformed into '*unreal*, objective moments of the Idea' (Marx, 1992, p. 62) and the state is transformed into the semblance of an earthly divinity, Hegel's speculative philosophy not only rationalises this upside-down reality, it also reveals it.

Marx argued that the rationality Hegel attributed to the state is contradicted at every point by its irrational reality. The illusion of the state, he wrote, is that 'the affairs of the people are matters of universal concern'; the truth is that 'the real interest of the people [...] is present only *formally*' (Marx, 1992, pp. 125, 129). The state admits the people only as '*idea*, fantasy, illusion, *representation*' (Marx, 1992, p. 134). It offers a 'ceremony' or 'spice' of popular existence. It delivers 'the lie [...] that the *state* is the *interest of the people*' (Marx, 1992, p. 129). Hegel idealises the bureaucracy as the ultimate purpose of the state and the state as the ultimate purpose of the universal. At the same time he empiricises 'public consciousness' as if it were a 'mere hotchpotch made up of "the thoughts and opinions of the Many"' (Marx, 1992, p. 124). Marx maintained that both Hegel and the political state must be 'turned on their head' if the people are to enter the political stage in *actuality* rather than in mere form.

The trope that enriches Marx's text is chiasmus, a figure of speech in which the order of words in one clause is inverted in a second. Thus Marx writes: Hegel's true interest is not in 'the logic of the subject-matter but the subject-matter of logic' (Marx, 1992, p. 73); it is 'not to discover the truth of empirical existence but to discover the empirical existence of the truth' (Marx, 1992, p. 98). Hegel 'does not provide us with the logic of the body politic' but 'provides his logic with a political body' (Marx, 1992, p. 109). Hegel 'does not say that the will of the monarch is the final decision, but that the final decision of the will is – the monarch' (Marx, 1992, p. 82). Marx wishes to put philosophy back on its feet: it is not the constitution that creates the people but the people that create constitutions; it is not the state that determines civil society but civil society that determines the state; it is not consciousness that determines life but life that determines consciousness; it is not the Idea that determines actuality but actuality that determines ideas. In a 'true democracy' philosophy would stand on its own two feet: '*matters of universal concern* are really matters of universal, public concern' (Marx, 1992, p. 125) and not the preserve of the class of officials; representatives of the people are delegates of the people and no longer a power over the people; 'man does not exist for the sake of the law, but the law exists for the sake of man' (Marx, 1992, p. 88). While Hegel 'proceeds from the state and conceives of man as the subjectivised state', Marx 'proceeds from man and conceives of the state as objectified man' (Marx, 1992, p. 87).

Marx's critique of Hegel's 'mystical' dialectic

The ghost of Hegel never ceased to haunt Marx's scientific and political writings. He praised Hegel for having discovered the 'correct laws of the dialectic'; he criticised him for presenting the dialectic in an idealistic and mystifying form. In 1858 Marx wrote to Engels that in leafing through Hegel's *Logic* 'I [...] found much to assist me in the *method* of analysis' (Marx and Engels, 1983, p. 50). In March 1868 he wrote to Kugelman: '[M]y method of argument is *not* Hegelian, since I am a materialist, Hegel is an idealist. Hegel's dialectic is the basis of all dialectic, but only *after* the disposal of its mystical form' (Marx and Engels, 1983, p. 126). In his 1873 'Postface' to the second German edition of *Capital* he comments: 'The *mystification* which the dialectic suffers in Hegel's hands by no means prevents him from being the first to present its general forms of motion in a comprehensive and conscious manner. With him it is standing on its head. It must be inverted in order to discover the rational kernel within the mystical shell' (Marx, 1990, p. 103).

Marx's representation of Hegel and his presentation of self were always intertwined. While Hegel transformed the process of thinking into an independent subject and the real world into the external appearance of the Idea, Marx recognised that 'the ideal is nothing but the material world reflected in the mind of man and translated into forms of thought'. While Hegel's 'mystical form of the dialectic' became the fashion in Germany because it functioned to 'glorify what exists', the 'rational form of the dialectic [...] is a scandal and an abomination to the bourgeoisie [...] because it includes in its positive understanding of what exists a simultaneous recognition of its negation, its inevitable destruction' (Marx, 1990, pp. 102–3). At the same time Marx thundered against 'pompous, pseudoscientific professors' and 'ill-humoured, arrogant and mediocre epigones' who understood nothing of Hegel, he remained loyal to the necessity of inverting the old master (Marx, 1990, p. 102; see also Marx and Engels, 1983, pp. 167–8).

With some exceptions, within Marxist scholarship most secondary discussions tend to follow Marx's equivocal construction of his relation to Hegel (e.g. Fraser, 1997, p. 103; MacGregor, 1998, pp. 2–4; McLellan, 1980, p. 13; Nicolaus in Marx, 1973; Rosdolsky, 1980, p. xiii; Smith, 1990, p. 17; Wood, 1993, p. 433). However, on the margins of Marx's own writings we find traces of an alternative reading. In the section on *the method of political economy* at the opening of the *Grundrisse* Marx refers in a much quoted passage to Hegel's confusion of the real and thought about the real and insists on the importance of distinguishing, as Hegel did not, between the process by which the concrete comes into being and the process by which thought appropriates the concrete:

> The concrete is concrete because it is the concentration of many determinations [...] It appears in the process of thinking, therefore, as a process of concentration, as a result, not as a point of departure, even though it is the point of departure in reality [...] Hegel fell into the illusion of conceiving the real as the product of the thought concentrating itself, probing its own depths and unfolding itself out of itself, by itself, whereas the method of ascending from the abstract to the concrete is only the way in which thought appropriates the concrete, reproduces it as the spiritually concrete. But this is by no means the process by which the concrete itself comes into being.
>
> (Marx, 1973, p. 101)

According to Marx the rational kernel of Hegel's method lies in its recognition of the dialectic, that is, the immanent movement of concepts and of the necessity of transition from one concept into another. The mystical shell consists of his confusion of the movement of concepts with that of reality. Hegel is charged with confusing 'the development of the moments of the notion' with the development of the concrete itself. Marx argues that the driving force of the dialectic is not logical but historical, not the 'notion' but the bourgeois economy, not a self-affirming movement from one logical category to another but a movement from one social form to another. Whereas in Hegel the dialectic is conceived as a closed system with natural presuppositions and a rational *telos*, Marx conceives the dialectic as a movement of contradictory social forms based on historical presuppositions and open to revolutionary change. In his 'Notes on Adolph Wagner' he writes:

> I do not start out from 'concepts', hence I do not start out from 'the concept of value' and do not have to 'divide' these in any way. What I start out from is the simplest social form in which the labour-product is presented in contemporary society, and this is the 'commodity'. I analyse it and right from the beginning, in the form in which it appears.
>
> (Marx, 1975, p. 198)

Simply put, Marx identifies Hegel with the transmutation of social relations into timeless logical categories, whilst he recognises the transitory character of capitalist social relations.

On closer examination we see that Marx himself casts doubt on this contrast. In the introduction to the *Grundrisse* Marx observes that it may seem correct to begin with the 'real and the concrete, with the real precondition, thus to begin in economics with e.g. the population'. However, it is false because the real and the concrete is itself 'the concentration of many determinations'. Population, for instance, presupposes classes; classes presuppose wage labour and capital; wage labour and capital presuppose money; money presupposes exchange value and the commodity form. These are the *elements* which make up the 'chaotic conception of the whole'. Marx writes:

> If I were to begin with population, I would then [...] move analytically toward ever more simple *concepts*, from the imagined concrete toward ever thinner *abstractions* until I had arrived at the simplest determinations. From there the journey would have to be retraced until I had finally arrived at the population again, but this time not as the chaotic conception of the whole but as a rich totality of many determinations.
>
> (Marx, 1973, p. 100)

Marx identifies the first option as the *analytical path* which he associates with economics at the time of its origins; he identifies the second as the *dialectical path* which he associates with the 'scientifically correct method'. Instead of starting with a category like population, it is necessary to ascend from the simplest and most abstract forms (value, exchange value, etc.) to the level of the concrete and complex totality (the state, the world market, etc.). Marx asks:

> [D]o not these simpler categories also have an independent historical or natural existence predating the more concrete ones? That depends. Hegel, for example, correctly begins the *Philosophy of Right* with possession, this being the subject's simplest juridical relation.
>
> (Marx 1973, p. 102)

In fact Hegel did not begin with the idea of possession in general but with abstract right, legal personality and private property. Nonetheless Marx sees himself as following in Hegel's footsteps when he observes that historically there are families in which there is possession but no private property but that to understand the *modern* family it must be seen in relation to private property. As Marx put it, the simpler category (say, private property) *may* have an historical existence before the more concrete category (say, the family), in which case the path of abstract thought, rising from the simple to the complex, would correspond with the real historical process. However, it would be wrong

> to let the economic categories follow one another in the same sequence as that in which they were historically decisive. Their sequence is determined, rather, by their relation to one another in modern bourgeois society [...] The point is not the historic position of the economic relations in the succession of different forms of society. [...] Rather, their order within modern bourgeois society.
>
> (Marx, 1973, p. 107)

The order of presentation is governed by logic, not history. Marx affirms here that the starting point of his analysis of capitalism, the commodity form, *may* correspond to some historical event – for example a barter between communities prior to all money relations – but it is the starting point only because it is the simplest economic form of capitalist society. He further acknowledges that this *mode of presentation* may give rise to idealist illusions:

> Of course, the mode of presentation must differ in form from that of inquiry. The latter has to appropriate the material in detail, to analyse its different forms of development and to track down their inner connection. Only after this work has been done, can the real movement be appropriately presented. If this is done successfully, if the life of the subject matter is now reflected in the ideas, then it may *appear as if* we have before us an *a priori* construction.
>
> (Marx, 1973, p. 102)

Scientific analysis of capitalist society, if done successfully, will *appear* as an *a priori* construction. Marx cannot, however, shake off the conviction that Hegel's *Philosophy of Right* really is a logical, *a priori* construction.

We have to question this conviction. For we cannot take it as given that the relation between Hegel and Marx accords with Marx's own account of it. Marx's own work opens up for us the possibility that Hegel did not after all reduce history to logic in his *Philosophy of Right*, that his 'science of right' was not a logical, *a priori* construction but a 'scientific treatment' of the social forms of modern society.

The dialectics of representation in Hegel's *Philosophy of Right*

Let us return to the young Marx and his charge that the older Hegel was an uncritical apologist for modern representative government. The older Hegel summed up his own work in a contrastive manner as an attempt to dispel the illusions of representation. In *Lectures on the Philosophy of History* he formulated his position thus: 'it was a great advance when political life became the property of everyone through the advent of representative government [...but] to associate the so-called representative constitution with the idea of a free constitution is the hardened prejudice of our age' (Hegel, 1975, p. 121). 'Hardened prejudice' is not the language of uncritical apology. Hegel saw himself rather as dispelling the aura of representative government.

In the *Philosophy of Right* Hegel's critique of representation in fact pre-figured Marx's own. Hegel pointed to the manifold 'guarantees' that restrict the principle of representation both as envisaged in republican thought and as practised in the modern state. Representation is restricted to one part of the state, the legislature, and to one House of the legislature, the Commons. Representatives are endowed with a privileged standing in relation to those they represent: they are not 'agents with a commission or specific instructions' but enjoy a relation of 'trust' with their electors which allows them to reach decisions on the basis of their own 'greater knowl-edge of public affairs' and 'the confidence felt in them'. Representatives are answerable to the executive and one of the principal duties of the executive is to curb the 'excesses' of the assembly (Hegel, 1991, §301R). The author-ity of representatives is restricted by the constitutional monarch endowed not only with formal powers of ultimate decision but also with powers over the survival of the state. Hegel put it ironically: it is as if there were an unwritten rule that 'public freedom in general and a hereditary succession guarantee each other reciprocally' (Hegel, 1991, §286R). The constitution allows representatives to make legislative changes but only in so far as they are 'imperceptible' and 'tranquil in appearance'. It demands that the con-stitution itself must not be regarded as '*something made*, even if it does have an origin in time', but rather as 'divine and enduring [...] exalted above the sphere of all manufactured things' (Hegel, 1991, §273R). Civil society is arranged in such a way as to 'ensure that individuals do not present themselves as a *crowd* or *aggregate* [...] and do not become a massive power in opposition to the organic state' (Hegel, 1991, §302) and to keep them under the 'higher supervision of the state' (Hegel, 1991, §255A). The key to representative government is that everything is done to ensure that the people at no point become a 'formless mass' uncontrolled by the state. Thus the 'democratic element' is refused admission to the state unless it goes through a system of mediations on the grounds that in an unmediated democracy 'the masses will always express themselves in a barbarous manner' (Hegel, 1991, §302A). Hegel highlights the *exclusions* practised by the modern state and justified in natural law theory: the exclusion at one time or another of workers, women, servants, the mad, the bad, children and foreigners. As Hegel observed, what we call 'universal suffrage' means in effect the participation of the Many, never of All (Hegel, 1991, §301R).

Hegel contrasted the purely conceptual thinking of Kant, who simply identified representative government with 'the united will of all' and who declared that 'every true republic is and can be nothing else than a representative system of the people', with the actual existence of representation in the modern state. He impelled Kant's critical philosophy beyond Kant to reveal what exists beneath the concept. He also explored the critique of representation associated with the name of Rousseau.

Hegel maintained that the Rousseauian critique of representation is expressed in two closely related propositions: the demand to abolish representation as such on the ground that I have a right to speak for myself and no one else has a right to speak on my behalf; and the demand to abolish the guarantees which restrict representation in the modern state and instead to make representation 'fully active and unrestricted'. Throughout his writings Hegel acknowledged the democratic impulse behind this principle, although his relation to it changed. In his *Early Theological Writings* Hegel simply celebrated 'the revolution in the spirit of the age' (Hegel, 1971, p. 152) ushered in by posing the general will as the principle of the modern state. It signified 'the right to legislate for one's self, to be responsible to oneself alone for administering one's own law' (Hegel, 1971, p. 145). Rousseau, as the young Hegel put it, rediscovered the ancient political principle according to which citizens 'obeyed laws laid down by themselves, obeyed men whom they themselves had appointed to office, waged wars on which they had themselves decided, gave their property, exhausted their passions and sacrificed their lives by thousands for an end which was their own' (Hegel, 1971, p. 154). In the *Philosophy of Right* Hegel continued to acknowledge the democratic principle contained in the general will: 'all individuals ought to participate in deliberations and decisions on the universal concerns of the state – on the grounds that they are all members of the state and that the concerns of the state are the concerns of everyone, so that everyone has a right to share in them with his own knowledge and volition' (Hegel, 1991, §308R). Rousseau, the older Hegel observed, was the first to put forward 'the will as the principle of the state, a principle which has thought not only as its form [...] but also as its content' (Hegel, 1991, §258R). The revolutionary implications of this principle were such that it 'afforded the tremendous spectacle [...] of the overthrow of all existing and given conditions within an actual major state and the revision of its constitution from first principles and purely in terms of thought' (Hegel, 1991, §258R). Now, however, reflecting on the phenomena of revolutionary Terror, Hegel maintained the more critical stance he developed in the *Phenomenology of Spirit*. He stated the principle in order to decode it.

In the *Phenomenology* Hegel explored the illusory form in which the general will expresses the relation of the individual to society: 'every personality [...] undivided from the whole, always does everything [done by the whole], and what appears as done by the whole is the direct and conscious deed of each' (Hegel, 1977, §584). Individuals are instructed to see their only purpose as the general purpose and individual personality is denied. Hegel explored the negativity inherent in this conception of freedom. Rather than build 'institutions of conscious freedom' (Hegel, 1977, §588), the general will experiences itself only through the annihilation of all particular and objective determinations. It expresses its power through destruction (Hegel, 1977, §589). In *Philosophy of Right* he observed that '[t]he subjective opinion which indivduals have of themselves may well find the demand for such guarantees, if it is made with explicit reference to "the people", superfluous and perhaps even insulting' (Hegel, 1991, §310R). In the name of the people, revolutionaries demand 'all power to the assembly' and declare an essential opposition between the assembly and the state executive, as if the assembly were all good and the executive all bad. However, Hegel commented that it could equally be said that 'since the Estates have their origin in individuality, in the private point of view and in particular interests, they are inclined to direct their efforts towards these at the expense of the universal interest, whereas the other moments in the power of the state are by their very nature dedicated to the universal end and disposed to the adopt the view of the state' (Hegel, 1991, §301R). Neither standpoint is justified. In the modern state the function of political representation, as Hegel sees it, is to admit the private interests of civil society into the organism of the state as one of its several elements and to serve as a middle term between civil society and the state. Its role is to embody the 'subjective moment in universal freedom' in order to prevent the isolation of the government which otherwise might become an arbitrary tyranny, and the isolation of civil society which might otherwise crystallise into a bloc in opposition to the state (Hegel, 1991, §301R). If representation is this middle term between civil society and the state, then the appropriation of the whole state by the principle of representation will not overcome the private point of view, it will totalise it. Hegel argued in effect that implanting the democratic element devoid of rational form into the organism of the state means that representation is not overcome, it is irrationally reproduced.

A related 'prejudice' Hegel identifies sets the general will in opposition to civil society on the grounds that the factions and parties of civil society are self-interested and thereby incapable of subsuming their private point of view to the good of the whole. The temptation then is to reject the alien institutions of representation so that the people might appear in the assembly in person. This attitude led in the course of the French Revolution to the suppression of the associations of civil society because they put the private point of view before the universal. It created a new mask beneath which the rule of the few and the indifference of the many remained intact. Hegel recognised that the demand that everyone should participate in the business of the state arises in opposition to the formal guarantees and substantive exclusions imposed by representative government. However, it is based on the assumption that everyone is '*an expert on such matters*' and on the instruction that everyone 'should participate in the concerns of the state' (Hegel, 1991, §308R). This 'pure' form of democracy means in effect that citizens are treated as an atomised mass and the state as the only legitimate association.

In his critique of Hegel's 'doctrine of the state', Marx was indebted to the Rousseauian proposition that 'sovereignty does not admit of representation' (Colletti, 1992). He argued that the meaning of the general will is that 'it is the will of *all* to be real (active) members of the state' and 'to give reality to their existence as something *political*' (Marx, 1992, p. 188). He acknowledged that Rousseau's treatment of the legislature as the *sole* focus of universal participation makes no sense in the modern age, not least for reasons of size, but argued it was necessary to go beyond this 'abstract view of the political state' (Marx, 1992, p. 189) and extend participation into *all* areas of the state and society until the very distinction between civil society and the state is dissolved.

As Richard Hyland noted, the young Marx still followed the reading of the *Philosophy of Right* drawn by the Young Hegelians (Hyland, 1989, 1735–831). For example, Arnold Ruge, who personified the revolutionary spirit of the 'Glorious Days' of 1830 and subsequently edited a journal with Marx, read the *Philosophy of Right* as a defence of the backward form of state current in Prussia and criticised Hegel for abandoning political action in favour of a philosophy of eternal forms. The problem for Ruge was Hegel's confusion of timeless logical categories with particular historical institutions. From the conservative side of the political spectrum F. J. Stahl protested against the inversion of subject and predicate in Hegel's theory of the state, the deduction of determinate institutions from abstract categories, and the conversion of irrationality and compulsion into the semblance of reason and freedom. Marx criticised the Young Hegelians for merely inverting Hegel and doing nothing to change the terms inverted. However, at this time he too followed suit. The inversion of Hegel meant a regression to Rousseau. For Marx to become 'Marx' and not just a more radical Young Hegelian, he had to move beyond this logic of inversion (Warminski, 1998, pp. 171–93).

Hegel's account of the dialectic in the *Philosophy of Right*

Hegel's recognition of the dialectic in the *Philosophy of Right* prefigured Marx's own recognition of the dialectic in *Capital*. Hegel turned philosophy towards a scientific approach to the subject matter at hand. Philosophy, as he construed it, does not prescribe 'what ought to be'; it is not a statement of the philosopher's own 'opinions, feelings or convictions'; it is not 'what *wells up from each individual's heart, emotion and enthusiasm*' (Hegel, 1991, p. 15); it is not about 'invent[ing] and propound[ing] *yet another theory*' of political community, as if the philosopher had to imagine that 'no state or constitution had ever previously existed or were in existence today' (Hegel, 1991, p. 12). It is 'the *comprehension of the present and the actual*, not the setting up of a *world beyond* [...] such instruction as it may contain cannot be aimed at instructing the state on how it ought to be, but rather at showing how the state [...] should be recognized' (Hegel, 1991, pp. 20–1). Hegel's repeated instruction is to read the *Philosophy of Right* as a 'scientific and objective treatment' of the actual legal and political order, not as a normative prescription for an ideal political order. Hegel presents the shift of emphasis as a theoretical leap from one kind of political philosophy to another – from natural law that prescribes what a reasonable political order should be to a critical philosophy that understands what the actual political order is: 'Hic Rhodus, hic saltus' (Here is Rhodes, here make the leap).

In the 'Preface' to *Philosophy of Right* Hegel described it as a great 'obstinacy' and achievement of the modern age that 'human beings [...] are unwilling to acknowledge in their attitudes anything which has not been justified by thought'. The peace he sought to establish with this world had fire in its belly: not quietism, cynicism or indifference; not 'that cold despair which confesses that, in this temporal world, things are bad or at best indifferent, but that nothing better can be expected here' (Hegel, 1991, pp. 22–3); but a refusal to accept any dogma or given authority: 'such thinking does not stop at what is *given*, whether the latter is supported by the external positive authority of the state or of mutual agreement among human beings, or by the authority of inner feeling and the heart [...It does not] adhere with trusting conviction to the publicly recognised truth' (Hegel, 1991, p. 11). Equally a science of right does not turn what '*diverges from what is universally acknowledged and valid*' into an oppositional principle of thought as if all that were necessary were to invert existing ideas (Hegel, 1991, p. 12). The task of philosophy is not to dissolve the experience of domination, not to declare that at some deeper level we have consented to whatever the state commands and not to say that the experience of oppression is superficial or that the rationality of the state is invisible to natural consciousness. The task of philosophy is, as Hegel put it, to 'recognise reason as the rose in the cross of the present' – to recognise reason in a world of alienation and domination (Hegel, 1991, p. 22).

Hegel's point of departure for his science of right is the idea of abstract right. It is a historical starting point in the sense that it is the end point of a historical process that falls outside the science itself. It is a 'determinate *starting point*, which is the *result* and truth of what *preceded* it' (Hegel, 1991, §2). The science of right, however, self-consciously foregoes the purely *historical* task of viewing 'the emergence and development of determinations of right *as they appear in time*' (Hegel, 1991, §3R). The starting point is not the 'highest instance' or the 'concretely true' such as the state itself, because the state is the result of many determinations and can only be understood if we break it down into simpler elements. The state may appear to be independent of its origins, but this appearance is deceiving since the determination of each concept and shape presupposes those determinations from which it results.

Hegel maintained that the science of right must start from the simplest and most abstract forms of contemporary society and work upwards toward the more complex and concrete. In exploring the various 'forms and shapes' of right taken by this starting point in the course of its development, the science of right seeks to uncover the laws that govern the movement by observing 'the proper immanent development of the thing itself' (Hegel, 1991, §2). The 'higher dialectic', as Hegel puts it, is the movement of right through its various 'concepts and shapes'. It is not an '*external* activity of subjective thought [...] but the *very soul* of the content which puts forth its branches and fruit organically' and which thought merely observes (Hegel, 1991, §31). In the process of 'self-division' and 'self-determination' the idea of right is not only the beginning but also 'the soul which holds everything together and which arrives at its own differentiation only through an immanent process' (Hegel, 1991, §32A). Hegel describes this dialectical approach thus:

[W]e merely wish to observe how the concept determines itself, and we force ourselves not to add anything of our own thought and opinions. What we obtain in this way, however, is a series of thoughts and another series of existent shapes, in which it may happen that the temporal sequence of their actual appearance is to some extent different from the conceptual sequence. Thus we cannot say, for example, that property existed before the family, although property is nevertheless dealt with first. One might accordingly ask at this point why we do not begin with the highest instance, that is, with the concretely true. The answer will be that we wish to see the truth precisely in the form of a result, and it is essential for this purpose that we should first comprehend the abstract concept itself.

(Hegel, 1991, §32A)

This is precisely the point Marx was later to echo in his critique of political economy. In seeking to discover the laws that determine the movement of right Hegel looks to the unfolding relation between form and content, concept and existence, rationality and actuality. The term 'idea' includes both the *concept* and its *existence*.

> Philosophy has to do with Ideas and therefore not with what are commonly described as *mere concepts*. On the contrary, it shows that the latter are one-sided and lacking in truth [...] The *shape* which the concept assumes in its actualisation, and which is essential for cognition of the *concept* itself, is different from its *form* of being purely as concept, and is the other essential moment of the Idea. The concept and its existence are two aspects [of the same thing], separate and united, like soul and body [...] The Idea of right is freedom, and in order to be truly apprehended, it must be recognisable in its concept and in the concept's existence.
>
> (Hegel, 1991, §1R)

Conceptual thinking considers only the concept and ignores its existence; or it turns the concept into an ideal against which it measures what actually exists; or in a more active mode it incessantly strives to bring existence up to the level of the concept. It does not recognise that the concepts themselves are one sided and lacking in truth. Hegel's critique of representation is at once a critique of the idealisation of the concept (Kant) and of the active political aim of bringing existence up to the level of the concept (Rousseau).

The manifold resemblances of Hegel's methodology to that which Marx was later to develop are striking and give substance to Marx's sense of indebtedness to Hegel's dialectical understanding. They cast some doubt, however, over Marx's claim that Hegel's dialectic was merely conceptual and therefore mystified.

Forms of right, forms of value: The unity of Hegel and Marx

It is more in their choice of subject matter than in their methodology that Hegel and Marx differ. The subject matter of the *Philosophy of Right* is the idea of right, by which Hegel refers to 'not merely civil right, which is what is usually understood by this term, but also morality, ethics and world history' (Hegel, 1991, §33A). Hegel begins with abstract right and its internal division into personality, property, contract and wrong. He moves from abstract right to morality (*Moralität*) and from morality to the forms of ethical life (*Sittlichkeit*) which include the family, civil society, the state and international society. Civil society is differentiated into the system of needs, laws and associations. The state is differentiated into the constitution, sovereign, executive and legislature. International right is differentiated into treaties, wars and finally into what Hegel calls the transition from the state to 'world history'. Every form and shape of right develops through an internal process into the next form and shape of right, displaying them all as a connected *system*. Each stage in the evolution of the idea of right represents the *existence* of freedom in one of its determinations. None, however, can be understood except in relation to the system as a whole. It is an error, Hegel argues, to consider a particular determination in isolation from the rest, as if right were embodied in this particular determination alone and all the rest were external to it. When property, morality, ethics and the state come into collision, this indicates that all forms of right are relative. 'Sublation' (*Aufhebung*) is the name Hegel gives to this metamorphosis of forms and Ovid is his inspiration. It indicates that the characteristics of simpler forms are transmuted in higher forms. They are not relations of progression (as if the state were a 'higher form' than individual personality); still less relations of transcendence (as if the emergence of the state makes individual personality redundant); nor are they relations of reconciliation (as if the state finally resolves the inequalities and conflicts that once divided civil society). Sublation indicates the indivisibility of preservation and transcendence. Hegel was the arch-diagnostician of how the violence inherent in the simplest forms of right is carried through to the most complex and concrete.

Let me now clarify my claim about the relation between what Hegel was doing in his *Philosophy of Right* and what Marx was doing in *Capital*. Hegel confronts the forms of *right* of modern society; Marx confronts the forms of *value*. For Hegel the subject matter comprises the forms taken by human subjects in the modern age (right, personality, ownership, contract, wrong, morality, family, civil society, state, the international, etc.); for Marx the subject matter comprises the forms taken by things, by objects, in modern capitalist society (value, exchange value, money, capital, profit, rent, interest, etc.). What is at issue is not idealism versus materialism but the fact that with Hegel we address the *ideal* forms of modernity and with Marx the *material* forms of capitalist society. Marx's critique of the forms of value of capitalist society complements Hegel's original analysis of the forms of right. When we read these texts together, rather than in opposition to one another, we access both the subjective and objective forms of modernity and construct a more holistic image of modernity than each offers in isolation. The modern age cannot be reduced either to its ideal or to its material aspects. An analysis which focuses on one rather than the other or treats one as essential and the other as merely epiphenomenal, mistakes the part for the whole. Each text supplements the other. Read together, they overcome the idealism which flows from identifying modernity exclusively with the ideal forms of legal and political life, and the materialism which flows from identifying modernity exclusively with the material forms of economic life. Hegel was an idealist only to the extent that he focused on the social forms of freedom and violence characteristic of the modern age; Marx was a materialist only to the extent that he focused on the material forms of economic determination characteristic of modern capitalist society. Hegel's 'idealism' and Marx's 'materialism' were wrong only inasmuch as they were one-sided; in their own spheres, they were equally valid.

Recognition of the unity of Hegel and Marx helps us confront the dichotomies of the modern age: subject and object, person and thing, freedom and determination, politics and economics, right and value. These dichotomies are in the world, not merely in how we look at the world, and they are explicable in terms of the specific conditions of our age. Each sphere gives rise to its own illusions: illusions of free will in the case of the political and illusions of determination in the case of the economic. Each sphere gives rise to abstract forms of domination: in one case morality, family, law and the state, in the other, the market, money and capital. Hegel's concern was with the pathologies of the system of right: personification, subjectivism and the fetishism of the subject. Marx's concern was over the pathologies of capitalist society: reification and the fetishism of the commodity. These concerns are not mutually exclusive. If we draw them together, we see that the achievement of the modern age to contain these divisions and oppositions and that an abyss opens up when political freedom and economic determination are cast adrift.

Bibliography

Colletti, Lucio (1992) 'Introduction', *Karl Marx: Early Writings* (London: Penguin and New Left Books).

Fraser, Ian (1997) 'Two of a Kind: Hegel, Marx, Dialectic and Form', *Capital and Class*, 61, 81–106.

Hegel, Georg Wilhelm Friedrich (1971) *Early Theological Writings*, trans. T. M. Knox (Philadelphia: University of Pennslvania Press).

—— (1975) *Lectures in the Philosophy of World History Introduction: Reason in History*, trans. H. B. Nisbet (Cambridge: Cambridge University Press).

—— (1977) *Phenomenology of Spirit*, trans. A. V. Miller (Oxford: Oxford University Press).

—— (1991) *Elements of the Philosophy of Right*, (ed.) Allen Wood (Cambridge: Cambridge University Press).

Hyland, Richard (1990) 'Hegel: A User's Manual', *Cardozo Law Review*, 10, 1735–831.

MacGregor, David (1998) *Hegel and Marx: After the Fall of Communism* (Cardiff: University of Wales Press).

Marx, Karl (1973) *Grundrisse: Introduction to the Critique of Political Economy*, foreword by Martin Nicolaus (Harmondsworth: Penguin).

—— (1975) *Texts on Method*, (ed.) Terrell Carver (Oxford: Blackwell).

—— (1990) *Capital Volume 1* (Harmondsworth: Penguin).

—— (1992), *Karl Marx: Early Writings*, (ed.) Lucio Colletti (London: Penguin and New Left Books).

Marx, Karl and Engels, Friedrich (1983) *Letters on 'Capital'*, (ed. and trans.) Andrew Drummond (London: New Park).

McLellan, David (1980) 'Introduction' to *Marx's Grundrisse* (London: Macmillan).

Rosdolsky, Roman (1980) *The Making of Marx's Capital* (London: Pluto).

Smith, Steven B. (1991) *Hegel's Critique of Liberalism: Rights in Context* (Chicago: Chicago University Press).

Warminski, Andrzej (1998), 'Hegel/Marx: Consciousness and Life', in Stuart Barnett (ed.) *Hegel after Derrida* (London: Routledge).

Wood, Allen (1993) 'Hegel and Marxism', in Frederick Beiser (ed.) *The Cambridge Companion to Hegel* (Cambridge: Cambridge University Press).

PART III MARX ON LABOUR, MONEY AND CAPITAL

7
Species-Being and Capital

Andrew Chitty

In this chapter I compare Marx's first conception of capital, in 1844, to his conception of the modern political state in 1843.[1] I argue that Marx in 1844 conceives capital as a realisation of human 'species-being', that is, of the universality and freedom inherent in human nature. However it realises this universality and freedom only in the form of 'abstract' universality and freedom, and therefore inadequately. The transition from capital to 'real community' consists in transforming this abstract universality and freedom into a 'concrete' universality and freedom.

Hegel on freedom and the state

In Aristotle's *Politics* humans are by nature rational animals, but they can only realise their rationality by entering into a certain kind of association with each other, the polis (Aristotle, 1981, pp. 54–61). This idea recurs in Rousseau, but now with a different conception of humans in which their essence is to be free. 'To renounce freedom is to renounce one's humanity' (Rousseau, 1968, p. 55). The social contract that initiates the legitimate state does not just preserve this essential human freedom, but brings about a 'remarkable change in man' which gives him a general will as well as a particular will, so that he thinks of himself as part of a larger whole as well as an individual. Thereby he acquires civil and moral freedom in place of natural freedom, and becomes truly free for the first time (Rousseau, 1968, p. 65). So Rousseau's legitimate state plays the same role as Aristotle's polis, of enabling humans to realise their own essence, although with a new conception of the human essence as freedom.

Fichte is a direct descendant of Rousseau. For him too the properly constituted state enables humans to realise their own essence as free. But whereas for Rousseau this freedom is brought into existence by a contract, for Fichte it is brought into existence by mutual recognition. It is by mutually recognising one another as free selves that individual human beings become free. Fichte calls the relation of mutual recognition the 'relation

of right' and sees the legitimate or rightful (*rechtlich*) state as institution-
alising that relation (Fichte, 2000, pp. 18–52). Therefore, as for Rousseau,
humans can only realise their essence as free by entering into a certain
kind of state.

Hegel follows Fichte in conceiving human freedom as achieved only
through mutual recognition, and in seeing this as institutionalised in a
rightful state. However he differs fundamentally from Fichte in his conception of recognition. When we achieve mutual recognition in Hegel we
recognise each other as free individual selves but *also* as part of a single
'universal' or collective self, which we bring into existence though this very
act of mutual recognition. Hegel calls this mutual recognition 'universal
self-consciousness':

> *Universal self-consciousness* is the affirmative knowing of one's self in
> the other self. Each has *absolute independence* as a free individuality, but,
> through the negation of its immediacy or desire, does not differentiate
> itself from the other, and so is universal and objective, and has real uni-
> versality as mutuality in that it knows itself to be recognised in the free
> other, and knows this in so far as it recognises the other and knows it to
> be free [...] the self-conscious subjects related to each other have through
> the supersession of their *dissimilar particular singularity* risen to the con-
> sciousness of their *real universality*, of their *freedom* which belongs to *all*,
> and thereby to seeing their *determinate identity with each other*.
> (Hegel, 1971, §436, 436A; 1986a, p. 225; t.m.[2])

This peculiar recognition – recognition of the other as at once distinct and
autonomous from me and yet at root identical to myself – is at the heart
of Hegel's concept of 'spirit'. He says as much when he first introduces the
concept in the *Phenomenology of Spirit*:

> What still lies ahead for consciousness is the experience of what spirit
> is – this absolute substance which, in the complete freedom and inde-
> pendence of its opposite, namely different self-consciousnesses existing
> for themselves, is the unity of them: *I* that is *We* and *We* that is *I*.
> (Hegel, 1977a, p. 110; 1986b, p. 144; t.m.)

Spirit is at once an 'I', a single universal or collective self, and a 'we', a
multiplicity of separate selves. As a universal self it is self-grounding, a
Spinozist 'substance' of which the individual selves are simply modes or
expressions, and yet at the same time these individual selves are themselves
'independent' and 'existing for themselves', so that the universal self is only
a union of them.

However fully realised (or 'absolute') spirit is constituted only when this
mutual recognition between individuals that brings into existence a universal

self is supplemented by a *second* mutual recognition between this universal self and the individuals that compose it, or between individuals acting as members of this universal self and the same individuals acting as particular individuals:

> The word of reconciliation is *existing* spirit, which sees the pure knowledge of itself as a *universal* essence in its opposite, in the pure knowledge of itself as absolutely being-for-itself *singularity* – a mutual recognition which is *absolute spirit.*
>
> (Hegel, 1977a, p. 408; 1986b, p. 492; t.m.)

For Hegel 'freedom is the one authentic property of spirit' (Hegel, 1975, pp. 47–8; 1955, p. 55), so humans become free through the double act of mutual recognition whereby they bring spirit into existence. Thus for Hegel, as for Rousseau and Fichte, human freedom is a joint achievement. As he says in his *Differenzschrift*:

> [T]he community of a person with others must not be regarded as a limitation of the true freedom of the individual but essentially as its enlargement. Highest community is highest freedom.
>
> (Hegel, 1977b, p. 145; 1986c, p. 81)

However, for Hegel if spirit and its essential freedom are to be properly realised this community must be given an institutional form, as a rightful state:[3]

> Man is free, this is certainly the substantial nature of man; and not only is this freedom not relinquished in the state, but it is actually in the state that it is first constituted. The freedom of nature, the disposition for freedom, is not real [*wirkliche*] freedom; for the state is the first realisation [*Verwirklichung*] of freedom.
>
> (Hegel, 1995, p. 504; 1986e, p. 307)[4]

Specifically, the rightful state realises spirit and its essential freedom by *objectifying* them. The state is 'objective spirit'.[5] In it 'freedom attains its objectivity and enjoys the fruits of its objectivity' (Hegel, 1975, p. 97; 1955, p. 116).

Finally, just as spirit combines universality and particularity, so does the freedom which is its essence, and so does the rightful state which objectifies them both. As Hegel says in the *Philosophy of Right*, the modern state

> allows the principle of subjectivity [i.e. the principle of individual freedom – AC] to attain fulfilment in the *self-sufficient extreme* of personal

particularity, while at the same time *bringing it back to substantial unity* and so preserving this unity in the principle of subjectivity itself.

(Hegel, 1991a, §260; 1986d, p. 406)

So for Hegel as for Fichte humans realise their freedom in a state that institutionalises relations of mutual recognition between them. But mutual recognition as Fichte understands it leaves individuals essentially separate, so that their freedom is a matter of their individual self-determination, even if it is dependent on their relations of recognition with others. By contrast mutual recognition as Hegel understands it forms individuals into a new complex kind of entity, an 'I that is we and a we that is I', and their freedom is their self-determination as members of this entity, which somehow combines individual and collective self-determination without reducing to either alone.

Thus when Hegel speaks of the individuals in relations of mutual recognition as having 'universal self-consciousness' and 'real universality', he has in mind not an 'abstract' universality which is opposed to particularity but a 'concrete' universality which is in fact a combination of universality and particularity as we normally understand those terms. The concrete universal 'contains the particular and the singular within it' (Hegel, 1991b, §164R; 1986f, p. 313; t.m.).[6] Similarly, spirit is concretely rather than abstractly universal, and the freedom which is its essential characteristic is 'concrete' rather than 'abstract' freedom: the freedom of individuals who are simultaneously part of a larger whole rather than of individuals considered in abstraction from that whole. As Hegel says, 'The state is the reality [*wirklichkeit*] of concrete freedom' (Hegel, 1991a, §260; 1986d, p. 405).

Marx and the modern state in 1843

In his 1842 writings Marx agrees with Rousseau, Fichte and Hegel that freedom is the essence of human beings, and that it is properly achieved only through an association between them:

> Freedom is so much the essence of man that even its opponents implement it while combating its reality.
>
> ('Debates on the Freedom of the Press';
> Marx and Engels, 1975a, p. 155; 1959, p. 50)

> The more ideal and thorough view of recent philosophy [...] considers the state as the great organism, in which rightful, ethical and political freedom gains its realisation.
>
> ('Leading article in no. 179 of the Kölnische Zeitung';
> Marx and Engels, 1975a, p. 202; 1959, p. 104)

Specifically, he agrees with Rousseau and Hegel that this freedom is insepa-rable from coming to see oneself as part of this larger whole:

> [T]he state itself educates its members in that it makes them into state-members, in that it converts the aims of the individual into universal aims, raw drive into ethical inclination, natural independence into spirit-ual freedom, in that the individual enjoys himself in the life of the whole and the whole [enjoys itself] in the disposition of the individual.
> (Marx and Engels, 1975a, p. 193; 1959, p. 95; t.m.)[7]

In so far as the human essence can only be realised through an association between human beings, we can say that this essence itself includes sociality. In the course of 1843 Marx follows this implication through and begins to reformulate his idea of the essence of humanity around the core idea that humans are essentially 'universal' beings: beings whose essence is to think and live from a universal or collective standpoint (he does not distinguish these two) rather than from the standpoint of their own particular self-interest (e.g. Marx, 1975, p. 148; Marx and Engels, 1959, p. 285). Although he continues to see freedom as an essential property of human beings, he now puts the emphasis on universality, while seeing freedom as inseparably bound up with this universality. So, while in the *Critique of Hegel's Philosophy of Right* he continues to assert that the state is 'the highest social realisation [*Wirklichkeit*] of the human being' (Marx, 1975, p. 98; Marx and Engels, 1959, p. 240; t.m.), he conceives it essentially as a realisation of human universality. The state (along with the family and civil society) is the '*realised* universality' of the individual; in it he 'achieves his true universality' (Marx, 1975, p. 99; Marx and Engels, 1959, pp. 241–2).[8]

Meanwhile, Marx now draws a sharp contrast between the modern or '*merely* political' state (Marx, 1975, p. 183; Marx and Engels, 1959, p. 319), as it is described by Hegel, and the form of human association that would *properly* realise human universality and freedom. As he puts it in *On the Jewish Question*, the former accomplishes only a 'political emancipation' (or liberation) of human beings, while only the latter can accomplish their 'human emancipation', i.e. can make them properly free.[9] In political eman-cipation 'the human being liberates himself from a restriction through the *medium of the state*, in a *political* way' (Marx, 1975, p. 218; Marx and Engels, 1959, p. 353). That is, human beings become free only through the medium of an association which is 'external' to them, and therefore only in an indi-rect and so unreal way, just as in Christianity they only see themselves as divine in an indirect way, through the medium of a particular human being (Jesus Christ) who is external to them:

> [I]n so far as he frees himself *politically*, man frees himself in a *roundabout way*, through a *medium*, even if it is a *necessary medium*. [...] he recognises

himself only by a roundabout route, only through a medium. Religion is precisely the recognition of man in a roundabout way, through *a mediator*. The state is the mediator between man and man's freedom.

(Marx, 1975, pp. 218–9; Marx and
Engels, 1959, p. 353; t.m.)

Likewise, in the modern political state humans realise their essential *universality* only in an indirect and so unreal way:

The perfected political state is, in its essence, the *species-life* of man as *opposed* to his material life [...] Where the political state has attained its true development, man – not only in his thought, in his consciousness, but in *reality*, in *life* – leads a twofold life, a heavenly and an earthly life: life in the *political community* [*politischen Gemeinwesen*], in which he counts to himself as a *communal being* [*Gemeinwesen*], and life in *civil society*, where he is active as a *private individual*. [In civil society,] where he counts to himself and to others as a real individual, he is an *untrue* appearance. In the state, on the other hand, where man counts as a species-being [*Gattungswesen*], he is the imaginary member of an imagined sovereignty, is deprived of his real individual life and endowed with an unreal [*unwirklichen*] universality.

(Marx, 1975, p. 220; Marx and Engels, 1959, pp. 354–5; t.m.)

Here for the first time Marx uses the term 'species-being' (or 'species-essence', *Gattungswesen*) to refer to the essential universality of human beings. Every entity that belongs to a species has a 'species-essence', if this means the characteristic which is universal to all members of the species. But in the case of human beings the *content* of this characteristic is universality. The feature that is universal to all human beings is universality itself. Marx expresses this by saying not just that a human being has a 'species-essence' (which would be the case for every entity that belongs to a species) but that it *is* a species-essence. This expression does not sound odd in German, since the word *Wesen* can mean 'a being' as well as 'an essence', but it does in English, hence the usual English translation 'species-being'.

In short, for Marx in 1843 the modern political state realises human universality and freedom in an indirect and unreal, or 'estranged', way. The political emancipation it brings about is an incomplete form of human emancipation. Nevertheless it is a step towards genuine human emancipation:

Political emancipation is, of course, a great advance. True, it is not the final form of human emancipation in general, but it is the final form of human emancipation *within* the hitherto existing world order.

(Marx, 1975, p. 221; Marx and Engels, 1959, p. 356; t.m.)

In fact Marx envisages human emancipation as an extension of the emancipation that has already been accomplished in the modern state. In the kind of association that accomplishes human emancipation, humans will relate to each other as universal and free beings, as they do as citizens of the modern state, but they will do so in their everyday lives. Thereby they will realise their universality and freedom in a real way:

> Only when the real individual man takes back into himself the abstract citizen, and has become a *species-being* as an individual man in his empirical life, in his individual labour, and in his individual relations, only when men have recognized and organized their 'own powers' as *social* powers, and, consequently, no longer separate social power from themselves in the shape of political power, only then will human emancipation have been accomplished.
>
> (Marx, 1975, p. 234; Marx and Engels, 1959, p. 370; t.m.)

If the essential characteristic of human beings for Marx is universality, then is this Hegel's 'abstract universality' or his 'concrete universality', that is, is it a universality that is opposed to particularity or is it a combination of universality and particularity? In the *Science of Logic* Hegel explicitly associates the idea of concrete universality with the term 'species' (*Gattung*),[10] so Marx's choice of the term 'species-being' already indicates that he has concrete universality in mind. This is confirmed by the above quote. Marx's vision of a society that realises human universality is one in which each individual realises that universality 'in his individual labour, and in his individual relations' rather than by adopting the role of a citizen whose motivations are counterposed to those he has as a particular individual.

In fact Marx's basic criticism of the modern political state can be stated by saying that in it individuals realise their own universality only in the form of an abstract universality that is opposed to their particularity, rather than in the genuine form of a concrete universality that includes their particularity. When Marx says that in this state individuals realise their universality in an 'estranged' way, he means that they realise it through an association that is 'external' to them, and to the realm of civil society in which they realise their particularity. But, I suggest, just because they realise their universality through this external association, they realise it in the form of an abstract rather than a concrete universality, in opposition to their particularity.[11] This is the essential difference between political and human emancipation.

It seems natural to conclude that for Marx the kind of association that will properly realise human universality as concrete universality will also realise human freedom as concrete freedom, the freedom of individuals who are simultaneously part of a larger whole, and that this is the kind of freedom that Marx has in mind when he says in *On the Jewish Question* that other humans are the 'realisation' rather than the 'limit' of my freedom (Marx, 1975, pp. 229–30; Marx and Engels, 1959, p. 365), or as he puts it in *The German Ideology*: 'In the real [*wirklichen*] community individuals obtain their freedom in and through their association' (Marx and Engels, 1976, p. 78; 1962, p. 74).[12] By contrast the modern state realises human freedom only as abstract freedom, the freedom of individuals whose status as members of a larger whole is counterposed to their status as particular individuals.[13]

In the second part of *On the Jewish Question*, Marx treats money in a similar way to the modern state. He suggests that in the market system, humans can realise their own essence only in the form of something external to them, namely money:

> Selling is the praxis of alienation [*Entäusserung*]. Just as man, as long as he is in the grip of religion, is able to objectify his essence only by turning it into an alien fantastic essence [or being, *Wesen*],[14] so under the domination of egoistic need he can be active practically, and practically produce objects, only by putting his products, like his activity, under the domination of an alien essence, and giving them the significance of an alien essence – money.
> (Marx, 1975, p. 241; Marx and Engels, 1959, pp. 376–7; t.m.)[15]

If the essence of human beings is universality and freedom, then it follows humans realise this essence in *two* 'estranged' and 'unreal' ways, first in the form of the modern political state and second in the form of money.[16]

Furthermore, Marx speaks of money here not just as the estranged essence of human beings but as an essence that *dominates* the activity of human beings: 'Money is the estranged essence of man's labour and man's existence, and this alien essence dominates him, and he worships it' (Marx, 1975, p. 239; Marx and Engels, 1959, pp. 374–5; t.m.). So in money human beings realise their essence in the form of something that is not only estranged from them but also dominates them.

Here too there is a parallel between what Marx says about the modern state and about money. Although he does not explicitly use the language of domination in describing the modern state in the *Critique of Hegel's Philosophy of Right*, Marx constantly accuses Hegel of inverting the proper relation between human beings and the state, saying for example that 'Hegel proceeds from the state and conceives of the human being as the subjectivized state' when the state should rather be conceived as the objectification of human beings (Marx, 1975, p. 87; Marx and Engels, 1959, p. 231). At the same time he also says that Hegel 'describes the essence of the modern state as it is' (Marx, 1975, p. 127; Marx and Engels, 1959,

p. 231). The clear implication is that the inversion in which individuals are reduced to nothing but expressions of the state they have produced is characteristic not only of Hegel's account of the modern state but of the modern state itself.[17] In this sense the modern state too dominates individuals.

Capital as estranged species-being

I will now argue that Marx's philosophical conceptions of the modern state and of money in 1843, as the means whereby humans realise their essential universality and freedom in an estranged and dominating form, provides the template for the conception of capital that he forms in 1844, when he first engages with political economy.

In the *Economic and Philosophical Manuscripts* Marx begins by adopting Adam Smith's concept of capital. For Smith capital is that part of a person's 'stock' or wealth, whether it consists in money or goods, which is used not for consumption but so as to 'derive a revenue' from it (Smith, 1956, p. 183). Capital can produce a revenue by being used to buy commodities at one price and sell them at a higher one (merchant's capital), but Smith is mainly interested in capital that produces a revenue by being used to buy 'useful machines and instruments of trade' and 'materials', and to pay 'workmen' who use these to produce commodities which are then sold for a sum of money larger than the capital invested (Smith, 1956, p. 184). In sum, capital is a sum of wealth that is used to generate more wealth. But in turn the measure of a sum of wealth is the amount of labour that it takes to produce it (Smith, 1956, p. 30-31). So we do not need to go far beyond Smith to understand capital as a quantity of labour, embodied in commodities or money, which is used to purchase living labour from labourers in order to generate a larger quantity of embodied labour.

This is how Marx officially understands capital in the *Economic and Philosophical Manuscripts*. Capital is 'accumulated labour' (Marx, 1975, pp. 285, 287; Marx and Engels, 1968, pp. 473, 476) or 'stored-up labour' which 'yields its owner a revenue or profit' (Marx, 1975, p. 295; Marx and Engels, 1968, p. 483), mainly by being used to hire labourer and to buy raw materials and instruments of production so as to produce commodities for sale on the market.[18]

But in these manuscripts Marx also characterises capital in terms similar to those he had used to describe the modern state and money the year before. To begin with, capital dominates the very human beings who have produced it. With the expansion of capital the worker's 'own labour increasingly confronts him as alien property', the accumulation of capital 'opposes the product of labour to the worker as something increasingly alien to him', and this leads to an 'enslavement to capital which piles up in threatening opposition to him' (Marx, 1975, pp. 285–6; Marx and Engels, 1968, pp. 473–4). Of course Marx expresses this idea most clearly in the section 'estranged labour' in the *Economic and Philosophical Manuscripts*:

> So much does the appropriation of the object appear as estrangement that the more objects the worker produces the fewer can he possess and the more he falls under the domination of his product, of capital [...] The *alienation* [*Entäusserung*] of the worker in his product means not only that his labour becomes an object, an *external* existence, but that it exists *outside him*, independently of him and alien to him, and becomes a self-sufficient power confronting him; that the life which he has given to the object confronts him as hostile and alien.

> (Marx, 1975, p. 324; Marx and Engels, 1968, p. 512; t.m.)

The result is 'the relationship of the worker to the *product of labour* as an alien object that has power over him', in which the worker becomes a 'slave of his object' (Marx, 1975, pp. 327, 325; Marx and Engels, 1968, pp. 515, 513). It is not the particular object that one worker produces that dominates him, but the totality of objects produced by all workers that, when these objects take the form of capital, dominates them all.

So Marx's characterisation of capital in the *Economic and Philosophical Manuscripts* involves the same domination that we saw in his accounts of the modern state and money in his 1843 writings. But it also involves the other central idea in these accounts, that of an estranged realisation of the human essence, of species-being.

In the *Economic and Philosophical Manuscripts* Marx introduces a substantial development of his conception of humans as 'species-beings', in which for the first time the idea of labour plays a central role:

> Man is a species-being, not only because he practically and theoretically makes the species – both his own and those of other things – his object, but also – and this is simply another expression for the same thing – because he relates to himself as the present, living species, because he relates to himself as a *universal* and therefore free being.
> (Marx, 1975, p. 327; Marx and Engels, 1968, p. 515)

At first sight this definition simply seems to reiterate Marx's 1843 conception of species-being. The only difference is that whereas before he had said that the essence of a human being is to *be* universal now he says that it is to *relate to oneself* as universal. In this Marx simply seems to be bringing his definition of the essence of human beings in line with the one in the first lines of Feuerbach's *Essence of Christianity* (Feuerbach, 1989, p. 1; 1960, p. 1). However, while Feuerbach only says that the essence of humans consists in their ability to take their own species as the object of their thought, Marx says that they make their species their object 'practically and theoretically', i.e. that they make it their object of their thought *and* activity. Correspondingly 'relates' in last part of the definition must refer to both thought and activity.

In fact Marx goes on to develop his conception of a species-being entirely in terms of the kind of activity in which humans engage, saying that: 'The whole character of a species, its species-character, resides in the nature of its life activity' (Marx, 1975, p. 328; Marx and Engels, 1968, p. 516). He identifies this specifically human kind of activity with labour. It is (1) universal, both in that it is oriented towards species, whether the human species or the species of other entities, and in that it is directed to any part of nature,[19] (2) consciously undertaken,[20] and (3) free.[21] But most importantly of all it is (4) 'world-producing', in that it refashions nature as a human-produced world in which humans can see their own essence:

> It is therefore in his fashioning of the objective world that man really proves himself to be a *species-being*. Such production is *his* active species-life. Through it, nature appears as his work and his realisation. The object of labour is, therefore, the objectification of the species-life of man: for man doubles himself not only intellectually, in his consciousness, but actively and actually, and he can therefore see himself in a world he himself has created.
> (Marx, 1975, p. 329; Marx and Engels, 1968, p. 517; t.m.)[22]

It is clear that Marx sees this creation of a human-produced world not just as *evidence* that humans are species-beings but as the process through which they *realise* themselves as species-beings. It follows that capital is an estranged realisation of the essence of human beings:

> Estranged labour, therefore, turns [...] man's *species-essence* – both nature and his intellectual species-power – into an *alien* essence.
> (Marx, 1975, p. 329; Marx and Engels, 1968, p. 517; t.m.)

Therefore in the *Economic and Philosophical Manuscripts* Marx says of capital just what he said of the modern state and money in 1843: that it is an estranged and dominating realisation of the human essence. However Marx has now characterised this essence in a new way. Whereas before the central features of the human essence were universality and freedom, now the central feature is labour, and universality and freedom are reduced to aspects of labour. In fact it is just because he has redefined the human essence in his way that Marx can now see capital, a mass of 'stored-up labour', as a realisation of this essence.

Let us leave aside the idea of domination for now (I return to it at the end of this chapter) and focus on estrangement. If capital is an estranged realisation of the human essence, then what is needed to genuinely realise this essence is to replace capital with something that retains its positive features but lacks its estranged character, just as what was needed in the 1843 writings was to replace the state with a form of association that would retain its positive features of universality and freedom but would lack its estranged character. In fact in the *Economic and Philosophical Manuscripts* Marx speaks of the genuine realisation of the human essence in just this way. It will be

> the *appropriation* of the objective essence through the supersession of its estrangement [...] the real appropriation of [man's] objective essence through the destruction of the estranged character of the objective world, through its supersession in its estranged existence.
>
> (Marx, 1975, p. 395; Marx and Engels, 1968, p. 583; t.m.)

Here the 'objective essence' means the essence of human beings in so far as it has been objectified by labour as a world of products, or as a refashioned nature. Currently, this objective essence takes the form of capital, and what is needed is not to destroy it but only to strip it of its estranged character.

Furthermore in the *Economic and Philosophical Manuscripts* Marx goes on to say not just that capital is an estranged realisation of the human essence, but that this estranged realisation is a *necessary means* towards the genuine realisation of the human essence, just as he suggested that political emancipation is a necessary means towards human emancipation in *On the Jewish Question*. Here it is worth mentioning Feuerbach's account of God in *The Essence of Christianity*, which parallels both of these. For Feuerbach, God is a misconception by human beings of their own human essence as a being external to them, but this misconception is not just an unfortunate error. Humans could only become aware of their own essence by first becoming aware of it in the shape of a being external to them:

> [R]eligion, the consciousness of God, [...] is the first, but indirect, self-consciousness of man [...] Man transfers his essence outside himself before he finds it within himself. His own essence is an object for him first as another essence.
>
> (Feuerbach, 1989, p. 13; 1960, p. 16; t.m.)

In the *Economic and Philosophical Manuscripts* Max directly draws an analogy between capital and God, although of course capital is a product of practical activity whereas God is a product of thinking (Marx, 1975, p. 324; Marx and Engels, 1968, pp. 512), and, in a way similar to Feuerbach's, he sees the estranged realisation of humans as species-beings in capital as a necessary step towards their genuine realisation as species-beings. He says this most clearly in his commentary on Hegel's *Phenomenology of Spirit*, which

he construes as expressing this basic insight (albeit in an 'estranged' form).
Thus he praises Hegel for seeing that

> religion, wealth, etc., are only the estranged realisation [*Wirklichkeit*] of
> *human* objectification, of *human* essential powers born into work, and
> therefore only the *way* to true *human* realisation [*Wirklichkeit*].
> (Marx, 1975, p. 385; Marx and Engels, 1968, p. 573; t.m.)

That is, Hegel sees that capital is a necessary step towards the realisation of
humans as species-beings:

> Hegel grasps man's self-estrangement, alienation of his essence, loss of
> objectivity, and de-realisation as self-discovery, expression of his essence,
> objectification and realisation. (In short, he sees [...] man's relating to
> himself as an alien essence and his activation of himself as an alien
> essence as the coming to be of *species-consciousness* and *species-life*.)
> (Marx, 1975, p. 395; Marx and Engels, 1968, p. 583; t.m.)

To summarise, then: in the *Economic and Philosophical Manuscripts* Marx
reworks his earlier conception of what it is to be a species-being so as to
organise it around the idea of universal, free, and conscious productive
activity. He gives a philosophical account of labour as this activity. Thanks
to this reworking, he is able to draw on Smith's implicit concept of capital
as consisting in 'stored-up labour' so as to give a philosophical account of
capital modelled on his earlier accounts of the modern political state and
money. Capital is the realisation of species-being in the estranged form of a
thing that dominates the very humans whose essence it realises.

Capital as abstract universality

This still leaves the question of the exact sense in which capital is an
'estranged' realisation of species-being. In the case of the modern political
state I have argued that it realises species-being in an estranged way because
it realises the concrete universality of humans in an association that is
external to them and in the form of an abstract universality. In the *Economic
and Philosophical Manuscripts* Marx clearly sees a genuine human association
as realising concrete universality:

> Man, however much he may therefore be a particular individual – and
> it is just this particularity which makes him an individual and a really
> *individual* communal being – is just as much the *totality*, the ideal
> totality, the subjective existence of society which has been thought and
> experienced for itself.
> (Marx, 1975, p. 351; Marx and Engels, 1968, p. 539; t.m.)[23]

This suggests that by contrast capital, like the modern political state in *On the Jewish Question*, realises human universality not only in an external thing but also in the form of an abstract universality. There is one passage where Marx implies just this. If we return to the *Critique of Hegel's Philosophy of Right*, Marx begins by rejecting the idea of a monarchy in which one person exercises political power, but then goes on to align it with 'the political republic' or what we would now call a constitutional democracy (Marx, 1975, p. 89; Marx and Engels, 1959, p. 232), saying: 'The struggle between monarchy and republic is itself still a struggle within the abstract form of the state'. By contrast Marx calls for a 'true democracy' in which 'the political state disappears' (Marx, 1975, p. 88; Marx and Engels, 1959, p. 232), or at least in which its separation from civil society is overcome (Marx, 1975, pp. 189, 234; Marx and Engels, 1959, pp. 325, 370). His point is that expanding the number of people who share in political power leaves untouched the fact that in so far as individuals share in this power they do so only as citizens, in counterposition to their status as a private individuals. Even if everyone is a legislator, the individual as a legislator thinking for the common good remains counterposed to the same individual as a private self-seeker. By gaining the status of legislator, the individual realises his or her universality only in a form that is counterposed to his or her particularity, that is, in the form of an abstract universality. So a constitutional democracy fails to overcome the estranged character of the political state. By contrast true democracy realises universality as concrete universality: it is 'the first true unity of the particular and the universal' (Marx, 1975, p. 88; Marx and Engels, 1959, p. 231).

In the *Economic and Philosophical Manuscripts* Marx makes an exactly parallel argument about 'crude communism', in which the ownership of social wealth is extended from a few individuals to the entire population, so that

> [j]ust as woman passes from marriage to general prostitution so the entire world of wealth, that is, the objective essence of man, passes from the relationship of exclusive marriage with the owner of private property to a relation of universal prostitution with the community.
> (Marx, 1975, p. 346; Marx and Engels, 1968, p. 534; t.m.)

Marx's objection is that extending the status of capital-owner to every member of the community does not overcome the fundamental duality between individuals as owners of capital and the same individuals as labourers:

> The community is only a community of labour and [is only] the equality of wages paid out by communal capital, by the community as the universal capitalist. Both sides of the relationship are raised to an imagined universality, *labour* as the determination in which every person is placed, and capital as the recognised universality and power of the community.
> (Marx, 1975, pp. 346–7; Marx and Engels, 1968, p. 535; t.m.)

So Marx's fundamental objection to capital is not that it consists in a wealth of human products which are the private property of a few persons, but that it consists in a wealth of products which are private property *as such* and thus which are 'external' to those who produce them.[24] If everyone became co-owners of the totality of human products, then all would realise their universality through these products, but only in the form of an abstract universality. For the individual as the co-owner of this totality of products, thinking of how to use them for the common good, would remain counter-posed to the same individual as a producer. 'Crude communism' would give everyone a share in the ownership of the products of the whole labour of the community, parallel to the share in political power that citizens of the political republic have, but they would possess this share only as capital-owners, in counterposition to their status as producers.

Accordingly what is needed is a more fundamental transformation, in which private property in the totality of the products of labour is not just extended to all but abolished. But the resulting society would not simply be the negation of capital. Rather it would be a 'positive supersession' of capital, in which the human universality (and thus the human freedom) which is realised in capital only abstractly would be realised as concrete universality.[25] Of course Marx never spells out exactly such a society would look like.

In arguing that Marx in 1844 criticises capital essentially on the grounds that it realises human universality only in an abstract way, I have left aside the idea that workers are *dominated*, indeed enslaved, by capital, and it might be said in objection that the domination of workers by capital was what over-whelmingly preoccupied Marx. But this preoccupation is not incompatible with the account that I have given, any more than a preoccupation with the way that people are dominated by the modern political state would be incompatible with the account I have given of that. Marx's aim in the *Economic and Philosophical Manuscripts* was not simply to protest against the domination of workers by capitalists, or even to show that the agent of this domination was ultimately capital itself. It was to give an account of the ultimate source of this domination. I suggest that he saw its source pre-cisely in the fact that capital realises the universality inherent in the human essence in an abstract way, in such a way as to counterpose the universal as something external to the particular. For if we make the Aristotelian assumption that the human essence exerts a power over human behaviour from within, it might follow that an external realisation of this essence will exert the same power over humans from outside. Specifically, it might establish a relation of power between those who personify the universal and those who occupy the position of the particular, between the legislator and the citizen, or the capitalist and the worker: a relation of power which would remain even if everyone became a legislator, or if the ownership of the world of human products were extended from individual capitalists to the whole community. Whether such a view of the source of the coercion endemic to capitalist production is ultimately convincing, it is at least plausible that Marx in 1844 could have held it.

Conclusion

It might be argued that Marx's first attempt to relate the concept of capital to that of human nature is of little interest, since within a year he had replaced it with a very different one. In *The German Ideology* Marx and Engels' vision of realised humanity becomes one of beings who engage in ever-developing productive activity, and the relation between capital (or rather the set of capitalist social relations) and this realised humanity is that it is the set of property-based social relations that least hinders the free development of human productivity, so that the next step beyond it in the history of human self-realisation must be the abolition of property as such. This makes the relationship between capital and human nature rather contingent: there is no philosophical reason why some other set of property-based social relations might not have played the role of the last and most productive in the historical series. Even the drive of capitalist social relations to expand to every part of the globe and continuously to expand and revolutionise the forces of production, emphasised further in the *Communist Manifesto*, seems to connect these relations only in a contingent way to Marx's conception of humans as beings who engage in ever-developing productive activity, for in principle some other set of social relations of production might have possessed these drives.

A suggestion, however, is that the idea of the human essence as consisting in concrete universality and freedom which is realised only in the form of abstract universality and freedom in capital and which can only be properly realised in communism, may have returned to inform Marx's mature economic writings.[26] In this case *Das Kapital* would be implicitly not just a theory of capital but also a philosophical anthropology. Whether this is the case, and, if it is the case, whether this helped or hindered Marx in his lifelong effort to grasp the nature of capitalism, can only be questions for future research.

Notes

1. An earlier version of this paper appeared in Chinese in *Social Sciences in Nanjing* 2, 2007, pp. 1–10.
2. Here and below 't.m.' indicates 'translation modified'.
3. The idea that for Hegel the state is the realisation of freedom is discussed in Franco (2000, pp. 154–87), Patten (1999) and Neuhouser (2000, pp. 82–174).
4. I have preserved the standard but sexist translation of Marx's *Mensch* as 'man' only because the alternatives have proved so clumsy. Unless otherwise mentioned, 'real' and 'realisation' in my translations always stand for *wirklich* and *Verwirklichung*.

5. In the *Encyclopaedia* this is Hegel's general term for the system of right that culminates in the state.

6. Cf. from the *Encyclopedia Logic*: 'What is universal about the concept is indeed not just something common against which the particular stands on its own; instead the universal is what particularises (specifies) itself, remaining at home with itself in its other, in unclouded clarity' (Hegel, 1991b, §163A; 1986f, p. 311). It is important to see that the underlying contrast between 'abstract' and 'concrete' here is not between mental concepts on the one hand and physical things on the other, but rather between what is separated from, and what is interconnected with, particulars. Unfortunately there is no space here for a full investigation of Hegel's idea of concrete universality. For a discussion, see Royce (1892, pp. 492–506).

7. For fuller investigations of Marx's 1842 view of the state see McGovern (1969) and Chitty (2006).

8. Cf. 'the essence of the 'particular personality' is not his beard, his blood, his abstract *physis*, but his *social quality*, and [...] the activities of the state, etc., are nothing but the modes of existence and action of the social qualities of human beings' (Marx, 1975, pp. 77–8; Marx and Engels 1959, p. 222; t.m.). For two recent discussions of Marx's 1843 view of the state, see Kouvelakis (2003, pp. 232–336) and Leopold (2007, pp. 17–182).

9. In *On the Jewish Question* Marx is referring specifically to emancipation from religion, but I take it that his basic points about freedom do not rely on this context.

10. E.g. at Hegel 1969, p. 655; 1986g, p. 340. In the English translation of this passage *Gattung* is translated as 'genus' and *Art* as 'species'. *Gattung* is associated with concrete universality.

11. This point is made by McCarthy (1990, p. 186), but he does not elaborate on the meaning of 'concrete universality' (cf. pp. 39, 108).

12. Cf. in *The Communist Manifesto* 'In place of the old bourgeois society, with its classes and class antagonisms, we shall have an association, in which the free development of each is the condition for the free development of all' (Marx and Engels 1976b, p. 506; Marx and Engels 1969, p. 482). On the idea that Marx's concept of species-being, and therefore the form of association that will realise it, combines universality and particularity, see Mahowald (1973).

13. Meanwhile Marx's essential criticism of Hegel's account of the modern system of political state and civil society is that Hegel misrepresents this system as realising concrete freedom by trying to bridge the fundamental divide between its two elements with 'mediations'. On Marx's critique of these mediations, see Leopold (2007, pp. 74–80).

14. As noted above, the word *Wesen*, translated as 'essence' here, can also be translated as 'a being', so the 'alien fantastic essence' is clearly meant to evoke the idea of God.

15. See also from the *Notes on James Mill*: 'the *human* social act [...] is estranged and becomes the property of a *material [materiellen] thing* external to man, i.e. money'; money is 'the alienated species-activity of man' (Marx, 1975, pp. 260, 261; Marx and Engels, 1968, p. 446).

16. Along with the idea of the modern state and money as estranged realisations of the human essence there is an implicit emphasis on their 'material' or thinglike character. Thus, clearly referring to the modern state, Marx says that the modern age 'separates the *objective* essence of the human being from him, treating it as something purely *external* and material [*materielles*]' (Marx, 1975, p. 148; Marx

and Engels, 1959, p. 285; t.m.). I am grateful to Jai Crookshanks for pointing this passage out to me. For a parallel reference to money as 'material', see the last note.

17. Cf. from the *Introduction to the Critique of Hegel's Philosophy of Right*: 'This state and this society produce religion, an *inverted world-consciousness*, because they are an *inverted world*' (Marx, 1975, 244; Marx and Engels, 1959, p. 378). In the *Critique of Hegel's Philosophy of Right* Marx focuses on the monarchical state as inverted in this way, but he implies that his critique applies equally to a 'political republic'. See the discussion in the section 'Capital as abstract universality' below.

18. Cf. Engels in his 1844 *Outlines of a Critique of Political Economy*: 'it becomes immediately evident that capital and labour are identical, since the economists themselves confess that capital is "stored-up labour"' (Marx and Engels, 1975b, p. 427; 1959, p. 508). Marx's and Engels' 1844 conceptions of capital are discussed by Oakley (1984, pp. 33–4, 36–9).

19. 'The universality of man manifests itself in practice in that universality which makes the whole of nature his inorganic body.' (Marx, 1975, p. 328; Marx and Engels, 1968, pp. 515–16)

20. '[M]an makes his life activity itself into an object of his willing and consciousness.' (Marx, 1975, p. 328; Marx and Engels, 1968, p. 516; t.m.).

21. '[F]ree conscious activity constitutes the species-character of man.' (Marx, 1975, p. 328; Marx and Engels, 1968, p. 516).

22. For an earlier attempt by the author to elucidate Marx's 1844 concept of species-being see Chitty (1997). See also Plamenatz (1975, pp. 36–86), Wallimann (1981, pp. 11–23), Wartenberg (1982), Wood (1981, pp. 16–43) and, for a recent 'modernist' interpretation, Dyer-Witheford (2004).

23. Similarly, communism is 'the true resolution of the conflict [...] between individual and species' (Marx, 1975, p. 348; Marx and Engels, 1968, p. 536) rather than the reduction of either to the other.

24. Of course human products will always be *physically* external to their producers, but this is not the kind of externality Marx has in mind.

25. Marx describes communism as the 'positive supersession of private property' at Marx, 1975, pp. 348, 349; Marx and Engels, 1968, pp. 536, 537. Unfortunately the question of the exact relation between capital and private property in the *Economic and Philosophical Manuscripts* cannot be addressed here.

26. For example, the idea that abstract labour, which in Marx's later economic writings is the source of value and therefore of capital, is characterised by 'abstract universality' has been developed by Rubin (1994) and Arthur (1978).

Bibliography

Aristotle (1981) *Politics* (Harmondsworth: Penguin).

Arthur, Christopher J. (1978) 'Labour: Marx's Concrete Universal', *Inquiry* 21(1), 87–104.

Chitty, Andrew (1997) 'First Person Plural Ontology and Praxis', *Proceedings of the Aristotelian Society*, 97 (1), 81–96.

—— (2006) 'The Basis of the State in the Marx of 1842', in D. Moggach (ed.) *The New Hegelians: Politics and Philosophy in the Hegelian School* (Cambridge: Cambridge University Press).

Dyer-Witheford, Nick (2004) '1844/2004/2044: The Return of Species-Being', *Historical Materialism*, 12 (4), 1–23.

Feuerbach, Ludwig (1960) *Sämtliche Werke*, (eds) W. Bolin and F. Jodl, Band 6 (Stuttgart: Frommanns Verlag).
—— (1989) *The Essence of Christianity*, trans. G. Eliot (Amherst, NY: Prometheus Books).
Fichte, J. G. (2000) *Foundations of Natural Right*, (ed.) F. Neuhouser (Cambridge: Cambridge University Press).
Franco, Paul (2000) *Hegel's Philosophy of Freedom* (New Haven and London: Yale University Press).
Hegel, G. W. F. (1896) *Lectures on the History of Philosophy*, trans. E. H. Haldane and F. H. Simson, 3 volumes (London: Kegan Paul).
—— (1955) *Die Vernunft in der Geschichte*, (ed.) J. Hoffmeister (Hamburg: Felix Meiner).
—— (1969) *Science of Logic*, trans. A. V. Miller (London: George Allen and Unwin).
—— (1971) *Philosophy of Mind*, trans. A. V. Miller (Oxford: Clarendon Press).
—— (1975) *Lectures on the Philosophy of World History. Introduction: Reason in History*, trans. H. B. Nisbet (Cambridge: Cambridge University Press).
—— (1977a) *Phenomenology of Spirit*, trans. A. V. Miller (Oxford: Oxford University Press).
—— (1977b) *The Difference Between Fichte's and Schelling's System of Philosophy*, trans. H. S. Harris and W. Cerf (Oxford: Oxford University Press).
—— (1986a) *Theorie Werkausgabe*, Band 10, (eds) E. Moldenhauer and K. M. Michel (Frankfurt am Main: Suhrkamp).
—— (1986b) *Theorie Werkausgabe*, Band 3, (eds) E. Moldenhauer and K. M. Michel (Frankfurt am Main: Suhrkamp).
—— (1986c) *Theorie Werkausgabe*, Band 2, (eds) E. Moldenhauer and K. M. Michel (Frankfurt am Main: Suhrkamp).
—— (1986d) *Theorie Werkausgabe*, Band 7, (eds) E. Moldenhauer and K. M. Michel (Frankfurt am Main: Suhrkamp).
—— (1986e) *Theorie Werkausgabe*, Band 20, (eds) E. Moldenhauer and K. M. Michel (Frankfurt am Main: Suhrkamp).
—— (1986f) *Theorie Werkausgabe*, Band 8, (eds) E. Moldenhauer and K. M. Michel (Frankfurt am Main: Suhrkamp).
—— (1986g) *Theorie Werkausgabe*, Band 6, (eds) E. Moldenhauer and K. M. Michel (Frankfurt am Main: Suhrkamp).
—— (1991a) *Elements of the Philosophy of Right*, (ed.) A. Wood (Cambridge: Cambridge University Press).
—— (1991b) *Encyclopaedia Logic*, trans. T. F. Geraets, W. A. Suchting and H. S. Harris (Indianapolis: Hackett).
—— (1995) *Lectures on the History of Philosophy*, vol. 3: Medieval and Modern Philosophy, trans. E. S. Haldane and F. H. Simson (Lincoln and London: University of Nebraska Press).
Kouvelakis, Stathis (2003) *Philosophy and Revolution: From Kant to Marx* (London: Verso).
Leopold, David (2007) *The Young Karl Marx: German Philosophy, Modern Politics, and Human Flourishing* (Cambridge: Cambridge University Press).
McCarthy, G. E. (1990) *Marx and the Ancients: Classical Ethics, Social Justice, and Nineteenth-Century Political Economy* (Savage, Maryland: Rowman and Littlefield).
McGovern, A. F. (1969) 'Marx's first political writings: The *Rheinische Zeitung*, 1842–43', in F. J. Adelman (ed.) *Demythologizing Marxism* (The Hague: Martinus Nijhoff).
Oakley, Allen (1984) *Marx's Critique of Political Economy: Intellectual Sources and Evolution. Volume 1: 1844 to 1860* (London: Routledge and Kegan Paul).

Mahowald, Mary B. (1973) 'Marx's *Gemeinschaft*: Another Interpretation', *Philosophy and Phenomenological Research*, 33, 472–88.

Marx, Karl (1975) *Early Writings*, (ed.) L. Colletti (Harmondsworth: Penguin).

Marx, Karl and Engels, Friedrich (1959) *Karl Marx Friedrich Engels Werke* (MEW), Band 1 (Berlin: Dietz Verlag).

—— (1962) *Karl Marx Friedrich Engels Werke* (MEW), Band 3 (Berlin: Dietz Verlag).

—— (1968) *Karl Marx Friedrich Engels Werke* (MEW), Ergänzungsband, erster Teil (Berlin: Dietz Verlag).

—— (1969) *Karl Marx Friedrich Engels Werke* (MEW), Band 4 (Berlin: Dietz Verlag).

—— (1975a) *Collected Works*, vol. 1 (London: Lawrence and Wishart).

—— (1975b) *Collected Works*, vol. 3 (London: Lawrence and Wishart).

—— (1976) *Collected Works*, vol. 5 (London: Lawrence and Wishart).

Neuhouser, Frederick (2000) *Foundations of Hegel's Social Theory: Actualizing Freedom* (Cambridge, Massachusetts and London: Harvard University Press).

Patten, Alan (1999) *Hegel's Idea of Freedom* (Oxford: Oxford University Press).

Plamenatz, John (1975) *Karl Marx's Philosophy of Man* (Oxford: Clarendon Press).

Rousseau, Jean-Jacques (1968) *The Social Contract*, trans. M. Cranston (Harmondsworth: Penguin).

Royce, Josiah (1892) *The Spirit Of Modern Philosophy* (Boston and New York: Houghton Mifflin Company).

Rubin, Isaak Illich (1994) 'Abstract Labour and Value in Marx's System', in S. Mohun (ed.) *Debates in Value Theory* (Basingstoke: Macmillan).

Smith, Adam (1956) *Wealth of Nations* (Raleigh, North Carolina: Hayes Barton Press).

Wallimann, Isodor (1981) *Estrangement: Marx's Conception of Human Nature and the Division of Labour* (Westport, Connecticut and London: Greenwood Press).

Wartenberg, Thomas E. (1982) '"Species-being" and "human nature" in Marx', *Human Studies*, 5, 77–95.

Wood, Allen W. (1981) *Karl Marx*, Arguments of the Philosophers (London: Routledge and Kegan Paul).

8
Labour in Modern Industrial Society

Sean Sayers

In recent years the character of work in advanced industrial society has been changing rapidly.[1] Production is being automated and computerized. The factory operated by massed workers is being superseded. Industrial labour is ceasing to be the dominant form of work. Work in offices that used to require intellectual skills is now done by computers. With the enormous growth of jobs in the service sector and the increasing use of information technology, new kinds of work are being created.

These changes are often summed up by saying that these societies are moving from the industrial to the post-industrial stage. In some important respects this notion is questionable. Arguably, the economy is still industrial, but it now operates on a global scale. If industry is ceasing to be the predominant form of work in Western Europe and North America, it is mainly because of its relocation to other parts of the world in a new global division of labour.

Nevertheless, it is beyond dispute that work is changing. With the widespread use of computers and information technology, new kinds of work have developed. Hardt and Negri's (2000; 2005) attempt to theorize these changes has been particularly influential. The older industrial forms of labour which produced material goods, they argue, are no longer dominant. They are being superseded by new 'immaterial' forms of work. Hardt and Negri situated their thought within the Marxist tradition. However, they maintain, Marx's ideas need to be rethought in the light of the new conditions of post-industrial society (Hardt and Negri, 2005, p. 140). Marx takes material production as the paradigm of work, his concept of labour is based on an industrial model. In order to describe the new post-industrial forms of work, Marx's account must be supplemented with the concepts of 'immaterial' labour and 'biopolitical' production.

My aim in this chapter is to criticize these ideas. First I will explain Marx's account of labour and show that Hardt and Negri's criticisms are based on a fundamental misreading of his thought. Then I will argue that Hardt and Negri's own account is confused and unhelpful. Properly understood and suitably developed Marx's concept of labour continues to provide a more satisfactory basis for understanding the nature of work in the modern world.

Marx's concept of labour

According to Marx, labour is an intentional activity designed to produce a change in the material world. In his early writings, he conceives of work as a process of 'objectification' through which labour is 'embodied and made material in an object' (Marx, 1975, p. 324). Later he describes labour as activity through which human beings give form to materials and thus realize themselves in the world.

> In the labour-process [...] man's activity, with the help of the instruments of labour, effects an alteration, designed from the commencement, in the material worked upon. The process disappears in the product, the latter is a use-value, Nature's material adapted by a change of form to the wants of man. Labour has incorporated itself with its subject: the former is materialized, the latter transformed.
>
> (Marx, 1961, p. 180)

This account is often taken to assume a 'productivist' model that regards work which creates a material product as the paradigm for all work. It is much criticized on this basis. Hardt and Negri along with many others point out that many kinds of work do not seem to fit this picture, some with which Marx was familiar, others that have newly developed.

There are two versions of the view that Marx has a 'productivist' model of the labour process. Some, like Hardt and Negri (2000, pp. 255–6, 92; 2005, pp. 140–2), accuse him of presupposing an industrial idea of labour. Others, by contrast, maintain that Marx's ideas are based on the paradigm of craft or even artistic work. In either case, the productivist account is treated either as self-evident (Adams, 1991) or as a 'plausible' reading of Marx's language and imagery (Habermas, 1987, pp. 65–6; Benton, 1989, p. 66). These interpretations are superficial and unsatisfactory. Marx's theory of labour is not self-evident, nor is it based upon mere metaphors or images. It is a central element of a systematic philosophical theory of the relation of human beings to nature in which the concept of labour plays a fundamental role.

This theory is never stated explicitly by Marx. Although he discusses the general character of labour in a number of places, he does not fully spell out his philosophical presuppositions (Marx, 1975; 1973; 1961; Marx and Engels, 1970). These are derived from Hegel. Hegelian assumptions underlie his thinking about labour, not only in his early writings where they are clearly evident, but throughout his work. For a valid understanding of Marx's concept of labour, as I shall demonstrate, it is essential to see it in this

Hegelian context. However, the critics I am discussing do not take this background into account. When Marx's thought is restored to its proper context and interpreted in this light, it becomes evident that the charge that he is in the grip of a 'productivist' paradigm is misconceived and unjustified. On the contrary, it is rather these critics who see all labour in these terms and project them onto Marx.

In particular, the theory that labour is a process of 'objectification' and a form-giving activity has a Hegelian origin and plays a central role in his philosophy. According to Hegel labour is a distinctively human ('spiritual') activity. Through it human beings satisfy their needs in a way that is fundamentally different to that of other animals. Non-human animals are purely natural creatures. They are driven by their immediate appetites. They satisfy their needs immediately, by devouring what is directly present in their environment. The object is simply negated and annihilated in the process. Appetites arise again, and the process repeats itself. Natural life is sustained, but no development occurs.

Human labour by contrast creates a mediated relation to our natural appetites and to surrounding nature. Work is not driven by immediate instinct. In doing it we do not simply devour and negate the object. On the contrary, gratification must be deferred while we labour to create a product for consumption only later. Through work, moreover, we fashion and shape the object, and give it a human form. We thus 'duplicate' ourselves in the world.

Through this process we establish a relation to the natural world and to our own natural desires which is mediated through work. We objectify ourselves in our product, and come to recognize our powers, embodied in the world. We develop as reflective, self-conscious beings. Moreover, Hegel maintains, relations with others are a necessary condition for these developments (Hegel, 1977, p. 118). Labour is not a purely instrumental activity to meet only individual needs, it is always and necessarily a social activity. It involves and sustains relations with others.

These ideas are taken over and developed by Marx (Sayers, 2003; 2007a). They apply not only to industrial or craft work, but to work in all its forms, as Hegel makes clear in the following passage.

> In empirical contexts, this giving of form may assume the most varied shapes. The field which I cultivate is thereby given form. As far as the inorganic realm is concerned, I do not always give it form directly. If, for example, I build a windmill, I have not given form to the air, but I have constructed a form in order to utilize the air [...] Even the fact that I conserve game may be regarded as a way of imparting form, for it is a mode of conduct calculated to preserve the object in question. The training of animals is, of course, a more direct way of giving them form, and I play a greater role in this process.
>
> (Hegel, 1991, p. 86, §56A)

Hegel here treats all these different kinds of work as form-giving activities in the sense that they are all ways of imparting form to matter. 'Productivist' types of work which create a material product, such as craft and manufacture, figure as particular kinds of labour, but it is quite clear that Hegel is not trying to assimilate all work to this model. On the contrary, he is emphasizing the great variety of forms that it may take. Its result need not be the creation of a material product, it may also be intended to conserve an object, to change the character of animals or people, to transform social relations, etc.

The wider purpose of Hegel's theory is to give a systematic account of the different forms of labour; and this is part of a still larger theme. One of Hegel's most fruitful and suggestive ideas is that subject and object change and develop in relation to each other. He thus questions the enlightenment idea that a fixed and given subject faces a separate and distinct external world. As the activity of the subject develops, the object to which the subject relates develops and changes too.

This is the organizing principle of Hegel's account of labour.[2] He conceives of different kinds of labour as different forms of relation of subject to object (nature). In characteristic fashion, moreover, the different forms of labour are arranged on an ascending scale according to the degree of mediation that they establish between subject and object. Marx draws extensively on these ideas. They provide an indispensable key to understanding Marx's account of labour, as I will now argue.

Direct appropriation

The simplest form of work, involving the most immediate relation to nature, is direct appropriation from nature, as in hunting, fishing, or the gathering of plants. In work of this kind, nature is taken as it is immediately given. This is the limiting case, still close to unmediated, natural appropriation in that it does not involve transformation of the object in itself. However, such work is a distinctively human rather than a purely natural and unmediated form of activity in that, in its human form, it is intentional, socially organized and usually involves the use of tools or weapons.[3]

Benton argues that such labour cannot be fitted into Marx's account (Marx, 1961, p. 180, quoted earlier).

> The conversion of the 'subject [i.e. object] of labour' into a use-value cannot be adequately described as 'Nature's material adapted by a *change of form* to the wants of man'. This conversion is rather a matter of selecting, extracting and relocating elements of the natural environment so as to put them at the disposal of other practices (of production or consumption). These primary labour-processes, then, *appropriate* but do not transform.
>
> (Benton, 1989, p. 69)[4]

This is not correct. Such labour does transform the object. Appropriation is a kind of transformation, it is wrong to oppose these as though they were exclusive of each other. According to Marx, direct appropriation transforms the object in that it separates it from nature (Marx, 1961, p. 178). The object is thus made useable: it is caught and killed, plucked, extracted, moved, etc. Labour is thereby embodied and objectified in it through a change of form.

It might be objected that a mere change of place affects only the object's 'external' relations and does not alter the thing itself. This objection assumes that an object's external relations are not part of its being. This view is questioned by Hegelian and Marxist philosophy which is often described as a philosophy of 'internal relations' for this reason (Sayers, 1990; Ollman, 1971). In the context of economic life the fact that game or fish have been caught makes a great deal of difference: 'a bird in the hand is worth two in the bush'.

Agriculture

As productive activity develops our relation to nature alters and subject and object are changed. This is a crucial theme in Hegel that is taken over and developed by Marx. It is overlooked by Benton, Habermas, Hardt and Negri and many other writers. With the development of agriculture we no longer relate to nature as a mere given, we cease to be entirely dependent on the contingencies of what is immediately present. We actively arrange the natural environment to meet our needs. Thus we begin the process of freeing ourselves from passive dependence on natural contingency.[5]

Furthermore, in agriculture, our relation to nature is mediated through previous work. Agriculture employs raw materials that are themselves the results of previous labour (seeds, cultivated land, livestock, etc.), and which are then used to create useful products (crops, animals), as well as the materials for future production. In the process, it satisfies not only present needs, it necessitates planning for the future and determining future needs. In these ways, agriculture involves a more mediated and developed relation of subject and object than direct appropriation.

Benton argues that agriculture is another case that does not fit the productivist model that he attributes to Marx. The products of farming are not created by forming the object but grow on their own.

> Human labour does not *bring about* the transformation of seed to plant to crop, but secures optimal conditions for an organic transformation to occur by itself. Contrast this with the carpenter who works with tools to change the form of a piece of wood.
>
> (Benton, 1992, p. 60)

Agriculture, he maintains, is primarily 'a labour of sustaining, regulating and reproducing, rather than transforming' (Benton, 1989, pp. 67–8).

Both Hegel and Marx are of course aware that farming depends on natural processes, but they do not regard this as conflicting with the view that agricultural work is a formative activity. In thinking that it must do, again Benton is taking the notion of form-giving activity to refer specifically to work which creates a material product. This is a misreading of this concept, as I have stressed. For both Hegel and Marx agriculture is 'formative' in that we realize our purposes in nature by means of it. It involves the control of natural conditions and processes for human ends.

Craft and industry

Craft work involves a further development of our relation to the object of labour and to nature. By comparison with agriculture, craft is less reliant on natural processes and less dependent on natural contingencies. It involves the creation of a material product by the direct activity of the worker. It is thus a directly formative activity. Nevertheless, as I have been arguing, it is not the only kind of formative activity. What differentiates it is that the worker uses his or her own skills to make the object from raw materials that are themselves the products of previous labour.

Craft work is the basis upon which industry develops. Under the impact of capitalism, first the division of labour and then the character of the labour process itself is transformed. There are two distinct phases to this process. The first involves what Marx (1976, pp. 25–34, 1019–23) terms the 'formal subsumption' of labour under capital. The traditional methods of work are not altered, but the social organization of work, the division of labour, is transformed.

With the introduction of machinery, the labour process itself is altered. This is what Marx (1976, pp. 34–8, 1023–5,) calls the 'real subsumption' of labour under capital. In craft production, the worker controls the tool. In industrial production, the tool is operated by the machine. The craft element is progressively eliminated from the labour process (Marx, 1973, p. 705), the industrial factory is created. Subject and object are again changed.

Moreover, with the transition from handicraft to manufacture and industry, labour becomes an intrinsically cooperative and social process. The product ceases to be something that the worker creates individually, it becomes the collective result of collective activity (Marx, 1973, p. 709). The scale of production also increases enormously. Production is no longer designed to meet particular and local needs, it becomes what Hegel (1991, p. 236, §204) calls a 'universal' process aimed at satisfying 'universal' needs by means of market exchange using the 'universal' medium of money. Thus both activity and product become more abstract and universal, and the relation of subject to object in work is further mediated and distanced.

The increasingly universal character of work is also a central theme in Marx's account. Craft labour is rooted in particularity. It involves specialized processes and skills tied to particular materials and products. Its products are designed to satisfy individual and local needs. Industry does away with these limitations.

> What characterizes the division of labour in the automatic workshop is that labour has there completely lost its specialized character [...] The automatic workshop wipes out specialists and craft-idiocy.
>
> (Marx, 1978, p. 138)

With the introduction of machinery, work is reduced to routine and mechanical operations dictated by the machine, or to the feeding, minding and maintaining of machines. However, the industrialization and mechanization of work prepares the way for still fuller forms of automation. The more mechanical work becomes, the more it can be taken over by machines altogether. In the end, the human being can 'step aside' (Marx 1973, pp. 704–5, echoing Hegel, 1991, p. 233, §198).

In this way, through the development of industry, the relation of worker to product becomes increasingly mediated and distanced. The labour process ceases to involve the direct transformation of the object by the worker. The craft element is almost entirely removed from the work activity itself. In the production process, machines act on their own, nature acts upon itself. Human purposes are realized through the use of science and technology and the application of knowledge. The craft model of production becomes less and less appropriate. However, that is not to say that the notion of labour as a form-giving activity is rendered inapplicable. On the contrary, industrial production is still formative in that it is intentional activity that gives form to materials and creates use values which embody human labour.

Universal work

Industry creates a highly mediated relation of the worker to nature and to the social world. Work become increasingly distant from the direct production process as such, and the product is no longer related in a direct way to the satisfaction of particular needs. However, even the automated industry is not the final stage of the process of development that I have been tracing, for modern industrial society has spawned entirely new kinds of work that seem to have no relation at all to the creation of material products or the satisfaction of material needs. These include commercial, administrative and other kinds of service work. Such work has become increasingly significant in modern society.

Hegel and Marx witnessed the beginning of these developments. Hegel treats commerce as a type of work essentially connected with and subordinated to manufacturing industry. However, he regards public administration and education as distinct spheres which involve the universal work of a separate class of public servants. Such work is universal in that it is abstracted from the creation of particular objects to meet particular material needs.

Furthermore, it is the outcome of the exercise of universal, intellectual and rational powers. Marx also sees such work as employing intellectual abilities and creating a more universal and abstract relation between the worker and the object.

Commerce, administration and service work do not have direct material products, yet both Hegel and Marx include these sorts of work under the same heading of formative activities as other kinds of work. As economic activity grows from a local to an industrial scale, mechanisms of administration, distribution and exchange are needed to organize production and to maintain the connections between producers and consumers. Commercial, administrative and service work are formative activities in that they create and sustain these economic and social relations.

Post-industrial work

How do these ideas stand up today with the great changes in work since Hegel and Marx's time? As we have seen, Hardt and Negri argue that Marx's concept of labour is a product of the industrial society that was emerging at the time. It must now be rethought.

What sort of rethinking is needed? Hardt and Negri are not clear about this. At times they suggest that their project is to develop and extend Marx's theory to comprehend work and politics in post-industrial society. They portray mechanization and automation as the paths along which industry has been developing since its inception, in the way that I have been arguing. Post-industrial forms of work using computers merely continue and extend this process (Hardt and Negri, 2000, p. 292). More commonly, however, they suggest that post-industrial forms of work are completely novel and necessitate a radically new theoretical approach. Marx's account of labour, they imply, presupposes an industrial and productivist model which is ceasing to apply. Industry is being superseded by the 'immaterial' production of the information economy (Hardt and Negri, 2005, pp. 107–15). New 'immaterial' forms of labour are becoming predominant.

Hardt and Negri (2000, pp. 281–5; 2005, pp. 107–9, pp. 40–3) have taken the concept of 'immaterial labour' from Lazzarato (1996) and extended it to become central to their account of post-industrial society. Immaterial labour, like all labour, they acknowledge, involves material activity: what makes it 'immaterial' is its product. Lazzarato (1996, p. 133) defines it as 'the labor that produces the informational and cultural content of the commodity'. According to Hardt and Negri (2005, p. 108), it creates 'immaterial products, such as knowledge, information, communication, a relationship, or an emotional response'. It makes not just objects but 'subjectivities' (Hardt and Negri, 2000, p. 32). It is 'biopolitical production, the production of social life itself' (Hardt and Negri, 2000, p. xiii).

These ideas have considerable initial appeal and plausibility. However, they will not bear detailed examination. Precisely what kinds of work are these concepts referring to? Hardt and Negri's account is hazy and shifting. In *Empire*, they distinguish three types of immaterial labour.

> The first is involved in an industrial production that has been informationalized and has incorporated communication technologies in a way that transforms the production process itself ...] Second is the immaterial labour of analytical and symbolic tasks [...] A third type [...] involves the production and manipulation of affect.
>
> (Hardt and Negri, 2000, p. 293)

More recently, the first of kind of work on this list has been dropped (Hardt and Negri, 2005, p. 108). Quite rightly so. Although industry uses computer control, this does not make it an 'immaterial' process. The fact that many aspects of car production, for example, are now computerized, does not mean that car making has ceased to be a material process, or that car workers are no longer engaged in material production. Although machines now do the work and shop floor workers no longer 'get their hands dirty', nevertheless, by controlling these machines, they still have material effects and produce material goods. Their work is still material and formative in character.

Symbolic labour

Hardt and Negri no longer include computerized industrial work under the heading of immaterial labour. That leaves two 'principle forms' of such work: 'symbolic' or intellectual labour and 'affective' labour, dealing with feelings or attitudes.[6] Both are types of immaterial labour, they maintain, in the sense they do not have material products nor are they designed to meet material needs. For this reason also such work seems to fall outside Marx's model of work as formative activity.

Symbolic work is primarily intellectual or artistic. It 'produces ideas, symbols, codes, texts, linguistic figures, images, and other such products' (Hardt and Negri, 2005, p. 108). It includes computer programming, graphic design, various sorts of media work, work in advertising and public relations, etc. Work of this kind, it is true, does not directly create a material product. In this respect it resembles commercial, administrative and other kinds of service work. However, it is wrong to think that a new category of immaterial labour is needed to comprehend it. The error here is to imagine that 'symbolic' work of this sort has no material result and that only work which directly creates a tangible product, like industry or craft, is material activity. It is not the case that symbolic work creates only symbols or ideas: products that are purely subjective and intangible. All labour operates by intentionally transforming matter in some way, as Marx maintains.

Symbolic labour is no exception: it involves making marks on paper, making sounds, creating electronic impulses in a computer system, or whatever. Only in this way is such activity objectified and realized as labour. In this way, all labour is material.

Economically speaking, symbolic work is not primarily concerned with creating a material product as such, but rather with the realization of value through distribution, exchange, marketing, etc. However, it is important to see that these activities are essential to the processes of material production in an industrial economy. They are needed in order to establish, maintain and facilitate the economic and social relations required for production. A modern economy cannot function without managers, accountants, computer programmers, designers, etc. Their work does not directly create a material product, nevertheless it has material effects which produce and reproduce social and economic relations and alter consciousness.

In this way, there is also an immaterial aspect to such labour, as Hardt and Negri maintain. However, the same is true for other kinds of work as well. All labour has an immaterial as well as a material aspect. For all labour takes place in a context of social relations. In altering the material world, labour at the same time sustains and alters these social relations. In the process, it affects – creates, alters – subjectivities. *All* labour, it must be stressed, does this. It is not peculiar to a special sort of 'immaterial' labour or 'biopolitical' activity alone.

> Social relations are just as much produced by men as linen, flax, etc [...] In acquiring new productive forces men change their mode of production; and in changing their mode of production, in changing the way of earning their living, they change all their social relations.
>
> (Marx, 1978, p. 103)

In a quite different way, Marx's account is also criticized by Habermas (1972, ch. 2; 1996). He conceives of work as a purely instrumental activity to meet individual needs, and he treats the sphere of communicative action and social interaction as a separate and autonomous realm. The result is a dualistic distinction between work on the one side and the sphere of social relations (communicative action and social interaction) on the other.

Hardt and Negri (2000, pp. 404–5) criticize Habermas for thus 'compartmentalizing' work and communicative action into separate spheres. In the post-industrial period with the development of immaterial labour, they argue, work has become 'biopolitical' and *essentially* communicative and social in character. By separating social relations from the sphere of work, Habermas detaches them from their real, material basis and idealizes them.

This criticism of Habermas is valid as far as it goes but it should be taken further, for it applies to his account of labour and social relations quite generally. By restricting their argument to 'immaterial' labour only, Hardt and

Negri end up reproducing a dualism between material and immaterial activity of the sort that they criticize in Habermas. All human labour is social and necessarily involves a communicative element; and at the same time all human social relations are rooted in material labour. This is Marx's theory, and neither Hardt and Negri nor Habermas presents a valid critique of it.[7]

Affective labour

There are similar problems with the account that Hardt and Negri give of their second form of immaterial labour, 'affective' labour. This is

> labor that produces or manipulates affects such as a feeling of ease, well-being, satisfaction, excitement, or passion. One can recognize affective labor, for example in the work of legal assistants, flight attendants, and fast food workers (service with a smile).
>
> (Hardt and Negri, 2005, p. 108)

Such affective labour also includes caring and helping work. According to Hardt and Negri this is a further form of 'immaterial' labour that cannot be accounted for by Marx since it has no material product.

To support their case they appeal to Hannah Arendt's philosophy. She maintains that there is a fundamental distinction between what she calls 'labour' and 'work' which Marx fails to make. What she terms 'labour' is activity to satisfy immediate consumption needs. It is concerned primarily with the maintenance of natural life, it creates no lasting products. Arendt's main examples of such labour are cleaning, cooking and other forms of housework, but her account applies to other kinds of service work as well. Hardt and Negri's 'affective' labour is 'labour' in this sense. What Arendt calls 'work', by contrast, makes an enduring object for 'use' rather than for immediate consumption. It thereby creates a 'world'. Arendt (1958, chs 3–4) criticizes Marx for treating all productive activity in terms applicable only to 'work' in this specific sense, and hence for ignoring the fact that much productive activity is devoted to 'labour' which has no enduring product.

Again we must avoid thinking that only work which results in a material product counts as work or form-giving activity for Marx. This is at the basis of both Arendt's and Hardt and Negri's criticisms of him. It is wrong to imagine that Arendt's 'labour', or Hardt and Negri's 'affective' labour have no products. Such work operates, as does all labour, by intentionally forming matter and altering the material environment in some way, including through speech and other forms of communicative action. It does not simply disappear, it is objectified in the world, it creates use values.

Affective labour is necessary in order to establish and maintain economic and social relations. Housework is needed to create and maintain a home, education to produce socialized individuals. Receptionists, social workers, cleaners, shop workers, etc., are needed to maintain social and economic relations in a modern economy. None of these activities directly creates a material product, yet they are formative activities and modes of objectification nonetheless. As with the other kinds of so-called 'immaterial' production discussed earlier, they have material results which serve to produce and reproduce social relations and subjectivity.

Hardt and Negri are aware of some of the problems with the concept of immaterial labour to which I have been pointing. The 'labor involved in all immaterial production', they admit,

> remains material [...] What is immaterial is *its product*. We recognize that *immaterial labor* is a very ambiguous term in this regard. It might be better to understand [it] [...] as 'biopolitical labor', that is, labor that creates not only material goods but also relationships and ultimately social life itself.
>
> (Hardt and Negri, 2005, p. 109)

The concept of 'biopolitical' labour does not resolves these problems, they go deeper than Hardt and Negri appreciate. As I have argued, just as all immaterial labour necessarily involves material activity, so all material labour has an immaterial aspect in that it alters not only the material immediately worked upon but also social relations and subjectivity. There is no clear distinction between material and immaterial labour in this respect. Resort to the concept of 'biopolitical' activity is no help. The same point applies. *All* productive activity is 'biopolitical' to some degree in that all labour transforms relationships and social life. In this way all labour is ultimately a form of self-creation (Marx, 1973, p. 712). In short the notion of 'biopolitical' activity is no more satisfactory than that of 'immaterial' labour as a way to distinguish post-industrial forms of work.

Political implications

Hardt and Negri are right to argue that work has changed radically since the industrial revolution. Despite the initial plausibility of their account, however, their categories of immaterial labour and biopolitical activity are little help in understanding these changes. Properly understood and suitably developed, Marx's theory of work as objectification and form-giving activity provides a more satisfactory and illuminating conceptual framework for understanding the nature of work, including its new post-industrial forms.

According to this theory, different kinds of labour involve different degrees of mediation in our relation to nature ranging from the most immediate relationship of direct appropriation to the most abstract and universal kinds of work. This is primarily a logical sequence rather than a historical one (though historical changes are associated with it). In Hegel's case, there is also an ethical and political dimension to his account. With the development of our relation to nature through labour comes the emergence of self-consciousness from immediate natural conditions towards a developed, reflective and mediated state and with that a growth of freedom.

It is not immediately clear whether Marx adopts a similar perspective. His theory of labour is developed in an economic context. In purely economic terms, Marx does not differentiate between different kinds of labour, still less make a hierarchy of them. Like other classical economists, in the labour theory of value he equates different forms of labour together as 'abstract' labour. This may appear to suggest that he does not rank different kinds of work morally or politically. But that is not the case: there is clearly an evaluative dimension to Marx's theory. The writers I have been discussing all criticize it in this respect, and they are not wrong in doing so. However, they fail to take account of the Hegelian dimension to Marx's thought and so misunderstand its implications.

The view that Marx's account relies on a 'romantically transfigured prototype of handicraft activity' (Habermas, 1987, pp. 65–6, cf. Benton discussed earlier) is a complete misconception. Marx could not be clearer in his rejection of the craft ideal. He is scornful of the 'idiocy' and small mindedness engendered by handicraft work (Marx, 1978, p. 138). His critical attitude is grounded on the account of the labour process that I have been describing which sees craft work as a limited and purely individual activity, aimed at the satisfaction of particular and local needs.

For Marx, the coming of industry means a liberation from these constraints. This is the positive aspect of its development. However, the change from craft to industrial production takes place under the contradictory conditions of capitalism in which the pressure towards universality inherent in industry comes into conflict with the system of private ownership and the free market in which it develops. The result is the 'devastation caused by a social anarchy which turns every economic progress into a social calamity' (Marx, 1961, p. 487). In the longer term, however, the coming of industry means the elimination of brute physical effort and the reduction of repetitive and mechanical toil. Work becomes more productive, rational, and universal, hence 'more worthy of [...] human nature' (Marx, 1971, p. 820).[8]

These points about Marx are widely understood. Marxism is thus often seen as a philosophy rooted in industrial conditions that idealizes industrial labour and the industrial working class. This is Hardt and Negri's position. However, the reading that I have been proposing suggests a different view. Marx is a historical thinker. At the time he was writing, industry was becoming the predominant form of production and the industrial proletariat was emerging as the most advanced political force. But things have moved on. Hardt and Negri are right to insist that Marx's ideas must be rethought and developed to take account of this.

Marxism should not be seen as eternally linked to an industrial perspective. Indeed, its underlying philosophy suggests that industry is not the highest development of our productive and creative powers. It points to higher forms of labour, beyond industry, in more universal kinds of work. Hegel assigns this mainly to a universal class of civil servants. This is not Marx's idea. Marx envisages the eventual emergence of forms of work in which the universal tendencies of modern industry are realized, and in which

> the detail-worker of to-day, crippled by one and the same trivial operation, and thus reduced to the mere fragment of a man, [will be replaced] by the fully developed individual, fit for a variety of labours [...] to whom the different social functions he performs, are but so many modes of giving free scope to his own natural and acquired powers.
>
> (Marx, 1961, p. 488)

It is easy to dismiss this as a utopian dream but that would be a mistake. Aspects of it are already coming true, though within the contradictory conditions of capitalism. In contemporary society, as Hardt and Negri observe,

> jobs for the most part are highly mobile and involve flexible skills [...] They are characterized in general by the central role played by knowledge, information, affect and communication.
>
> (Hardt and Negri, 2000, p. 285)

As I have argued, Marx's concept of labour, properly understood, continues to provide a more helpful basis than the concepts of immaterial labour and biopolitical production for understanding these developments. In more favourable conditions, such universal work might extend our rational and creative powers. It could become something we do not only because we are forced by economic necessity but as a free activity. This is Marx's ideal (Marx, 1971, p. 820).

Notes

1. This is an edited and revised version of Sayers, 2007b. An earlier draft was first read at a Marx and Philosophy Society Seminar on 28 May 2005. I am grateful to David McNally for his comments.
2. This is also the organizing theme in Hegel's accounts of the development of 'spirit' (Hegel, 1977; 1975; 1988). The first seeds of this theory of labour appear very early in Hegel's work (Hegel, 1979). It is well worked out by time of the Jena lectures (Hegel, 1983). It is presented again in Hegel, 1991, pp. 231–39, §§196–207. This work was well known to Marx. The earlier accounts were not published in Marx's time and would not have been available to him.

3. 'All those things which labour merely separates from immediate connexion with their environment, are subjects [i.e. objects] of labour spontaneously provided by Nature. Such are fish which we catch and take from their element, water, timber which we fell in the virgin forest, and ores which we extract from their veins' (Marx, 1961, p. 178). Such work is mentioned briefly by Hegel (1997, pp. 179–80, §103).
4. Cf. Grundmann, 1991; Benton, 1992, p. 59ff.
5. Of course, agriculture remains dependent on the natural contingencies of the seasons, climate, weather, etc. until we begin to free ourselves from these factors too.
6. The distinction between these forms is not clear cut, as Hardt and Negri (2005, p. 108) acknowledge, 'most actual jobs involving immaterial labor combine these two forms'.
7. I am grateful to David McNally for suggesting this line of argument to me.
8. This is the logic of Marx's account. It should be Hegel's outlook too, but Hegel does not fully accept the implications of his own theory (Sayers, 2003).

Bibliography

Adams, William (1991) 'Aesthetics: Liberating the Senses', in T. Carver (ed.) *The Cambridge Companion to Marx* (Cambridge: Cambridge University Press).
Arendt, Hannah (1958) *The Human Condition* (Chicago: University of Chicago Press).
Benton, Ted (1989) 'Marxism and Natural Limits: An Ecological Critique and Reconstruction', *New Left Review*, 178, 51–86.
—— (1992) 'Ecology, Socialism and the Mastery of Nature', *New Left Review*, 194, 55–74.
Grundmann, Reiner (1991) 'The Ecological Challenge to Marxism', *New Left Review*, 187, 103–20.
Habermas, Jürgen (1972) *Knowledge and Human Interests* (London: Heinemann).
—— (1987) *The Philosophical Discourse of Modernity: Twelve Lectures*, trans. F. G. Lawrence (Cambridge: Polity).
—— (1996) 'Labor and Interaction: Remarks on Hegel's Jena Philosophy of Mind', in J. O'Neill (ed.) *Hegel's Dialectic of Desire and Recognition* (Albany, NY: SUNY Press), pp. 123–48.
Hardt, Michael and Negri, Antonio (2000) *Empire* (Cambridge, MA, London: Harvard University Press).
—— (2005) *Multitude: War and Democracy in the Age of Empire* (London: Hamish Hamilton).
Hegel, G. W. F. (1975) *Aesthetics*, trans. T. M. Knox (Oxford: Clarendon Press).
—— (1977) *Phenomenology of Spirit*, trans. A. V. Miller (Oxford: Clarendon Press).
—— (1979) *System of Ethical Life (1802/3) and First Philosophy of Spirit (Part III of the System of Speculative Philosophy 1803/4)*, trans. H. S. Harris and T. M. Knox (Albany: State University of New York Press).
—— (1983) *Hegel and the Human Spirit*, trans. L. Rauch (Detroit: Wayne State University Press).
—— (1988) *Lectures on the Philosophy of Religion. One-Volume Edition. The Lectures of 1827*, trans. R. F. Brown, P. C. Hodgson and J. M. Stewart (Berkeley: University of California Press).
—— (1991) *Elements of the Philosophy of Right*, trans. H. B. Nisbet (Cambridge: Cambridge University Press).

—— (1997) *Lectures on Natural Right and Political Science*, trans. J. M. Stewart and P. C. Hodgson (Berkeley: University of California Press).

Lazzarato, Maurizio (1996) 'Immaterial Labor', in P. Virno and M. Hardt (eds) *Radical Thought in Italy: A Potential Politics* (Minneapolis: University of Minnesota Press).

Marx, Karl (1961) *Capital*, vol. 1, trans. S. Moore and E. Aveling (Moscow: Foreign Languages Publishing House).

—— (1971) *Capital*, vol. 3 (Moscow: Progress).

—— (1973) *Grundrisse*, trans. M. Nicolaus (Harmondsworth: Penguin).

—— (1975) 'Economic and Philosophical Manuscripts of 1844', in *Early Writings* (Harmondsworth: Penguin).

—— (1976) 'The Result of the Immediate Process of Production', in *Capital*, vol. 1 (Harmondsworth: Penguin).

—— (1978) *The Poverty of Philosophy* (Peking: Foreign Languages Press).

Marx, Karl and Engels, Friedrich (1970) *The German Ideology Part I* (New York: International Publishers).

Ollman, Bertell (1971) *Alienation: Marx's Conception of Man in Capitalist Society* (Cambridge: University Press).

Sayers, Sean (1990) 'Marxism and the Dialectical Method: A Critique of G. A. Cohen', in S. Sayers and P. Osborne (eds) *Socialism, Feminism and Philosophy: A Radical Philosophy Reader* (London: Routledge), pp. 140–68.

—— (2003) 'Creative Activity and Alienation in Hegel and Marx', *Historical Materialism*, 11, 1, 107–28.

—— (2007a) 'Individual and Society in Marx and Hegel', *Science and Society*, 71, 1, 84–102.

—— (2007b) 'Marx's Concept of Labor', *Science and Society*, 71, 4, 431–54.

9
The Concept of Money

Christopher J. Arthur

In the history of philosophy the greatest minds have been aware that the existence and power of money poses a problem. One need only mention Aristotle. Of course, if it is accepted that *Capital* is as much a work of philosophy as it is of economics, then pride of place must go to Marx. That money is a philosophically interesting phenomenon might seem surprising when we consider its familiarity to us. But what is always at hand physically may yet be hard to fathom ontologically.

Within economics proper there has always been a split between those who dismiss money as a veil occluding the 'real economy' and those who grasp that what is new about the modern world is the hegemony of monetary relations. Orthodox readings of Marx place him in the former camp, but he is better understood as recognising the importance of money in shaping economic processes.

However, here I do not enter into exegetical disputes; I present my own take on the concept of money. I argue that value is a peculiar social form which arises out of the practice of exchange in such a manner that value exists only when the dialectic of commodity relations results in money. The main point of the chapter is that the concept of money requires elucidation through drawing on the resources of Hegel's logic.[1]

Systematic dialectic

This discussion is part of a broader project (see Arthur, 2002) to provide a systematic dialectical reconstruction of the categories of Marx's *Capital*, for which it is a crucial case. *Systematic* dialectic is a method of exhibiting the inner articulation of a given whole. Science in treating such a totality must take the shape of *a system* comprising a set of categories capturing the forms and relations constitutive of the totality. Hence the presentation of the totality in thought is a *systematic dialectic of categories*.

However, more than method is at issue. Hegel's logic has two characteristics besides its systematicity: (1) the forms of thought are said to be sufficiently autonomous to be *self-moving*, (2) the conceptual framework is therefore said to be 'the truth' of reality. This is why he called himself an idealist. I believe that capital has a similar ideality, but it is a real ideality which imposes itself on the content of economic life.

The relevance of Hegel's logic to my reconstruction of Marx's categories flows from the *reality* of that 'practical abstraction' in exchange predicated on the *identification,* as 'values', of *heterogeneous* commodities. The different goods concerned play the role of *bearers* of this new social determination. They become subject to the *value form*. So the value form of the commodity rests on a split between value as the *identity* of commodities premised on their equivalence in exchange and their material *diversity* differentiating them from each other as use-values.

Hegel's logic, too, springs from the evacuation of contingent empirical instantiations to leave the category as such. In my view a significant homology obtains between the movement of exchange, generating a *practical* abstraction from the natural specificity of commodities, and the movement of thought, generating a system of *logical* categories. In both, the self-moving forms impose themselves on the real material they address. As a result, it is possible to illuminate the forms of value with the categories of Hegel's logic. At the same time, whereas the forms of thought may be considered 'free-standing', the forms of value require always material bearers. Hence there is a limit to the ideality of value.

Value as a social form

This approach to critical political economy claims that the determinant of economic categories is *social* form, not the *natural* basis of the economic metabolism. I reject the naturalistic approach that sees in labour, its allocation, and its productivity, the natural determinations reflected in forms of social recognition such as prices and profits. Instead, I see social practice *constituting* social forms, centrally the value form, within which is inscribed productive activity. Following from this, value itself is not given *prior* to its forms, but is rather constituted in and through the development of exchange relations.

The 'value-form' theory of money holds that money is no 'veil' of the 'real' material content of economic relations; it is essential to value relations, not merely the shape in which an underlying matter is expressed. Only money makes value *actual*. What is essential to commodities is not to be found *in* them through some reductive abstraction. It arises only in exchange relations and hence must be discovered in the *relation* of one commodity to another, as determined in and through their *outward* forms, and especially their relation to money. So the search for value may take two routes: one route is to go *into* commodities to find in each the same substratum, for example 'abstract labour'; the other route is to go *out* from commodities to their relations to see if these relations posit value as a form of their social existence. Because production units are dissociated one from another, labours become social only in so far as their products are exchanged. Although labour always naturally takes the form of *concrete* labour, which is as heterogeneous as commodities themselves, the consequence is that these labours are socially cognised in value only as abstract. In truth the peculiar abstractness of the labour producing commodities is the *result* of the social reality of exchange, not its ground. Moreover the process of exchange takes hold of many things that are not products, and in so far as it circulates products, these are given value forms, such as price, that do not make explicit their origin in production. In its immediacy the commodity has a pure form.

If naturalism were correct, then money would be no problem for theory. Since all commodities would be inherently valuable, including gold, then gold money would be merely a numeraire, a typical commodity in being a value, but special in its designated function as a measure of the others, and as medium of their circulation. However, it makes no sense to presuppose that a commodity in isolation *has* value. Value has a purely social reality, and it emerges from commodity relations.

If, however, value is a socially constituted form, its concept cannot be glossed in the usual way, for example by analogy with a natural feature of commodities, such as weight. Because of this, money has a peculiar role in ensuring that the actuality of value is posited in practice. The universal aspect of commodities is secured only in so far as it is posited through their common relation to a universal equivalent, namely money. This money form does not *represent* the presupposed 'value' of commodities, rather, it *posits* it as their form of social being.

One way of thinking about this is by analogy with Kant's 'Copernican revolution' wherewith he made the objects conform to their cognition. In our case the commodities must conform to how they are *practically* known through the forms of value. Instead of commodities being given as values and measured in money, money is what allows commodities to be known as values in the first place, through transcendentally synthesising the commodity manifold. Money is not simply the provision of a standard of comparison for commodities already inserted in the value dimension; it *constitutes* the value dimension. The monetary form is the condition of possibility of a unitary sphere of value relations.

Let us examine more closely the form of value. From the observation that all commodities are exchangeable, directly or indirectly, in definite proportions arises the postulate that all the many exchange values possessed by a commodity share a unitary essence, an *inherent* value. But is this presupposition well-founded?

The simplest form of value implicit in commodity relations is: '*The value of A is B*'. I follow Marx in seeing the commodity in 'relative' form (A) as the commodity whose value is manifested, and the commodity in 'equivalent' form (B) merely as the material shape of the value of A. Moreover, as Marx insightfully observes, B is present here as a *natural body*, it is not present as a value. It is not a value, because there is not yet posited the presupposition that there *is* any such thing as value prior to this relation. Even if we assume this is a *value relation*, value cannot be present in the natural body of either commodity because the heterogeneity of such bodies requires the form of value to abstract such features away. In this sense value is what the commodity as a natural body is *not*. As Marx saw, if A cannot thus express value in its own body, it yet posits the body of B as the locus of the value it must exclude from itself.

Ideally value is determined in opposition to the heterogeneity of use-value. But value must *appear* if it is to have any actuality. Immediately a commodity appears as a use-value; but, because the value of a commodity is defined in opposition to its own use-value, it cannot appear *there*. However, in the *form* of exchange-value, the value of A appears as the natural body of B. So there are here two worlds, which predicate themselves on use-value in *inverted* fashion. In essence value *is not-use-value* (of A), but as appearance value *is use-value* (of B). The peculiarity of the equivalent form is that in it the commodity's natural body counts not as itself but as value. So the two worlds, the 'sensuous and supersensuous'[2], are here immediately one. This duality is the germ of money. 'It is, so to speak, the cell form or, as Hegel would say, the *in-itself of money*' (Marx, 1983a, p. 28).

Money is posited as the universal equivalent form of value. The commodity serving as the universal equivalent is necessarily present as a natural body. But it secures the actuality of value by virtue of its relations to commodities, unifying them in their common relation to what they are not. All commodities must exclude one commodity, say gold, from the relative form in order to serve as the universal equivalent. The natural body of gold is equivalent to *value as such* according to the commodities in relative form. However, this is not like pieces of iron counting as weight as such, because iron already has weight, hence serves as representative of the class of weighty things. But gold is not yet known to have a value, rather it is posited as all commodities' value by them. The expression 'iron weight' is merely metonymic because weight is simply a property of iron, but in the case of 'gold money' it really is the case that gold is simply the shell of a 'social substance' posited in the relation of commodities and money, rather than gold naturally having value. In weight, weighing is secondary to the givenness of weight, but in value, the expression of value in a price is primary and the reflection of value into commodities is secondary.

Since value is not naturally grounded, it is not possible to take gold as *already* value, hence a suitable measure for commodities. Gold can figure here only as it *immediately appears*, namely as a natural body. Its goldenness is not the utterance of its own value, but the outward manifestation of the commodities' value. So commodities can actualise their identity in value only *outside* them since they are not instantiations of a *pre-given* essence. Thus money, as their universal equivalent, opposes itself to commodities by appearing as a commodity alongside them designated as the actuality of value.

The concrete universal

In the first edition of *Capital*, Marx draws a very illuminating analogy to make the strangeness of the relation between money and commodities clear: 'It is as if alongside and external to lions, tigers, rabbits, and all other actual animals [...] there existed also in addition the *animal*, the individual incarnation of the entire animal Kingdom' (Marx, 1983a, p.37). This example is a reminiscence of Hegel's point:

> 'Animal as such' cannot be pointed out; only a definite animal can ever be pointed at. 'The animal' does not exist; on the contrary, this expression refers to the *universal* nature of single animals, and each existing animal is something that is much more concretely determinate, something particularised. But 'to be animal', the kind considered as the universal, pertains to the determinate animal and constitutes its determinate essentiality. If we were to deprive a dog of its animality we could not say what it is. Things as such have a persisting, inner nature, as well as an outward existence.
>
> (Hegel, 1991, §24A)

Now the peculiarity of (gold) money is that as 'the universal commodity' it *can* be 'pointed out'. The universal aspect uniting commodities is presupposed to be value, and in money this 'inner nature' is posited as 'a thing' *beside* them.

Is value a 'concrete universal' in Hegel's sense of the term? Hegel rejects the analytic opposition between the universal as wholly abstract and the singular as concrete. His dialectical view is that the universal is no mere abstraction, no mere abstract commonality, it is a *concrete universal* that comprehends within itself its particularisations. Now, as we have just seen in the passage where Hegel discussed 'the animal', it is not the case that the concrete universal exists *alongside* the individuals. The universal is understood as the *inner* essence of the singulars, making them what they are. Why, with the concept of value, if this is to be considered as such a concrete universal, is it not found *within* the commodities but outside them, incarnate in a money commodity that reflects their universal essence? It is because commodities as materially heterogeneous are not essentially values. The *generation* of value as a concrete concept is secured only when money as its material existence gives commodities a universal form in price. While the universal thought-form comprehends its particularisations *in thought*, the value form comprehends its particularisations through the *objective relation* in which such money stands to commodities. This is why a material bearer of the value concept is required *alongside* the commodities it comprehends as values.

Hegel explicitly mocks the idea that the universal exists as particular apart from its instantiations. He writes:

> The *universal* must be distinguished from the *particular*, according to its proper determination. Taken formally, and put *side by side* with the particular, the universal itself becomes something particular too [...] as if someone who wants fruit, for instance, were to reject cherries, pears, raisins, etc., because they are cherries, pears, raisins, but *not* fruit.
>
> (Hegel, 1991, §13)[3]

However, in the case of value just this situation obtains. Marx writes: 'Though a commodity may, alongside its real shape (iron for instance), possess an ideal value-shape or an imagined gold-shape in the form of its price, it cannot simultaneously be both real iron and real gold' (Marx, 1976, pp. 197–8). The owner of the iron cannot go to the owner of some other earthly commodity, and refer him to the price of iron as proof that it is as good as gold.

The peculiar necessity for value, as a concrete universal, to appear in the relations of commodities means money must take the shape of the analogue of 'the animal', namely a locus of value as such *alongside* the commodities. For goods to have 'value' as their 'inner nature' requires that this presupposition be *imposed* on them through the commodity-form, and more precisely through their external relation to money. Yet the opposite appears to be the case: that money recognises a value they already have.

Fetishism

In *Capital* the derivation of money, as value in autonomous form, is followed by the section on 'the fetishism of commodities'. However, it is worth remark that originally, in the Appendix to the first edition, fetishism was listed as the fourth 'peculiarity of the equivalent form'. The lessons of this are twofold: (1) that fetishism has its origin in the simple equivalent form and (2) that fetishism appears in its most dazzling shape with money.

Fetishism is a metaphor taken from anthropology, in which some material object is given human, or even superhuman, powers. It is very apposite, therefore, to the power of money. But Marx argues the commodity itself is a fetish. The political economists argued that gold is no more special than pots and pans. But insofar as they thought all commodities inherently valuable, they remained prisoners to fetishism.

The germ of fetishism, as we just said, lies in the peculiarity of the equivalent form of value, in which the natural body of one commodity serves as the value of another. 'The natural form of the commodity becomes the value-form' (Marx, 1976, p. 148; translation corrected). But at this point it is not hard to see that this results from the relation in which the commodity in relative form stands to it; indeed Marx says that the one in equivalent form is purely 'passive' here, when it is posited by that in relative form as its equivalent. With the universal equivalent form things are more developed, because all commodities now express their value in the same body; the latter therefore appears relative to any single commodity as already the appropriate material in which value is to be expressed. With money, the inversion of active and passive is completed. Now commodities are recognised as values only if money deigns to grant validity to these supplicants. It exerts a force of *attraction* on commodities, so to speak, rather than being passive. Having direct exchangeability it can metamorphose into each and every commodity at will. This social power is *intrinsic* to it, and when it measures the value of other commodities, it acts as if they too naturally possess intrinsic value. However, it is important to take on board Marx's insight that this is no mental confusion; this derangement has objective validity when systemically posited (Marx, 1976, p. 169).

Value and price

In what follows I explore the homology between the value categories and those of Hegel's logic. To illuminate the role of money I shall draw on Hegel's 'Doctrine of the Concept'. I begin with its initial sections that together make up the so-called Subjective Concept: The Concept as Such, the Judgement and the Syllogism. First I recapitulate Hegel's presentation; then I show its relevance to money.

'The Concept as Such' has three moments, Universality, Particularity and Singularity. Since the Concept as Such is purely formal, Hegel stresses that 'Singularity' is not to be taken to mean single things, *singulars*; (the latter appear in judgements, we shall see, when the formal moments split into distinctly separate finite instances). Now an important subtlety flowing from the difference between 'Singularity' and 'the singular' is that the movement of particularisation is doubled. At a purely *formal* level the Concept particularises itself to 'Singularity', but at the level of *reality* there are many identical *singulars*, each of them particularisations of the Concept. Each is numerically different from others. Yet as the implicit instantiation of a universal each is capable of reflecting it.

This reflection of the moments of the Concept takes shape as judgement. The judgement is the stepping of the concept into finite determination, says Hegel, that is, the parting of Universality/Particularity/Singularity. But in the Judgement the separate moments of the Concept are yet related of course.

The abstract paradigm of the Judgement is 'The Singular is the Universal'. The moment of particularity validates this Judgement if the Singular is in truth a determinable particularisation of the Universal. From this form the Concept passes into the 'Syllogism'.

Hegel says this about the relation of the conceptual and the real:

> Everything is a concept, the existence of which is the differentiation of its *moments* in such a way that its *universal* nature gives itself outward reality through *particularity*, and in this way [...] makes itself *singular*. Or, conversely, the actual is a *singular* which raises itself by means of *particularity* to *universality* and makes itself identical with itself.
>
> (Hegel, 1991, §181; my translation)

Now let us see how all this can be drawn upon to analyse the form of value, more specifically the form of price. The 'Value Concept' must be articulated formally as Universality/Particularity/Singularity we know. We have also seen earlier that there must be a material bearer of this concept, alongside the commodities. But since, at first, the only relation commodities have is to other commodities, a single commodity must be posited in this role. Paradoxically, in order for their value to be posited as the essence of commodities, it has to be incarnate in a unique commodity, such as gold. This is money. Moreover because 'amount' is the only particularisation of value logically possible, the singularity of the concept is given as *an amount* of money.

This brings us to the Judgement, which in our material instantiation of Hegel's paradigm is: 'This commodity is valuable'. The determinate judgement 'how valuable?' can be expressed only in money. Thus a singular commodity is shown to be valuable in virtue being equated to so much money. As Hegel says of the Judgement: '[We] see one and the same object double, first as its singular actuality, and then in [...] its Concept: the single raised into its universality.' (Hegel, 1969, pp. 630–1; translation emended).

This doubling requires in our case a *material* separation; money is really present apart from the commodity because only thus can the value of the commodity be presented to it. Both sides are required for the concept to realise itself. It is impossible for value to exist only in pure form, adequately captured by money; there has to be something *to be valued* in the first place. This means there are two kinds of particularisation of value. The commodity as priced is particularised ideally as a simple sum of value incarnated in money; but the commodity as material object is multiply particularised concretely in *bodies* of value. There are *multiple* similar coats of the same value, where there is only *one* coat price. In the coat, commodity value exists consubstantially with use value as if, like use value, it existed naturally in this material form. There are, as it were, bits of value in the world. As tied to a material shell these values are numerically distinct and can be destroyed both materially and through revolutions in market conditions.

As for money: gold is itself a particular commodity which, in order to exchange with a single commodity, must itself appear as another such singular. But a piece of gold presents itself as the *absolute singularity* of value because it is not, like other commodities, a single locus of value among others; it is *uniquely* posited as incarnating in itself value as a substance. In a sum of money the value universal hence appears as its own instance.

The following diagram (Diagram 9.1) shows how these sides of value, money and commodities, interpenetrate.

Diagram 9.1

'*Concept*' *of Value*

Universality

|

Particularity (amount)

Single commodities   Singularity (an amount of money)

The Judgement of Worth

The value of this commodity is two ounces of gold

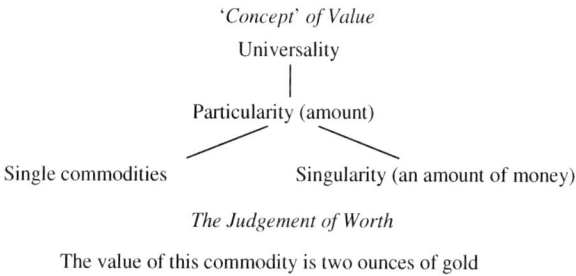

In Diagram 9.1 the double movement of particularisation results in both the presence of money as an amount of itself and the presence of single commodities, which in virtue of the parallel particularisation, contain an amount of value. These moments are explicitly reflected against one another when a commodity is worth such and such an amount of money.

The commodity as always materially singular seems opposed to value because of its immediacy as a natural body. Money as *pure form* of value appears opposed to commodities. However, the link exists in the judgement of worth. Here value has particularised itself to a definite amount of *money*. Conversely, *commodities* are raised above their status as material singulars to that of particular embodiments of value. But there is no immediate *identity* in these particular shapes of value, only a *relation*, because one side of the equation is the value in ideal shape, as a moment of a universal concept, and on the other value is posited in single material shapes. Thus, when money, as the tangible concept of value, appears as a particular sum, it is not therewith constituted as *a* singular, it remains a *notional* particularisation. Conversely the commodity *is a singular* because of its material difference from others, and it is 'a value' only because it is valued by a particular amount of money. However, as 'a value' the commodity cannot be itself *immediately* an *instance* of the universal, just because it is *not* value *outside* the mediation of the price form. Albeit it is implicitly value, its actual *valuation* requires money.

We see that the two-way determination of the Concept I cited from Hegel is here present in Diagram 9.1. He spoke of the universal determining itself through particularity to the singular, and said its complement is the rising of the singular by means of particularity to universality. But the value concept is not inherent to a specific thing (in the way that 'animality' is to a dog); its ideal and material moments fall apart because they are *distributed* across money and commodities. The mediating moment between value as universal and the commodity as singular instance is particularisation when the right amounts of value are equated.

While money is the bearer of the pure concept of value, the real determinacy of value is given in judgements of worth. But for a commodity to be elevated to a value through such a judgement, money must meet it halfway by appearing in an empirically operational form; this requires a *standard of price*. There is a conceptual distinction between money as measure of value and money as standard of price. The former *constitutes* value as a measurable entity; the latter, on the presupposition that value *is* measurable, supplies a common standard for comparing values of commodities. At the level of the pure concept money notionally grants dimensionality to value, that is, it is measure-giving. At the level of finitude, commodities must be confronted with an operational standard of price in order to make judgements of worth possible, a money measure. Money appears as a finite amount of itself that can be set equal to every commodity, as if it were one among them; as if price were just souped-up barter.

However, there is still a difference of form that is significant, even in the case where money takes shape as a standardised commodity, for example a gold coin. The singular commodity *has* a value recognised in the form of its price. The gold coin by contrast *is* value, as incarnating the singularity of the concept. It mediates in finite form the value dimension, so as to allow the valuation of commodities. This function does not depend on any value its material 'has', if any. Thus it is common for there to be a discrepancy between an identical nominal, and variable real, value of metal coins; yet they continue to function as a standard of price indifferently. (Abrasion, clipping and debasement reduce the value of the gold content; but the ideality of money requires its emancipation from such material problems.)

In the form of price all sorts of commodities worth £3 are worth an identical £3, which shows that money is their materially existent concept, whereas commodities are the real world instantiations of value, each separately worth £3, and all together they are worth a multiple of this (that is, another *particular* amount, not a *class* of separate amounts).

The provision of such a determinate *standard of price*, and the practice of its use, then generates the illusion that money is just a numeraire. Money as a 'piece' of itself pretends to be something that *has* value (which may be claimed of gold, just to confuse things) rather than being the necessary *form* of value. In price, money acts *as if* it were just a numeraire, and commodities acts *as if* they were inherently valuable. But in truth value achieves conceptual determinacy only through price.

We do not need to consider most of the judgement-forms covered by Hegel because we are concerned only with the quantitative determination of value, there being no qualitative difference. Similarly, when we pass to the forms of the Syllogism, the only form relevant is that which Hegel calls the syllogism of equality. Given in our case, it is the inference that if the value of A equals the value of B, and the value of B equals the value of C, then the value of A equals the value of C. Since value is actual only in price, this implies the transitivity of prices.

Hegel argues that a self-sustaining system of truth is achieved when the premises of every syllogism are results of other syllogisms. This is obviously true if we shuffle the order of the syllogism of equality of price. Whatever two equalities are taken first, transitivity ensures the third. We have a consistent value space instead of a set of contingent prices, still less a mess of ad hoc barters. In the set of complementary prices, the concept of value is thus articulated as a unitary whole. It has universal range of reference and singleness of form as the totality itself.

This brings me to the end of the first section of the logic of money, its 'formal' concept in price. Next we shall draw on the second section of Hegel's 'Doctrine of the Concept', 'Objectivity', in thematising exchange.

The Metamorphoses of Commodities

When judgements of worth coincide, they may result in an exchange. This move from the 'subjective' conceptuality of value to its positing in real transactions corresponds to Hegel's logic of 'Objectivity'. Hegel's first category of Objectivity is that of an immense collection or heap of things. He then develops the logical order of their interactions in 'Mechanism', 'Chemism', and 'Teleology'. The heap becomes a universe governed by an inherent dynamic.

In thematising the dialectic of exchange, and 'the metamorphoses of commodities' (Marx, 1976), we begin with the simple exchange of one commodity for another. This corresponds to Hegel's logic of 'Mechanism'. He begins with such a primitive notion of objective movement because this sphere is marked by the explicit difference of things from each other as mere numerical difference. The unity of the Concept is thus not yet explicitly posited.

In our terms, the social instantiation in exchange and circulation of a homogeneous sphere of value is not secured if agents have discrepant ideas about judgements of worth because no objective principle is at work. The 'action' of giving commodity A for commodity B requires the 'reaction' of giving commodity B for commodity A. However, just as logically correlated judgements allow a conclusion to be drawn, agreement in judgements of worth may allow a bargain to be concluded.

But the form of commensuration is required for a 'law' of exchange to obtain. Even if it is presupposed that both commodities are of identical value and thus share common ground, this 'centre of attraction' remains too implicit to have effect. Only given the presence of money as 'value for itself' is a principle of unity explicitly put; that buyer and seller accept the same price expresses the identity of value with itself objectively.

Hegel's principle of 'Chemism', pertaining to the affinity of complementary determinations, is the parallel here. The identity of action and reaction in exchange is refigured as the complementarity of purchase and sale. As a dyadic transaction a bargain may lack social validity; but just as the ideality of value implies the necessity of transitive prices, so in reality the activity of arbitrage realises the unity of markets.

The two opposite movements, sale and purchase, exist at the same time in every transaction; but if they are differentiated sequentially as a sale followed by a purchase, a new logic, and a new function of money emerge. This is when I sell one commodity (C) *in order* to have the money (M) to buy another. This sequence (C—M, M—C) is the objective correlate of the notion of value just discussed. Marx is more specific in his 1859 *Contribution to the Critique of Political Economy*:

> The C at each of the two extremes of the circuit C—M—C has a different formal relation to M. The first C is a particular commodity which is compared with money as the universal commodity, whereas in the second phase money as the universal commodity is compared with an individual commodity. The formula C—M—C can therefore be reduced to the abstract logical syllogism P—U—I; whereas particularity forms the first extreme, universality characterises the common middle term and individuality signifies the final extreme.
>
> (Marx and Engels, 1987, pp. 330–1)

This use of the syllogistic form by Marx may not be immediately perspicuous unless it is thought of in terms of the point of the two exchanges. In the first C—M, the C as such has no interest for the exchanger who is endeavouring to gain money (which itself exchanges against *all* commodities); what interests him from this point of view is merely that the C be *some* particularisation of the universal. In the second exchange M—C, by contrast, the point is to secure, not just any C but that whose individual characteristics will satisfy a certain need, and hence leaves circulation as a singular.

With money as a mediator, commodities are brought together within circulation. Here the function of money as measure of value in price gives a ground for the ability of money to serve as 'the universal commodity', hence one with immediate exchangeability.

C—M—C is an example of 'Teleology' because the C—M serves as a means for the M—C. But the aim here is still the aquisition of a use-value as in simple exchange. Having served its purpose as medium, money drops away. Or does it? In fact since every purchase is a sale the mediator money stays always in circulation, albeit further and further removed from the original purchase. The following diagram (Diagram 9.2) shows three successive exchanges; while commodities arrive and depart, money keeps on trucking.

Diagram 9.2

The metamorphoses of commodities

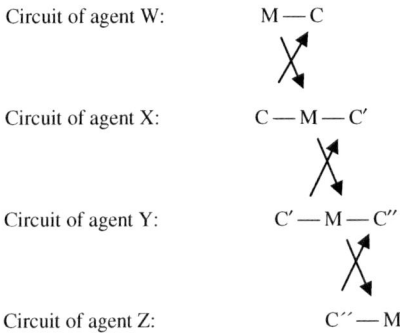

Circuit of agent W: M — C

Circuit of agent X: C — M — C′

Circuit of agent Y: C′ — M — C″

Circuit of agent Z: C″ — M

Here money that circulates endlessly has a kind of immortality; but as medium of circulation, this still appears as an emergent property of the exchange system; it does not *direct* it. However, if this 'bad infinity' recoils back on itself in the circuit M—C—M, money makes itself the origin and aim of its circuit. In this way the implicit unity of the 'Concept' of value is grounded in the objective intermediation of its moments. Buying in order to sell reverses the teleological positing of C—M—C. The mediator takes over from the extremes. Money now liberates itself from use value in setting the aim of exchange as its own. A system structured in this way is centred on the valorisation of value.

However, we jumped too quickly. For money to be the aim requires that it be posited 'for itself' rather than as mediator. This points to money's functions as means of payment and store of value, for which its real presence is required. (Measure may be merely notional, the medium may be replaced with tokens of itself.) In this form money is separated from commodities and counterposes itself to their circulation. Marx even says that in this shape it is fixed as the sole existence of value in the face of commodities as use values (Marx, 1976, p. 227). But, of course, no moment of the concept can subsist on its own. The miser thinks he accumulates wealth, but his hoard is just a metal dump apart from circulation.

In M—C—M value is referred to itself, particularising itself from money to a single commodity and then recovering its universal form through realising the particular value of that commodity. The self-reference of money in the circuit constitutes a new form of value, capital, which realises itself through the metamorphoses of money and commodities. The superiority of the capitalist over the miser is that he accumulates by throwing his money again and again into circulation. This iteration is absolutely necessary if the movement of M—C—M is to realise capital, the truly infinite as against the finitude of the world of commodities. Simply to be itself capital must become ever larger. Posited as the totality of its determinations, capital is the 'Subject' of its own movement. Now commodities and money are its *own* determinations. Marx says 'capital is money, capital is commodities' (Marx, 1976, p. 255). Commodities and money continue to act *as* commodities and money; but the circuit as a whole is further determined as capital, that is to say, money in search of money. In fine, capital is money in motion. Capital has become 'Idea' in Hegel's terms.

Nonetheless there is a difference between Hegel's logic and the value form. As we have seen, in contrast to Hegel's closed totality of categories, the forms of value require material bearers. Marx himself remarks this contrast when he says: 'It is only the Hegelian "Concept" that manages to objectify itself without external stuff' (Marx, 1983a, p. 31). He quotes Hegel: 'The Concept, which is initially only subjective, proceeds to objectify itself by virtue of its own activity and without the help of an external material or stuff.' (Hegel, 1991, §194A)

This comment occurs precisely in a discussion of the necessity for value to appear in the material of the equivalent commodity, itself the determinate product of a particular useful form of labour. As we have argued, the money commodity gives tangible reality to the concept of value.[4] (It remains to stress that the necessity for money to exist alongside the commodities is not affected when gold is replaced by electronic dots.)

Conclusion

I have argued that the categories of Hegel's logic may be deployed in understanding the nature of capital because material practice has generated a model of Hegel's logic of the concept. Yet, for such a concept to be really present, the logical moments of value have to be distributed over its material bearers, namely, commodities and money. This idea is the most novel, and difficult, aspect of what I here propose. There is no 'given' of which one forms a concept, namely the concept of value, rather value is a concept given to us from practice, having been generated 'behind our backs'. Value is a concept *objectively presented* to us in the circuit of capital. It is not through some externally applied method that the nature of capital is identified and defined; capital defines its own identity through the circuit of the determinations of its concept that it itself presents.

Notes

1. An earlier version of this paper (containing also a section on 'labour money') was published in *Radical Philosophy* 134, Nov/Dec 2005.
2. In *Capital* Marx says the commodity is '*ein sinnlich übersinnliches Ding*'. (Marx, 1983b, pp. 85, 86). The Fowkes translation, 'a thing which transcends sensuousness', is wrong (Marx, 1976, p. 163).
3. Marx takes 'the fruit' as his example when mocking Hegelian 'Speculative Construction' in *The Holy Family* (Marx and Engels, 1975, pp. 57–60).
4. It is extraordinary that Hegel anticipated this in one of his unpublished early works as follows: 'their [commodities] universal concept must become a thing like them, but one which as a universal represents all; *money* is this materially existing concept, the form of unity or the possibility of all things needed' (Hegel, 1979, p. 249). It is a pity Hegel did not reflect further on this peculiarity of money.

Bibliography

Arthur, Christopher J. (2002) *The New Dialectic and Marx's 'Capital'* (Leiden/Boston: Brill).

Hegel, G. W. F. (1969) *The Science of Logic*, trans. A. V. Miller (London: George Allen and Unwin).

—— (1979) *System of Ethical Life and First Philosophy of Spirit*, trans. H. S. Harris and T. M. Knox (Albany, NY: State University of New York Press).

—— (1991) *The Encyclopaedia Logic*, trans. T. F. Geraets, W. A. Suchting, and H. S. Harris (Indianapolis: Hackett).

Marx, Karl (1976) *Capital Volume 1*, trans. B. Fowkes (Harmondsworth: Penguin).

—— (1983a) 'Das Kapital Erster Band 1867', in Karl Marx and Friedrich Engels *Gesamtausgabe* (MEGA) Zweite Abteilung, Band 5 (Berlin: Dietz Verlag).

—— (1983b) *Das Kapital* Band I, *Marx-Engels Werke* Band 23 (Berlin: Dietz Verlag).

Marx, Karl and Frederick Engels (1975) *Collected Works Volume 4* (London: Lawrence and Wishart).

—— (1987) *Collected Works Volume 29* (London: Lawrence and Wishart).

10
Value, Money and Capital in Hegel and Marx

Patrick Murray

Some years ago I was surprised to receive a package in the mail from a former student.[1] It took me a moment to recognize what was inside, a green ceramic **ΔM**. I had a good laugh. From our study of *Capital*, the student had gotten the idea loud and clear how preoccupied Marx is with ΔM, or what he calls 'surplus value'. In thinking over Hegel's treatment of property, contracts of exchange and civil society in the *Philosophy of Right* and earlier writings, I am struck by a simple fact: *Hegel just does not seem to be interested in ΔM*.[2] Hegel is aware that 'gain' or 'profit' motivate what he calls the 'reflective estate' of trade and industry. And he recognizes that civil society is naturally expansive, with firms developing products and technologies in order to accumulate wealth. But the topic of surplus value simply does not move Hegel on grounds either of science – where does ΔM come from? – or social justice – what justification can be offered for ΔM?

Why didn't ΔM strike a chord in Hegel?[3] Aristotle had posed the problem of its source plainly enough in Book 1 of his *Politics*, a passage to which Marx responds in *Capital*. And in his treatment of contracts of exchange, Hegel strongly affirms the principle of commutative justice, namely, that items of equal value be exchanged.[4] Yet that basic principle of commercial justice appears incompatible with capital's circuit, M—C—M+ΔM. Aristotle judged it to be exactly that (Marx, 1976, p. 267).[5] Let me propose, tentatively, two possible reasons why ΔM didn't stir Hegel.

(1) After a period of wrestling with the phenomena of modern commercial life as a young man, Hegel reconciled himself to it; ΔM comes with the territory, including ΔM in the form of interest paid to lenders.
(2) The key to understanding the source of ΔM is to draw the distinction between labour and labour-power and to comprehend the class distinction between capitalists and wage workers. Like John Locke, Hegel gave wage labour the moral stamp of approval; Marx quotes him on that point (Marx, 1976, pp. 271–2 n. 3). But Hegel neither drew

the distinction between labour and labour-power nor did he think of capitalists and wage workers as two classes. Rather, Hegel clumps them together under the rubric of the 'estate of trade and industry' [*Stand des Gewerbs*] (Hegel, 1991, §204).[6] That categorization is doubly antiquated because Hegel is still thinking in terms of estates [*Stände*] rather than classes [*Klassen*] and because he does not distinguish between capitalists and wage labourers as classes.[7]

Hegel's disinterest in ΔM is one manifestation of a fact about his social theory that has been dawning on me for some time: Hegel does not have an adequate, clearly articulated concept of capital.[8] Readers of T. M. Knox's translation of *Hegel's Philosophy of Right* will object that the third subsection under the heading 'The System of Needs' is entitled 'Capital [and class-divisions]' and that, in §199, Hegel refers us back to an earlier discussion of 'capital' in connection with the family (Hegel, 1952, §§199, 170). But Hegel's term here is not '*Kapital*' but rather '*Vermögen*'. (Also, the term that Knox refers to with 'class-divisions' is not '*Klassen*' but rather '*Stände*'.) H. B. Nisbet's translation improves on Knox by translating '*Vermögen*' as 'resources' and '*Stände*' as 'estates' (Hegel, 1991, §199). Paragraph §199 recalls Adam Smith, as Hegel points to the way the universal necessarily mediates the particular (Smith's 'invisible hand'). The self-interested efforts of the butcher, the brewer, the baker and others simultaneously allow them and countless strangers to meet their needs while they all maintain and augment (*vermehrt*) the 'universal and permanent resources' (*allgemeine, bleibende Vermögen*).[9] This is as close as Hegel comes to adequate concepts of capital and surplus value, including the idea of the aggregated social capital and its accumulation process. But resources are not necessarily capital, not even resources that accumulate. That the category of resources appears within civil society, however, means that Hegel conceives of them as in the commodity form. Still, capital is more than resources in the commodity form that pile up, like the 'heap of commodities' to which Marx refers in the opening sentence of *Capital*. Capital, in Marx's concise phrase, is 'self-valorizing value'; it is a peculiar social form of wealth that is inherently, and boundlessly, dynamic.[10]

Capital and Marx's critique of bourgeois philosophy of right

In *Marx's Theory of Scientific Knowledge*, I argued that Hegel's *Philosophy of Right* is a crucial book for students of Hegel and of Marx (Murray, 1988, pp. 27–43). The *Philosophy of Right* is where Hegel's way of doing philosophy should really pay off. Of his four published books, the *Phenomenology* introduces the system; the *Science of Logic* confines itself to the shadowy realm of pure abstractions; and the *Encyclopaedia of the Philosophical Sciences* treats logic and the 'real sciences' of nature and spirit in, well, encyclopaedic fashion. The *Philosophy of Right*, then, is Hegel's only full-dress version of a philosophical real science (*Realwissenschaft*). Here is where he had better deliver. And it was to Hegel's *Philosophy of Right* that the young Marx turned in 1843 after his abbreviated career as editor of the *Rheinische Zeitung*.

In the period between his dissertation and the *Grundrisse*, Marx was perhaps never more intellectually engrossed than in his uncompleted critique of Hegel's *Philosophy of Right*, which he considered the best book bourgeois social theory had to offer. Characteristically, Marx saw here an opportunity to criticize simultaneously the leading theory of the modern world along with that world itself:

> The critique of the German philosophy of right and of the state, which received its most consistent, its richest, and its final comprehension through Hegel, is [...] the critical analysis of the modern state and of the actuality connected with it.
>
> (Marx, 1970, pp. 136–7)

Marx's work on the *Philosophy of Right* set his future course. (1) It locked him to Feuerbach's critique that Hegel imposed logic onto reality. (2) It convinced Marx that the key to comprehending modern life lay in the anatomy of civil society. (3) It educated him more deeply in certain of Hegel's ways of thinking, notably, to attend to the content and dialectic of social forms. (4) The series of 'brochures' that Marx announced in the 'Preface' to his *Paris Manuscripts* had their roots in his encounter with Hegel's *Philosophy of Right*, and the six-'book' scheme that he projected in the *Grundrisse* descends from those youthful plans. *Capital* is the first, and last, instalment of Marx's mature critique of Hegel's *Philosophy of Right* and bourgeois philosophy of right generally. The concept of capital is central to that mature critique.

Closely linked to his focus on ΔM is Marx's choice to organize his presentation of capitalist society in terms of two spheres, the sphere of commodity circulation and the sphere of capital's circulation. Lacking an explicit, articulated concept of capital, Hegel does not draw this distinction. *Value* is the dominant concept in the first sphere, *surplus value* in the second. Already Marx's *Grundrisse* is structured in terms of two books, the book on money and the book on capital. Upon finishing the *Grundrisse*, Marx wrote the 'Original Text' (*Urtext*) and then rewrote it for publication as the *Contribution to the Critique of Political Economy*. Both texts concerned commodities and money, the sphere of simple circulation.[11] One reason why Marx took this approach was because he expected his theory of capital to create a furore.[12] Though he first presented his account of the sphere of circulation separately, in the *Critique*, one of *Capital's* chief claims is that the sphere of simple commodity circulation is an abstraction from the sphere of capital's circulation; there is a conceptual distinction between the two, not a real one. As Chris Arthur has urged, *Capital* does not posit the existence of some precursor to capitalism called simple commodity production (Arthur, 2002, ch. 2, especially p. 19). Rather, *Capital* shows that generalized commodity circulation, value and money are insepa-rable from capital, surplus value and wage labour. There are not two spheres actually; there are two ways of conceiving the marketplace.

Marx has several reasons for adopting the two-sphere mode of presentation. One concerns his phenomenologically based, systematic dialectical presen-tation; another concerns ideology critique. In the 'Original Manuscript' (*Urtext*) and again in *Capital*, Marx makes the dialectical argument that the sphere of simple commodity circulation cannot stand alone; rather, it pre-supposes production on a capitalist basis. Marx's approach in *Capital* to the bourgeois theory of right is to show that it is an ideology and to reveal how the peculiar social forms of capitalist society present themselves in ways that naturally foster this ideology. Here is where the two-sphere construc-tion figures in: because commodity circulation is an easily recognizable and understandable moment of the circulation of capital where liberty, equality, property and Bentham appear to reign, it is easily mistaken for an independ-ent sphere and even for the full reality of capitalist society.[13] Marx discloses bourgeois theory of right to be, in the main, the ideology of the sphere of simple commodity circulation wrenched from the circulation of capital, of which it is, in truth, only an aspect.

The two spheres are coupled by ΔM. In *Capital* 1, Marx devotes Part 2, 'The Transformation of Money into Capital', first to setting up the puzzle posed by the circuit of capital, $M—C—M+\Delta M$ – how can ΔM arise without offend-ing commutative justice? – and then to supplying the distinction between labour and labour-power required to solve it.

> The form of circulation within which money is transformed into capital contradicts all the previously developed laws bearing on the nature of commodities, value, money and even circulation itself.
>
> (Marx, 1976, p. 258)

When he completes the solution late in Chapter 7, 'The Labour Process and the Valorization Process', Marx insists on the point that capital's valoriza-tion process can leave the sphere of commodity circulation's rule of justice intact.

> Every condition of the problem is satisfied, while the laws governing the exchange of commodities have not been violated in any way. Equivalent has been exchanged for equivalent.
>
> (Marx, 1976, p. 301; see also p. 731)

Hegel, by contrast, makes no distinction of spheres and pays the puzzle no heed. Hegel's attention never turns to ΔM.

Marx pulls up the two main planks of the bourgeois conception of right, both of which are incorporated into Hegel's *Philosophy of Right*.

One concerns the principle of appropriation, the other the principle of exchange. The bourgeois principle of appropriation was famously enunciated by Locke in Chapter 5 of his *Second Treatise of Government*: my labour entitles me to property. Hegel restates it in the *Philosophy of Right*: 'To give form to something is the mode of taking possession most in keeping with the Idea, inasmuch as it combines the subjective and objective' (Hegel, 1991, §56R).[14] The bourgeois principle of exchange is that of commutative justice: equal values are to be exchanged. Hegel enunciates this principle in connection with contracts of exchange:

> Since each party, in a real contract, retains *the same* property with which he enters the contract and which he simultaneously relinquishes, that property which remains *identical* as having being *in itself* within the contract is distinct from the external things [*Sachen*] which change owners in the course of the transaction. The former is the *value*, in respect of which the objects of the contract [*Vertragsgegenstände*] are equal to each other, whatever qualitative external differences there may be between the things exchanged; it is their *universal* aspect.
>
> (Hegel, 1991, §77)

Marx accepts that definition, saying, 'The law of exchange requires equality only between the exchange-values of the commodities given in exchange for one another' (Marx, 1976, p. 731).

Marx argues that the bourgeois principle that property is acquired through one's own labour necessarily reverses itself. Those who labour, the wage labourers, acquire no property in their product, while all property goes to those who do not labour, namely, the capitalists. Property, which appeared, necessarily, as 'grounded in a man's own labour', now

> turns out to be the right, on the part of the capitalist, to appropriate the unpaid labour of others or its product, and the impossibility, on the part of the worker, of appropriating his own product.
>
> (Marx, 1976, p. 730)

As for the bourgeois principle of exchange, Marx shows that surplus value, which derives from the surplus labour that the capitalist class can extract from the working class, need not entail any violation of the standards of commutative justice. In revealing that the sphere of commodity circulation depends upon the circulation of capital, however, Marx exposes the irony that the whole framework and rationale of commutative justice, inasmuch as it appeals to the existence of value, rests on the exploitation of the class of wage workers. For without surplus value, there is no value.

Moving on to the reproduction of capital and its accumulation, Marx demonstrates that, as the capitalist's original investment – at first assumed to be the result of his own labour – is replaced by accumulated surplus value, the exchange between capitalist and wage labourer devolves into 'the legal fiction of a contract' (Marx, 1976, p. 719). Marx summarizes the shocking outcome of his investigation of the concept of capital for bourgeois theory of right:

> Therefore, however much the capitalist mode of appropriation may seem to fly in the face of the original laws of commodity production, it nevertheless arises, not from a violation of these laws but, on the contrary, from their application.
>
> (Marx, 1976, p. 730)

These points that Marx makes against bourgeois philosophy of right all turn on the concept of capital.

In the treatment of the process of 'so-called primitive accumulation' in the concluding part of *Capital* 1, Marx closes the circle of his mature critique of bourgeois philosophy of right by removing the assumption that the capitalist's original investment funds were the consequence of his own labour. To the contrary, Marx's exposé of the secret of the 'so-called primitive accumulation' of capital reveals the process to have been one of bloody usurpation.

Value, money and the market

It is a profound misreading of *Capital* to think that the critical element of the book enters with the shift from the sphere of commodity circulation to the sphere of capital's circulation. That is the Ricardian reading of Marx. Marx's theory of value exclusively concerns the social form of labour peculiar to capitalist societies, a topic that is not on Ricardo's radar screen. The point of *Capital* is not to redistribute surplus value, as with the Ricardian Socialists; it is to abolish value. The Ricardian interpretation misses Marx's critique of bourgeois theory of right: surplus value is not the result of violating commodity exchange's law of equality, on the contrary, it is the presupposition and necessary consequence of generalized commodity exchange. Surplus value is the condition for the existence of the law of value. But Marx's conceptions of value and of simple commodity circulation are already deeply critical already at the level of commodity circulation. Obstructions to human freedom and community already populate the sphere of simple commodity circulation.

Hegel's ideas about commodity exchange, value, and money anticipate many of Marx's points: both see modern commercial life as marked by abstraction (of needs, labour and social relations); cynical levelling; egoism and excess; poverty and dangerous inequalities of wealth; and the domination of individuals by blind, unstable abstract forces. Certain of Hegel's (early) formulations surpass Marx's language in vehemence. Here is Hegel's description of the system of needs from the Jena *First Philosophy of Spirit*:

> Need and labour, elevated into this universality, then form on their own account a monstrous system of community and mutual interdependence in a great people; a life of the dead body, that moves itself within itself, one which ebbs and flows in its motion blindly, like the elements, and which requires continual strict dominance and taming like a wild beast.
>
> (Hegel, 1979, p. 249)[15]

By comparison, this correlative passage from *Capital* is rather tepid:

> The owners of commodities therefore find out that the same division of labour which turns them into independent private producers also makes the social process of production and the relations of the individual producers to each other within that process independent of the producers themselves; they also find out that the independence of the individuals from each other has as its counterpart and supplement a system of all-round material dependence.
>
> (Marx, 1976, p. 203)

Though Hegel's and Marx's ideas regarding commodity circulation overlap a good deal, substantial differences remain. First, as we have seen, Hegel does not articulate a concept of capital; so, he draws no distinction between the sphere of commodity circulation and the sphere of capital's circulation. Neither, then, does Hegel see capital's circulation as the presupposition of commodity circulation. As a result, he does not recognize the challenges to bourgeois philosophy of right or the fresh obstacles to human freedom and community that Marx's exposition of capital disclose. Second, as critical as Hegel is about modern commerce (civil society), he reconciles himself to it. That is true from his first Jena writings through the *Philosophy of Right*, almost 20 years later.

> Thus in this system what rules appears as the unconscious and blind entirety of needs and the modes of their satisfaction. But the universal must be able to master this unconscious and blind fate and become a government.
>
> (Hegel 1979, pp. 167–8)

In the *Philosophy of Right*, Hegel counts on several different mediating institutions, above all, the state, to buffer the ill effects of the clash of the particular and universal in what Smith called 'the great scramble' of the marketplace.

In thinking about Hegel as a philosopher of reconciliation, it may be helpful to distinguish where Hegel believes that he has found reconciliation *in* actuality and where he reconciles himself *to* social realities that resist reconciliation. Hegel's approach to civil society incorporates reconciliation in both senses. Like Smith, Hegel sees a certain reconciliation of self-seeking and the good of the community as inherent to the system of trading the products of the division of labour,

> In this dependence and reciprocity of work and the satisfaction of needs, *subjective selfishness* turns into a *contribution towards the satisfaction of the needs of everyone else.*
>
> (Hegel, 1991, §199)

He finds further conciliatory aspects to civil society in the expansion and refinement of wealth, capabilities and permanent resources available to members of civil society. Memberships in *estates* (*Stände*) and *corporations* are also important in reconciling self-interest and the common good. Hegel cautions that the estates

> are of special importance, because private persons, despite their selfish-ness, find it necessary to have recourse to others. This is accordingly the root which links selfishness with the universal, i.e. with the state, which must take care to ensure that this connection is a firm and solid one.
>
> (Hegel, 1991, §201)

Last, but definitely not least, Hegel counts on the intervention of the state in multiple ways.

All the same, civil society's discontents are not uprooted: 'civil society affords a spectacle of extravagance and misery as well as of the physical and ethical corruption common to both' (Hegel, 1991, §185); poverty, in particular, 'agitates and torments' civil society without end. There remains much about civil society that Hegel believes we must reconcile ourselves *to* if we intend to defend the modern world's great advance, namely, 'the principle of the self-sufficient and inherently infinite personality of the individual [*des Einzelnen*], the principle of subjective freedom' (Hegel, 1991, §185R). Though Hegel reconciles himself to civil society, like Marx, his conception of value and the peculiar social form of labour that produces value is profoundly critical. Let us turn then to Hegel's ideas about value and money.

Hegel does not write a great deal about value, and it is hard to draw conclusions even about basic aspects of his theory of the kind of value that money measures: does he have a labour theory of value, or a utility theory, or neither?[16] In particular, the question of how value is determined quantitatively is left hanging.[17] Still, we can identify a number of features of value as Hegel conceives of it. Unlike classical political economists, Hegel sees value as bound up with the particular way that the production and distribution of wealth is organized in civil society, whose emergence 'belongs to the modern world' (Hegel, 1991, §182A). Value is thoroughly modern, a feature of the bourgeois world. Before Marx, Hegel has a 'truly social' concept of value (see Murray, 2000). Hegel's approach to value is cut from different cloth than that of political economy: it is historical and dialectical.[18] Value presupposes private property (Hegel, 1991, §63A). Value presupposes an advanced division of labour. Value presupposes commodity exchange, a social practice of abstraction that validates all labours in abstraction from their concrete purposes and methods. Value presupposes a public, authoritative system of recognition of commodity exchangers as equals. Value presupposes that a multiplicity of needs, use-values, and labours are comparable, indeed comparable quantitatively, and commodity exchange actually treats them as abstractions (Hegel, 1979, p. 118; Hegel, 1991, §80). Value is something public, universal; it is substantial even though utterly abstract. (Marx writes of value's 'ghostly objectivity'.) Value is the subject matter of contracts; it can be owned in contradistinction to owning particular use-values. Those who lend money at interest own only the value lent, not the specific thing (Hegel, 1983, p. 89). Value is changeable; it is 'a perpetual wave, surging up and down' (Hegel, 1979, p. 167). More specifically, Hegel recognizes that value is responsive to demand and to technological change. The former suggests that Hegel recognizes that value and price are inseparable, the latter indicates that Hegel has at least a rudimentary idea of the 'value treadmill', whereby the increasing productive power of labour does nothing to increase the rate at which value is produced.[19]

Something remarkable is taking shape here. As Chris Arthur successfully argues in his provocatively titled essay 'Hegel's Theory of the Value Form', Hegel, like Marx, is a value-form theorist (Arthur, 2002; see Hegel, 1991, §§63A, 203, 204). Value-form theory represents a fundamental break with classical political economy in that it recognizes the inner connectedness of the commodity, value and money. Money is the necessary form of appearance of value, whose 'ghostly objectivity' is a consequence of the social sort of labour that produces commodities. Money is no mere technical device, a convenience to facilitate barter; money plays a role in the constitution of commodities and value. Hegel distinguishes barter from purchase and sale, which is the 'exchange of a commodity for money [*Geld*], i.e., a thing that is not specific but universal, or a commodity that only has value, with no other specific determination as to use' (Hegel, 1995, pp. 87–8). This suggests that Hegel grasps a key feature of the value form, namely, the necessary polarity of the expression of value: the commodity functions as a particular use-value (in what Marx calls the 'relative value-form'), while money functions as value incarnate (in what Marx calls the 'equivalent value-form'). Hegel conceives of the relation between money and value such that we cannot speak of value in a barter system, 'since money abstracts from the [specific] commodity to pure value, a primitive people does not yet have money, and makes do with inconvenient barter' (Hegel, 1995, pp. 88).

Here is a passage on commodity exchange in which Hegel captures fundamentals of value-form theory:

> The universality of labour or the indifference of all labour is posited as a middle term with which all labour is compared and into which each single piece of labour can be directly converted; this middle term, posited as something real, is *money*.
>
> (Hegel, 1979, p. 154)

Commodity-producing labour is socially validated as labour in the abstract, establishing abstract labour as the inner measure of the value of commodities that is necessarily expressed in money, value's outer measure. Hegel, of course, also recognizes money's function as a means of circulation. With his well-articulated account of how credit emerges naturally from commodity exchange, creating the necessity for money as means of payment in addition to money as means of circulation, Hegel again anticipates Marx.

Conclusion

Hegel thought deeply about commodities, value and money as a young man and kept thinking about them. How close he was to arriving at an adequate conception of capital is suggested by a passage from his early Jena *System*. Here Hegel conceives of the capacity of value to maintain itself in commodity exchange in terms of the logic of the concept (which belongs to Hegel's subjective logic):

> This is exchange [...] Property enters reality through the plurality of persons involved in exchange and mutually recognizing one another. Value enters in the reality of things and applies to each of them as surplus [i.e. as a commodity, rather than a product to be used by the producer – P.M.]; the concept enters as self-moving, annihilating itself in its opposite, taking on the opposite character in place of the one it possessed before.
>
> (Hegel, 1979, p. 121)

Hegel here has the exchange of two commodities (presumably mediated by money) in mind; ΔM does not come into the picture. By contrast, in *Capital* 1 Marx makes quite a similar observation but with respect to the circuit of capital, $M—C—M+\Delta M$. He writes,

> [B]oth the money and the commodity function only as different modes of existence of value itself, the money as its general mode of existence, the commodity as its particular or, so to speak, disguised mode.

It is constantly changing from one into the other, without becoming lost in this movement; it thus becomes transformed into an automatic subject.

(Marx, 1976, p. 255; compare Marx, 1987, p. 501)

Marx argues that this self-movement of value in and out of the money and commodity forms makes sense only if it leads to offspring in the form of ΔM (Marx, 1976, pp. 250–1, 255–6). What is the point of something as abstract and qualitatively homogeneous as value preserving itself in the course of its circulation unless that process results in a quantitative increase – ΔM?

Marx makes a powerful argument here based on the very considerations that Hegel identifies as operative in commodity exchange. Marx combines his insight (which Hegel shares) that money is the sole adequate form in which value can express its identity or its change over time with the idea of value becoming a 'dominant subject' within commodity circulation to argue that money is necessarily the starting point and end point of the circuits that value dominates:

As the dominant subject [*übergreifendes Subjekt*] of this process, in which it alternately assumes and loses the form of money and the form of commodities, but preserves and expands itself through all these changes, value requires above all an independent form by means of which its identity with itself may be asserted. Only in the shape of money does it possess this form. Money therefore forms the starting-point and the conclusion of every valorization process.

(Marx, 1976, p. 255)

When, in Hegel's words, 'value enters in the reality of things [commodities]' and value becomes 'self-moving', M—C—M+ΔM is the only circuit of its movement that makes sense.[20] Money must beget money (Marx, 1976, p. 256).

How important is Hegel's failure to articulate the concept of capital to his standing as a theorist of modern life? Marx's discoveries regarding the implications of capital for bourgeois philosophy of right suggest that it is very important. Hegel's treatment of modern commercial life (civil society) in the *Philosophy of Right* and its several forerunners remains a dense, brilliant and honest account of modern commercial life. But Hegel's disinterest in ΔM and his failure to articulate the concept of capital cast doubt on Allen Wood's unfettered praise:

Hegel is an important philosopher; his penetrating analysis of the human predicament in modern society is perhaps unsurpassed among social observers of the past two centuries.

(Wood, 1991, p. xxvii)

No doubt, the *Philosophy of Right* is full of remarkable insights into modern life, but can a book that articulates no clear concept of capital be the most penetrating analysis of modern society to date? Is the concept of capital so trifling?

Notes

1. An early version of this paper was presented to the Marx and Philosophy Society Annual Conference on 10 September 2005. Joe McCarney, one of the originators of the society, kindly sent me helpful, thought-provoking remarks on the presentation. I regret that his untimely death put an end to our exchange.
2. Those earlier writings include the Jena *System of Ethical Life* of 1802/3 and the Jena *First Philosophy of Spirit* of 1803/4 (both in Hegel, 1979), along with the Jena *Lectures on the Philosophy of Spirit* of 1805/6 (Hegel, 1983), and the recently unearthed Heidelberg lectures on *Natural Right and Political Science* (Hegel, 1995), the earliest version of the *Philosophy of Right*. Jerry Muller observes, 'For Hegel, the market was the central and most distinctive feature of the modern world' (Muller, 2002, p. 139). Hegel and Marx are alike in that they both thought and wrote about topics related to modern commerce throughout their adult lives.
3. Hegel writes about the 'surplus' in the Jena *System* (Hegel, 1979, p. 118ff.), but he is referring to commodities, not to surplus value.
4. In rejecting the objectivity of value, Richard Winfield rejects Hegel's view here. Instead, for Winfield, commutative justice, if we can use the term, reduces to the requirement that exchanges be voluntary. See Winfield, 1988, pp. 109ff.
5. In particular, Aristotle railed against usury, whose circuit is compressed to M—M+ΔM.
6. Winfield (1988) criticizes Hegel for putting estates into the fabric of his philosophy of right.
7. Hegel divides the estates 'in accordance with *the concept*' into three: 'the *substantial* or immediate estate, the reflecting or *formal* estate, and lastly, the *universal* estate', corresponding to agriculture, commerce and industry, and the state, respectively (Hegel, 1991, §202). Hegel subdivides the 'reflecting or *formal* estate', the estate of trade and industry, into (1) the estate of craftsmanship, (2) the estate of manufacturing and (3) the estate of commerce. He draws no distinction between merchant capital and financial capital.
8. Winfield argues that Hegel is right to conceive of the commodity, not capital, as the centrepiece of modern commerce and industry (civil society). He writes, '[Hegel] works out the total structure of commodity relations without subsuming them under a system of capitals whose profit derives from wage labour commodity production. Although Hegel does make brief mention of the relationship of capital and labour, he treats it as a subordinate element within the market economy. In contrast to Marx, he does not view it as a privileged determining structure that envelops and orders all commodity relations within its process of capital accumulation' (Winfield, 1988, p. 99).
9. In the same vein Locke and Smith wrote of the 'common stock of mankind'.
10. Moishe Postone writes, 'Marx's category of capital refers to an alienated, dualistic structure of labour-mediated relations in terms of which the peculiar fabric of modern society, its abstract form of domination, its historical dynamic, and its characteristic forms of production and work can be understood systematically.

For Marx, capital, as the unfolded commodity form, is the central, totalizing category of modern life' (Postone, 1993, p. 352). It may seem ironic for me to charge that Hegel lacks a concept of capital, since, with Postone, Chris Arthur, and others, I have argued (Murray, 1988) that Marx sees Hegel as the philosopher of capital. But the 'of' in this case means that Hegel was unwittingly expressing in his logic of the concept – and more particularly of the idea – the logic of capital's subsumption of nature and humanity. Having capital on the brain did not require Hegel to undertake an exposition of capital and its consequences.

11. The 'Original Text' contains several pages of a draft of Chapter 3, on capital. This part was dropped in the *Contribution to the Critique*.
12. See Marx's letter of 28 March 1859 to Lassalle.
13. In the final paragraph of the part of *Capital* 1 dealing with the transformation of money into capital, Marx writes, 'this sphere of simple circulation or the exchange of commodities ... provide[s] the "free-trader *vulgaris*" with his views, his concepts and the standard by which he judges the society of capital and wage-labour' (Marx, 1976, p. 280).
14. Bernard Cullen observes that Hegel's first reference to economic activity was due to his reading of Locke and 'the Lockean concept of property as the embodiment of the personality of the labour was to reappear – practically unmodified – in vitally important sections of the *Philosophy of Right*, almost 30 years later (see Hegel, 1991, §151)' (Cullen, 1979, p. 16).
15. Compare the toned-down version in Hegel, 1991, §186. See also Hegel, 1979, pp. 153–4.
16. For a sophisticated account of Hegel's theory of value that explores a range of his uses of the concept of value, see Deranty, 2005.
17. While perhaps frustrating for his readers, it may be to Hegel's credit that his theory of value remains indeterminate, since there are serious problems with both subjective utility theories of value and with the classical labour theory of value.
18. Winfield (1988) rightly makes much of this point.
19. On the 'value treadmill', see Marx, 1976, p. 137. As Marx observes, this effect is one of the important consequences of the fact that the substance of value is *abstract* labour.
20. This means that simple commodity circulation presupposes the circulation of capital, one of the most important points Marx makes in *Capital*. This is why, as against Winfield, Marx sees the commodity as subordinate to capital and views capital 'as a privileged determining structure that envelops and orders all commodity relations' (Winfield, 1988, p. 99.)

Bibliography

Arthur, Chris (2002) *The New Dialectic and Marx's 'Capital'* (Leiden, Boston, Köln: Brill).

Cullen, Bernard (1979) *Hegel's Social and Political Thought: An Introduction* (New York: St. Martin's Press).

Deranty, Jean-Philippe (2005) 'Hegel's Social Theory of Value', *The Philosophical Forum*, XXXVI, No. 3, 307–31.

Hegel, G. W. F. (1952) *Hegel's Philosophy of Right*, trans. by T. M. Knox (Oxford: Oxford University Press).

—— (1979) *System of Ethical Life (1802/3) and First Philosophy of Spirit (Part III of the System of Speculative Philosophy 1803/4)*, (ed. and trans.) by H. S. Harris and T. M. Knox (Albany: State University of New York Press).

—— (1983) *Hegel and the Human Spirit: A Translation of the Jena Lectures on the Philosophy of Spirit (1805–6)* with commentary by Leo Rauch (Detroit: Wayne State University Press).

—— (1991) *Elements of the Philosophy of Right*, (trans.) H. B. Nisbet and (ed.) Allen W. Wood (Cambridge: Cambridge University Press).

—— (1995) *Lectures on Natural Right and Political Science: The First Philosophy of Right* (Heidelberg 1817–1818), (trans.) J. Michael Stewart and Peter C. Hodgson (Berkeley and Los Angeles: University of California Press).

Marx, Karl (1970) *Critique of Hegel's 'Philosophy of Right'*, trans. Annette Jolin and Joseph O'Malley, ed. Joseph O'Malley (Cambridge: Cambridge University Press).

—— (1976) *Capital Volume 1*, trans. B. Fowkes (Harmondsworth: Penguin).

—— (1987) 'Original Text' (*Urtext*) in 'Economic Manuscripts of 1857–58', in *Marx and Engels Collected Works*, vol. 29 (London: Lawrence and Wishart).

Muller, Jerry (2002) *The Mind and the Market: Capitalism in Modern European Thought* (New York: Alfred A. Knopf).

Murray, Patrick (1988) *Marx's Theory of Scientific Knowledge* (Atlantic Highlands, NJ: Humanities Press International).

—— (2000) 'Marx's "Truly Social" Labour Theory of Value: Part I, Abstract Labour in Marxian Value Theory', *Historical Materialism*, 6, 27–65.

Postone, Moishe (1993) *Time, Labor, and Social Domination: A Reinterpretation of Marx's Critical Theory* (Cambridge: Cambridge University Press).

Winfield, Richard (1988) *The Just Economy* (New York and London: Routledge).

Wood, Allen W. (1991) 'Editor's Introduction' to G. W. F. Hegel, *Elements of the Philosophy of Right*, (trans.) H. B. Nisbet, (ed.) Allen W. Wood (Cambridge: Cambridge University Press).

11
Abstraction and Productivity: Structures of Intentionality and Action in Marx's Capital

William Clare Roberts

In Johnny Cash's 'The Ballad of John Henry' (1963), John's father, before being hauled off to jail, admonishes his son to learn all the skills of a railroad worker, ending with this promise: 'And take that hammer; it'll do anything you tell it to.' However, when John goes to the foreman of the railroad crew and enumerates his skills, he responds to the foreman's question, 'Can you swing that hammer?' by saying, 'I'll do anything you hire me to.' John's father thought he was bequeathing to his son the means by which John could provide for the family and do what he wanted. The hammer and John's skill in using it were supposed to be the vehicles of the worker's desires. The hammer was supposed to obey him. Instead, John, with his hammer and his skill, ends up serving only the desires of his boss. John himself becomes a tool and, in the end, works himself to death to prove that he can be a more effective instrument than the steam drill brought in to replace him. The promised instrumentality of the hammer is transmuted into the instrumentality of the worker.

The song provides us with a marvellous image of the transition from concrete labour to abstract labour, the way labour functions within capital. Employment by capital transforms the end of labour. Production for the sake of surplus-value is the formula of capital. This immediately entails the use of labour for something other than labour's own, self-posited end; that is, it entails the exploitation of labour for the end of valorization. In the *Grundrisse*, Marx writes; 'It is easy to understand how labour can increase use-value; the difficulty is, how it can create exchange-values greater than those with which it began' (Marx, 1973, pp. 317–18). This judgment has been verified time and again in the intervening history. Most economists since Marx, including many 'Marxist' economists, have denied that labour produces value at all. It is a self-proclaimed Marxist who declared that 'the errors in the labour theory of value are Ptolemaic' (Roemer 1985, p. 65). Much of the trouble has been caused by a dearth of attention to the distinction between concrete and abstract labour, a distinction Marx thought to be 'the origin, around which the understanding of political economy revolves' (Marx, 1976, p. 132; translation modified). Concrete labour is the purposeful production of useful things, which Marx describes at the beginning of Chapter 7 of *Capital*. It makes given material over into something useful for human life by forming it according to a preconceived idea of functionality. The Greeks called this sort of making *technê*, and I will have cause to mention it in what follows. It is abstract labour, however, that presents itself as exchange-value, and it is abstract labour that will be my focus here.[1]

An inquiry into abstract labour is an inquiry into the productivity of capitalism. The difficulty that besets attempts to understand how abstract labour produces value is identical with the difficulty of understanding how capital – which is not identical with any individual or group – can be the most formidable agent of modernity, with its own means and ends. My examination will amount to an argument that capital names a completely different structure of intentionality than does concrete labour, and that this form of intentionality has come to dominate and displace the intentionality of concrete labour. This has the surprising consequence that capital necessarily expresses itself as a form of universal society. That is, capital, and the categories that go along with it (the commodity, money, abstract labour, and so on), are essentially collective to the point of being all-encompassing. There is no such thing as a single commodity, an individual act of abstract labour, or an individual capitalist. These modes of human life cannot, without grave distortion, be broken down into or analysed in terms of individual agents performing individual actions for the sake of individual goals. What Marx calls the real subsumption of labour under capital is nothing other than the becoming real of a social imagination that renders nonsensical any methodological, ethical, or ontological individualism, including logical or semantic atomism. Capital, this collective actor – this 'animated monster' – has displaced (and continues to displace) the Promethean individual from the stage of history's production.

In order to understand this collective productivity, I want to trace Marx's own discussion of the abstraction of labour, which is also the story of its subsumption under the capital-form. In the next section I will draw a distinction between conceptual abstraction and social abstraction, arguing that abstract labour must be understood as the latter. I will then illustrate the social abstraction of labour by examining the abstraction implicit in commodity exchange. This will not suffice, however, for an understanding of capitalism, so, in 'The subsumption of labour', I will turn to the processes of abstraction proper to capitalist production, which are theorised by Marx as the formal and real subsumption of labour. I want to examine what follows both directly from the fact that capital has control over labour and bends it to the end of valorization and from the further fact that capital modifies the labour process to suit its new purpose. In the final section,

I will discuss the productivity of capital as a form of society, and contrast it to the productivity of concrete labour.

The social abstractions of the market

Diane Elson's claim, made 30 years ago, remains true today; 'debate over Marx's theory of value has been hampered by a mutual incomprehension on matters of method' (Elson, 1979, p. ii). I hope to clear up some of this incomprehension by identifying and dissecting certain social practices that amount to mechanisms of social abstraction. I will begin with commodity exchange before turning, in 'The subsumption of labour', to the capitalist production process.

   Marx begins *Capital* by analysing the 'cell-form' of bourgeois wealth into two aspects; every commodity is both a useful object, and an object of exchange. Marx makes clear that this latter aspect of commodities is possible only by means of an 'abstraction from their use-values' (Marx, 1976, pp. 127–8). For this to be a social abstraction, it must take place in actual social intercourse, not merely in the heads of economists. How, then, does commodity exchange abstract from use-values? Marx writes:

> A certain commodity, a quarter of wheat, e.g., is exchanged with x blacking, or with y silk, or with z gold, etc., in short with other commodities in various proportions. The wheat thus has many exchange-values instead of only one. But the x blacking, and y silk, and z gold, etc., are replaceable by one another or are equally great exchange-values. It therefore follows, firstly: The current exchange-values of these commodities express an equality.
>
> (Marx, 1976, p. 127; translation modified)

This equality or commensurability is a condition posited by the practice of exchange. In order for there to be markets, diverse commodities with diverse use-values must be treated as commensurable. But *qua* use-values, they are incommensurable, since every use-value is defined by its specific function. Food is for eating, books are for reading, and I can no more satisfy my hunger for knowledge with a sandwich than I can fill my stomach with the written word. How is it possible, then, for eating and reading, which are not interchangeable, to be exchanged for one another in the commodity-forms of a meal and a book? It seems that two commodities can only appear as exchangeable insofar as their particular use-values are bracketed by the agents of exchange. Hence, wherever the concrete particularity of an object cannot be ignored (e.g. the ox that provides the sole means of ploughing my field, or the locket that is the only physical reminder of my mother), neither can that object be fairly appraised and exchanged. Such irreplaceable objects are 'invaluable', or 'priceless'.

So long as the investigator of social life focuses on use-value, the commensuration that conditions actual practices of exchange remains invisible. Commentators confuse matters greatly when they take Marx's dismissal of use-value to be a dismissal of 'utility'. It is precisely the situation wherein incommensurable uses appear as quanta of utility in general that must be explained, and this situation cannot be explained by reference to itself. In his 1861 manuscripts Marx already complained about economists who 'have no difficulty in overlooking the fact that no 2 use values are absolutely identical [...] and even less difficulty in judging use values, which have no common measure whatever, as exchange values *according to their degree of utility*' (Marx and Engels 1989a, p. 232).

Once we recognize that the practice of exchange must abstract from use-value, it is only a short step to the realization that this abstraction is also, indirectly, an abstraction from the useful character of the labour that made the commodity. Wherever the market is dominant, the particularity of function that rules over concrete labour is suspended, and the most diverse labours mingle and change places. As Marx wrote in the 1861 manuscript, 'the basis of *value* is the fact that human beings relate to one another's labour as equal, as general, and in this form social, labour' (Marx and Engels 1989a, p. 232).

Marx's qualification of 'social' in this sentence requires some attention. Many of the difficulties of the first parts of *Capital* are generated by the circumstance that capitalist society is a market society. Commerce can be fairly widespread in non-capitalist societies, but capitalism cannot exist in non-market societies. In order for Marx to arrive at the specific mechanisms of capitalism, he must first deal with the mechanisms of commodity exchange. The trouble is that commodity exchange throws up a screen in front of capitalism, a screen of things. Because of this, the abstraction of labour is initially mediated through the abstraction of use-value. When we buy and sell things, we do not *directly* exchange our social labour. Instead, this labour – which Smith called the 'co-operation and assistance of great multitudes' (Smith, 1976, p. 18) – must be exhibited in something else. Commodities are the containers in which we exchange our efforts and energy with the efforts and energy of everyone else.[2] Therefore, while we do actually disregard the particularity of our labours, we do so by circumlocution, only in so far as these labours are already embodied in products.

Because capitalism presupposes commodity exchange, commerce mediates the processes of capitalism (except the division of labour within the firm, a crucial exception to which I will return in a moment). That's why Marx has to deal with exchange right away, instead of starting with the labour process, as he had planned to do when working on the *Grundrisse* (Marx 1973, pp. 298, 320). In capitalism, labour-power is a commodity like any other, and the relations between employer and employee are mediated by money, the most developed form of the commodity's exchange-value. The 'thingly veil' remains in place (Marx 1970, p. 34; translation modified). Nonetheless, there is a qualitative difference between the commodity-mediated abstraction of labour definitive of the market and the money-mediated abstraction of labour peculiar to capitalism. Moreover, there is a further abstraction of labour that develops within this latter, and this final abstraction is *not* mediated by commodities, for it is connected to the division of labour within the firm. It is this third abstraction that has the greatest ontological 'density,' since it directly alters the material–technological basis of capital relations. The section of this chapter titled 'The animated monster' of this chapter will trace out how these two factors intensify the abstraction of labour. This will set the stage for a consideration, in the Conclusion, of capital's distinctive mode of productivity: the generativity of this abstract labour.

The subsumption of labour

In the drafts of his 'Critique of Political Economy', Marx gives extensive treatment to capital's twofold control over labour, naming it with the distinction between the formal and the real subsumption of labour.[3] In its final form, however, *Capital* mentions the distinction only in passing (Marx 1976, pp. 645–6). I believe this shift may have been due to certain difficulties in Marx's formulation of the distinction, difficulties I will discuss below. Nonetheless, Marx aligns formal subsumption with the production of absolute surplus-value and real subsumption with the production of relative surplus-value, and this latter pair – what Marx calls the 'material expression' of subsumption (Marx, 1976, p. 1055) – retains an absolute centrality in *Capital*, occupying all of Parts 3 through 5. Therefore, while the *phrases* are largely absent, the *processes* of subsumption are an integral feature of Marx's discussion of capital's production process. Marx's categories of subsumption are especially important from the point of view of this study because they are 'categories for sorting the ways capital makes labour abstract' (Murray, 2000a, p. 30).

Labour is formally subsumed under capital as soon as surplus labour is extracted from the worker through 'a purely *sale and purchase relationship* or *money relationship*' (Marx, 1976, p. 1027; translation modified). Production has to fit into the M—C—M′ formula in order to be capitalist production, and this entails that everything required for production, including the workers' ability to work, must enter into production through sale and purchase. Capitalists control the production process not because of any personal qualities they may have, not because they are favoured by the gods nor because they have conquered, but only because they have hired workers for a wage. Marx calls this control of the labour process by a capitalist 'formal subsumption' 'because it is only *formally* distinct from earlier modes of production' (Marx, 1976, p. 1025; translation modified). In other words, if you enter into a formally capitalist business, you won't be able to tell by examining the labour taking place therein whether it is run by a capitalist or not. The work being done is in no way distinguishable from the work of independent artisans or apprentices, serfs or small peasants. 'The *labour process, technologically* viewed, goes on as before' (Marx, 1976, p. 1026; translation modified).[4]

There are, however, other changes. When labour is hired by capital, it is subordinated to capital's end of creating surplus-value. This subordination manifests itself in the lengthening of the working day and in the close supervision of the labour process by the capitalist. Both of these follow directly from the fact that labour-power is a commodity used by capital for capital's purpose. What this means for labour is that its particular concreteness is further disregarded. Capital, as a form, is 'indifferent to every particularity of its substance', and thus 'the labour which confronts it likewise subjectively has the same totality and abstraction in itself'. Capital moves around to where the rate of profit is high; it 'can come into relation with every *specific* labour; it confronts the *totality* of all labours *dunamei*, and the particular one it confronts at a given time is an accidental matter' (Marx, 1973, pp. 296–7). Patrick Murray passes on a telling example. Explaining the decision of US Steel to change its name to USX, then president of the company James Roderick stated, 'The duty of management is to make money, not steel' (Murray, 2000b, p. 113 n. 46).[5] The labour that management hires to make money is not any labour in particular, for the field of labour that makes money today may not make money next year.[6] Capital that remains loyal to one sort of labour at the expense of profitability will cease to be capital; it will be driven from the field by competition. This abstraction from the particularity of labour is obviously not a theoretical construction, but is carried out in social life.

These developments are not the end, however, but only the beginning of the changes wrought by capital. Formal subsumption does not yet change the technical process of labour, but it is only a matter of time before the controlling power of capital begins to modify its means in view of their new end. Marx calls this reconstruction of the labour process in order to align it more perfectly with the purposes of capital 'real subsumption'.

Valorization demands a reconstruction of labour along two fronts. First, the goal of surplus-value imposes a regime of economy upon the use of all commodities entering into production. For the means and materials of labour, this means a reduction in waste, efforts to find cheaper equivalents,[7] increases in the scale of production, and so on. For the use of labour-power, it entails work speedups and the rearticulation of the labour process itself, through both an infinitesimal division of labour within the workshop, and the mechanization of production. Intimately bound up with this economization is a second transformation, the socialization of labour. Marx is categorical; 'Capitalist production first begins in fact [...] where each individual capital simultaneously employs a comparatively large number of workers', a change which, all alone, 'effects a revolution in the objective conditions of the labour process'; quantitative growth becomes qualitative transformation, for the co-operation of many workers is 'the creation of a productive power, which must be in and for itself a power of the masses' (Marx, 1976, pp. 439, 441, 443; translation modified). No one makes anything in a truly capitalist business, except insofar as they are part of a collectivity. Efficiency always demands cooperation, a division of labour, and, hence, a coordinated effort by many.

This complex of changes in the production process radically reconfigures what workers make and how they make it and, in the process, renders their labour abstract in immediately palpable ways. First, real subsumption deepens the sense in which labour is abstract from the standpoint of capital. Because of the increase in productivity that attends subsumption, the product of the specifically capitalist mode of production 'is not individual goods, but a *mass of commodities*'. Therefore, 'The labour expended on each commodity can no longer be calculated – except as an average, i.e., an ideal estimate' (Marx, 1976, p. 954). In the collective worker, each individual figures only as an aliquot part of the whole. Moreover, the abstraction of labour comes to have both a phenomenal reality for workers and an objective reality within the process of production itself. Because the labour process is broken down into component movements, working really does become an abstract activity, an activity that is not subordinated to a concrete end. From an identity attested in surnames, one's field of labour becomes a matter of no personal import. *What* one makes doesn't matter, only that one has a job and *makes a wage*. Furthermore, the labour process itself comes to be increasingly indifferent to the specificity of what is being made. This begins at the site of the individual worker as a point within that process. Because the final product is only the result of the entire system of movements, no individual worker needs to attend to the function of the product.[8] As Marx writes; 'labour loses all its characteristics of art; as its particular skill becomes something more and more abstract and irrelevant, and as it becomes more and more a *purely abstract* activity, a purely mechanical activity, hence indifferent to its particular form' (Marx, 1973, p. 297).[9]

The real subsumption of labour, therefore, is the creation of a form of labour that is not *technê*. The work we do when we're at work no longer produces useful things according to a mental preconception. Its products are only use-values in the context of the system within which it is embedded. Only social labour can create anything useful. The variety of purposes that defined the myriad branches of *technê* has been melted down into an 'all-purpose' abstract labour, a labour that disregards its own ends in favour of the end of capital.

Marx repeatedly describes the creation of this abstract labour as capital's incorporation of labour. In the *Grundrisse*, he calls capital an 'organic system', and writes; 'This organic system itself, as a totality, has its presuppositions, and its development to its totality consists precisely in subordinating all elements of society to itself, or in creating out of it the organs which it still lacks' (Marx, 1973, p. 278). The processes of subsumption I have just outlined are the mechanisms whereby capital makes labour into its own organ. Since we have seen how this incorporation comes about, I want now to investigate the functioning of the social body created thereby. In other words, I will now turn to capital as a form of society, and ask how this society functions as a whole.

The animated monster

The precise difference between formal and real subsumption seems to elude Marx at times; the reader of 'Results of the Immediate Process of Production' encounters a tendency for formal subsumption to slide ineluctably into real subsumption. The difficulty is in trying to isolate capital's direct control of the production process from any changes in the production process that follow from that control. For example, Marx allows that formal subsumption immediately includes economizing on the means and materials of production (Marx, 1976, p. 1026). Yet, any economy beyond what is called for by the technical requirements of the work – for example, cutting leather to maximize the number of shoes one can make rather than with an eye to the material best suited to protecting the feet – is an alteration of the labour process itself and ought, therefore, to belong only to real subsumption. As I suggested above, this difficulty in fixing the distinction may explain Marx's decision to largely drop the terminology of subsumption from the published version of *Capital*.

Nonetheless, I believe there is a very real distinction at work, one which comes to light if we excavate below the mystification whereby 'the value-creating power of labour appears as a self-valorizing power of capital' (Marx, 1976, pp. 1020–1; translation modified). In this 'capital fetish', capital is identified with the conditions of labour, thereby rendering capital both an eternal necessity and the condition of labour's productivity. Marx claims that this mystification is already present in formal subsumption, but that it 'is greatly intensified' by real subsumption (Marx, 1976, pp. 1020, 1024). I believe, however, that this relative difference in the intensity of mystification marks a fundamental difference between the status of formally subsumptive capital and that of really subsumptive capital. This difference can be brought out by looking first at those 'antediluvian' forms of capital that existed before formal or real subsumption began: usurer's capital and merchant's capital. Both usury and commerce satisfy the general formula for capital; they use money to get more money. So long as these were the only forms of capital in existence in the West, they were generally condemned by the dominant philosophical and moral traditions. Plato, Herodotus, and Thucydides all viewed merchants, and the ports and ships that accompanied them, with suspicion.[10] Aristotle considered commerce to be 'expertise in exchange', which 'is justly blamed since it is not according to nature but involves taking from others' (Aristotle, 1984, p. 49). Much more recently, Benjamin Franklin, usually a fount of capitalist common sense, declared as well that 'commerce is cheating' (cited in Marx, 1976, p. 267). The condemnation of usury is even more sustained and intense.

I want to call attention to the dominant motif in these attacks. Capital that has not subsumed labour is condemned for being either unproductive or unnaturally productive, largely by unfavourable comparison to *technê*. Merchants and usurers are not respectable because they do not subordinate their activity to a concrete function. They don't make anything useful. As Aristotle puts it, 'usury is most reasonably hated because one's possessions derive from money itself and not from that for which it was supplied. For it came into being for the sake of exchange, but interest actually makes more of it' (Aristotle, 1984, p. 49). Dante makes the contrast with *technê* more explicit in Virgil's words from *Inferno*; 'art follows nature as much as it can, [and] from these two we must draw our life and advance our people; and because the usurer holds another way, he scorns nature in herself and in her follower' (Alighieri, 1996, pp. 175–6). Usury and commerce don't produce anything useful for human life, but parasitically insert themselves between the works of others, drawing life and wealth from the social body.[11]

Contrast this ignominy with the position of capital once it has formally subsumed labour. Where the merchant and usurer were solitary parasites on the social body, the early capitalists are able to engage in a spirited polemic to show that they are productive organs of that body, together with the farmers and artisans, and as opposed to the real parasites, the aristocracy, the government, and their servants (Smith, 1976, pp. 351–71; Bataille, 1991). Capital becomes respectable by becoming productive, but it only becomes productive by subsuming labour. There is a marvellous passage from Franklin, that neatly measures the distance travelled from pre-subsumptive to subsumptive capital. Franklin writes:

> Remember, that money is of the prolific, generating nature. Money can beget money, and its offspring can beget more, and so on. Five shillings turned is six, turned again it is seven and threepence, and so on, till it becomes a hundred pounds. The more there is of it, the more it produces every turning, so that the profits rise quicker and quicker. He that kills a breeding-sow, destroys all her offspring to the thousandth generation. He that murders a crown, destroys all that it might have produced, even scores of pounds.
>
> (quoted by Bataille, 1991, p. 126)

By taking direct control of labour, capital incorporates labour, and 'begins to 'work,' as if its body were by love possessed' (Marx, 1976, p. 302). Despite

Franklin's enthusiasm, this can only happen where capital can purchase labour-power on the market. With this purchase, the worker 'surrenders [labour's] creative power, like Esau his birthright for a mess of pottage' (Marx, 1973, p. 307). Capital gets a complete makeover. It has purchased its passage out of the ghettos and ports into polite society, and it has done so only to the extent that the intentionality definitive of production has become abstract.

However, this newfound acceptability can be quite sharply differentiated from capital's status once it has *really* subsumed labour. Real subsumption renders capital's productivity overwhelming and hegemonic in whichever arena the subsumption takes place. Instead of sharing the field with *technê*, capital becomes the only recognized productive power. Within any branch of industry really subsumed under capital, the stubborn intransigence of an independent artisan or small farmer appears as unproductive as the usurer or merchant seemed in ancient Greece. Furthermore, this sentence of social irrelevance is quite ruthlessly enforced by the invisible hand, for an independent artisan cannot possibly compete on the basis of such a mode of life for any length of time, much less expect it to flourish and spread. Far from defining productivity in late modernity, non-subsumed labour, with its concrete aims, has become an exercise in futility.

There is thus a difference of kind between formal and real subsumption. The formal subsumption of labour renders capital productive, but the real subsumption of labour negates the productivity of non-subsumed labour. Capital thereby gains a monopoly on productivity. 'The only worker who is productive is the one who produces surplus-value for the capitalist, or in other words contributes to the self-valorization of capital' (Marx, 1976, p. 644). This monopoly on productivity corresponds to capital becoming the whole of the social body. Capital is the collective labourer, whose organs are the multitude of its productive employees.[12] It is the 'organic system', appropriating social material to its own functions. The socialized totality of production now 'presents itself as the *productive power of capital*, not as the productive power of labour, or even as the productive power of labour so far as it is identical with capital, and in any case not as the productive power of the individual workers or of the workers combined in the production process' (Marx, 1976, p. 1024; translation modified). Marx here declares the end of the era of *technê*, the end of the era in which individual, concrete intentions matter. Under the regime of real subsumption, 'the question whether capital is productive or not is absurd. Labour itself is *productive only* if it is absorbed into capital' (Marx, 1973, p. 308).

Conclusion

But if the productivity of capital is ascendant, right across the face of the globe, this productivity is nonetheless rather odd. Marx is very clear that 'the production of the normal capitalist, of the industrial capitalist as he ought to be, is production for the sake of production' (Marx and Engels 1989b, p. 179). This is not, however, the production of things for the sake of producing things; it is the production of surplus-value for the sake of producing surplus-value. The capitalist 'becomes more or less unable to fulfil his function', Marx writes, 'as soon as he wants the accumulation of pleasures instead of the pleasure of accumulation' (Marx and Engels, 1989b, p. 180). Since capitalist accumulation as such has no object, it is most true to say that capital produces only itself. Capital is self-valorising value, self-reproductive and ever-expansive. Value 'thus appears as a *self* – the incarnation of this self is the capitalist – *the selfhood of value*'. So 'personified' value 'has become a will in its own right, being-for-itself, a conscious end in itself' (Marx and Engels 1989b, pp. 39, 93).

Analytically inclined Marxologists hate it when Marx starts talking like this. Capital sounds like Hegel's *Geist*. It is a mysterious speculative construction that cannot be reduced to any set of lower-order mechanisms, a supra-individual intentional actor, a piece of providence in a godless universe – in short: nonsense.[13] I hope that tracing the various practical mechanisms of abstraction has removed some of the sense of mystery from Marx's presentation. It is clear, for example, that Marx himself wanted to trace the shape of capital as a social totality back to the interactions of its members. Thus, in *Theories of Surplus Value*, he approvingly cites Hodgskin. 'The *capitalist* is the *oppressive middleman*' between the different labourers. If he is put out of view, 'it is plain that *capital* [...] and *co-existing labour* are one; [...] consequently capital and the labouring population are precisely synonymous' (Marx and Engels 1989c, p. 446). This is perfectly in line with his statement from the 'Theses on Feuerbach' that the human essence 'is no abstraction inherent in the single individual. In its actuality, it is the ensemble of social relations' (Marx and Engels 1976, p. 7).

What cannot be reduced, however, is the logic of the capital-form itself, for this is what defines the specificity of *this* ensemble of relations. The intentionality of capital is different from the intentionality of concrete labour. Capital doesn't aim at any good, but at the abstraction from any good. The pursuit of this aim by individual capitalists puts out of view the particularities of the human actors, of their needs, of their products. It cares for these things only so far as they can be reduced to something else (value), only so far as they can be exhibited in money. This is what it means to say that capital is based upon processes of social abstraction; the logic of action that is capital makes abstractions into social forces by treating the abstraction from function as the goal of social practices. Abstraction becomes both the substance and subject of modernity.[14]

This movement whereby abstractions become embodied cannot simply be dismissed as ludicrous[15] or irrational[16] or metaphorical.[17] Marx's own insistence on the mysticism, obfuscation, and fetishism of the capital relation needs to be held together with his insistence that the mystery is real and very effective; 'those who demonstrate that the productive force attributed to capital is a *displacement*, a *transposition of the productive force* of labour, forget precisely that capital itself is essentially this *displacement, this transposition*, [...] this *transubstantiation*' (Marx, 1973, p. 308). Marx more than once refers to capital's processes of abstraction as transubstantiations[18] and, more broadly, illustrates his critique of economics by referring the workings of capitalism to the workings of religion. In this regard, the earliest such cross-reference by Marx is illuminating. In a footnote to his dissertation, Marx dismisses as irrelevant Kant's critique of the ontological argument for the existence of God. Marx writes (Marx and Engels 1975, p. 140; translation modified):

> [T]he ontological argument means nothing but: 'what I really imagine is an actual idea for me', that works on me, and in this sense *all* gods, heathen as well as Christian, have possessed a real existence. [...] Here, also, Kant's critique means nothing. If someone imagines that they possess a hundred dollars, if this idea is no arbitrary, subjective idea to him, if he believes in it, then the hundred imagined dollars have as much value as a hundred actual dollars. He will, e.g., make debts on his imagination, they will *work, as the whole of humanity has made debts on its gods*. Actual dollars have the same existence as imagined gods. Has the dollar another existence than in the imagination, if the general, or rather, social imagination of humanity?

In another footnote, written 26 years later, Marx seems to continue this thought: 'It is, in fact, much easier to find by analysis the earthly kernel of religious fog-formations than to do the opposite, to develop from the always actual relations of life their deified forms. The latter is the only materialist, and, thus, the only scientific method' (Marx, 1976, p. 494n; translation modified). Marx attempts in *Capital* to do just this, to develop from the structure of our active interrelations – buying and selling goods, hiring labour, looking to make a profit, etc. – the coming into being of an abstract, spiritual subject, which we embody as its moments, but the logic of which we do not control.

Marxism is sometimes accused of presenting a collective action problem for a world of self-interested individual actors. I think this is misleading. The problem that confronts us, according to Marx, is not an absence of or insuperable barriers to collective action. Instead, capitalism confronts us with a compulsive form of collective action. This form of collective action, the abstract labour that forms capital, is not difficult to engage in, but difficult to refuse. Nonetheless, if Marx is right, refuse it we must. The problem, then, is how to escape from compulsive collective action. Here is Rhodes.

Notes

1. I am indebted to the work of Postone (1993), Arthur (1986), Murray (2000a, b) and Reuten (1993), who have opened up these areas of inquiry before me.
2. This account meets the condition Carver (1998, p. 80) lays out for the acceptability of Marx's thesis that labour is objectified in value: 'the thesis is only acceptable if there are good reasons for believing that the participants in a capitalist economy generally avow that value is itself a substance, or that it represents something substantial, or if they could be shown in general to have presupposed such views in their social action.' My account meets the third version of Carver's condition.
3. See Marx, 1976, pp. 1019–38 and Marx and Engels, 1989a, pp. 92–3, 233–306.
4. Cf. Marx and Engels, 1989a, p. 92 and Marx, 1976, p. 425.
5. Cf. Marx, 1976, pp. 372–3.
6. See 'Wage Labour and Capital' in Marx and Engels, 1977, p. 212.
7. See Marx, 1976, p. 359 for some particularly gruesome examples.
8. See Marx, 1976, pp. 482, 475 n. 34 and 1973, p. 693.
9. Cf. Arthur, 1986, p. 347.
10. The cities of both the Republic and the Laws are purposefully placed inland, away from any harbors. Herodotus' History can be read as an extended allegory of the corruption that attends ship-building, and the consequent imminent downfall of the Athenian empire. Thucydides provides further grist for this mill.
11. Cf. Marx, 1976, p. 267.
12. See Marx, 1976, pp. 457, 643–4.
13. See e.g. Elster, 1985; cf. Postone, 1993, p. 75.
14. See Murray, 2000a, p. 61.
15. Cf. Murray, 2000a, p. 58.
16. Cf. Wolff, 1988, p. 52.
17. Cf. Reuten, 1993, p. 102.
18. See Reuten, 1993.

Bibliography

Alighieri, Dante (1996) *Inferno: Volume 1 of The Divine Comedy of Dante Alighieri*, (trans. and ed.) R. M. Durling (Oxford: Oxford University Press).

Aristotle (1984) *The Politics*, (trans.) C. Lord (Chicago: University of Chicago Press).

Arthur, C. (1986) *Dialectics of Labour: Marx and His Relation to Hegel* (Oxford: Basil Blackwell).

Bataille, G (1991) *The Accursed Share: An Essay on General Economy*, vol. 1, (trans.) R. Hurley (New York: Zone Books).

Carver, T. (1998) *The Postmodern Marx* (University Park, PA: Pennsylvania State University Press).

Cash, Johnny (1963) 'The Ballad of John Henry', *Blood, Sweat and Tears* (Columbia Records).

Elson, D. (ed.) (1979) *Value: The Representation of Labour in Capitalism* (London and Atlantic Highlands, NJ: CSE Books and Humanities Press).

Elster, J. (1985) *Making Sense of Marx* (Cambridge and Paris: Cambridge University Press and Editions de la Maison des Sciences de l'Homme).

Marx, Karl (1970) *A Contribution to the Critique of Political Economy*, (trans.) S. Ryazanskaya, (ed.) M. Dodd (London and New York: Lawrence and Wishart and International Publishers).

—— (1973) *Grundrisse: Foundations of the Critique of Political Economy*, (trans.) M. Nicolaus (New York: Vintage Books).

—— (1974) *Early Writings*, (trans.) R. Livingstone and G. Benton, (ed.) Q. Hoare (New York: Vintage Books).

—— (1976) 'The Production Process of Capital', in Karl Marx and Friedrich Engels *Capital: A Critique of Political Economy*, vol. 1, (trans.) B. Fowkes (New York: Vintage Books).

—— (1995) *The Poverty of Philosophy*, (trans.) H. Quelch (Amherst, NY: Prometheus Books).

Marx, Karl and Engels, F. (1975) *Collected Works*, vol. 1 (London and New York: Lawrence and Wishart and International Publishers).

—— (1976) *Collected Works*, vol. 5 (London and New York: Lawrence and Wishart and International Publishers).

—— (1977) *Collected Works*, vol. 9 (London and New York: Lawrence and Wishart and International Publishers).

—— (1989a) *Collected Works*, vol. 30 (London and New York: Lawrence and Wishart and International Publishers).

—— (1989b) *Collected Works*, vol. 31 (London and New York: Lawrence and Wishart and International Publishers).

—— (1989c) *Collected Works*, vol. 32 (London and New York: Lawrence and Wishart and International Publishers).

Murray, P. (2000a) 'Marx's "Truly Social" Labour Theory of Value: Part I, Abstract Labour in Marxian Value Theory', *Historical Materialism: Research in Critical Marxist Theory* , 6 (1), 27–66.

—— (2000b) 'Marx's "Truly Social" Labour Theory of Value: Part II, How is Labour that is under the Sway of Capital *Actually* Abstract?', *Historical Materialism: Research in Critical Marxist Theory* , 7 (1), 99–136.

Postone, M. (1993) *Time, Labor, and Social Domination: A Reinterpretation of Marx's Critical Theory* (Cambridge: Cambridge University Press).

Reuten, G. (1993) 'The Difficult Labor of a Theory of Social Value: Metaphors and Systematic Dialectics at the Beginning of Marx's *Capital*', in F. Moseley (ed.) *Marx's Method in Capital: A Reexamination* (Atlantic Highlands, NJ: Humanities Press, 1993).

Roemer, J. (1985) 'Should Marxists be Interested in Exploitation?', *Philosophy and Public Affairs*, 14 (1), 30–65.

Smith, A. (1976) *An Enquiry into the Nature and Causes of the Wealth of Nations*, (ed.) E. Cannan (Chicago: University of Chicago Press).

Wolff, R. P. (1988) *Moneybags Must Be So Lucky: On the Literary Structure of Capital* (Amherst, MA: University of Massachusetts Press).

PART IV   TWENTIETH-CENTURY MARXISM

12
The Subject and Social Theory: Marx and Lukács on Hegel

Moishe Postone

It is very difficult to imagine addressing the relation of Marx and Hegel – and, relatedly, the question of the Subject and critical social theory – without considering the towering figure of Georg Lukács.[1] In *History and Class Consciousness*, written in the aftermath of the Russian Revolution and the failure of revolution in central Europe, Lukács (1971) effects a fundamental theoretical break with Second International Marxism by reasserting the Hegelian dimension of Marx's thought. On this basis, he fundamentally criticized scientism and faith in linear historical progress, arguing that such positions were the deep theoretical grounds for the world-historical failures of Social Democracy to prevent war in 1914 and bring about radical historical change in 1918–19.

In appropriating Hegel, Lukács places the issue of subjectivity and the notion of praxis at the centre of the Marxian project in ways that broaden and deepen the critique of capitalist society. His essays grasp Marx's critique as a dialectical theory of praxis, on the basis of which he develops a rich theory of history, culture, and consciousness, a powerful revolutionary social theory very different from the mechanical, affirmative, and reductionist Marxism of the Second International.

Hegel and the Hegelian turn in Marxism, as powerfully represented by Lukács, however, have been strongly criticized more recently by structuralists and poststructuralists for whom concepts such as totality and the historical Subject, which are central to Lukács's project, are anti-emancipatory, concepts of domination. Nevertheless, the global historical transformations of recent decades – including the crisis of the Fordist/Keynesian welfare state, the collapse of Soviet communism, and the emergence of a neo-liberal capitalist global order – have underlined the importance of the issue of historical dynamics, and cannot be elucidated adequately by the poststructuralist and postmodernist theories that were dominant in the 1970s and 1980s. They suggest the need for a renewed theoretical concern with capitalism.

I am going to outline a reading of Marx that, while indebted to Lukács, seeks to get beyond the opposition of Hegelian and anti-Hegelian critical approaches. The relation of Marx's mature theory to Hegel, I argue, is different from that which Lukács presents. Indeed, Marx's critical appropriation of Hegel provides the basis for a critique both of Lukács as well as of poststructuralism in ways that can avoid the weaknesses of each while incorporating their strengths.

The critique of capitalism as a critique of modernity

Lukács's theory of praxis – especially as developed in his essay, 'Reification and the Consciousness of the Proletariat' – does not grasp the categories of Marx's mature critique, such as the commodity, simply as economic categories. Instead, Lukács interprets them as determinations of both subjective and objective dimensions of modern social life.[2] On the basis of this argument, that the subjective and objective dimensions of social life are intrinsically interrelated, Lukács develops a sophisticated social theory of consciousness and of knowledge entailing a fundamental critique of Cartesianism, of subject–object dualism. His theory of praxis allows him to argue that the subject is both producer and product of the dialectical process (Lukács, 1971, p. 142). Consequently:

> Thought and existence are not identical in the sense that they 'correspond' to each other, or 'reflect' each other, that they 'run parallel' to each other, or 'coincide' with each other (all expressions that conceal a rigid duality). Their identity is that they are aspects of the same real historical and dialectical process.
>
> (Lukács, 1971, p. 204)

Within the framework of Lukács's categorial analysis, then, 'consciousness … is a necessary, indispensable, integral part of that process of [historical] becoming' (Lukács, 1971, p. 204).

In analysing the interrelatedness of consciousness and history, Lukács's primary concern is to delineate the historical possibility of revolutionary class-consciousness. At the same time, he presents a brilliant social and historical analysis of modern western philosophy. Such thought, according to Lukács, attempts to wrestle with the problems generated by the peculiar abstract forms of life characteristic of its (capitalist) context, while remaining bound to the immediacy of the forms of appearance of that context. Hence, philosophical thought misrecognizes the problems generated by its context as transhistorical and ontological (Lukács, 1971, pp. 110–12). Marx, according to Lukács, was the first to adequately address the problems with which modern philosophy had wrestled. He did so by changing the terms of those problems, by grounding them historically in the social forms of capitalism expressed by categories such as the commodity.

Recovering this mode of analysis, Lukács provides a social and historical analysis of modern philosophical and sociological thought. Significantly, he does not do so first and foremost with reference to considerations of class interest. Rather than focusing on the *function* of thought for a system of social domination, such as class domination, Lukács attempts to ground the *nature* of such thought in the peculiarities of the social forms constitutive of capitalism such as the commodity.

By intrinsically relating social and cultural aspects of life, this appropriation of Marx's categorial analysis breaks decisively with classical Marxist base–superstructure conceptions. Such conceptions are themselves dualistic – the base being understood as the most fundamental level of social objectivity, the superstructure being identified with social subjectivity. Lukács's approach also differs from that of the other great theorist of praxis, Antonio Gramsci, inasmuch as it relates forms of thought and social forms intrinsically and does not treat their relation as extrinsic or in a functionalist manner. It not only elucidates the hegemonic function of those forms, but also delineates an overarching framework of historically determined forms of subjectivity within which class-related differentiation takes place. Lukács's approach, in other words, can serve as the point of departure for an analysis of the nature of modern, capitalist cultural forms themselves.

In addition to providing the basis for a sophisticated historical theory of subjectivity, Lukács, in his 'Reification' essay, also shifts the focus of the critique of capitalism, rendering it more adequate to the significant social, economic, political, and cultural features of twentieth-century capitalism. His reading of Marx's categories goes far beyond the traditional critical analysis of capitalism in terms of the market and private property. Instead, he regards as central the processes of rationalization and bureaucratization emphasized by Max Weber, and grounds those processes in Marx's analysis of the commodity as the basic structuring form of capitalist society. Lukács argues that the processes of rationalization and quantification that mould modern institutions are rooted in the commodity form (Lukács, 1971, pp. 85–110). Like Marx, he characterizes modern capitalist society in terms of the domination of people by time, and treats the factory as a concentrated version of the structure of capitalist society as a whole (Lukács, 1971, pp. 89–90). This structure is also expressed in the nature of modern bureaucracy (Lukács, 1971, pp. 98–100), and gives rise to a determinate form of the state and of law (Lukács, 1971, p. 95). By grounding these features of modernity in Marx's categories, Lukács seeks to show that what Weber described as the 'iron cage' of modern social life is a function of capitalism and, hence, transformable.

Lukács's essay on reification demonstrates the power and rigour of a categorially based critical theory of modern capitalist society, both as a theory of the intrinsic relatedness of culture, consciousness, and society and as a critique of capitalism. His critique extends beyond a concern with issues of class domination and exploitation. It seeks to critically grasp and socially ground processes of rationalization and quantification, as well as an abstract mode of power and domination that cannot be understood adequately in terms of concrete personal or group domination. The conception of capitalism implied by Lukács's analysis is much broader and deeper than the traditional one of a system of exploitation based on private property and the market. Indeed, his conception implies that the latter ultimately may not be the most basic features of capitalism. On the other hand, Lukács's analysis provides a level of conceptual rigor absent from most discussions of modernity. It indicates that 'modern society' is basically a descriptive term for a form of social life that can be analysed with greater rigour as capitalism.

Yet, in spite of the depth he introduces to the critique of capitalism, Lukács misrecognizes central aspects of the remarkable theoretical turn effected by Marx and fails to realize the promise of the sort of categorial critique he outlines. Consequently, although Lukács's approach presents a critique of capitalism fundamentally richer and more adequate than that of traditional Marxism, it ultimately remains bound to some of that theory's fundamental presuppositions. This weakens his attempt to formulate a more fundamental critique of capitalism, one that would be adequate to the twentieth century.

Hegel and the historical subject

In order to elaborate these contentions let me briefly outline what I regard as a fundamental difference between Lukács's appropriation of Hegel and that undertaken by Marx in his mature works. As is well known, Hegel attempted to overcome the classical theoretical dichotomy of subject and object, arguing that reality, natural as well as social, subjective as well as objective, is constituted by practice – by the objectifying practice of the *Geist*, the world-historical Subject. The *Geist* constitutes reality by means of a process of externalization; in the process, it reflexively constitutes itself. Inasmuch as both objectivity and subjectivity are constituted by the *Geist* as it unfolds dialectically, they are of the same substance. Both are moments of a general whole that is substantially homogeneous – a totality.

For Hegel, then, the *Geist* is at once subjective and objective; it is the identical subject–object, the 'substance' that is, at the same time, 'Subject': 'The living *substance* is, further, that being which is [...] *Subject* or, what is the same thing, which is [...] actual only insofar as it is the movement of positing itself, or the mediation of the process of becoming different from itself with itself' (Hegel, 1966, p. 28; translation modified, emphasis added).

The process by which this self-moving substance/Subject, the *Geist*, constitutes objectivity and subjectivity as it unfolds dialectically is a historical one grounded in the internal contradictions of the totality. The historical process of self-objectification, according to Hegel, is one of self-alienation, and leads ultimately to the reappropriation by the *Geist* of that which had been alienated in the course of its unfolding. That is, historical development has an end point: the realization by the *Geist* of itself as a totalizing and totalized Subject.

In 'Reification and the Consciousness of the Proletariat', Lukács translates Hegel's concept of the *Geist* anthropologically, identifying the proletariat in a 'materialized' Hegelian manner as the identical subject–object of the historical process, as the historical Subject, constituting the social world and itself through its labour. Relatedly, Lukács analyses society as a totality, constituted by labour, traditionally understood as a social activity mediating humans and nature. The existence of this totality, according to Lukács, is veiled by the fragmented and particularistic character of bourgeois social relations. By overthrowing the capitalist order, the proletariat would realize itself as the historical Subject; the totality it constitutes would openly come into its own. The totality and, hence, labour, provide the *standpoint* of Lukács's critical analysis of capitalist society (Lukács, 1971, pp. 102–21, 135, 145, 151–3, 162, 175, 197–200).

Lukács's interpretation of the categories and his reading of Hegel, in particular his identification of the proletariat with the concept of the identical subject–object and his affirmative view of totality, have frequently been identified with Marx's position.[3] A close reading of *Capital*, however, indicates that Marx's appropriation of Hegel in his mature works differs fundamentally from Lukács's affirmation of totality as the standpoint of critique and his identification of Hegel's identical subject–object with the proletariat. This, in turn, suggests that their understandings of a critical theory of modern, capitalist society are very different.

At the beginning of *Capital*, Marx refers to value as having a 'substance', which he identifies as abstract human labour (Marx, 1976, p. 128). Marx no longer considers the concept of 'substance' to be simply a theoretical hypostatization, as he did in his early works, but now conceives of it as an attribute of value – that is, of the peculiar, labour-mediated form of social relations that characterizes capitalism.[4] 'Substance', for Marx, is now an expression of a determinate social reality. He investigates that social reality in *Capital* by unfolding logically the commodity and money forms leading to the complex structure of social relations expressed by his category of capital. Marx initially determines capital in terms of value, as self-valorizing value. At this point in his exposition, Marx presents the category of capital in terms that clearly relate it to Hegel's concept of *Geist*:

It [value – M.P.] is constantly changing from one form into the other without becoming lost in this movement; it thus transforms itself into an *automatic subject* [...] In truth, however, value is here the *subject* of a process in which, while constantly assuming the form in turn of money and of commodities, it [...] valorizes itself [...] [V]alue suddenly presents

itself as a *self-moving substance* which passes through a process of its own, and for which the commodity and money are both mere forms.
(Marx, 1976, pp. 255–6; translation modified, emphasis added)

In *Capital*, then, Marx explicitly characterizes capital as the self-moving substance that is Subject. In so doing, he implicitly suggests that a historical Subject in the Hegelian sense does indeed exist in capitalism. Note, however, that he does not identify that Subject with any social grouping, such as the proletariat, or with humanity. Instead, Marx grasps it with reference to the social relations constituted by the forms of objectifying practice expressed by the category of capital.

Marx's interpretation of the historical Subject with reference to the category of capital suggests that the social relations that characterize capitalism are of a very peculiar sort – they possess the attributes that Hegel accords the *Geist*. This, in turn, indicates that the most fundamental social relations at his critique's centre cannot be adequately understood in terms of class relations but as forms of social mediation expressed by categories such as commodity and capital. Marx's Subject is like Hegel's: it is abstract and cannot be identified with any social actors; moreover, it unfolds temporally independent of will.

As the Subject, capital is a remarkable 'subject'. Whereas Hegel's Subject is transhistorical and knowing, in Marx's analysis it is historically determinate and blind. As a structure constituted by determinate forms of practice, capital, in turn, is constitutive of forms of social practice and subjectivity; as a self-reflexive social form it may induce self-consciousness. Unlike Hegel's *Geist*, however, it does not possess self-consciousness. Subjectivity and the socio-historical Subject, in other words, must be distinguished in Marx's analysis.

Marx's identification of the identical subject–object with determinate forms of social relations has very important implications for a theory of subjectivity. With this theoretical move, Marx recasts the epistemological problem from a consideration of the knowing individual (or supra-individual) subject and its relation to an external (or externalized) world, to one of forms of social mediation (constituted by praxis), considered as determinations of social subjectivity as well as objectivity.[5] The problem of knowledge now becomes a question of the subjective dimension of determinate forms of social mediation.

This reading of *Capital* appropriates Lukács's understanding of Marx's categories as subjective and objective, and cultural and social. Yet it also indicates that those categories have a different meaning than that accorded them by Lukács, who implicitly posits 'labour' (labour in general, transhistorically conceived) as the constituting substance of a Subject, which is prevented by capitalist relations from realizing itself. Lukács's historical Subject, it should be noted, has the same basic attributes as the subject theorized by, for example, John Locke and Adam Smith: it constitutes itself and the world through 'labour'. In that sense, the historical Subject in Lukács can be understood as a collective version of the modern, bourgeois subject. This, in turn, is related to an underlying conception of socialism as the realization of the ideals of the great bourgeois revolutions. (I am arguing, in other words, that the transhistorical concept of 'labour' and the notion of the [bourgeois] subject – whether interpreted as the individual or as a class – are intrinsically related.)

Note that Lukács's interpretation implicitly treats capitalist relations as extrinsic to labour. Although *History and Class Consciousness* does contain criticisms of the structure of factory labour, its underlying presuppositions are consonant with traditional approaches to capitalism essentially in terms of the market and private property – that is, in terms extrinsic to labour.

Marx's critique of Hegel breaks with the presuppositions of such a position (which, nevertheless, became dominant within the socialist tradition). Rather than viewing capitalist relations as extrinsic to the Subject, hindering its full realization, Marx analyses those very relations, characterized by their quasi-objective form, as constituting what Hegel grasped as a historical Subject. This theoretical turn means that Marx's mature theory is not bound to the notion that social actors, such as the proletariat, constitute a historical meta-Subject that will realize itself in a future society. Indeed, it implies a critique of such a notion.

A similar difference between Marx and Lukács exists with regard to the Hegelian concept of totality. For Lukács, a social totality is constituted by 'labour', but is veiled, fragmented, and prevented from realizing itself by capitalist relations. It represents the *standpoint* of the critique of the capitalist present, and will be realized in socialism. Marx's categorial determination of capital as the historical Subject, however, indicates that the totality and the labour that constitutes it have become the *objects* of his critique. The capitalist social formation, according to Marx, is unique inasmuch as it is constituted by a qualitatively homogeneous social 'substance'. Hence, it exists as a social totality. Other social formations are not so totalized; their fundamental social relations are not qualitatively homogeneous. They cannot be grasped by the concept of 'substance', cannot be unfolded from a single structuring principle, and do not display an immanent, necessary historical logic.

The idea that capital, and not the proletariat or the species, is the total Subject clearly implies that, for Marx, the historical negation of capitalism would not involve the *realization*, but the *abolition*, of the totality. It follows that the contradiction driving the unfolding of this totality does not drive the totality forward towards its full realization, but, rather, towards the possibility of its historical abolition. That is, the contradiction expresses the temporal finiteness of the totality by pointing beyond it.

The determination of capital as the historical Subject grounds capitalism's dynamic in historically specific social relations (commodity, capital) that are constituted by structured forms of practice and, yet, are alienated: they acquire a quasi-independent existence and subject people to quasi-objective constraints. Capital, as analysed by Marx, is a dialectical process that, by virtue of being quasi-objective, quantifiable, and independent of will, presents itself as a logic. The existence of a historical logic is not, within this framework, a characteristic of human history as such but, rather, a historically specific, distinguishing feature of capitalism that Hegel (and Lukács, and most Marxist thinkers) projected transhistorically onto all of human social life as History. Marx's mature analysis, then, changes the terms of debate regarding history. He neither treats historical logic affirmatively, nor as an illusion, but as a form of domination rooted in the social forms of capitalism.

Paradoxically, this historically specific understanding of history possesses an emancipatory moment not available to those positions that, explicitly or implicitly, identify the historical Subject with the labouring class. Such 'materialist' interpretations of Hegel which posit the class or the species as the historical Subject seek to enhance human dignity by emphasizing the role of practice in the creation of history. Within the framework of the interpretation outlined here, however, such positions are only apparently emancipatory, for the very existence of a historical logic is an expression of heteronomy, of alienated practice. Accordingly, the call for the full realization of the Subject could only imply the full realization of an alienated social form.

It should be evident by now that the critical thrust of Marx's analysis, according to this reading, is similar in some respects to that of poststructuralist approaches inasmuch as it entails a critique of totality, of the Subject, and of a dialectical logic of history. However, whereas Marx grasps these conceptions as expressions of the reality of capitalist society, poststructuralist approaches deny their existence. Seeking to expand the realm of human freedom, such positions ignore the reality of alienated social relations and cannot grasp the historical tendencies of capitalist society. Consequently such approaches are, contrary to their intentions, profoundly disempowering.

Those positions that assert the existence of a totality, but do so in an affirmative fashion, then, are related to those that deny totality's very existence in order to save the possibility of freedom. Both positions are one-sided: they posit, albeit in opposed fashion, a transhistorical identity between what is and what should be, between recognizing the existence of totality and affirming it. Marx, on the other hand, analyses totality as a heteronomous reality in order to uncover the historically emergent conditions for its abolition.

Totality and history

At this point I shall briefly outline a reading of Marx's categories very different from that presented by Lukács. Although indebted to Lukács's focus on the categories, this reading could serve as the basis for a critical theory of capitalism that is able to overcome the dualism of his specific approach as well as its traditionalist assumptions.

Lukács analyses central aspects of modernity – for example, the factory, bureaucracy, the form of the state and of law – with reference to processes of rationalization grounded in the commodity form. He describes these processes in terms of the subsumption of the qualitative by the quantitative, arguing, for example, that capitalism is characterized by a trend towards greater rationalization and calculability, which eliminates the qualitative, human, and individual attributes of the workers (Lukács, 1971, p. 88). Relatedly, he maintains that time loses its qualitative, variable, and flowing nature and becomes a quantifiable continuum filled with quantifiable 'things' (Lukács, 1971, p. 90). Because capitalism entails the subsumption of the qualitative under the quantitative, according to Lukács, its unitary character is abstract, general, and formalistic.

Nevertheless, although the rationalization of the world effected by the commodity relation may appear to be complete, Lukács argues, it actually is limited by its own formalism (Lukács, 1971, p. 101). Its limits emerge clearly in periods of crisis, when capitalism is revealed as a whole made up of partial systems that are only contingently related, an irrational whole of highly rational parts (Lukács, 1971, pp. 101–2). The crisis, in other words, reveals that there are qualitative conditions attached to the quantitative relations of capitalism, 'that it is not merely a question of units of value which can easily be compared with each other, but also use-values of a definite kind which must fulfil a definite function in production and consumption' (Lukács, 1971, p. 106). Hence, capitalism cannot be grasped as a rational totality. Indeed such knowledge of the whole would amount to the virtual abolition of the capitalist economy, according to Lukács (1971, p. 102).

Lukács, then, grasps capitalism essentially in terms of the problem of formalism, as a form of social life that does not grasp its own content. This suggests that when he claims the commodity form structures modern, capitalist society, he understands that form solely in terms of its abstract, quantitative, and formal dimension – its value dimension. He thereby posits the use-value dimension as the 'real material substratum', as a quasi-ontological content, separable from the form, which is constituted by labour, transhistorically understood.

Within this framework, getting beyond bourgeois thought means getting beyond the formalistic rationalism of such thought, that is, beyond the diremption of form and content effected by capitalism. And this, Lukács argues, requires a concept of form that is oriented towards the concrete content of its material substratum; it requires a dialectical theory of praxis (Lukács, 1971, pp. 121–42). It is Hegel, according to Lukács, who points the way to such a theory by turning to history as the concrete and total dialectical process between subject and object. Yet, Lukács claims, although Hegel develops the dialectical method, which grasps the reality of human history and shows the way to the overcoming of the antinomies of bourgeois thought, he is unable to discover the identical subject–object in history (Lukács, 1971, p. 145). Instead, he locates it idealistically, outside of history, in the *Geist*. This results in a concept mythology, which reintroduces all the antinomies of classical philosophy (Lukács, 1971, pp. 145–8).

Overcoming those antinomies entails a social and historical version of Hegel's solution, according to Lukács. The adequate 'solution' is provided by the proletariat, which is able to discover within itself, on the basis of its life experience, the identical subject–object (Lukács, 1971, p. 149). Lukács then proceeds to develop a theory of the class-consciousness of the proletariat (Lukács, 1971, pp. 149–209). I shall not discuss this theory at length other than to note that, unlike Marx, Lukács does not present his account with reference to the development of capital – for example, in terms of possibilities that emerge as a result of changes in the nature of surplus value (from absolute to relative surplus value) and related changes in the development of the process of production. Instead, he outlines a dialectic of immediacy and mediation, quantity and quality, which could lead to the self-awareness of the proletariat as subject. His account is curiously devoid of a historical dynamic. History, which Lukács conceives of as the dialectical process of the self-constitution of humanity, is indeterminate in this essay; it is not analysed with reference to the historical development of capitalism.

Indeed, Lukács treats capitalism as an essentially static, abstract quantitative form that is superimposed on, and veils, the true nature of the concrete, qualitative, social content. Within the framework of his account, the historical dialectic, constituted by praxis, operates on the level of the 'real' social content, that is, class relations; it is ultimately opposed to the categories of capitalism. Those categories, then, veil what is constituted by praxis; they are not themselves categories of praxis. The opposition Lukács draws between 'the developing tendencies of history' and 'the empirical facts', whereby the former constitutes a 'higher reality', also expresses this understanding (Lukács, 1971, p. 181).[6] History here refers to the level of praxis, as Lukács understands it, to the 'real' social content, whereas the empirical 'facts' operate on the level of the economic categories.

How, then, does Lukács deal with capitalism's dynamic? He does refer to the immanent, blind dynamic of capitalist society, which he characterizes as a manifestation of the rule of capital over labour (Lukács, 1971, p. 181). Nevertheless, Lukács does not ultimately take seriously that dynamic as a historical dynamic, a quasi-independent social reality at the heart of capitalism. Instead he treats it as a reified manifestation of a more fundamental social reality, as a ghostly movement that veils 'real history':

> This image of a frozen reality that nevertheless is caught up in an unremitting ghostly movement at once becomes meaningful when the reality

is dissolved into the process of which man is the driving force. This can be seen only from the standpoint of the proletariat because the meaning of these tendencies is the abolition of capitalism and so for the bourgeoisie to become conscious of them would be tantamount to suicide.

(Lukács, 1971, p. 181)

'Real' history, according to Lukács, is the dialectical historical process constituted by praxis. It operates on a more fundamental level of social reality than what is grasped by the categories of capitalism, and points beyond that society. This 'deeper', more substantive, level of social reality is veiled by the immediacy of capitalist forms; it can only be grasped from a standpoint that breaks through that immediacy. And this standpoint, for Lukács, is a possibility that is available structurally to the proletariat (Lukács, 1971, p. 149). The historical overcoming of capitalism by the proletariat, then, would involve overcoming the formalistic, quantitative dimension of modern social life (value), thereby allowing the real, substantive, historical nature of society (the dimension of use-value, labour, the proletariat) to emerge openly and come into its own historically.

Lukács, then, presents a positive materialist version of Hegel's dialectical method. Lukács affirms the dialectical process of history constituted by the praxis of the proletariat (and, hence, the notions of history, totality, dialectic, labour, and the proletariat) *in opposition* to capitalism. We have seen, however, that Marx interprets the Hegelian identical subject–object *in terms of* the category of capital. This indicates, as already noted, that precisely what Lukács appropriates from Hegel as pointing beyond capitalism – the idea of a dialectical historical logic, the notion of totality, the identical subject–object – are analysed by Marx as characteristics of capital. What Lukács understands as socially ontological, outside the purview of the categories, is grasped critically as intrinsic to capital by the categories of Marx's critique of political economy.

Lukács's analysis in the 'Reification' essay separates and opposes the quantitative and the qualitative and, relatedly, form and content. These oppositions are bound to his understanding of the relation of value and use-value and, hence, of the commodity form. Lukács, as we have seen, interprets the commodity as a historically specific abstract form (value) superimposed upon a transhistorical concrete substantive content (use-value, labour), which constitutes the 'real' nature of society. For Lukács, the relation of form and content is contingent in capitalism. Relatedly, a concept of form that is not indifferent to its content would point beyond capitalism.

This, however, is not the case with Marx's analysis of the commodity. At the heart of Marx's analysis is his argument that labour in capitalism has a 'double character': it is both 'concrete labour' and 'abstract labour' (Marx, 1976, pp. 128–37). 'Concrete labour' refers to the fact that some form of what we consider labouring activity mediates the interactions of humans with nature in all societies. 'Abstract labour' does not simply refer to con-crete labour in the abstract, to 'labour' in general, but is a very different sort of category. It signifies that labour in capitalism also has a unique social function that is not intrinsic to labouring activity as such: it mediates a new, quasi-objective form of social interdependence (Postone, 1993, pp. 123–85). 'Abstract labour', as a historically specific mediating function of labour, is the content or, better, 'substance' of value (Marx, 1976, p. 128). Form and content are indeed intrinsically related here as a fundamental determination of capitalism.

Labour in capitalism, according to Marx, then, is not only labour, as we transhistorically and commonsensically understand it, but also is a histori-cally specific socially mediating activity. Hence its products – commodity, capital – are both concrete labour products and objectified forms of social mediation. According to this analysis, the peculiar quasi-objective, for-mal social relations that fundamentally characterize capitalist society are dualistic: they are characterized by the opposition of an abstract, general, homogenous dimension and a concrete, particular, material dimension, both of which appear to be 'natural', rather than social, and condition social conceptions of natural reality. Whereas Lukács understands the commodity only in terms of its abstract dimension, Marx analyses the commodity as both abstract and concrete. Within this framework, Lukács's analysis falls prey to a fetish form; it naturalizes the concrete dimension of the commod-ity form.

The form of mediation constitutive of capitalism, in Marx's analysis, gives rise to a new form of social domination – one that subjects people to impersonal, increasingly rationalized structural imperatives and constraints. It is the domination of people by time. This temporal domination is real, not ghostly. It cannot be grasped adequately in terms of class domination or, more generally, in terms of the concrete domination of social group-ings or of institutional agencies of the state and/or the economy. It has no determinate locus and, although constituted by determinate forms of social practice, appears not to be social at all.[7] Moreover, the temporal form of domination analysed by Marx in *Capital* is dynamic, not static. Whereas Lukács affirms history as a dynamic reality that is veiled by capitalism, Marx analyses it critically as heteronomous, as a basic characteristic of capital-ism. In *Capital*, the unstable duality of the commodity form generates a dialectical interaction of value and use-value that gives rise to a very com-plex, non-linear, historical dynamic underlying modern capitalist society (Marx, 1976, pp. 283ff.). The use-value dimension here is not outside of the basic structuring forms of capitalism, but is one of their integral moments (Postone, 1993, pp. 263–384). The dynamic generated by the dialectic of value and use-value is characterized, on the one hand, by ongoing trans-formations of production and, more generally, of social life. On the other hand, this historical dynamic entails the ongoing reconstitution of its own fundamental condition as an unchanging feature of social life – namely that social mediation ultimately is effected by labour and, hence, that living labour remains integral to the process of production (considered in terms of society as a whole), regardless of the level of productivity. The historical dynamic of capitalism ceaselessly generates what is 'new', while regenerating what is the 'same' (Postone, 1993, pp. 287–306). This dynamic both generates the possibility of another organization of social life and, yet, hinders that possibility from being realized.

Marx's mature critique, therefore, no longer entails a 'materialist', anthropological inversion of Hegel's idealistic dialectic of the sort undertaken by Lukács. Rather, it is, in a sense, the materialist 'justification' of that dialectic. Marx implicitly argues that the so-called 'rational core' of Hegel's dialectic is precisely its idealist character. It is an expression of a mode of social domination constituted by structures of social relations that acquire a quasi-independent existence vis-à-vis the individuals and that, because of their peculiar dualistic nature, are dialectical in character. The immanent dynamic they generate cannot be understood directly with reference to individual or group action. Rather, the historical Subject, according to Marx, is the alienated structure of social mediation constitutive of the capitalist formation (capital), whose contradictions point to the abolition, not the realization, of the Subject.

According to this interpretation, the non-linear historical dynamic elucidated by Marx's categorial analysis provides the basis for a critical understanding of both the form of economic growth as well as the proletarian-based form of industrial production characteristic of capitalism (Marx, 1976, pp. 645, 657–8; Marx, 1981, pp. 953–4). That is, it allows for a categorial analysis of the processes of rationalization Lukács critically described. This approach neither posits a linear developmental schema that points beyond the existing structure and organization of labour (as do theories of postindustrial society), nor does it treat industrial production and the proletariat as the bases for a future society (as do many traditional Marxist approaches). Rather, it indicates that capitalism gives rise to the historical possibility of a different form of growth and of production; at the same time, however, capitalism structurally undermines the realization of those possibilities.

The structural contradiction of capitalism, according to this interpretation, is not one between distribution (the market, private property) and production, between existing property relations and industrial production. Rather, it emerges as a contradiction between existing forms of growth and production, and what could be the case if social relations no longer were mediated in a quasi-objective fashion by labour. (As an aside: by grounding the contradictory character of the social formation in the dualistic forms expressed by the categories of the commodity and capital, Marx implies that structurally based social contradiction is specific to capitalism. In light of this analysis, the notion that reality or social relations in general are essentially contradictory and dialectical can only be assumed metaphysically, not explained.)

The reinterpretation of Marx's theory I have outlined constitutes a basic break with and critique of more traditional interpretations. Such interpretations understand capitalism in terms of class relations structured by the market and private property, grasp its form of domination primarily in terms of class domination and exploitation, and formulate a normative and historical critique of capitalism from the standpoint of labour and production (understood transhistorically in terms of the interactions of humans with material nature). I have argued that Marx's analysis of labour in capitalism as historically specific seeks to elucidate a peculiar quasi-objective form of social mediation and wealth (value) that is constitutive of a form of domination. This form structures the process of production in capitalism and generates a historically unique dynamic. Hence, labour and the process of production are not separable from, and much less opposed to, the social relations of capitalism, but constitute their very core.

Marx's theory, then, extends far beyond the traditional critique of the bourgeois relations of distribution (the market and private property); it grasps modern industrial society itself as capitalist. It treats the working class as the basic element of capitalism rather than as the embodiment of its negation, and does not conceptualize socialism in terms of the realization of labour and of industrial production but in terms of the possible abolition of the proletariat, of the organization of production based on proletarian labour, and of the dynamic system of abstract compulsions constituted by labour as a socially mediating activity (Postone, 1993, pp. 307ff). This reinterpretation of Marx's theory thus implies a fundamental rethinking of the nature of capitalism and of its possible historical transformation. Shifting the focus of the critique away from an exclusive concern with the market and private property provides the basis for a critical theory of post-liberal society as capitalist and also of the so-called actually-existing socialist countries as alternative (and failed) forms of capital accumulation, rather than as social modes that represented the historical negation of capital, in however imperfect a form. This approach also allows for an analysis of the newest configuration of capitalism – of neo-liberal global capitalism – in ways that avoid returning to a traditionalist Marxist framework.

Critique and the historical configurations of capitalism

It has become evident, considered retrospectively, that the social/political/ economic/cultural configuration of capital's hegemony has varied historically – from mercantilism, through nineteenth-century liberal capitalism, and twentieth-century state-centric Fordist capitalism, to contemporary neo-liberal global capitalism. Each configuration has elicited a number of penetrating critiques – of exploitation and uneven, inequitable growth, for example, or of technocratic, bureaucratic modes of domination.

Each of these critiques, however, is incomplete. As we now see, capitalism cannot be identified fully with any of its historical configurations. By outlining the differences between Lukács's critical appropriation of Hegel and that of Marx, I have sought to differentiate between an approach that, however sophisticated, ultimately is a critique of one historical configuration of capital and an approach that allows for an understanding of capital as the core of the social formation, separable from its various surface configurations.

The distinction between capital as the core of the social formation and historically specific configurations of capitalism has become increasingly important in the course of the past century. Conflating the two has resulted in significant misrecognitions. Recall Marx's assertion that the coming social revolution must draw its poetry from the future, unlike earlier revolutions that, focused on the past, misrecognized their own historical content (Marx, 1979, p. 106). In that light, Lukács's critical theory of capitalism, grounded in his 'materialist' appropriation of Hegel, backs into a future it does not grasp. Rather than pointing to the overcoming of capitalism, Lukács's approach entails a misrecognition that conflates capital and its nineteenth-century configuration. Consequently he implicitly affirms the new state-centric configuration that emerged out of the crisis of liberal capitalism. Although, paradoxically, Lukács's rich critical *description* of capitalism is also directed against the bureaucratization of society, his specific understanding of the categories of Marx's critical theory does not adequately ground that critical description.

The unintended affirmation of a new configuration of capitalism can be seen more recently in the anti-Hegelian turn to Nietzsche characteristic of much poststructuralist thought in the 1970s and 1980s. Such thought, arguably, also backed into a future it did not adequately grasp. In rejecting the sort of state-centric order Lukács implicitly affirmed, it did so in a manner that was incapable of critically grasping the neo-liberal global order that has superseded Fordist state-centric capitalism, East and West; on a deep theoretical level, it affirmed, in turn, that order.

By rethinking Marx's relation to Hegel in ways that illuminate his conception of capital as the essential core of the social formation, I have sought to contribute to the reconstitution of an adequate critique of capitalism today, freed from the conceptual shackles of approaches that identify capitalism with one of its historical configurations.

Notes

1. This article is based, in part, on Postone (2003). I would like to thank Mark Loeffler for critical feedback.
2. Thus, Lukács (1971, p. 293) criticized Ernst Bloch for assuming that the critique of capitalism is only economic (rather than an analysis of the system of forms that

defines the real life of humanity), and, therefore, supplementing it with religious utopian thought.
3. See, e.g. Piccone, 1982, p. xvii.
4. For an extensive analysis of Marx's conception of abstract labour as constituting a historically specific, abstract form of social mediation, see Postone (1993).
5. Habermas (1984, p. 390) claims that his theory of communicative action shifts the framework of critical social theory away from the subject-object paradigm. I am suggesting that Marx, in his mature works, already effects such a theoretical shift. Moreover, I would argue – although I cannot elaborate here – that Marx's focus on forms of social mediation allows for a more rigorous analysis of capitalist modernity than does Habermas's turn to communicative action.
6. The distinction between the tendencies of history and empirical 'facts' is implicitly related by Lukács to the difference in logical levels between Marx's analysis of value and surplus value in Volume 1 of *Capital* and his analysis of price, profit, rent and interest in Volume 3 of *Capital*, whereby the latter categories veil the former (Lukács, 1971, pp. 181–5). What is significant here is that Lukács reads the concrete dimension of the underlying categories of Volume 1 such as 'labour' and 'use-value' as ontological and affirmative.
7. This analysis provides a powerful point of departure for analyzing the pervasive and immanent form of power that Michel Foucault (1984) described as characteristic of modern Western societies.

Bibliography

Foucault, Michel (1984) *Discipline and Punish: The Birth of the Prison*, (trans.) A. Sheridan (New York: Pantheon).
Habermas, Jürgen (1984) *The Theory of Communicative Action Vol. 1*, (trans.) T. McCarthy (Boston: Beacon Press).
Hegel, Georg Wilhelm Friedrich (1966) 'Preface to *The Phenomenology of Spirit*', in W. Kaufmann (ed.) *Hegel: Texts and Commentary* (Garden City, NY: Anchor Books).
Lukács, Georg (1971) *History and Class Consciousness*, trans. R. Livingstone (Cambridge, MA: MIT Press).
Marx, Karl (1976) *Capital Vol. 1*, trans. B. Fowkes (Harmondsworth: Penguin).
—— (1979) 'The Eighteenth Brumaire of Louis Bonaparte', in Karl Marx and Friedrich Engels, *Collected Works*, vol. 11 (New York: International Publishers).
—— (1981) *Capital Vol. 3*, trans. D. Fernbach (Harmondsworth: Penguin).
Piccone, Paul (1982) 'General Introduction', in A. Arato and E. Gebhardt (eds) *The Essential Frankfurt School Reader* (New York: Continuum).
Postone, Moishe (1993) *Time, Labor and Social Domination: A Reinterpretation of Marx's Critical Theory* (Cambridge: Cambridge University Press).
—— (2003) 'Lukács and the Dialectical Critique of Capitalism', in R. Albritton and J. Simoulidis (eds) *New Dialectics and Political Economy* (Basingstoke, Hampshire, and New York: Palgrave Macmillan).

13
Multiple Returns: Althusser on Dialectics

John Grant

Any periodization of Louis Althusser's work ought to reveal continuous and acute transformations as well as multiple returns to the same determining points.[1] My concern is with Althusser's shifting positions on dialectical thought via Hegel, which forms part of his ongoing engagement with the composition of critique and how it can contribute to radical politics. Tracing some of these careful modifications reveals an underappreciated nuance: the ruthless interrogator of Hegel is also quietly respectful, so much so that his own conception of dialectical critique came to depend increasingly on Hegelian insights. While Althusser stood to benefit from this tendency, additional difficulties with his conception of dialectics stand to be resolved in other ways. These include isolating the root of the determinism in Althusser's dialectics, as well as introducing a greater existentialist sensibility that expands the scope of dialectical analysis. Collectively, these issues are among the most immediate of those raised by reading Althusser today.

The term of a project: Anti-Hegelianism and Marxism

In this chapter I do not address Althusser's posthumously published work in *Philosophy of the Encounter* (2006), which is deserving of its own separate treatment on these issues. I do begin, however, with an early text that Althusser produced while studying under Maurice Merleau-Ponty that reveals a sympathetic disposition toward Hegel. Because it was written in 1947, well before his mature work, 'On Content in the Thought of G. W. F. Hegel' cannot be awarded sufficient authority to overturn his later writings. What makes this text useful, however, is that it shows how Althusser recognized some of the critical potential in Hegel's dialectic. From this it is possible to trace how Althusser's understanding of dialectics turned significantly on his reading of Hegel.

In light of his more well-known anti-humanist work, it is surprising to find Althusser contending that because it gives philosophical priority to matter, 'the Marxist movement' represents not only materialism, 'but also a humanism, since this matter is human matter, struggling against inhuman forms' (Althusser, 1997, p. 156). It is also unexpected to find him emphasizing Hegel's superiority over Marx as a philosopher. Althusser maintains that both Hegel and Marx knew, as philosophers, that they were prisoners of their times and could not transcend them. Where Marx went wrong, according to Althusser, was in treating labour as the 'origin' of history, 'as a necessity which goes beyond the present content, anticipates its own future, and discovers its anticipatory character in, precisely, the future that it commands even before that future appears' (Althusser, 1997, pp. 134–5). This is as near to a reversal of roles as one could expect to find in Althusser, with Marx as the target of the critique usually reserved for Hegel and his description in the *Phenomenology of Spirit* of the ontological unfolding of the categories of thought. Contrary to his view of Marx, Althusser claims that there is no given content of thought that would constitute an origin for Hegel's dialectic.

> Such is the lesson of the *Phenomenology*: the given content is destroyed in the very act by which I seek to take possession of it, but it does not elude me *qua* content, it eludes me only *qua* given. And the very act by which I destroy what is given in the content is the initial movement of a dialectic at the end of which the content I aimed at will be restored to cognition – not, this time, as an original given, but as a mediated result.
>
> (Althusser, 1997, p. 66)

At the conclusion of the *Phenomenology*, Hegel even claims that for all the toil that Spirit has put forth and for everything it has learned, that it can only proceed by renewing its pursuit of self-knowledge as if from the very beginning – precisely in light of what it now knows about itself (Hegel, 1977, §808).

My own reading of Hegel shares much with the young Althusser. Without forgetting the *Phenomenology's* concern with the ontological categories of thought, it is also the case that its ongoing dialectical motion is experienced as the most desperate of existential struggles (see Merleau-Ponty, 1964, pp. 63–70; Hyppolite, 1969, pp. 22–32). The intertwining of these thematics allows for the reconciliation of a universal process with a subject's feeling 'that all its defences have broken down, that every part of its being has been tortured on the rack and every bone broken' (Hegel, 1977, §539). But a thematic reconciliation does not carry over to the content of those themes. Althusser claims that Hegel's most profound idea in the *Phenomenology* is the identity of truth and reality (or of subject and object, or concept and thing). The accomplishment of that idea is never realized, according to Althusser, because 'man's attempt to recreate in his mind the totality he does not experience in reality culminates in failure' (Althusser,

1997, p. 82). For Althusser, this reflects the untranscendable finitude and contingency of the dialectic, which 'is neither a rule nor fixed laws, because the object and its measure vary over the course of the process' (Althusser, 1997, p. 113; slightly amended). The dialectic's permanent motion is not only the result of contradiction or the inability to achieve a closure of representation, but also because its object and the standard of analysis applied to it are fluid; the dialectic is always *in process*. Thus, Hegel's dialectic seems suspended between, on the one hand, the identity of truth and reality, and on the other, a process that cannot be completed, rendering impossible the reconciliation of truth and reality.

If Althusser is correct that Hegel's dialectic is more equivocal than is often presumed to be, this is also precisely the point where the critical nature of Hegel and the beginnings of a radical dialectics can be located. By reading Hegel against himself, the inability to unite reason with experience indicates the (negative) dialectical conditions that are capable of supporting critical insights into our lived experience and the precarious nature of existence. It is here where the young Althusser's reading of Hegel's dialectic displays all its potential for social and political critique, which the mature Althusser works vigorously to erase. Indeed, in the essays that comprise *For Marx* and *Reading Capital*, Althusser intends to show how Hegelian philosophy has virtually no critical value. Even Marx's materialist solution of inverting Hegel's dialectic so it no longer stands on its head, as the famous metaphor claimed, is deemed inadequate. Althusser is certain that this produces nothing more than an 'idealist anthropology' ('Contradiction and Overdetermination' in Althusser, 1969, p. 89). Escaping this fate means establishing an absolute break with Hegel.

> If we clearly perceive the *intimate and close relation* that the Hegelian structure of the dialectic has with Hegel's 'world outlook', that is, with his speculative philosophy, this 'world outlook' cannot really be cast aside *without our being obliged to transform profoundly the structures* of that dialectic.
>
> (Althusser, 1969, p. 104, original italics)

It is necessary, then, to specify exactly which structures of the Hegelian dialectic Althusser wanted to transform.

One of the most predictable targets is the Hegelian *Aufhebung*. This is Hegel's term for the dialectical process where contradictions internal to a particular stage of consciousness lead to its demise, yet the truth content of that stage is integrated into the following one. For Althusser, as well as others such as Jacques Derrida, the *Aufhebung* operates as a process of preservation where nothing can count against it, which would seem to negate the possibility that the *Phenomenology's* progression of consciousness toward self-consciousness could be anything other than certain. Althusser highlights how it was only through a retreat from this process that Marx freed himself from speculative German philosophy to concentrate on real history ('On the Young Marx' in Althusser, 1969, p. 76). If one is to grasp Marx, or comprehend the fluctuations of the real, the following is necessary:

> [T]o renounce the spirit of Hegelian logic implied in the innocent but sly concept of 'supersession' (*Aufhebung*) which is merely the empty anticipation of its end in the illusion of an immanence of truth, and to adopt instead a *logic of actual experience and real emergence*, one that would put an end to the illusions of *ideological immanence*; in short, to adopt a logic of *the irruption of real history in ideology itself*.
>
> ('On the Young Marx' in Althusser, 1969, p. 82, original italics)

Althusser imagines the *Aufhebung* transforming history into its own show trial, bending the nuance of every event to fit its own truth and purpose. He is arguing, in short, that Hegel's dialectic cannot account for historical transformations or discontinuities. In terms of the critical potential of dialectical thought, nothing could tame it more than if it went silent at precisely those historical moments.

Although there is no space for it here, it is worth noting that there is sufficient evidence to doubt Althusser's reading of dialectical movement in Hegel (see Adorno, 1993, pp. 4–5). Althusser is, in any case, compelled to set out his own criteria for how dialectical contradictions function. He argues that a contradiction is 'inseparable from the total structure of the social body in which it is found', and because it is both determining of and determined by the plurality of elements that constitute any particular social formation, 'it might be called *overdetermined in its principle*' ('Contradiction and Overdetermination' in Althusser, 1969, p. 101, original italics). Rather than being opposed to contradiction, overdetermination designates specific characteristics about contradictions and the conditions under which they occur. Overdetermination indicates that at any given moment a complex social totality contains multiple contradictions, which are the result of a multitude of different constituent elements. In other words, any effect has multiple causes. The distinguishing feature of this complexity is a 'structure in dominance' that assumes the principal role in organizing and articulating the specific shape of any social formation. Althusser's clearest explanation of the term structure is in *Reading Capital*, where he describes it as the unity of a 'specific combination of peculiar elements', which through its effects expresses an immanent essence rather than a universal-expressive one (Althusser and Balibar, 1970, p. 189). The structure in dominance counts as 'the most profound characteristic of the Marxist dialectic' ('On the Materialist Dialectic' in Althusser, 1969, p. 206), and is responsible for the 'uneven' (read: unequal) development of the structures that constitute each social formation. It is for this reason that the characteristic of dominance is designated as the 'specific difference of a Marxist contradiction' (Althusser, 1969, p. 217). One of the reasons why Hegel's dialectic is deemed to be insufficient is because it is organized around a 'simple original unity' that lacks complexity (Althusser, 1969, p. 197). This deprives the dialectic of 'the structure in dominance which is the absolute precondition for a real complexity to be a unity and really the object of a *practice* that proposes to transform this structure: political practice' (Althusser, 1969, p. 204, original italics). In the tradition of Marx and critical theory after him, the relationship between critique and practice is a serious preoccupation for Althusser, and it is one that his reconceptualization of dialectical critique after Hegel *and Marx* is meant to address.

One of the most enduring aspects of Althusser's complex social totality is that he designates the economy as the structure in dominance of any social formation, although famously it is only dominant 'in the last instance'. The last instance is a vital feature of the dialectic that allows one to 'escape the arbitrary relativism of observable displacements by giving these displacements the necessity of a function (Althusser and Balibar, 1970, p. 99). If the economy is only dominant in the last instance, this means that in principle it is possible for a different structure to be dominant in any other instance, albeit for economic reasons. Curiously, it might even be the case that the economy never occupies a dominant position. 'From the first moment to the last', claims Althusser, 'the lonely hour of the 'last instance' never comes' ('Contradiction and Overdetermination' in Althusser, 1969, p. 113). This contingency is what invests overdetermination with such theoretical importance. At any given moment the structures that make up the social totality constitute a complex unity, governed by a specific structure in dominance. The productivity of overdetermination rests in the notion that the specific shape of a social formation is constantly developing (in response to the dominant structure), which requires an infinite return to the specific moment of conjuncture in order to articulate its form.

Althusser's intention is to give an account of the dialectical reciprocity between each particular element of a social whole and the social whole itself. Each conjuncture assigns a role to individual structures and their practices, the combined effects of which work either to reaffirm or alter established relations and logics. Examining such relations requires discovering the effects of contradictions within a particular structure – say capital – as well as between them – say capital and patriarchy. Within these conjunctural relations, which are at once mutually constitutive, antagonistic, and therefore productive, one can discover historically specific relations of political struggle. The significance of Althusser's dialectic can be counterposed to much of what is found in Hegel. Althusser excludes any appeal to the subject or its experiences and focuses instead on structures and institutions. He would also reject any suggestion that he mimics the onto-structural side of Hegel's dialectic. Althusser makes it clear that he considers Hegel to have relied on a simple contradiction described in the Preface to the *Phenomenology* – the estrangement of Being from itself – that unfolds teleologically and prohibits dialectical categories from offering any insights into socio-structural organization (see Hegel, 1977, §36). Althusser avoids these Hegelian traits by deploying concepts such as overdetermination, structure in dominance, and determination in the last instance, which allow him to grasp how social formations are complex and always in flux. Further, Althusser's attempt to establish a type of 'scientific' Marxist philosophy is predicated upon the assumption that these concepts articulate the objective nature of each social conjuncture. This obliges him to make a distinction between science and ideology, which I introduce here because it forms a vital part of Althusser's project.

Although Althusser's most extended analysis of ideology is in his essay 'Ideology and Ideological State Apparatuses', I restrict this discussion to his statements in *For Marx* and *Reading Capital* because they have the most direct impact on dialectics. In 'Marxism and Humanism', Althusser defines ideology as a '*lived* relation between men and their world', except that in ideology 'men do indeed express, not the relation between them and their conditions of existence, but *the way* they live the relation between them and their conditions of existence: this presupposes both a real relation and an '*imaginary*', '*lived*' relation' (Althusser, 1969, p. 233, original italics). Although ideology identifies certain existing relations, unlike science it does not contain the concepts required for *knowing* those relations. In *Reading Capital*, Althusser uses the example of the humanist subject to demonstrate an ideological relation (Althusser and Balibar, 1970, p. 27). The humanist subject, which conceives of itself as a constitutive subject, suffers an ideological relation to its conditions of existence because it imagines that it controls its surroundings, that its relationship to its conditions of existence is shaped predominately by its ability to determine its own life opportunities. Indeed, the subject is constituted as a humanist subject by bourgeois society and it thinks and acts accordingly. The humanist subject depends also on an idea of human essence and origin. To wit, subjects have an original essence from which they are presently estranged, and our foremost concern must be to reestablish conditions that will allow this essence to flourish. In typically provocative fashion, Althusser explains how the 'theoretical anti-humanism' with which Marx responds to humanist ideology constitutes a philosophical revolution. 'It is impossible to *know* anything about men except on the precondition that the philosophical (theoretical) myth of man is reduced to ashes' ('Marxism and Humanism' in Althusser, 1969, p. 233, italics in original). Quite simply, Althusser believes that when it comes to understanding social relations and change, the individual, or the category of the subject, is an inadequate unit of analysis (indeed an ideological one) compared with, say, classes, ideology, or the mode and relations of production. This is why his attack on ideology as well as his break with Hegel take place 'in the dialectical crisis of a mutation of a theoretical structure in which the 'subject' plays, not the part it believes it is playing, but the part which is assigned to it by the mechanism of the process (Althusser and Balibar, 1970, p. 27). Rather than producing social structures, the subject is instead one of their effects.

Althusser's attempt to break the dominance of ideology is pursued through an attack on empiricism, which he sees as an ideological expression of the supposed correspondence between what is real and what is thought. Althusser proposes a radical break between concepts and their objects, emphasizing Spinoza's claim that 'the concept dog cannot bark' to demonstrate the permanent disjunction between the object of knowledge and the real object (Althusser and Balibar, 1970, pp. 88, 105, 115). This critique sees Althusser shift his attention away from the concept of the origin to focus on mediation, which he treats as an empiricist term and not a dialectical one. Whereas earlier he praised the way mediation helps to undermine the notion of philosophical origins, Althusser is now hostile to the argument that there is always a mediating term or element that complicates any simple concept–object dichotomy (in the *Phenomenology* I would argue that language, subjectivity and labour all play mediating roles). Althusser writes: 'The concept of mediation is invested with one last role: the magical provision of post-stations in the empty space between theoretical principles and the "concrete", as bricklayers make a chain to pass bricks' (Althusser and Balibar, 1970, p. 63). Because Althusser thinks the socio-political field as a series of objects, any claim to knowledge must be posed 'in terms which exclude any recourse to the ideological solution contained in the ideological characters Subject and Object, or to the mutual mirror-recognition structure, in the closed circle of which they move (Althusser and Balibar, 1970, p. 55). This type of ideological closure where the real is reduced to the theoretical unity of idea and object is precisely what Althusser sees as the product of Hegel's dialectic.

There is now an extensive difference between the conceptual resources of the Hegelian dialectic and a properly Marxist dialectic, at least according to Althusser. The latter is uniquely characterized by the following: a complex set of overdetermined contradictions; a structure in dominance that is determined, in the last instance, by the economy; the uneven development of contradictions; a form of theoretical anti-humanism that rejects the concepts of the constitutive subject, origin, essence, and mediation; a committed resistance to the teleology associated (rightly or wrongly) with the *Aufhebung*; and the concept of a process without a Subject (this will be discussed more later). Together this contributes to a scientific Marxism that is designed to overcome various ideologies (humanism and empiricism, e.g.) by producing a non-speculative philosophy capable of knowing our real conditions of existence.

A slow thaw: New readings and shifting evidence

After *For Marx* and *Reading Capital*, Althusser gradually entered into a period of self-criticism prompted by attacks from humanist Marxists and non-Marxists alike. He produced a set of essays that reconsidered some of his most familiar theses, even if their anti-humanist, anti-empiricist, and broadly structuralist implications were maintained. One of the most notable shifts occurred in Althusser's stance toward the Hegelian dialectic, which became less strident and more nuanced. Before I discuss that shift, I want to articulate what I think are some of the shortcomings of Althusser's own dialectic. One of its most problematic (and unintended) features, which Althusser himself acknowledged in order to overcome it, was what he called 'theoreticism'.

> Theoreticism here means: primacy of theory over practice; one-sided insistence on theory; but more precisely: *speculative-rationalism*. To explain only the pure form: to conceive matters in terms of the contrast between truth and error was in fact *rationalism*. But it was *speculation* to want to conceive the contrast between established truths and acknowledged errors within a General Theory of Science and Ideology and of the distinction between them.
>
> (Althusser, 1976, p. 124, n. 19)

Theoreticism's most serious consequence, beyond the implication that the thesis of the difference between science and ideology could not be strictly upheld, was that it pushed Althusser toward a type of theorizing in which political struggles, and class struggle in particular, were marginalized. The concept of structure became reified while the subject was bracketed out so that the ideological nature of its lived relations (Althusser's terminology) was treated epistemologically rather than politically. Although I think it is important not to classify Althusser simply or reductively as a structuralist, this is the point at which his structuralist tendencies are the strongest.

In fact, Althusser's rewriting of the dialectic contains a theoretical incompatibility between overdetermined social formations, the structure in dominance, and determination in the last instance. The result of this incompatibility is that Althusser's dialectic assumes determinist tendencies over and against its anti-essentialist commitments. To take each concept in turn, the overdetermination of social formations means that they have no shared and innate essence; each formation is the result of an ensemble of determining factors that are peculiar to it. In contrast, the concept of a structure in dominance suggests a mild form of historically specific determinism. If any structure can dominate, then presumably determinism can be avoided by maintaining the dialectical reciprocity between the social whole and individual structures. However, the tension between overdetermination and structural causality in Althusser maintains the possibility of a determinist tendency. In the case of determination in the last instance, a fully determinist structuralism is unavoidable. It presumes, ultimately, that the constitution of social structures results from a determining essence. In turn, this makes the supposedly overdetermined nature of social relations look like it is *underdetermined*, which is the type of dialectical logic that Althusser criticized in Hegel. Since the concept itself is invalid, carrying with it the very characteristics that Althusser's anti-essentialism was intended to do away with, exactly which structure is determinant in the last instance is of no consequence. Althusser finesses this awkward position by claiming that the last instance never comes, but this sleight of hand does nothing to alter the implications I have described. If the last instance truly never comes then it is superfluous to Althusser's project and should have no place. But quite the opposite, the last instance was present from the very start because it performs a constant function: Althusser calls it the 'absolute precondition' of any explanation about the hierarchical ordering of structural effectivity (Althusser and Balibar, 1970, p. 99). The inclusion of this causal factor produces a deterministic understanding of how the social is constituted, negating the deconstructive implications overdetermination would have on Marxist thought – the end of all economism and determinism. The result for social critique is that the possibility of a dialectics has been written out because all contradictions can be traced back to a source that has been determined in advance.

If this sounds suspiciously similar to the critique that Althusser levelled at Hegel, his work after *Reading Capital* also reduces their critical distance from one another, but for positive reasons. This should not be entirely surprising. It would have been almost impossible for Althusser to revise some of the theses in essays like 'On the Materialist Dialectic' and 'Contradiction and Overdetermination', which are the most critical of Hegel, without reconsidering his reading of Hegel too. Even prior to his *Essays in Self-Criticism*, Althusser made a significant admission in his 1968 essay 'Marx's Relation to Hegel': 'Everything we have published on Hegel in fact leaves out the positive heritage Marx, by his own confession, owed to Hegel' (Althusser, 1977, p. 174). Just before his famous statement in *Capital* that Hegel is standing on his head and needs to be turned right side up, Marx also wrote how the 'mystification that the dialectic suffers in Hegel's hands, by no means prevents him from being the first to present its general form of working in a comprehensive and conscious manner' (Marx and Engels, 1978, p. 302). Written in 1873, the sentiment of that passage is strikingly similar to one written in the *1844 Manuscripts*, where Marx declares that Feuerbach's are 'the only writings since Hegel's *Phänomenologie* and *Logik* to contain a real theoretical revolution' (Marx and Engels, 1978, p. 68). By contrast, Althusser is at first content to claim only that Marx owed Hegel *'the idea of the dialectic'* (Althusser, 1977, p. 174, original italics). Apparently there were no other concessions to be made. However, the implications of Marx's claim that Hegel provided the dialectic's general form of working, and Althusser's assertion that Hegel was only responsible for the idea of the dialectic, are of two different orders: one concrete and one abstract. As if aware of this discrepancy, Althusser began to concede more and more to Hegel.

Jumping ahead for one moment, Althusser elaborates in his *Essays in Self-Criticism* how Spinoza's work had already avoided so much of what Marx had to reject in Hegel: idealism, teleology, transitive, or expressive causality. What Spinoza also lacked was a concept of contradiction, which Marx had no choice but to assume from Hegel (Althusser, 1976, pp. 140–1). In his earlier essay 'Marx's Relation to Hegel', Althusser had, in a certain way, already anticipated this insight. He did so, first, by submitting Hegel to another biting critique.

> Of course, as we can now begin to say, what irremediably disfigures the Hegelian conception of History as a dialectical process is its *teleological* conception of the dialectic, inscribed in the very *structures* of the Hegelian dialectic at an extremely precise point: the *Aufhebung* (transcendence-preserving-the-transcended-as-the-internalized-transcended), directly expressed in the Hegelian category of the *negation of the negation* (or negativity).
>
> (Althusser, 1977, p. 181, original italics)

Take away the *Aufhebung* and the teleology, Althusser argues, and what 'Marx owes Hegel [is] this decisive philosophical category, *process*' (ibid, original italics). Note the change in Althusser's language: Hegel has not merely provided the idea of the dialectic, but a decisive philosophical category. Textual evidence from Marx is available to support this claim. In the *1844 Manuscripts* he describes the 'the dialectic of negativity' as the 'outstanding thing in Hegel's *Phenomenology'* (Marx and Engels, 1978, p. 112). To put together these different terms that Althusser and Marx find in Hegel, negativity is the prime characteristic of the process of dialectical contradiction. Negativity is not a logical category or procedure, but rather the hallmark of critical thought that permanently unsettles the relationship of thinking and experience. According to a reading of Hegel, which I alluded to earlier, his dialectic is a constant and perpetual one that cannot account for any of the supposed reconciliations between subject and object, idea and experience, and so on. The young Althusser recognized this negativity in Hegel; Marx saw it too, but considered Hegel to have betrayed it (see Marx and Engels, 1978, pp. 112–14). The question for the later Althusser, who gradually allowed for this appeal to Hegel's negativity to re-enter his thought, is whether his own conception of dialectics became unsustainable almost for the same reasons he attributed to Hegel?

Étienne Balibar has described how the radical openness of negativity is crucial to Althusser's own project. 'The question [of negativity] is important because, from Hegel onward, this notion was a criterion of demarcation between dialectics and positivism'. He continues: 'Without such a concept, there is no real possibility of formulating structural antagonism as something irreconcilable, rooted in the experience of the unbearable and taking the forms of a 'radical' resistance' (Balibar, 1996, pp. 118–19). Negativity designates an ongoing movement and critique that Althusser's dialectic would seem to lack. The reason becomes clearer as Althusser describes in more detail the specific characteristic of the category of process that is most important to Hegel and Marx.

> Once one is prepared to consider just for a moment that the whole Hegelian teleology is contained in the expressions I have just stated, in the categories of alienation, or in what constitutes the master structure of the category of the dialectic (the negation of the negation), and once one accepts, if that is possible, to *abstract* from what represents the teleology in these expressions, then there remains the formulation: history is *a process without a subject*. I think I can affirm: this category of *a process without a subject*, which must of course be torn from the grip of the Hegelian teleology, undoubtedly represents the greatest theoretical debt linking Marx to Hegel.
>
> (Althusser, 1977, pp. 182–3, italics in original)

To keep up with Althusser, Hegel has now been credited with supplying the 'idea' of the dialectic, contradiction, process, and process without a subject (Marx added the dialectic's general form of working as well as negativity). It is worth noting that in his formulation Althusser does not mention whether the category of a process without a subject needs to be torn also from the grip of a Marxian teleology: the proletariat as the subject of history as it develops toward a communist and classless society. Althusser's remarks on the idea of a process without a subject are consistent, from this first statement in January 1968, through the essay 'Lenin before Hegel' in April 1969, to his 'Reply to John Lewis' in May 1973. There Althusser explains in greater detail the implications of his position.

> In my opinion: men (plural), in the concrete sense, are necessarily subjects (plural) *in* history, because they act *in* history as subjects (plural). But there is no Subject (singular) *of* history. And I will go even further: 'men' are not 'the subjects' *of* history [...] The question of the constitution of individuals as historical *subjects*, active *in* history, has nothing in principle to do with the question of the *'Subject* of history', or even with that of the *'subjects* of history' [...] That human, i.e. social individuals are *active* in history – as *agents* of the different social practices of the historical process of production and reproduction – that is a fact. But, considered as *agents*,

human individuals are not 'free' and 'constitutive' subjects in the philosophical sense of these terms.
                                                (Althusser, 1976, pp. 94–5, italics in original)

Althusser's first claim is that history has no absolute Subject or metanar-
rative. His second claim allows for the fact that subjects act in history, but
still without considering subjects to be anything more than the supports of
social structures and the relations of production and reproduction. They do
not, therefore, acquire any status as subjects *of* history, above and beyond
their existence as subjects *in* history. So much seems acceptable. However,
since one of Althusser's main goals was to account for political struggles in
a way that the theoreticism of his earlier work had prevented, it is not at all
clear whether he addresses the appropriate registers of inquiry.

The impact of Althusser's theoreticism is that it interfered with the work
of thinking about radical politics, including questions pertaining to experience, resistance and praxis. Despite the sense we get from Althusser about
the objective dominance of structures in the constitution of social relations,
his hope for radical social change still requires the subjective intervention of
a popular uprising. Structures do not, after all, take to the streets (although
there is no decisive evidence to suggest that the working class takes to the
streets, either). Even Althusser's staunchly anti-humanist Marxism cannot
prevent him from admitting the importance of agents committed to revolution. 'Everything depends, in the last instance, not on techniques but on
militants, on their class consciousness, on their devotion, and on their courage' (in Ferry and Renaut, 1990, p. 29). Presuming that the 'last instance' in
this case is one that might actually arrive, Althusser still situates the dialectic
on a conceptual register that cannot account for these questions of political practice. What is necessary, I believe, is for the structuralist category of
a process without a Subject to be complemented by an account of existence
that employs the more existentialist category of *subjects in process*. Although
Althusser might not need such an account in order to explore *how* individuals become subjects, without one he cannot investigate the specific realities
of lived ideological relations and experience. Nor can he account for why
people might revolt, which is a concern that *he* raised by appealing to the
issue of their consciousness, devotion, and courage and to which his commitment to class struggle, both as a primary political tactic as well as something
that should orient philosophical inquiry into the nature of social relations,
compels a response. In short, Althusser has done nothing less than invoke
the need for an account of experience without being able to satisfy it.

Subjects in process

The idea that subjects are in process has a double meaning: first, that they
are caught up in, and subject to, the structural processes of society and

history and second, that subjects are not static, but are themselves an ongoing process of becoming that occurs, in part, through their own (limited) capacities of critique and experimentation. This double meaning sets the parameters for what is, essentially, an investigation into the dialectical constitution of subjects (and is not in any way intended to challenge Althusser's argument that there is no Subject of history). As Althusser points out, just because subjects are not self-constituting and are not alienated from some essential nature does not impact on their empirical existence in history as agents of different social practices. But this reference to social practices is what makes the idea of subjects in process all the more necessary. Earlier, Althusser described ideology as a 'lived relation', which is both real and imaginary, between men and their conditions of existence. His attempt to account for the gap between existential experience and supposedly real (or scientific) knowledge broke down not only as a result of his theoreticism, but also because he attempted to establish this gap as a permanent void: experience could never touch science. The absence of any suitable existentialist categories means that Althusser tacitly upheld the ideology–science distinction even after it had proven unsustainable. Thus, even though the general theory of ideology's functioning is properly understood in a structuralist sense, the concrete movements of specific ideologies that depict how subjects relate to and exist in present conditions remain unaccounted for (despite its persuasiveness, the critique of humanism remains at the level of generality). Ultimately, this ruled out a dialectical understanding of subjects' ideological existence.

There is a way to remedy Althusser's impact on dialectics. One suggestive approach is made by Paul Ricoeur:

> [I]deology has a certain ethical function; it attempts to make sense of the accidents of life, the painful aspects of existence. We must introduce an existential language; when we speak of contradiction, it is not a logical contradiction, a conflict between structures, but a lived contradiction, a contradiction between our capacity to adjust and the demands of reality.
>
> (Ricoeur, 1994, p. 57)

Ricoeur usefully points out the existentialist register that Althusser was ill-equipped to address. However, in making his point Ricoeur commits to exactly the same difficulty, only at a different level of inquiry. Althusser prioritizes contradictions between structures; Ricoeur stresses contradictions at the lived, everyday level; neither cares to account for the other or particularly for contradictions between these two levels, which anyway should be approached as dialectically related rather than juridically detached. It seems to me that the idea of subjects in process is a productive way to capture these relations. Althusser's positing of subjects as the agents of social practices suggests that they are not just automatons or the mechanical parts of structural processes, although he clearly does not believe that they are autonomous actors, either. Similarly, I want to stress again that this idea of subjects in process does not imply a humanist, voluntaristic, or constitutive notion of the subject. However, given that Althusser is concerned with the potential for action by political radicals, such action cannot take place if the constituted role of subjects in reproducing capitalist structures is so strong that it prevents them from engaging in critique or exploiting alternative subject positions that might be available to them at more than an individual level. The first sense of subjects in process is indeed one where they are subjected to and constrained by impersonal structural processes. The second sense is one where the constant movement of these processes, along with the capacity of subjects to act within conditions that are set for them, results in a state of becoming in which the subject positions and potential practices available to subjects are in constant flux. There is, I believe, a strong tradition of this type of dialectical analysis, but it is not Althusser's. Marx continually made statements that indicate the importance of investigating subjects in process. There is no better example than the one found in *The German Ideology*, where Marx contends, famously, that 'circumstances make men just as much as men make circumstances (Marx and Engels, 1978, p. 165). Even though Marx did not use the term 'subjects in process', Althusser was certainly correct that he privileged the category of process. Throughout the first volume of *Capital*, Marx describes labour, the production of surplus value, and even capital itself, as processes – a set of related actions directed toward a particular outcome. This understanding of process is precisely what we discover when we investigate the logic of certain structures – capital, the state, the education system, say – as well as the logic of certain organized political actions. There is, as Pierre Bourdieu has described it, an ongoing dialectic that internalizes the external – the logics of impersonal structures are internalized into subjects' practices – and externalizes the internal – the practices of agents are externalized into the structural field, affecting its constitution (Bourdieu, 1977, p. 72). What this shows is that the dialectical idea of subjects in process is not an investigation into subjects only using concepts specific to the subject. Instead it displays a concern for both the constitution and capabilities of subjects within the totality of social conditions. Subjects in process are not just the effects or supports of structures because structures are simultaneously the effects and supports of the practices of subjects. It is a false dichotomy, then, to set totally determining structures against free willing subjects. Instead, the processes that (re)produce the structures and practices that constitute social existence can be conceived of more fully by including the idea of subjects in process and the experiences they live through.

To conclude, I will not take time to insist on my point that Althusser's position Hegel and on dialectics is more complex than is usually believed, perhaps even by Althusser himself. His texts do this for me. Where I will attempt to prevail is on the implications that I think this evidence discloses. Allowing that Althusser does not need concepts such as subjects in process or experience in order to explain structural proliferation or the general functioning of ideology, I believe that he does need them in order to avoid theoreticism and to account for the lived experiences of agents that engage in radical political practices. This is where some of Althusser's limits are met: his excellent work on the role and influence of social structures is overcome by the idea of determination in the last instance, which grips and steers his conception of dialectics. Of perhaps greater consequence is that Althusser leaves too little space for the agency of human subjects, whether in the form of a class, individuals, or otherwise. With no little irony then, we now relate to Althusser as he did to Marx and Hegel: as inheritors of a provocative but inadequate version of dialectical critique that will compel our own multiple returns.

Note

1. A version of this chapter was presented at the Marx and Philosophy Society seminar on 5 March 2005.

Bibliography

Adorno, T. W. (1993) *Hegel: Three Studies*, (trans.) S. Nicholsen (London: The MIT Press).

Althusser, L. (1969) *For Marx*, (trans.) B. Brewster (London: Penguin Books).

—— (1976) *Essays in Self-Criticism*, (trans.) G. Lock (London: NLB).

—— (1977) 'Marx's Relation to Hegel', in B. Brewster (trans.) *Politics and History: Montesquieu, Rousseau, Hegel, Marx*, (London: NLB).

—— (1997) *The Spectre of Hegel*, (trans.) G. M. Goshgarian (London: Verso).

Althusser, L. and Balibar, E. (1970) *Reading Capital*, (trans.) B. Brewster (London: NLB).

Balibar, E. (1996) 'Structural Causality, Overdetermination, and Antagonism', in A. Callari and D. F. Ruccio (eds) *Postmodern Materialism and the Future of Marxist Theory* (London: University Press of New England).

Bourdieu, P. (1977) *Outline of a Theory of Practice*, (trans.) R. Nice (Cambridge: Cambridge University Press).

Ferry, L. and Renaut, A. (1990) *French Philosophy of the Sixties: An Essay on Anti-Humanism*, (trans.) M. Cattani (Amherst, MA: The University of Massachusetts Press).

Hegel, G. W. F. (1977) *Phenomenology of Spirit*, trans. A. V. Miller (Oxford: Oxford University Press).

Hyppolite, J. (1969) *Studies on Marx and Hegel*, (trans.) J. O'Neill (London: Heinemann).

Marx, K. and Engels, F. (1978) *The Marx-Engels Reader*, 2nd edn, R. Tucker (ed.) (New York: W.W. Norton and Company).

Merleau-Ponty, M. (1964) *Sense and Non-Sense*, (trans.) H. L. Drefus and P. A. Dreyfus (Evanston, IL: Northwestern University Press).

Ricoeur, P. (1994) 'Althusser's Theory of Ideology', in G. Elliott (ed.) *Althusser: A Critical Reader* (Oxford: Blackwell).

14
The Rationality of Analytical Marxism

Roberto Veneziani

During the 1970s, following the descending trajectory of structuralist Marxism and the renaissance of liberal egalitarianism, a strong wave of interest in Marxist themes emerged among Anglo-American analytical philosophers (Miller, 1983; Levine, 2003).[1] The debate focused mostly on topics that were most congenial to analytical philosophy, such as the relationship between Marxism and ethics (see, e.g. Cohen, Nagel and Scanlon, 1980). At the culmination of this process, in 1978, *Karl Marx's Theory of History: A Defence* appeared, in which G. A. Cohen reconstructed historical materialism guided only by 'two constraints: on the one hand, what Marx wrote, and, on the other, those standards of clarity and rigour which distinguish twentieth-century analytical philosophy' (Cohen, 1978, p. ix). The book marks the birth of Analytical Marxism as a self-conscious school.[2] In the following three decades, Analytical Marxism has provided some of the most controversial and sophisticated contributions on a number of core substantive and methodological issues in political philosophy and the social sciences.[3]

The contribution of Analytical Marxism to critical social theory is controversial, though, and it is unclear whether Analytical Marxism identifies a *distinctive*, progressive (in Lakatos's sense) research programme in explanatory social science, as claimed by some of its proponents. The core tenet of Analytical Marxism is the denial of a specific Marxist methodology and the adoption of the tools of mainstream social science and analytical philosophy, in order to discover the rational kernel of Marxist theory, and then reconstruct Marxism on that basis. Starting from these premises, Analytical Marxism has indeed been able to translate some Marxist ideas 'into terms that bear scrutiny according to the most demanding disciplinary standards in [mainstream] philosophy or in appropriate social science' (Levine, 2003, p. 132). Analytical Marxism analyses, however, have led to the rejection, or the radical revision, of a number of concepts and propositions, such that the viability of a distinctively Marxist, or indeed Analytical Marxist, perspective in social theory is arguably put into question.

Most critics reject Analytical Marxist conclusions on *a priori* methodological and exegetical grounds, arguing that they follow from the adoption of mainstream tools that are extraneous to Marx's theory. This approach is arguably questionable, because many innovations in Marxist theory have derived from the encounter with non-Marxist traditions. Analytical Marxism should be judged by whether it illuminates central questions of social theory, and, as acknowledged by critics, it does provide interesting insights on a number of crucial issues, such as the theory of history, the existence of exploitation in socialism, and the paradox of the middle classes. Besides, Analytical Marxism propositions are interesting even when they are unconvincing. The clarity and rigour of Analytical Marxism writings greatly facilitate constructive criticism by exposing the crucial assumptions and grey areas of Analytical Marxist theoretical constructions. Finally, Analytical Marxism should be distinguished from the narrower approach also known as Rational Choice Marxism. Many critics illegitimately proceed from the critique of Rational Choice Marxism to the rejection of Analytical Marxism.

This chapter adopts a different approach. First, Analytical Marxism and Rational Choice Marxism are rigorously defined and clearly distinguished. It is argued that Analytical Marxism has reconstructed a set of core Marxist propositions that are central in social theory and may contribute to a revival of socialist theory. By contrast, Rational Choice Marxism has given rise to a fertile literature on normative issues, but its contributions to Marxism are mainly negative and suggest that the role of Marxism in the social sciences is exhausted.

Second, various doubts are raised on Rational Choice Marxism's methodological prescriptions – in particular, on methodological individualism and rational choice theory – but the debate on alternative approaches is unlikely to be settled uniquely at an abstract methodological level. A focused critique of Rational Choice Marxism is provided, which highlights the importance of the social determination of individuals; that is, of the *endogeneity* of agents' preferences and beliefs. This is not to suggest that the methodological postulate that individual identities are given, unrelated, and unchanging – in short, the *exogeneity* of agents' preferences and beliefs – is the *only* shortcoming of Rational Choice Marxism. The focus on this issue is motivated by its central role in social theory, as acknowledged by all Analytical Marxists. This provides an immanent criticism of Rational Choice Marxism: despite Rational Choice Marxism's claims on the importance of endogenous preferences, they play hardly any role in Rational Choice Marxist models. Further, the endogeneity of preferences and beliefs raises a number of well-known problems for the reductionist methodology endorsed by Rational Choice Marxism. Instead, an approach that emphasises individual rational choices, but takes into account the social formation of individuals, is consistent with an antireductionist Analytical Marxism approach.[4]

Third, it is argued that the neglect of endogenous preferences reduces the explanatory power of Rational Choice Marxist models and the robustness of Rational Choice Marxism's negative conclusions on Marxist propositions – focusing in particular on the Rational Choice Marxist analysis of collective action, a crucial topic in social theory. This suggests some directions for further research, which may substantiate a research agenda that is consistent with, and builds upon, the core of Marxism reconstructed by Analytical Marxism.

Analytical and rational choice Marxism

Given the substantial heterogeneity of Analytical Marxists, it is difficult to define Analytical Marxism, either theoretically or in terms of membership. Attempts to identify a set of substantive propositions shared by all Analytical Marxists are necessarily vague and ultimately unconvincing. To be sure, no analytical Marxist 'accepts the law of the tendency of the rate of profit to fall [...] and [...] only one, Brenner, [...] still holds the labour theory of value expounded in volume I to be true' (Callinicos, 1987, p. 68). But this by no means identifies Analytical Marxism as a distinct approach in Marxist thought.

There are some common traits, however, that define a style of theorising, if not a school of thought. The core tenet of Analytical Marxism, and its main departure from classical Marxism, is the denial of a specific Marxist methodology, dialectical or otherwise. According to Analytical Marxism, 'Dialectical logic is based on several propositions which may have a certain inductive appeal, but are far from being rules of inference' (Roemer, 1986b, p. 191). More precisely, Wright (1989, pp. 38–9) proposes the following definition of Analytical Marxism.

Definition 1. Analytical Marxism is defined by the analysis of Marxist issues and:

C1. 'A commitment to *conventional scientific norms* in the elaboration of theory and the conduct of research.'
C2. 'An emphasis on the importance of *systematic conceptualisation.*'
C3. 'A concern with a relatively fine-grained specification of the steps in the theoretical arguments linking concepts.'
C4. 'The importance accorded to *the intentional action of individuals.*'

Definition 1 forcefully shows the rather wide range of methodological and substantive positions consistent with Analytical Marxism. Therefore, it encompasses all self-defined Analytical Marxists, but it is sufficiently general to include, in principle, a number of other analytically oriented Marxist phi-losophers and quantitative social scientists. C1–C4 are by no means trivial, though. The emphasis on conventional scientific norms and the rejection of a distinctive Marxist methodology have been questioned on philosophical and methodological grounds. According to critics, the analytical method is based on a framework of rigid and exclusive dichotomies, and produces 'not clarity and rigour, but systematic misunderstanding and misinterpretation' (Sayers, 1989, p. 82). Analytical philosophy essentially distorts Marxist theory and the negative results of Analytical Marxism prove 'the dangers of using philosophical tools especially designed to bury Marxism' (Kennedy, 2005, p. 341). Against Analytical Marxism, many authors have defended a specific Marxist methodology, based on dialectics and/or methodological holism.

This is a deep issue, and a proper analysis is beyond the scope of this chapter, but there are many reasons to question wholesale rejections of Analytical Marxism on *a priori* grounds. The most relevant, perhaps, is that there is no proof that *no* part of Marx's theory can be fruitfully exam-ined using analytical philosophy. Cohen's theory, for example, provides a recognisably Marxist, if not orthodox, version of historical materialism, as acknowledged by critics (e.g. Kennedy, 2005). More importantly, Analytical Marxism has provided a rigorous reconstruction of what it deems the dis-tinctive, rational kernel of Marxist theory, which comprises at least three core components.[5] First is Marx's theory of history, or historical materialism, which detects 'an endogenous process that supplies history with a determi-nate trajectory from one *mode of production* [...] to another' (Levine, 2003, p. 33). The fundamental contribution of Analytical Marxism, emerging from Cohen's (1978) seminal book, and the subsequent debate, according to Andrew Levine, is the reconstruction of a rigorous version of historical materialism, articulated into two main theses. The first states that the level of development of productive forces functionally explains the nature of the economic structure. The second states that '*economic structures* [functionally] explain *legal and political superstructures and also ways of thinking or forms of consciousness*' (Levine, 2003, p. 151). In recent contributions Analytical Marxism interprets historical materialism as 'a theory of historical possi-bilities opened up by the development of 'productive forces'' (Levine, 2003, p. 164), with an important role for class struggle. Historical materialism is an account of a *possible* communist future, which can 'unify what would otherwise be a motley of well-meaning, but mainly reactive, causes into a movement with a serious prospect of changing life for the better' (Levine, 2003, p. 171). Historical materialism is thus 'the foundational theory of sci-entific socialism, [...] the core upon which any future Marxism must build' (Levine, 2003, p. 34).

The second component is Marx's theory of the state. According to Levine, in Marxist theory, states are class dictatorships expressing the rule of the eco-nomically dominant class; with each economic structure, there corresponds a different form of state. The proletarian state is the only state whose histori-cal aim is to eliminate the need for states. The socialist revolution should establish institutions that are progressively self-effacing, a notion that is incompatible with 'the statism endemic to all strains of modern political philosophy' (Levine, 2003, p. 163).

Third, Levine identifies self-realisation, autonomy, community and equality as normative values typical of Marxism, even though they do not amount to a distinctive ideology, because 'the normative commitments of socialists are hardly different from those of the majority of nonsocialists' (Levine, 2003, p. 27).

These propositions represent positive, substantive contributions of Analytical Marxism to Marxist theory. Actually, Analytical Marxists suggest that they may provide the foundations for a distinctive Marxist research programme in the social sciences and for a revival of socialist theory. A thor-ough analysis of this crucial issue goes beyond the boundaries of this chap-ter, but as argued later, *any* satisfactory analysis of this question must start from a clear distinction of Analytical Marxism from the narrower approach also known as Rational Choice Marxism.

Definition 1 cannot really explain the controversy Analytical Marxism has generated. In fact, in order to identify the minimum common denominator of Analytical Marxism, it is not necessary to include the most contentious axioms, which are endorsed by some of its most prominent exponents, in particular Jon Elster, Adam Przeworski, and John Roemer, and which distin-guish Rational Choice Marxism as a sub-school of Analytical Marxism.

Definition 2. Rational Choice Marxism is defined by C2 and C3 plus a com-mitment to:

C1'. The use of 'state of the arts methods of analytical philosophy and 'positivist' social science' (Roemer, 1986c, pp. 3–4).
C4'. (i) Methodological Individualism and (ii) Rational choice explanations (Elster, 1985, pp. 5–9).

Definition 2 incorporates a strong, reductionist methodological position and, contrary to a common misconception, it does not apply to all Analytical Marxists. C1' and C4' are much stronger than C1 and C4, and they repre-sent only one way to get the analytical purchase advocated by Analytical Marxism. As is well known, for example, Cohen's (1978) reconstruction of historical materialism relies on functional explanations. Wright, Levine and Sober (1992) propose an antireductionist view of explanation that allows for supra-individual postulates. In Wright's (1997) theory of classes, the pivotal concepts are class relations and class structure.

The main *methodological* corollary of Definition 2 is that Methodological Individualism is the only legitimate foundation for the social sciences, and the only parts of Marx's theory which 'make sense' are those that can be analysed consistently with Methodological Individualism or, more narrowly, with standard 'rational choice models: general equilibrium theory, game theory and the arsenal of modelling techniques developed by neoclassical economics' (Roemer, 1986b, p. 192). Elster argues that Marx was 'committed to methodological individualism, at least intermittently', but, largely due to the influence of Hegelian philosophy, he was methodologically inconsistent (Elster, 1985, p. 7).

Rational Choice Marxism typically reaches two kinds of *substantive* conclusions on Marxian propositions and concepts. Some are considered either wrong or impossible to conceptualise consistently with C4' – including some of the core propositions identified by Analytical Marxism – and thus are discarded, such as most of Marxian economic theory (Roemer, 1986a; Elster, 1985); the theory of productive forces and relations of production (Elster, 1986a); the theory of the state; and the theory of revolution (Elster, 1985; Przeworski, 1985a). Other concepts can be analysed within a rational choice framework, but need substantial revision. For example, Roemer (1986a) provides microfoundations to exploitation and classes, thanks to (possibly at the cost of) a reduction of Marx's theory to an almost exclusive emphasis on asset inequalities.

Therefore the distinction between Analytical Marxism and Rational Choice Marxism is not important only for exegetical purposes. The two approaches have different implications concerning the future of Marxism and the definition of a distinctive approach in social theory. According to both Analytical Marxism and Rational Choice Marxism, *a* core legacy of Marxism is a set of normative commitments, which are hardly different from liberal egalitarianism. For Rational Choice Marxism, however, this is the *only* legacy of Marxism, which has instead exhausted its role in explanatory social theory: its valuable insights have been incorporated into the mainstream, the rest should be discarded. After reformulating Marxian economics in neoclassical terms, Roemer argues that 'even if one estimates that not much is left [...], or that what is left is not particularly Marxian, that is not damaging, to this enterprise at least' (Roemer, 1986a, p. 3). Similarly, in the closing paragraph of *Making Sense of Marx*, Elster concludes that 'It is not possible today, morally or intellectually, to be a Marxist in the traditional sense' (Elster, 1985, p. 531).

In the next section, several doubts are raised on Rational Choice Marxist propositions. This is crucial in order to question the Rational Choice Marxism conclusion that Marxism has exhausted its role in the social sciences. It is also important for those Analytical Marxists who hold that Analytical Marxism 'more than [its] traditional or contemporaneous rivals, "discovered" [...] what remains vital in the Marxist tradition' (Levine, 2003, p. x). In fact Rational Choice Marxist conclusions imply that the Analytical Marxist reconstruction of the core of Marxism outlined above is either flawed, or at best a brilliant but sterile logical exercise which cannot promote progress in social theory.

Methodological Individualism and rational agents

The general methodological prescriptions incorporated in C4′ have raised substantial controversy.[6] To be sure, many Analytical Marxist criticisms of functionalism seem compelling, especially if strong variants are considered, according to which the beneficial consequences of some institution or social practice are sufficient to explain it. Yet, criticisms of methodological holism and functionalism do not automatically lend support to C4′. For 'methodological collectivism is the contrary of Methodological Individualism not its contradictory' (Callinicos, 1987, p. 83). Conversely, to reject Methodological Individualism does not imply the adoption of a collectivist ontology: it only implies the existence of irreducible social structures, so that not all social phenomena can be explained *only* in terms of individuals. Besides, pace Przeworski (1985b, p. 400), rational choice theory is not the only reasonable way to 'close the loop' of functional explanations and many critics have rejected both functionalism and the reductionist Rational Choice Marxism conception of individual agency. C4′ should be evaluated *per se* as the proper explanatory strategy in the social sciences, rather than in opposition to functionalism and holism. Neither Rational Choice Marxist arguments nor the debates in the philosophy of science, however, provide decisive support for C4′.

C4′ (i) entails neither an atomistic perspective, since it allows for inherently relational properties in the description of individuals, nor that everything about the social outcomes of behaviour can be explained only in terms of individual intentions. As forcefully argued by Weldes, however, it does require that 'ultimate ontological and explanatory priority is accorded to the individual' (Weldes, 1989, p. 356). The rationale for C4′ (i) can be stated as follows. 'If the goal of a science is to *explain by means of laws*, there is a need to reduce the time span between explanans and explanandum – between cause and effect – as much as possible, in order to avoid spurious explanations' (Elster, 1985, p. 5). The specification of a micro-mechanism is necessary for the credibility of a macro law, because it shows how it 'actually works'. The process of micro reduction also enhances our understanding of an explanation. According to Ester, 'To explain is to provide a *mechanism*, to open up the black box and show the nuts and bolts, the cogs and wheels, the desires and beliefs that generate the aggregate outcomes' (Elster, 1985, p. 5).

Moreover, actions are the outcome of the decisions of subjects endowed with consciousness and only individuals possess consciousness. Analytical Marxism rejects those structuralist and functionalist conceptions, dominant in some strands of Marxism, which reduce agency to structure by viewing agents as bearers of social norms; or by conceiving of individual choice as severely limited, if not entirely determined, by structural constraints on individual feasible sets. These approaches seem inadequate, but it is unclear that Methodological Individualism provides a satisfactory alternative, as '[t]he tension between individual and structural explanations is [...] resolved (or dissolved), by fiat, by denying ontological and explanatory status to social structures' (Weldes, 1989, p. 356). This reductionist stance seems problematic.

At the ontological level, it is unclear where the process of reduction should end: individuals can be understood as structures liable of further decomposition in more elementary parts (e.g. cells), while even neoclassical economics admits supra-individual decision-makers, such as households, or trade-unions. More importantly, 'ontological reducibility (decomposability without remainder) does not *entail* explanatory reducibility' (Levine, 1986, p. 724). On the ontological claim that societies are collections of individuals, there is no necessary disagreement between holists and individualists. To deny the possibility of purposive action to supra-individual entities is arguably a basic requirement of any materialist ontology, but it does not imply Methodological Individualism.

In general, macro-level theories might provide a satisfactory answer to some questions, and a micro-mechanism need not improve an explanation. 'World War II was, in the sense in question, just an aggregation of subatomic particles in motion. But knowing all there is to know about these subatomic particles would not help us, in all likelihood, in knowing, say, the causes of World War II' (Levine, 1986, pp. 724–5, n. 12). The appropriate level of explanation depends on the object of analysis; for instance, a macro approach seems appropriate to analyse the dynamics of animal populations, where what matters is the behaviour of aggregates, not the choices of single individuals. Wright, Levine and Sober (1992) distinguish between *tokens* and *types* and argue that token-reductionism – the micro-reduction of specific instances of social types – is desirable and consistent with a materialistic approach. But type–type reductionism is impossible in the case of *supervenient* properties and relations, where many distributions of properties of individuals can realise the same social type.

C4' (ii) considerably strengthens C4' (i), but they are logically independent. As already noted, Methodological Individualism does not preclude non-intentional explanations of human behaviour. In turn, intentional explanations *only* require the specification of a goal for the sake of which an action is undertaken, rational choice requires in addition that the beliefs guiding behaviour be internally consistent, plausible, and caused by the available evidence. More precisely, standard rational choice theory requires that '(1) preferences are weakly ordered (i.e. complete and transitive); (2) beliefs are updated efficiently (that is, are consistent with Bayes's Rule [...]) and knowledge satisfies logical omniscience (i.e. full awareness of all logical implications of all statements that are held true); and (3) choices are expectationally rational, given their preferences and beliefs' (Landa, 2006, p. 436).

In Rational Choice Marxism, there is a presumption in favour of (standard instrumental) rationality, but it is not grounded in any substantive assumptions about human nature. The assumption that people behave rationally 'is largely a methodological one. One cannot even start to make sense of people unless one assumes that they are by and large rational' (Elster, 1986b, p. 210). Although C4' does not imply selfish behaviour, in Rational Choice Marxism there is a similar methodological presumption in favour of selfishness, because, according to Elster (1985, p. 9) 'Non-selfish behaviour is logically parasitic on selfishness' and because a realistic description of society, with differently motivated individuals 'may make any deductive analysis next to impossible. The strength of [Methodological Individualism] is methodological: it lies in the willingness [...] to ignore all complications that would impede getting answers to central questions' (Przeworski, 1985b, pp. 386–7).

But then, to list a set of well-known violations of the axioms of rational choice theory (including issues of intransitivity, satiation, incompleteness, etc.) *per se* is not sufficient to dismiss Rational Choice Marxism, let alone Analytical Marxism, pace Philp and Young (2002). Violations in the axioms of a theory do not automatically warrant its wholesale rejection.[7] For the criticisms to be convincing, one ought to show how taking account of such violations would improve explanations. It is not obvious, though, how, say, intransitivity would be helpful in this sense.[8]

This does not mean that standard rational choice theory cannot be criticised on *methodological* grounds, and it is certainly not the only way of capturing the assumption that agents are 'by and large rational'. Indeed, some methodological doubts on C4' (ii) and on the standard concept of rationality can be found in the Analytical Marxism literature itself. Much of Elster's work actually shows the limitations of rational choice theory and the importance of other notions of rationality, social norms, and so on (e.g. Elster, 1979, 1989a). Analytical Marxists acknowledge that the conception of 'undifferentiated, unchanging, and unrelated "individuals" typical of rational choice theory is limited and 'the theory of individual action must contain more contextual information than the present paradigm of rational choice admits' (Przeworski, 1985b, p. 381).

These issues are neglected in Rational Choice Marxist models, which are based on a conventional view of individual agency and on the identification of intentionality with standard instrumental rationality. This may be legitimate in some contexts, and Elster suggests that, despite all problems, 'there is a hard core of important cases where the rational choice model is indispensable [...] [T]his model is logically prior to its alternatives' (Elster, 1979, p. 116). These issues, however, raise further doubts on the validity of C4' as a general methodological prescription and they suggest that alternative conceptions of individual behaviour may provide a better explanation of a given social phenomenon.

Rationality, revolution, and endogenous preferences

The section 'Methodological Individualism and rational agents' critically evaluates the methodological tenets of Rational Choice Marxism and raises doubts on the view that it is the only scientific approach to Marxist theory. A wholesale rejection of Rational Choice Marxism, let alone Analytical Marxism, on *a priori* methodological grounds, however, seems unwarranted. The debate on C4' is far from being settled in the philosophy of science, and an analysis of Rational Choice Marxism uniquely at a general methodological level is unlikely to lead very far. This section takes a different perspective and focuses on a specific issue, namely the social formation of agents, which is of foremost importance in social theory, as acknowledged by Analytical Marxism. To be sure, that rational choice theory cannot properly deal with endogenous preferences and beliefs is well-known and no claim of originality is made here. The aim of the analysis is to provide a robust (indeed immanent), but focused, critique of Rational Choice Marxism and to identify relevant directions for further research in social theory that are consistent with the set of core propositions reconstructed by Analytical Marxism.

The social formation of individuals is central in social theory. Among the defining features of Marxism is the belief that 'in some way life – the things that human beings in their acting do and accept – conditions consciousness so that "life" does not arise out of "consciousness" but "consciousness" out of life' (Nielsen, 1989, p. 537). This is acknowledged by Rational Choice Marxism: the causal explanation of mental states, such as desires and beliefs, for example, is central in Elster's theory of scientific explanation (Elster, 1985, p. 4). Similarly, according to Roemer, crucial to Marxism, and to Rational Choice Marxism, is 'a commitment to the malleability of human preferences, to the social formation of the individual' (Roemer, 1986b, p. 201). There is no proper analysis of preference formation in Rational Choice Marxism, however. In general, preferences are taken as given for theoretical or technical convenience: 'once the issue of the formation of preferences has been settled, then the most convincing and fundamental explanation of a social phenomenon is [...] one that explains [it] as the result of individuals pursuing their interests [...] subject to the constraints they face' (Roemer, 1989, p. 378). The formation of preferences is treated as de facto secondary, at least methodologically.

This treatment (or, rather, lack of treatment) of preference and belief formation seems unsatisfactory. First of all, it raises an issue of consistency: if endogenous preferences can be abstracted away in most cases, it is unclear in what sense they are deemed a core feature of Marxism. Conversely, if these issues are central to Marxist theory, then it seems odd to draw general conclusions on Marx's propositions based on models in which they play no role.

Furthermore, Rational Choice Marxism does not address the methodological challenges that the social formation of individuals poses to C4'. Methodological Individualism arguably requires an asocial view of agents, whereby individuals are logically prior and their attributes and beliefs are determined only by the actions and properties of individuals, or else structural features would play a fundamental explanatory role, via their effect on preferences and beliefs. To acknowledge the relevance of the social formation of individuals blurs the very distinction between individual and social predicates, and it implies acknowledging that 'the individual-level predicates relied on by the individualist have built into them salient features of the relevant social context' (Weldes, 1989, p. 361). As for C4' (ii), it is well-known that 'the formation of the individual by society [...] arise[s] as a challenge since the rational choice model assumes the maximisation of utility subject to constraint' (Roemer, 1986b, p. 195).[9]

Substantively, the rational choice model with exogenously given preferences and beliefs seems inadequate to analyse a number of core topics in social theory. Consider the issue of collective action, which is central in Marxism, due to the relevance of class struggle and revolution. To be sure, as noted by Przeworski, 'The relation between social relations and individual behaviour is the Achilles heel of Marxism' (Przeworski, 1982, p. 307). Often an excessive malleability of agents is postulated by assuming that class positions lead to class behaviour,[10] which does not explain why class struggles and revolutions do not take place as often as predicted without resorting to an unsatisfactory appeal to ideology and deception. Rational choice theory explains some of the difficulties of collective action.

In his classic analysis of revolutionary motivation and rationality, Allan Buchanan (1982, ch. 5) argues that a subset of agents is sufficient to generate a revolution, whose costs are borne by individuals, whereas the benefits are a public good. Further, the gains for each agent are higher than their share of the cost of participating to a successful revolution. Then, assuming self-interested rational agents, a classic free-rider problem arises as abstention from action is a dominant strategy for each and every worker. This is a general result because in collective action situations 'it often pays to defect [...] [because] there are always private costs associated with organization, whereas the benefits typically are public goods' (Elster, 1985, pp. 347–8).

Rational choice theory, however, is unable to explain why collective action often *does* take place, in the form of strikes, rebellions, and even revolutions. As forcefully put by Buchanan; 'The point is not that inaction is *compatible* with rationality. Rationality *requires* inaction' (Buchanan, 1982, p. 90). A conception of self-interested, instrumentally rational individuals makes it difficult to account for collective action, except by appealing to repeated interaction or to side payments (or punishments). Neither solution seems fully satisfactory. Many instances of collective action are not repeated games, and in any case, it is well-known that in repeated games cooperation emerges as *one* possible equilibrium, and only if agents do not know when the interaction will end. Instead, to assume the existence of side payments/punishments 'is of no avail if we address the question of how trade unions came to be formed in the first place' (Elster, 1986b, p. 211). Besides, it implies an unrealistic view of workers' organisations as a pure centre of command, primarily devoted to the policing of their members.

Therefore, in order to explain collective action, it seems necessary to depart from the assumptions of the rational choice model. According to Elster, the methodological primacy of rational choice theory requires that individual-level explanations 'be constructed according to the following heuristic principle: first assume that behaviour is both rational and self-interested; if this does not work, assume at least rationality; only if this is unsuccessful too should one assume that individual participation in collective action is irrational' (Elster, 1985, p. 359).

So, first, he notes that agents normally do not choose in isolation from one another, and there may be externalities in the utility function, due to altruism or a preference for equality. Assuming these effects not to be so strong as to make cooperation a dominant strategy, a set of conditional preferences for collective action (conditional on other agents cooperating) 'might transform the Prisoner's Dilemma into an Assurance Game, in which the cooperative behaviour would be the solution outcome' (Elster, 1986b, p. 213). This is an interesting proposal: although Buchanan argues that a Marxian approach to revolution should only appeal to the material self-interest of workers (Buchanan, 1982, pp. 100–2), Cohen has forcefully rejected this view (Cohen, 1988, ch. 4). Non-selfish motives can (and, arguably, should) play a role in a Marxian analysis of collective action. Further, Elster suggests an interesting view of workers' organisations as the providers of information that may enable coordination in the assurance game. Nevertheless, this approach leaves the *explanandum* essentially unexplained, because 'these games function as tools that can highlight the fact that a change has occurred' (Weldes, 1989, p. 375), but the change that produces the shift from a prisoner's dilemma to an assurance game is located outside the theory. Elster actually claims that it 'must be explained by social psychology, not by game theory' (Elster, 1982, p. 480, n. 46). Besides, defection remains an equilibrium of the assurance game, and thus the circumstances under which cooperation is selected should be explained, noting that the informational role of leadership *per se* does *not* guarantee this outcome.

Second, Elster analyses explanations of collective action that rely on non-fully rational behaviour, such as unrealistic or irrational beliefs about other players' actions or even the inability to understand all the implications of one's decisions. Yet an appeal to emotional or irrational behaviour seems weak ground to found an analysis of collective action, much like some appeals to ideology and deception in order to explain the passivity of the proletariat. Besides, this approach provides limited insight as to why (and when) workers display the 'irrational' behaviour that makes collective action possible.

These arguments raise doubts about the possibility of explaining collective action consistently with C4', and indeed about the methodological primacy of rational choice theory. The problem with Elster's heuristic principle is that, by taking the rational choice model as *the* proper explanatory model in the social sciences, it suggests that social scientific theorising cannot really explain the behaviour leading to collective action, which should be investigated by some other discipline, and/or conceived of as irrational. This seems rather worrying given that, as acknowledged by Elster, 'there is no problem in the social sciences that is more important than that of explaining why people cooperate' (Elster, 1985, p. 366). Elster implicitly admits the limitations of C4' and argues that collective action 'may simply be too complex for individual-level explanations to be feasible at the current stage' (Elster, 1985, p. 359). To be sure, this claim is intended to be only a warning against the dangers of 'premature reductionism'. On the basis of the above arguments, however, it is unclear that a proper micro-analysis of collective action can be developed consistently with the methodological tenets of Rational Choice Marxism, even 'at a later stage'. In the remainder of this section, two main problems of C4' and some lines for further research which depart from the rational choice model are briefly discussed.

First, agents normally do not contemplate their choices in the fiction of a pre-strategic situation, before they actually interact with others. As acknowledged by Przeworski, '[t]he appropriate view is neither one of two ready–to–act classes nor of abstract individuals, but of individuals who are embedded in different types of relations with other individuals within a multidimensionally described social structure' (Przeworski, 1985b, p. 393). This suggests a more detailed analysis of the social structure shaping the interaction between agents and of how individual decisions change as interaction unfolds. A first step in this direction is made, within Analytical Marxism, by Christopher Bertram and Alan Carling who suppose that '[t]he real choices that individuals make are against the background of choices others make and practices they engage in' (Bertram and Carling, 1998, p. 286) and each individual's choices have external effects on other agents' decisions.

Bertram and Carling assume that individuals have different subjective attitudes towards collective action and each agent participates only if (at least) a minimum fraction of the population participated in the previous period. This generates a dynamic process whereby increases in the number of agents engaging in revolutionary activity raise the probability of other agents acting, and vice versa. Under rather weak assumptions concerning the distribution of agents' types (i.e. of individual preferences for action), Bertram and Carling derive a dynamic process in which mass collective action can emerge as the cumulative product of small-scale struggles. This result is quite insightful, and the model has the merit of treating collective action as a dynamic process, rather than 'a cost-benefit calculation by individuals contemplating an all-or-nothing struggle for socialism' (Bertram and Carling, 1988, p. 279). It should be noted, however, that agents are simply *assumed* to have preferences for action itself, and their preferences concerning the *outcomes* of action are not analysed. Moreover, although individual decisions can change over time, their preferences and beliefs – for example the threshold value for participation – are exogenously given and unchanging.

Second, the standard notion of instrumental rationality (outlined in the previous section) seems inadequate to understand even the simplest instances of collective action. Voting behaviour, for example, 'provides one of the strongest cases against the omnipotence of rational-choice explanation. Voting does seem to be a case in which the action itself, rather than the outcome it can be expected to produce, is what matters' (Elster, 1986b, p. 18). This suggests that in collective action problems the rational or causal determination of *ends*, and thus norms and identity, may play a crucial role. Elster has acknowledged the importance of social norms and norm-following behaviour, where rational choice theory is necessary to understand the means–end nexus but norms are not necessarily chosen according to the axioms of rational choice theory and may have an irreducibly social dimension (Elster, 1989b). These forms of collective identification are 'distinct from both self-interest and altruistic concern as normally conceived' (Graham, 1989, p. 305) and do not entail any irrational behaviour since agents are 'engaged in goal-oriented, purposive, self-interested action – i.e. each is acting rationally' (Wolff, 1990, p. 482). A growing literature exists which questions rational choice theory and develops alternative conceptions of rationality that emphasise the importance of social factors by dropping the assumption of Bayesian updating (e.g. Dickson, 2006; Skillman, 2008) or by emphasising the role of norms on choices (e.g., Landa 2006). Although no widely accepted explanation of collective action has been proposed yet, these approaches seem promising and should be of interest for critical social theorists, as they conceive of rationality as a feature of social, rather than individual-level phenomena, and analyse the emergence of cooperation as a product of the evolution of a social system.

Conclusion

The above discussion is not meant to provide an exhaustive treatment of collective action. It should suggest, however, some promising lines for further research which may depart from existing Rational Choice Marxist models but are consistent with Definition 1. Methodologically, to acknowledge the importance of the social formation of agents raises doubts about standard models of agency, but it supports an Analytical Marxist antireductionist perspective that emphasises individual intentional actions, but allows for irreducible supra-individual predicates. Thus, the analysis of endogenous preferences and beliefs might lead to a more satisfactory concept of agency which emphasises normative concerns and non-instrumental rationality.

Substantively, whereas Rational Choice Marxist contributions are mostly negative, the Analytical Marxist reconstruction of some core Marxist propositions outlined in Section 1 above is a significant, positive contribution, which may play an important role for a revival of socialist theory. This chapter suggests that the analysis of endogenous preferences may lead to a critical revision of Rational Choice Marxist results and it can provide the outline of a research agenda in explanatory social theory that builds on, and is complementary to, the core of Marxism identified by Analytical Marxism.

Notes

1. I am grateful to Meghnad Desai, Ben Fine, Andrew Levine, Simon Mohun, Erik Olsen, Steven Rigby, Robert Sugden, and Robert Ware for discussions and comments on an earlier draft of the paper. The usual disclaimer applies.
2. It is worth noting that Nowak (1998) identifies a Polish analytical Marxist school in the 1950s and 1960s.
3. For a thorough review of Analytical Marxism, see Veneziani (2008a,b).
4. Veneziani (2008a,b) argues that a similar argument applies to the Rational Choice Marxism neglect of structural constraints on individual action.
5. The following, rather schematic, account draws largely on Levine (2003). Wright et al. (1992) also include class analysis as a distinctive component of Marxism. For a more detailed analysis of the Analytical Marxism reconstruction of the rational kernel of Marxism, see Veneziani (2008a,b).
6. The Rational Choice Marxist adoption of neoclassical tools, or even formal models has also been questioned. For a thorough critique of *a priori* rejections of Rational Choice Marxism on these grounds, see Veneziani (2008a,b).
7. See, for instance, Schotter (2006) for a particularly clear defence of rational choice theory from an epistemological viewpoint, even when its axioms are proved to be false.
8. If preferences are intransitive, then, given three alternatives A, B, and C, the fact that an agent prefers A to B, and B to C, does not imply that s/he prefers A to C.
9. Roemer (1986c, pp. 198–9) suggests that endogenous preferences can be analysed within a rational choice framework by postulating some apparatus of meta-preferences from which agents optimally choose their conception of welfare. This is an interesting but undeveloped suggestion, which also raises the issue of infinite regress concerning the formation of meta-preferences.
10. This may derive from the determinism implicit in some interpretations of Marx's thesis of the 'inevitability' of the transition to socialism. For a discussion, see Cohen (1988, ch. 4).

Bibliography

Bertram, C. and Carling, A. (1998) 'Stumbling into Revolution: Analytical Marxism, Rationality and Collective Action', *Poznan Studies in the Philosophy of the Sciences and the Humanities*, LX, 277–97.

Buchanan, A. E. (1982) *Marxism and Justice* (Totowa: Rowman and Allanheld).

Callinicos, A. (1987) *Making History* (London: Polity).

Cohen, G. A. (1978) *Karl Marx's Theory of History: A Defence* (Princeton: Princeton University Press).

—— (1988) *History, Labour, and Freedom* (Oxford: Oxford University Press).

Cohen, M., Nagel, T., and Scanlon, T. (eds) (1980) *Marx, Justice and History* (Princeton: Princeton University Press).

Dickson, E. (2006) 'Rational Choice Epistemology and Belief Formation in Mass Politics', *Journal of Theoretical Politics*, XVIII, 454–97.

Elster, J. (1979) *Ulysses and the Sirens*, (Cambridge: Cambridge University Press).

—— (1982) 'Marxism, Functionalism, and Game Theory', *Theory and Society*, Vol. 11, 453–82.

—— (1985) *Making Sense of Marx* (Cambridge: Cambridge University Press).

—— (1986a) *An Introduction to Karl Marx* (Cambridge: Cambridge University Press).

—— (1986b) 'Further Thoughts on Marxism, Functionalism and Game Theory' in J. E. Roemer (ed.) *Analytical Marxism* (Cambridge: Cambridge University Press).

—— (1989a) *Solomonic Judgments: Studies in the Limitations of Rationality* (Cambridge: Cambridge University Press).

—— (1989b) *The Cement of Society* (Cambridge: Cambridge University Press).

Graham, K. (1998) 'Collectives, Classes and Revolutionary Potential in Marx', *Poznan Studies in the Philosophy of the Sciences and the Humanities*, LX, 299–314.

Kennedy, S. (2005) 'G. A. Cohen and the End of Traditional Historical Materialism', *Historical Materialism*, XIII, 331–44.

Landa, D. (2006) 'Rational Choices as Social Norms', *Journal of Theoretical Politics*, XVIII, 434–53.

Levine, A. (1986) 'Making Sense of Marx. Review', *The Journal of Philosophy*, LXXXIII, 721–8.

—— (2003) *A Future for Marxism?* (London: Pluto Press).

McCarney, J. (1989) 'Elster, Marx and Methodology,' *Canadian Journal of Philosophy*, Suppl. Vol. xv, 135–61.

Miller, R. W. (1983) 'Marx in Analytic Philosophy: The Story of a Rebirth', *Social Science Quarterly*, LXIV, 846–61.

Nielsen, K. (1989) 'Afterword: Remarks on the Roots of Progress', *Canadian Journal of Philosophy*, Suppl. Vol. XV, 497–539.

Nowak, L. (1998) 'The Adaptive Interpretation of Historical Materialism: A Survey. On a Contribution to Polish Analytical Marxism', *Poznan Studies in the Philosophy of the Sciences and the Humanities*, LX, 201–36.

Philp, B., and Young, D. (2002) 'Preferences, Reductionism and the Microfoundations of Analytical Marxism', *Cambridge Journal of Economics*, XXVI, 313–29.

Przeworski, A. (1985a) *Capitalism and Social Democracy* (Cambridge: Cambridge University Press).

—— (1985b) 'Marxism and Rational Choice', *Politics and Society*, XIV, 379–409.

Roemer, J. E. (1986a) *Value, Exploitation, and Class* (New York: Harwood Academic Publishers).

—— (1986b) '"Rational choice" Marxism: Some Issues of Method and Substance', in J. E. Roemer (ed.) *Analytical Marxism* (Cambridge: Cambridge University Press).

—— (1986c) 'Introduction', in J. E. Roemer (ed.) *Analytical Marxism* (Cambridge: Cambridge University Press).

—— (1989) 'Marxism and Contemporary Social Science', *Review of Social Economy*, XLVII, 377–91.

Sayers, S. (1989) 'Analytical Marxism and Morality', *Canadian Journal of Philosophy*, Suppl. Vol. XV, 81–104.

Schotter, A. (2006) 'Strong and Wrong', *Journal of Theoretical Politics*, XVIII, 498–511.

Skillman, G. (2008) 'Coordination Failures, Norms, and the Evolution of Strategic Confidence', paper presented at the Second APE Workshop, QMUL, May 2008.

Veneziani, R. (2008a) 'A Future for (Analytical) Marxism?', *Philosophy of the Social Sciences*, Vol. 38, pp. 388–399.

—— (2008b) 'Analytical Marxism: A Critical Appraisal', COE/RES Discussion Paper series No. 253, Hitotsubashi University.

Weldes, J. (1989) 'Marxism and Methodological Individualism: A Critique', *Theory and Society*, XVIII, 353–86.

Wolff, R. P. (1990) 'Methodological Individualism and Marx: Some Remarks on Jon Elster, Game Theory, and Other Things', *Canadian Journal of Philosophy*, XX, 469–86.

Wright, E. O. (1989) 'What is Analytical Marxism?', *Socialist Review*, XIX, 35–56.

—— (1997) *Class Counts: Comparative Studies in Class Analysis* (Cambridge: Cambridge University Press).

Wright, E. O., Levine, A., and Sober, E. (1992) *Reconstructing Marxism* (London: Verso).

Part V Marx and Feminist Philosophy

15
Marxism and Feminism: Living with Your 'Ex'

Terrell Carver

Having shacked up in the 1980s, Marxism and feminism are never going to get away from each other.[1] While this relationship was a worldwide 'item' for a time, the fact that it has cooled does not mean that it is over. Like mud, history sticks, and this couple will always have a history. The more interesting question, of course, is what kind of future they will have. The perhaps (un)surprising answer is that they will each turn into someone else – as we all do anyway.

Some like it hot

In the glory days, what was the attraction? This couple was beautifully matched – structurally speaking, made for each other. Leaving aside the April–September age difference, and the innumerable variations on a theme within Marxism and feminism, there are nonetheless structural similarities. These are hardly accidental, as feminism (second wave) developed in a political and intellectual context, especially in France, where Marxism was inescapable, and the 'forms of life' that went on within it created an overwhelming normality. Or they did if you were male, or – as we would say now – masculine-identified. Both Marxism and feminism

- are theories of emancipation/liberation
- appeal explicitly to theory to inform and guide practice
- invoke a linkage between intellectuals and 'ordinary' people
- employ extra-parliamentary tactics
- are founded on a view of a group/class that can act in a world-historical way if properly 'conscious' (or 'consciousness-raised')
- have a historical sensibility that tends towards the universal and the universalising
- generate intellectual problems and trends (particularly philosophical and historical ones) independent of political projects (and perhaps at the expense of them)

255

- appeal to worldwide majorities
- have problems with imperialism/colonialism in terms of leadership/ identity (but not 'race') as a constitutive concept
- create a canon of major writers, authoritative documents and heroes
- cause major revisions to history as it is written and understood as an activity
- tend to validate a 'method' or search for same
- support mass revolution, and a new understanding of same.

Of course there are differences, and major misfits. Feminism generates political action and activism, but hardly any political parties, or even very stable institutional caucuses or coalitions (why?). Marxism has a very strained (though not necessarily hostile) relationship with (bourgeois) democracy, liberal rights and values, and democratic regimes. Perhaps owing to the widening of 'the political' to include the 'private' and the 'personal', feminism has sidestepped almost all of the practicalities of regime-change, state-building, and national defence (on which Marxism has famously foundered and then imploded). Marxism was always more successful with its (so-called) 'materialism' than it was with its economics, except in so far as it merged (eventually) with liberal reformers, social democrats, and other non-Marxist socialists. If feminism has any economics, it is borrowed, and once borrowed, it looks suspiciously like updated Marxism (as just discussed) anyway. Marxism cut itself off from religions of all kinds, or any kind; surely this is the one area that feminists find most problematic of all, because so many overtly or covertly promote women's oppression in the first place. Where is the female Feuerbach arguing that God really is a projection of man-as-male? Marxists might say that feminists have no 'theory of history' reflecting inevitabilities in human societies over the *longue durée*; feminists might retort that Marxist theories have been wrong in practice and are no doubt wrong in principle.

In sum, despite the differences, feminism in most forms articulated itself on a model loosely derived from Marxism, and has been benefiting from many of its major concepts and methods. Marxism has reacted almost wholly defensively, either not asking feminism out at all, or proposing union on one-sided and patronising terms.

Man in the middle/muddle[2]

Engels is famously in the middle of all this. He wrote his short book *The Origin of the Family, Private Property and the State* (1884) just after the re-publication of August Bebel's *Women and Socialism* (1879, 2nd edn 1883). That book, now little known, was already a (banned) success and very soon became one of the best-selling and most influential socialist tracts of the nineteenth century. It is likely that Engels's title comes from a line in

Bebel's book (Lopes and Roth, 2000, pp. 29–39, 73, 82 n. 55). Having got his start as a polemical and highly political journalist, Engels was well used to writing ripostes, in some cases inflammatory and satirical, and in other cases more rigorous and serious-minded. *The Origin of the Family* may be one of the latter, and unlike his already well known *Anti-Dühring* (1878–9)[3], for instance, it is possible that it rather belies its original format as a riposte altogether, because Bebel and his book get no mention. Alternatively it is possible that Engels was not writing a riposte or a supplanting account, and was happy instead with his positioning as a kind of addendum or footnote to Bebel's more radical work (Lopes and Roth, 2000, pp. 73–5).

Certainly the latter argument would be more persuasive, if Engels had featured Bebel's work in his own, though there may have been political risks here – Bebel's work had been immediately and afterwards suppressed in successive editions under the anti-socialist laws in Germany, whereas Engels's more heavy-weight scholarly study was not. Rather than self-censor it for publication in the 'theoretical' monthly of German socialism, Karl Kautsky's Berlin-based *Die Neue Zeit*, Engels published it in Switzerland, from whence it was clandestinely distributed. Bebel's tract is no longer widely read, and it seems to have faded nearly as fast as it flowered, not least because Marxist historiography has triumphed over it in producing an Engels-centred account of socialist theory and practice (and so marginalising Bebel).

Engels's 'light touch' strategy in not foregrounding Bebel's work in *The Origin of the Family* was perhaps to spare the worthy trade unionist Bebel any discouragement, as he was very much an ally and friend rather than a rival and threat, like the academician Eugen Dühring. Bebel subsequently and modestly bowed to Engels's (supposed) greater expertise in theoretical matters, and so never mounted any counter-challenge (Lopes and Roth, 2000, p. 82 n. 55). Perhaps there was for Engels an element of being caught off-guard, and of damage-limitation, as well, in that he already had a clear agenda for intervention on 'major' theoretical questions to do with philosophical foundations, method, history, class struggle, and revolution, on which he aimed to set people straight. The 'woman question', on which he had had some experience, however (cf. *The Communist Manifesto* and some very early writings, and cartoons),[4] was never a central interest, nor included prominently in any previous overview of substantial issues for Marxists. It may be that Engels was not keen to publicise the matter all that much and thus to make it a central question of the age, since it would necessarily distract, in his view, from the central and singular focus on class politics (which we now see as masculinised) that Marxists had always argued was their mark of distinction. Moreover it might pose awkward questions of organisation, even *separate* organisation in some sense, which from the (male) leadership's perspective could only be unwelcome and divisive. Certainly the text of *The Origin of the Family* overall is rather concerned to add women to the conception of history, philosophy, and politics that Engels attributed to Marx, and that he himself had expounded in his various works and introductions to the master's writings since 1859 – but then to stir the mix as little as possible.

Even merely 'adding' women raises the issue of gender, that is, ways that sex and sexuality become power relations in society (Carver, 1998a, pp. 18–24). Such discussions are bound to raise issues of sexuality (typically through comments on marriage in some form and 'the family') and about men as men, being the 'other half' of gender relations. Engels rose splendidly to the task, and indeed *The Origin of the Family* is remarkable for its sweep, taking the story of human reproductive and caring relationships from their earliest origins through to a post-capitalist future that he identified as socialism. It was very widely circulated in German and in translation, and by 1891 it was in its fourth edition. Certainly the terms of the title – 'family', 'private property', 'state' – would have had a familiar, safe ring to them for male socialists and trades unionists, at whom the book was primarily directed. Engels, knowingly I think, did not repeat the 'woman' signifier of Bebel's title (*Die Frau und der Sozialismus*), with its overt reference to the 'woman question' and the issues raised in, and by, the feminist movements of the time, diverse as they were, inside and outside of socialism.

In short, Engels was the safe (male) pair of hands through which Marxism could meet any challenge, and if it needed any amendment or revision, he was the one authorised to make the changes. Engels not only lived his relationship with Marx, when the master was alive, he was also the first biographer of that relationship, as well as Marx's literary executor (though not the sole owner of his papers), and from those unimpeachable credentials he brooked no rivals in speaking for Marx, nor during his own lifetime did any emerge. He went from 'second fiddle' and 'junior partner' to quite another role, that of near co-author and posthumous collaborator, though his self-acknowledgement in that regard was characteristically self-effacing (Carver, 1983, pp. 118–51, 152–8; Carver, 1998b, pp. 163–80). Only now, with full publication of Marx's manuscripts and scholarly tracking of Engels's treatment of them, is this becoming an issue that cannot be avoided or explained away (Carver, 1996a, pp. 79–85).

And changes there were in *The Origin of the Family*. Engels adapted Marx's concept of 'material' production to include human re-production, and attempted to build on this revision an apparatus of twin-track 'determination' in history, involving sex-oppression, as well as class-oppression. Moreover this was also the occasion on which Engels made public his incorporation of Charles Darwin's 'great discovery' into the actual conception of history bequeathed by Marx from the pre-Darwinian 1840s, and indeed to build it into Marx's historical account of the transitions from one epoch to another that had been elaborated in published form (by both Marx and

Engels, separately) in 1859.[5] Bebel's intervention on the 'woman question' was thus the occasion for no small revision to the 'outlook' which Engels attributed to Marx, but of which he was now in sole charge, Marx having died just the year before the first publication of Engels's little book.

Ritually Engels linked his own work with unpublished manuscripts on anthropology that Marx had left behind, though without actually claiming that those writings were in any sense drafts of a work (by Marx), or indeed of Engels's actual work as he conceived it, and as eventually published. The manuscripts themselves, while acknowledged at the outset, were not specifically cited in Engels's text, and so the work has come down in the interpretive tradition as Engels's alone. Moreover scholarly analysis has shown that Engels's claim, both vague and extravagant in terms of an overlap in content or imprimatur for the ideas, does not stand up to scrutiny. It is clear that Marx was interested in Engels's main source, Lewis Henry Morgan, but it is not particularly clear why or what he thought about it (Krader, 1972; Carver, 1982, pp. 144–5). What the interpretive tradition has *not* grappled with very extensively, though, are Engels's revisions and amendments to the 'guiding thread' that Marx had left behind in his 1859 'Preface' to *A Contribution to the Critique of Political Economy*, and had then briefly cited in the first volume of *Capital* (1867), in order to help readers understand his published critiques of political economy, the economic theory of the day (Carver, 1982; Marx, 1986, pp. 175–6 n. 35).

This reluctance within the interpretive tradition to address Engels's remarkable revisions to the very fundamentals of Marxism – and thus to rewrite one of Marx's most famous texts, the 1859 'Preface', which was of course famously rehearsed yet again by Engels in *Anti-Dühring* – must be due to an association between those amendments, and the 'woman question', gently transmuted by Engels into 'family', 'private property' and 'state' in his title and in the structure of his short book. No (male) commentator on Marxism has taken *The Origin of the Family* as methodologically central to Marxism and to understanding Marx.[6] Rather the work has occupied a place well down the line in the *Engels* canon, with its (shocking?) content recounted, but not critically assessed, and certainly not promoted to pride of place over Marx's 'Preface' to *A Contribution to the Critique of Political Economy* (1859) – on the place of epochal 'modes of production' in history – or over the jointly written *Manifesto of the Communist Party* (1848) – on the nature of class struggles. Other late works by Engels, e.g. *Ludwig Feuerbach and the End of Classical German Philosophy* (1886), did not attempt anything so ambitious, rather the reverse, in fact, as Engels argues there that Marx's philosophical position can be traced back developmentally, in a smooth sweep, to the philosophical and political controversies of the 1840s, in which Engels was himself involved.

The Origin of the Family thus has two strikes against it. One is that it complicates what was otherwise a settled and (reasonably) simple story of historical 'determination' by an identifiably singular factor (production, albeit of its 'means' and 'relations') – as opposed to the obviously dual-factor 'production' and 're-production' of *The Origin of the Family*. The other is that it raises issues to do with women which the (presumptively male) leadership were only too happy to shelve, preferably in a book whose title gave scant advertisement to the feminist cause, and whose argument, read as a whole, did not support separate organisations for women nor take sex-oppression in class society more seriously than class-oppression. In short Engels is the feminists' Marxist; but left to his own devices, he was not much of a feminist by argument or action. *The Origin of the Family* thus poses problems for Marxism, in terms of its fundamental tenets, but those problems have rarely, if ever, been addressed outside the feminist context, and given the airing they evidently merit.

Engels's book also poses problems for feminism, though these were explicitly taken up at length, and in depth, only in the 1980s. The main issues were the validity and utility of a 'dual systems' approach that would find social 'determination' in gender dynamics, *and* in class dynamics, equally or at least even-handedly. Moreover the status and content of pre-historical accounts as such came under scrutiny in this literature, as Engels had made bold claims in this area and had constructed a highly readable, and widely read, discussion. Lastly the extent to which Engels's vision of a socialist future corresponded to any widely shared feminist ideals came under scrutiny. Was his claim that most gender-oppression would vanish, once class-oppression had been expunged through proletarian revolution, well supported with theory or sadly facile in practice? Was he really in a position to theorise 'woman' and 'women's experience' at all? Had he in fact articulated a sufficiently nuanced, and in particular emotionally sensitive, vision of future familial and sexual relations?

As a feminist text Engels's work suffered from minority status – few works (perhaps no works?) by men could, by definition, count as central and essential feminist reading. While there is no particular reason why Marxism should not have been more influential in second- and third-wave feminism than, say, psychoanalysis – and just as many reasons why both traditions carried heavy baggage of feminist-unfriendly, not to say misogynist associations – nonetheless few commentators would say that Marxism has counted for more in feminist thought than psychoanalytic theory. In general, feminist history, feminist research and feminist theory do not take Engels all that seriously (Marxist feminists to the contrary, of course), and when they do, the upshot is that he is insufficiently interested in gender to deliver on his promises, or to show exactly how someone (more feminist) could do so.

Despite this, Engels's *The Origin of the Family* has become a minor point of reference for feminist theory, even if it is not in itself a feminist classic. For some it is evidence why feminists should reject Marxism, or even Marx's work, and for others it is the foundation of a Marxist feminism, its deficiencies notwithstanding. Michèle Barrett comments:

> Scarcely a Marxist-feminist text is produced that does not refer somewhere to Engels's argument, and if one had to identify one major contribution to feminism from Marxism it would have to be this text.
>
> (Barrett, 1983, p. 214)

More strongly, I would argue that any text that self-identified as Marxist-feminist, or which figured as such by treating gender and class in tandem as determining social structures, would strike an odd note if it did not cite and then revisit Engels's *The Origin of the Family*. Over the years it has been regularly re-issued in English with appropriately updated introductions linking it to contemporary feminist politics, as well as to Marxist scholarship.[7]

Few commentators, feminist or otherwise, would defend very much of the anthropological material cited by Engels or very many of the anthropological points he makes independently. Too much has happened in the intervening years, both in terms of empirical research and fieldwork, and in terms of the scope and presumptions of anthropology itself, to sustain the certainties through which Engels wrote his text. The text is rightly described by Barrett as 'flawed and disputed' (Barrett, 1983, p. 214). Moreover the kind of Marxism through which Engels conceived his account, and to which he aimed to contribute in *The Origin of the Family* in a quite fundamental and foundational way, has itself been subject to several generations of critique, rooted in issues to do with science, causation, knowledge, determinism, class, leadership, and revolution. *The Origin of the Family*, in Marxist terms, has fallen somewhat to one side in all these Marxist critiques, without – as has been mentioned above – ever becoming truly central, or perhaps as central, as it should have been, given its relationship to the 'materialist interpretation of history', the foundational concepts of production and labour, and Marxist predilections for developmental historical periodisations.

In terms of gender studies more broadly, and in particular with reference to studies of men and masculinities, Engels's work should have a lot to offer. He gives a gendered account of men (as men) in the famous sections on pre-history which cover the development of sexual and family relationships, something in which men figure by definition and with which, in practice, they are still involved. He also writes Darwinian concepts of sexual selection into this account, which necessarily make claims about male behaviour (and the 'nature' of men as men), an area in which males have an important stake in self-knowledge, never more so than today, given feminist and other challenges.[8] And his account of private property and government in the historical and contemporary age is itself gendered (and not merely generic), in that he details the roles of both men (as men) and women in bringing those institutions about, and in enjoying (or suffering) the consequences.

Why, then, is Engels's *The Origin of the Family* not one of the foundational texts of men's studies?

Unfortunately, it takes some considerable work of analysis to make Engels's views on these matters apparent. In common with other texts Engels's *overtly gendered* account of men tends to slip into the background, as he also rather typically states his views and conclusions in apparently generic and gender-neutral terms. That is, Engels's text moves rather easily from an overtly gendered concept of man to an apparently de-gendered one, without alerting anyone very markedly to the difference. He is hardly alone in this, as the analytical distinction has only recently been developed, and is not yet widely appreciated, by any means (Pateman, 1988, pp. 1–18; Pateman, 1999; Carver, 1996b). Nonetheless, despite remarking on men in overtly gendered terms, and theorising their nature and behaviour in explicitly drawn ways, Engels is hardly a gender pioneer in men's studies, precisely because he does so little argumentatively with what he exposes to view. His text has no purchase on any *critique* of men as men, nor any exposure of generic man as male (rather than female), feminist or otherwise. Nor is there any evident suggestion that politically or personally he would have had any sympathy for such a notion (few men do, even now). Rather Engels derived considerable political and personal benefit, as men still do, from not raising transformative issues in any very serious way, and for reinforcing this complacency through a discursive strategy that 'flickers' between overtly gendered accounts of men as husbands and fathers, and covertly gendered accounts of 'man' as generic and gender-neutral. The overall effect is thus to rehearse certain naturalised and naturalising presumptions about men, but without making them at all problematic with reference to culture and change. Politically this then leaves men where they were, secure in their 'nature', and immune from the challenges posed by feminisms, and by transformative thinking about what manners maketh man, and what masculinities are acceptable.

Engels's *The Origin of the Family* has been taken seriously by at least one men's studies scholar, somewhat in the hope that Marxism will be taken seriously within gender studies, just as some feminists have found theoretical and political mileage in a critical engagement with Marx and Marxists. Jeff Hearn has argued that transformative thinking about labour could follow from the suggestion in *The German Ideology* (a manuscript work of 1845–6 by Marx and Engels) that human labour is materially productive and species-reproductive. Working from a feminist standpoint on maternal labour, Hearn suggests a revisioning of human labour as both emotionally nurturing and technologically developmental (Hearn, 1987, pp. 59–118). The 'other' to this conception is the narrow view of labour, inscribed within modern economics, as mere factor of production, a commodity with a market-value, albeit one rather inconveniently located in human bodies and brains, rather than in raw materials and machinery. The advantage of taking this earlier location for 'dual systems theory', that is, a view that Marxism incorporates a gendered concept of labour related to human re-production, is that *The German Ideology* does not pose issues about pre-history and anthropology in quite the explicit way that the later text, *The Origin of the Family*, poses so directly and at considerable length. Moreover Engels's later work is inscribed within overt presumptions about social theory that incorporate a positivist view of science within a deterministic view of human behaviour, or at least his outlook seems to tip more that way than towards the more speculative and hermeneutic discourse of the 1840s. *The German Ideology* bravely calls for empirical studies to fill out the conceptual framework that the joint authors have sketched in, but an identification of some notion of factual illustration for the 1840s with the positivistic notions of science that Engels himself developed only later during the 1860s and 1870s would surely be anachronistic (Carver, 1989, pp. 232–52).

The upshot is that Engels's *The Origin of the Family* is an undiscovered text for men's studies and theoretical work on masculinities, as indeed are numerous classics in all fields of social studies written by male authors. Generally these are replete with overtly stated yet unexamined presumptions about 'what men are like' (as men), and why that aspect of 'human nature' is simply factual, natural and cannot be made problematic. An important discursive strategy that ensures this outcome is the 'flickering' that the texts incorporate between overtly gendered and apparently de-gendered conceptualisations of 'man'. This not only naturalises gendered behaviour as necessarily (because 'biologically') inherent in the 'male of the species' but also then generalises this to humans as such through the (supposedly) generic concept of 'man', in which much of this masculinised behaviour is said to inhere 'in the species'. Of course at certain moments in these texts the feminine 'other' pops up, notably when the mechanics (literally) of pregnancy, parturition, and lactation are in view, not to mention the 'need' (of men, of course) for sexual partners and domestic 'partnership'. Engels's text is a particularly thorough portrayal of this typical and effective discursive strategy.

Engels's text has been vastly influential, but not for the right reasons. Studies of pre-history and historical teleologies are not as convincing as they once were (or least that is my hope), given that we are rightly focused today more on processes than on origins, and more on contingency than on over-determination. His feminism is just what we might expect from a man: full of knowingness about women, and near-deliberate recalcitrance about men. In so far as Marxism can be identified with a reductionist determinism (whether of one or two fundamental factors), Engels's revisions in *The Origin of the Family* have not been much debated. In so far as Marx's own views can be identified with a theoretical outlook that is more nuanced, and less deterministic, Engels's sketchy discussion (a tissue of assumptions, really) looks even less satisfactory. As Gayle Rubin said, 'Eventually, someone will have to write a new version of *The Origin of the Family, Private Property and the State*, recognizing the mutual interdependence of sexuality, economics and politics'(quoted in Scott, 1999, p. 202). Altogether *The Origin of the Family* as it stands is a triumph of assertion and self-assertiveness over all else. In particular it tells us a great deal about one man in particular – Friedrich Engels.

Back to the future of Marxism and feminism

Having reviewed this foundational text, and having thanked feminism for making it visible, where does this leave us with respect to our opening question? What is the future of the relationship between Marxism and feminism?

The first point to consider is that Marxism is no longer what it was. Just as feminism has pluralised into feminisms, so is Marxism becoming plural, various, celebrating differences. The best example of this is still Laclau and Mouffe (1985), which tackled the concept of class, the proletarian subject, political 'consciousness' or subjectivity, and the evident failure of various self-styled Marxist revolutions to maintain their links either with the liberal traditions and formalities of democracy or with some form of widely supported mass political practice that would replace defective 'bourgeois' institutions. Critiques that simply argued that the world had moved on were always subject to a hopeful rejoinder: perhaps the world could be put back on its track, if only 'we' tried hard enough. Much more radically (if not always very clearly) Laclau and Mouffe tackled a critical point of weakness in theory, namely the slide in 'traditional' Marxism between 'the material' (so solid-sounding, so scientific-sounding) and 'the economic' (surely a realm of 'material' goods and services), via Engels's frequent (and Marx's very occasional) self-identifications as 'materialists'. Marxists tended to skip over Marx's own complaints about 'traditional materialism' completely, and in order to make his confession to 'flirting' with Hegelian idealism consistent with 'hard science' (as in Engels's grandiose scheme for a 'system' covering 'nature, history and thought'). Laclau and Mouffe simply blew that away by arguing that 'class' was only a descriptive concept because, and when, it was in a prior sense a subjective and performative one. In some respects this merely returns Marxism to the world of the *Manifesto* and to *Wage-labour and Capital*, and other polemical, interventionist, consciousness-raising works, read as such, and not as treatises on 'theory' or repositories of (previously identified) doctrine and orthodoxy. Laclau and Mouffe thus pose a very stark question about Marxism, namely can it be divorced from its own Engelsian history as a 'science', or rather, can it be prised loose just enough to give it an alternate identity (given that it will never escape this history)?

While feminism(s) did not embrace the views of science and history that had seemed so rock-like to Marxists, they had certainly founded themselves on a concept of 'woman' (women, female, feminine etc.), and its binary opposition from 'man' (men, male, masculine etc.). Again, the nagging critiques that woman was not really 'there' as a matter of anatomy, chromosomes, practice etc. did not really bite. The more radical critique was again the conceptual one, or rather, the critique that enunciated a new understanding of concepts, and hence of theory/practice/knowledge. The move here was to argue that 'woman' was itself a category of oppression (not a descriptor of a 'group'), rather as Laclau and Mouffe had argued with 'class'. The conclusions were much the same. Political consciousness and programmatic politics did not flow from, nor could they be 'read off of', objects or facts or phenomena (e.g. 'woman', 'class') that are said indubitably to be 'there' ('materially') in the world. It followed that consciousness-raising in both cases had to be more profound, and to grapple more intensively with subjectivity, than had previously been acknowledged. Finding facts, fitting them into theories and drawing the 'inevitable' conclusions concerning (rather self-interested) action could no longer function as a recipe for political activity. While many Marxists and feminists regard this in very vocal terms as deplorable, it is clear that the alternative 'linguistic' ontologies and epistemologies are gaining ground in academic circles, and that agitprop of the traditional kind has no real grip on 'the masses'.

Conclusions

Marxism and Feminism will exist together as historical shadows in their 'unhappy marriage'. Shadows are very real and they accompany us around (outdoors, on sunny days, at least, and just occasionally in bright moonlight, if you're lucky). History is never over as it only exists because we constantly invoke it as a matter of experience; our experiences simply move forward, as we occupy our imaginations with thoughts on what 'was' or 'might have been'. It will always be a marriage of sorts, because people thought it was, during the 1980s.

In so far as anyone now sees Marxism that way, and feminism that way, this relationship is still flickering. The structural similarities that I listed at the beginning should ensure that. My excursus into Engels's *The Origin of the Family, Private Property and the State* was to demonstrate that – ironically – Engels himself was the author of (apparently) major revisions to Marx's theoretical work, introducing both reproductive labour (alongside productive labour) and Darwinian sexual selection (alongside economic development) into the 'theory of history'. Marxist monism swiftly closed ranks on this (and you can fast-forward swiftly to Cohen, 1978), whereas feminists got the rap for introducing 'dual-systems' theory (which was bound to be untidy and indeterminate-sounding in any case).

The feminist case that gender-oppression had a different origin from, but was intertwined with, class oppression, foundered in never quite explaining what 'gender' was in this context (not 'woman', surely, nor power-relations as such, nor – except for radical feminists – anything biological or necessary about men). Dual-systems theory worked best when it aligned two oppressions together and made a coalition of (all?) women with some men look possible. Politics intervened here, quite dramatically, as (white, liberal, middle-class) feminists themselves came under attack from women whose views arose from quite different nationalist aspirations, (global) class aspirations, and (variously) sexual, religious and cultural aspirations, all of which drastically undermined previous assurances that women's experiences were similar, universal and urgent. While the parallel case was less dramatic, the effect was much the same: communist and class-based politics and parties have been losing ground in industrialised (and even in less developed countries) for many, many years. 'Class' as an imaginary, perhaps very regrettably, does not seem to be coming back (other than as a ghostly or spectral *l'a-venir*, as Derrida, 1994, puts it). The really potent imaginaries of today's politics lie elsewhere.

'Class' *is* an imaginary, as it functions in politics, even if (and often because) it falls under the metaphorical slide 'material'/'economic'. If people are going to be a class, and act as a class, they have to have this, one way or another, in their subjectivity. But it doesn't get there, merely by being 'there' as some 'material reality', to which theorists think they can point (whilst pronouncing the metaphor 'material' or appealing to 'economic' determination, in whatever instance). This seems to me to be quite a reasonable (and practical) way of transcending (supposed) philosophical dichotomies and doing politics at the same time, but it does push the questions of 'truth' and 'science' into a firmly Foucauldian frame, where power and persuasion create a regime in which political identity and action make things 'true' and 'real'.

Feminists are the ones to bite the bullet here, ironically so, since 'woman' is, if anything, more 'material' even than 'class' (i.e. 'class' is rather more obviously an abstraction than is 'woman'). On the other hand, a political perspective seems to flow more directly from 'class' than from 'woman' (i.e. since the eighteenth century 'class' has been constructed politically as a category of oppression, whereas feminists are still having to work hard to establish this). It's also the case that 'woman' will never stand, or be made to stand, for 'humanity' in quite the same generic way that 'working class person' has been made to do (cf. Marx's (1975) early essay on the subject, 'A Contribution to the Critique of Hegel's Philosophy of Right: Introduction'). Given the hierarchical and binary nature of the man–woman gender–power dichotomy, there would appear to be conceptual limits to any universalisation of feminist liberation: what would men/masculinity look like in a feminist utopia where emancipation is achieved? We might understand what institutions would be in place to protect and empower women ... but would then a woman (in the words of Henry Higgins), 'be more like a man'? How much more? And vice versa. Or would gender disappear altogether (as the occasional feminist has suggested) (Grant 1993)? Would that then abolish this power-ridden binary, leaving us then with various power-relevant and power-neutral 'differences' – just not that big one?

Marxist politics, and socialist politics generally, has foundered on a somewhat more mundane issue, namely how far towards democratisation and equalisation does a capitalist economy have to go in order to count as socialism, at least at stage one? Ultimately, then, does further development require the abolition of the money economy? If so, what are the signs, and indeed what would it be like? The re-evaluation of leisure time (not leisure-time *consumption*) is about the only hope here, not simply revulsion at the waste, inequality and pollution that capitalism licences, encourages, and requires.

Perhaps we are all socialist-feminists now, and that's as good as it gets.

Notes

1. An earlier version of this chapter was published as 'Marxism and Feminism: Living with your "Ex"', *Studies in Marxism*, 10 (Carver, 2004), 67–83.
2. The following section is adapted from Carver, 2004, Chapter 10.
3. The title in full was *Herr Eugen Dühring's Revolution in Science*, with fully intended irony. On the early Engels, see Carver, 1989, pp. 31–9; on *Anti-Dühring*, see pp. 241–4.
4. Carver, 1989, pp. 10–12, and illustration no. 10 (between pp. 120–2), 145–8, 244–5; Carver, 1983, pp. 78–95.
5. Karl Marx, 'Preface' to *A Contribution to the Critique of Political Economy*, in Marx, 2002, pp. 160–1; these transitions are critically discussed in Carver, 1982, pp. 38–57.
6. The modern *locus classicus* for this version of Marxism, deriving from the terms of the 1859 'Preface', and thus this way of reading Marx through this 'central' text, is Cohen, 1978, which does not take up the question of Engels's revisions to this 'outlook' in *The Origin of the Family*.
7. This begins with the English translation (Chicago: C. H. Kerr, 1902); see also Leacock, 1972, and Barrett, 1985.
8. Engels's 'biological' and Darwinian framing (never mind his lifelong heterosexism) could make the text an interesting object of critique from the gay male standpoint, but to my knowledge no one has taken this up directly. Concentrating on the bio-graphical evidence for Engels's misogyny and homophobia, Parker (1993) touches on *The Origin of the Family* only very briefly and does not use this text to explore Engels's masculinised heterosexism from which the misogyny and homophobia proceed.

Bibliography

Barrett, M. (1983) 'Marxist-Feminism and the Work of Karl Marx', in B. Matthews (ed.) *Marx: 100 Years On* (London: Lawrence and Wishart).
—— (1985) Introduction to F. Engels, *The Origin of the Family, Private Property and the State* (Harmondsworth: Penguin).

Carver, T. (1982) *Marx's Social Theory* (Oxford: Oxford University Press).

—— (1983) *Marx and Engels: The Intellectual Relationship* (Brighton: Wheatsheaf).

—— (1989) *Friedrich Engels: His Life and Thought* (Basingstoke: Macmillan).

—— (1996a) '"Marx-Engels" or "Engels v. Marx"', *MEGA-Studien*, 1996/2, 79–85.

—— (1996b) '"Public Man" and the Critique of Masculinity', *Political Theory*, 24, 673–86.

—— (1998a) 'A Political Theory of Gender: Perspectives on the Universal Subject', in *Gender, Politics and the State*, (ed.) V. Randall and G. Waylen (London: Routledge)

—— (1998b) *The Postmodern Marx* (Manchester: Manchester University Press).

—— (2004) *Men in Political Theory* (Manchester: Manchester University Press).

Cohen, G. A. (1978) *Karl Marx's Theory of History: A Defence* (Oxford: Oxford University Press).

Derrida, J. (1994) *Specters of Marx: The State of the Debt, the Work of Mourning, and the New International*, trans. P. Kamuf (New York and London: Routledge).

Grant, J. (1993) *Fundamental Feminism: Contesting the Core Concepts of Feminist Theory* (New York and London: Routledge).

Hearn, J. (1987) *The Gender of Oppression: Men, Masculinity and the Critique of Marxism* (Brighton: Wheatsheaf).

Krader, L. (1972) Introduction to *The Ethnological Notebooks of Karl Marx: Studies of Morgan, Phear, Maine, Lubbock* (Assen and New York: Van Gorcum and Humanities Press).

Laclau, E. and Mouffe, C. (1985) *Hegemony and Socialist Strategy: Towards a Radical Democratic Politics* (London: Verso).

Leacock, E. B. (1972) Introduction to F. Engels, *The Origin of the Family, Private Property and the State* (London: Lawrence and Wishart).

Lopes, A. and Roth, G. (2000) *Men's Feminism: August Bebel and the German Socialist Movement* (Amherst, NY: Humanity/Prometheus).

Marx, K. (1975) 'A Contribution to the Critique of Hegel's Philosophy of Right: Introduction', in *Karl Marx: Early Writings*, (trans.) R. Livingstone and G. Benton (Harmondsworth: Penguin).

—— (1986) *Capital Volume 1*, (trans.) B. Fowkes (Harmondsworth: Penguin).

—— (2002) *Later Political Writings*, (ed. and trans.) T. Carver (Cambridge: Cambridge University Press).

Parker, A. (1993) 'Unthinking Sex: Marx, Engels, and the Scene of Writing', in Michael Warner (ed.) *Fear of a Queer Planet: Queer Politics and Social Theory* (Minneapolis MN and London: University of Minnesota Press).

Pateman, C. (1988) *The Sexual Contract* (Cambridge: Polity).

—— (1999) 'Beyond the Sexual Contract?', in G. Dench (ed.) *Rewriting the Sexual Contract*(New Brunswick, NJ: Transaction).

Scott, J. W. (1999) *Gender and the Politics of History*, rev. edn (New York: Columbia University Press).

16
Breaking Waves: Feminism and Marxism Revisited

Gillian Howie

In her revised introduction to *Women's Oppression Today*, Michèle Barrett writes that she shelved her original project – the attempt to consider alliances between a non-reductive Marxism and feminism – in response to the impact of postmodernism on the intellectual environment.[1] She cites as her reason for shelving, rather than resolving, the difficult relationship between Marxism and feminism the fact that postmodernism calls into question the status of all 'grand projects'; a definition that she saw applying to both socialism and feminism. However, she concludes, because postmodernism is a cultural climate as well as an intellectual position, a political reality as well as an academic fashion, it is not something one could have avoided but rather represented the key positions around which a newly invigorated feminist theory would have to revolve (Barrett, 1988, p. xxxiv).

Along with Diana Leonard, Seyla Benhabib, and Sylvia Walby a slightly later Barrett identifies a 'cultural turn' within feminist theory (Barrett, 1992, p. 204). At this point, feminist theory became more closely associated with cultural theory, specifically discourse analysis, than with social science. In addition, a corresponding trend could be detected within what was left of the social sciences: a movement away from social structure models to phenomenology and hermeneutics. In *The Condition of Postmodernity* David Harvey makes a similar but broader point. He assesses the impact of the 'cultural turn' made by the New Left and suggests that the push into cultural politics connected better with anarchism and libertarianism than with traditional Marxism (Harvey, 1989, p. 354). As a consequence of embracing new social movements, whilst abandoning its faith in the historical materialist principle that the proletariat is an agent of change, the left undermined its ability to critique either itself or social processes.

This move into cultural politics brought to the fore issues concerning: gender and race; politics of differences; politics of disability; the barbarism of colonization and the politics of aesthetic representation. As such the cultural move proved undeniably fruitful. The underlying question, though, is whether or not cultural theory – or postmodernism – was also a mask for deeper transformations in the culture of capitalism. Postmodernism has been variously defined and signifies many different things. For the sake of this essay the critical distinction is between the definition of postmodernism as an historical era and a new mode of production and its definition as an aesthetic or attitude – a way of presenting and experiencing very modern if developed modes of production. I shall be assuming that the conditions of modernity have been loosely continuous and that 'postmodernity' does not signify a new mode of social production or form of social organization, despite new alignments. Further, I shall be arguing that there is a correlation between certain formal features of postmodernism and the development of multinational capitalism.

The type of postmodern feminist theory that has blossomed, particularly within the UK, has presented distinct and well-documented challenges. It has destabilized previously secure categories, and encouraged theorists to analyse the meaning and relationships of power in a way that has called into question unitary, universal concepts and opened radical discussions concerning subjectivity, sex and gender. But this attempt to destabilize universal concepts has also been accused of 'pulling the rug from under the feet of feminism', for if individuals cannot be conceived as belonging to a distinct group, then they cannot be expected to mobilize around common concerns, shared political identities or allegiances (Stone, 2004, p. 136). Indeed, unsettling concepts in this way have also left feminists unable to discuss the 'structural' context of power and the conditions of subjectivity: be they economic, social, psychological or linguistic. This is particularly awkward for some third-wave feminists, basing their work on Leslie Heywood and Jennifer Drake, who contextualize third-wave feminist perspectives by showing how they are shaped both by material conditions created by economic globalization and technoculture and by bodies of thought associated with postmodernism and poststructuralism (Heywood and Drake, 2004, p. 13).

The description of various and disparate theories as 'postmodern' may strike some as a scandalous totalizing move. But, as Fredric Jameson notes, it is only recently that such a theoretical move has been considered scandalous; previously abstraction had been considered to be one of 'strategic ways in which phenomena, particularly historical phenomena could be estranged and defamiliarized' (Jameson, 1988, p. 35). The aim of this chapter is to indicate, via this 'abrupt distance afforded by the abstract concept', what has been subsumed, elided and erased in the recent canonization of feminist theory and to suggest that the exclusion of materialism, associated with socialist feminism, has led to a form of 'cultural' feminism within which is a particular thread of anti-realism that has left feminism unable to articulate, investigate or analyse its own conditions. These formal epistemic features of feminist cultural texts correlate to the context of production and reception of those texts.

Yet one must be careful not to throw the baby out with the bathwater. The contradictions internalized by feminist theory express something true about the situation of its emergence which cannot be addressed simply by calling for a return to old knowledges; for a reduction of all social relationships to their 'material' or economic origin. Indeed, the recent discussions in the journal *Historical Materialism* about the economic crisis in the late 1990s demonstrate that arguments within socialist and Marxist feminism were outside the 'mainstream' and were abandoned rather than resolved. The impulse to move beyond, to be *de mode* and grasp the new – the anxiety of influence – suffuses the academic terrain and encourages us to leave behind insights which have not exhausted their capabilities.

Recent history of feminist theory: Constructing a canon

The recent story of feminist struggles and generations has been most clearly staged by Julia Kristeva in her now seminal essay 'Women's Time'. She argues that the feminist movement can be divided into three distinct phases: Liberal (existentialist), Marxism and radical, and postmodern (Kristeva, 1982, p. 32–5). Since Kristeva's essay, a new generation of women has grown up, and new terminology with which to reflect on feminism has emerged. From its early formation (1991–95) this third stage – now described as a 'wave' – focused on exclusivist tendencies within the first-and second-wave feminist theory of the 1970s and 1980s. Broadly, the argument is that first- and second-wave *essentialism* led to an eradication of differences. Third-wave feminists believe that they must resist the seductive promise of inclusive identity because, far from providing the grounds for political agency, the assertion of commonalities among women leads to the neglect, and even erasure, of differences (Shildrick, 2004, p. 68). The force of these arguments has since led to 'an increasingly paralysing anxiety over falling into ethnocentrism or "essentialism"' (Bordo, 1990, p. 142; see also Howie, 2005, for a discussion of Spelman, Fuss and Stoljar). Layered into this is a tendency – most clearly articulated by Elizabeth Spelman and Elizabeth Grosz – to identify universal and general terms with essentialism (Grosz, 1990, p. 333; Spelman, 1990). As a consequence any discussion about the structural common grounds among women – what used to be the conditions of oppression – has been de-legitimized.

The blanket description and rejection of feminist theory particularly of the 1960s and 1970s but also 1980s as essentialist is then a real problem. Aside from the political consequences, the occlusion of some very careful discussions concerning social relations, economic determinants and mediation results in a rather peculiar account of culture. Writing at the very beginning of the 1980s, Lydia Sargent noted that history was being rewritten and replayed, that college students had never heard of Shulamith Firestone but they had heard of panty raids (Sargent, 1986, p. xxx). Today we can concur with this sentiment; students will probably never have heard of Firestone – although they will have heard of Judith Butler, Grosz and Monique Wittig – and this seems to confirm the view of the history of feminist theory as undulating waves, one giving way to the next.

The wave metaphor actually suggests two quite different theoretical approaches (Gillis, Howie and Munford, 2004). On the one hand it evokes the idea of fluid theoretical intersections. On the other, it suggests something altogether more teleological; where each phase gives way to, or is sublated, in the next. But if the arguments located within these 'waves' are incommensurable, or the social problems left unresolved, then there can be no sense to the linear historical progression implied by the wave metaphor. I am going to briefly point us back to radical feminism, to remind us why it was thought imperative to solve the problem of conceiving intersections between economic and sex-based exploitation and then see how materialist – socialist and Marxist – feminists attempted to resolve the same problems. My intention here is to break apart the wave or generational framing of feminist theory and to recover a rich stream of (social) critical theory.

Inheriting an extremely variegated enlightenment, post-war – second wave – feminists recognized that women had never been simply excluded from the social contract (Howie, 2002, p. 178–9).[2] Modern social structures, it was agreed, managed to include women in the political order in such a way that formal demands could be met without the substantial changes that liberal feminists thought would necessarily follow. Influenced by American feminist theorists, such as Betty Friedan, Kate Millett and Firestone, radical feminists began to analyse the family, sexuality and forms of cultural representations.[3] They concluded that the political gains of the first wave had been quite empty because traditional structures and values had been left in place, and it is these very structures which define the roles of men and women and give femininity and masculinity different values. Patriarchy was defined as a set of social relations between men, which have a material base, and which, though hierarchical, establish or create interdependence and solidarity among men that enable them to dominate women.

Radical feminism is characteristically concerned with the differences between men and women, differences in power and authority as well as different dispositions and characteristics. The 'problem with no name' – the 'women's question' – unwrapped a number of issues around sex and power including rape, domestic violence, pornography, low pay, division of labour, domestic labour, child abuse, social and political exclusions and the connection between all these and sexualized representations.[4] Essentialists and anti-essentialists agreed that the liberal political slogan 'equal but different' mystifies the fact that masculinity is valued over femininity and men guaranteed sanctioned domination over women. The structures themselves would need to be revised according to different values. Some argued that the appropriate values would be those associated with femininity. Others argued that characteristics associated with femininity are a product of the very system to be replaced, hence a 'revaluation of all values' would be required. Connecting these arguments is a belief in the real moral equality and value of men and women. This belief, in the 'metaphysical' equality of all human beings, co-existed within 'second wave' feminism with the opposing ideas that the two sexes are biologically different and that, because social systems change over time, the human subject – who is a result of such social processes – also changes. The theory of the nurtured human subject, constituted through her social relations, inaugurated a break from the 'abstract individualism' of liberalism and existentialism. This break would, in the end, remove from the feminist project its ability to defend its humanist moral position. The distance between the second and the third waves, described by Ann Brooks seems premised on a very rough description of the variety of positions within radical feminism as essentialist and a-historical (Brooks, 1997, pp. 16–17).

Socialist and Marxist feminists took part in these radical arguments within the women's movement, which explains why arguments concerning the nature of patriarchy and the causal origin of oppression came into focus. Emphasizing this discursive character of feminist theory, Lise Vogel notes issues of sexuality, economic distribution and the sex-based division of (domestic) labour were always at least implicit within radical feminism (Vogel, 1983, p. 5). But whereas radical feminists considered men – or male privilege – to be the root of oppression and the main obstacle to liberation, socialist and Marxist feminists dug deep within Marxism to address the demands of women's liberation. That said, as early as 1971, Juliet Mitchell made an incontrovertible case against traditional Marxism: it would have to be a transformed Marxism.

Fundamentally socialist/Marxist feminists wished to analyse the material structures of women's oppression but had to first decide whether or not patriarchy should be analysed as a set of social institutions distinct from capitalism, with its own history and causal origins. If capitalism could be defined as the appropriation and exploitation of labour by one class of another, could patriarchy be defined as the appropriation of labour and sexuality by one class (men) of another (women)? If so, what specifically is the relationship between production and reproduction? Is male dominance the creation of capitalism or is capitalism one expression of male dominance? Marxist feminists attempted to identify gender relations in the context of production and reproduction as understood within historical materialism; women are important in the struggle as workers not as women. So, Marxist unified systems theorists argued that theories of capitalism and patriarchy describe aspects of a single social system. Whereas dual systems theorists, more commonly associated with socialist feminism, argued that patriarchy and capitalism are two distinct systems that contingently intersect and that feminism and Marxism complement one another; each making up for the deficiency in the other.

There is a tendency within the current feminist canon to describe unified systems theory – Marxist feminism – as economistic, but in fact Marxist feminists themselves recognized that the categories of economic analysis tend to reduce questions of power to the simple matter of who owns and controls the means of production and who has surplus labour extracted. Indeed, setting themselves the task of redressing this, Marxist feminists tried to identify the operation of gender relations as and where they may be distinct from, or connected with, the process of production and reproduction, understood by historical materialism. Traditional socialist theory was inadequate, they believed, to the task of explaining the apparent cross-class and trans-historical character of women's oppression, sex-based division of labour, and the parallels between oppression based on race, gender and class.

Although Marxist feminism is described as unified system theory, various unified systems theorists, such as Alison Jagger, Lise Vogel, and Iris Young, introduced the idea that gender distinctive oppression is a necessary feature of capital. Vogel stressed that Marxism is actually inadequate as it stands because it is unable to account for the particular (sexed) dynamics of the labouring process and so it must be transformed to make it properly adequate. Explaining how sex-benefits are only apparent and not in the long-term interests of working class men, she offered a convincing account of how capitalism incorporates men through a process of sanctioned domination and privilege. Importantly, though, she stressed the point that contradictions may arise within capitalism – and reverberate through the working class – as capitalism strives both to maximize productive labour, and so encourage women into the workforce, and retain women's unpaid domestic labour.

Substituting division of labour theory for class analysis, Young attempted to develop a theory of gender-biased capitalism where class and gender relations had evolved together. By concentrating on the division of labour, she believed that it would be possible to be sensitive to the ethnic distinctions of a racist labour market. She also argued that marginalization of women, and our function as a secondary labour force, is an essential and fundamental characteristic of capitalism. Ellen Wood, a Marxist feminist, argued otherwise, stating that capitalism is uniquely *indifferent* to the social identities of people it exploits, undermining differences and diluting identities such as race and gender (Wood, 1988, p. 167). According to this argument, when the least privileged sectors of the working class coincide with 'extra-economic' identities – such as gender and race – it may appear that the cause of the oppression lies elsewhere. In fact, however, racism and sexism function so well in capitalist society because they work to the advantage of some members of the working class in the competitive conditions of the labour market. In other words, the cause of oppression can be explained in terms of economic categories.[5]

Dual systems theorists, often referred to as socialist feminists, tended to separate out economic and sex relations, thereby accommodating gender analysis within an exposition of patriarchy, rather than forcing the economic analysis of Marxism to answer the questions outlined above. Patriarchy and capitalism were considered analytically distinct, with their own interests, laws of motion and patterns of contradiction and conflict resolution. The intersection of the systems is a contingent fact and can be less than smooth. But this twin track approach can supplement the sex-blind Marxist categories and make explicit the systematic character of oppressive relations between men and women. Marxism cannot answer why women are subordinate to men inside and outside the family and why it is not the other way round, whereas, according to Heidi Hartmann, feminist analysis can expose the fact that patriarchy has a material basis in men's control over women's labour-power (Hartmann, 1981, p. 9). The family wage debate noted above is one example of the resolution of conflict over women's labour-power occurring between patriarchal and capitalist interests. Juliet Mitchell contended that the two systems are theoretically irreducible and argued that there had been a tendency in Marxism towards reductionism, such that the function (and role) of reproduction, sexuality and socialization was taken to be determined by the economic base. Indeed, in *Psychoanalysis and Feminism* she suggested that the causes of women's oppression are buried deep in the human psyche and that psychoanalysis is the way into understanding ideology and sexuality (Mitchell, 1974).[6]

In one of the most well known articles comparing Marxism with feminism, dual systems theorist Catharine MacKinnon drafts out a systematic typology of the distribution of power that allows us to read across from one to the other (MacKinnon, 1982). Within Marxism, she claimed, work has class as its structure, production as its consequence, capital as its congealed form and its main concern is control. Sexuality within feminism is a similar organizing principle: heterosexuality is its structure, gender and family its congealed forms, sex roles its qualities, reproduction a consequence and, likewise, its main concern is with the issue of control. Retaining the integrity of each theoretical system, MacKinnon recognizes the limitations of each:

> [W]omen with feminist sympathies urge attention to women's issues by left or labour groups: Marxist women pursue issues of class within feminist groups; explicitly socialist feminist groups come together and divide, often at the hyphen (MacKinnon, 1982, p. 10).

She suggests that instead of engaging the debate over which came – or comes – first, sex or class, the task for theory is to explore the conflicts and connections between the methods that found it meaningful to analyse social conditions in terms of those categories in the first place (MacKinnon, 1982, p. 13).

Analysing the ways in which sexual desirability is fetishized, MacKinnon argues that sexuality comes to be seen as something independent from social relations. Estrangement, objectification and alienation are synonymous from the point of the view of the object: 'because women have not authored their objectifications'. Pushing this a little further, she notes that 'the alienated who can only grasp self as other is no different from the object who can only grasp self as a thing' (MacKinnon, 1982, p. 28). She believes that underlying this is a fundamental 'ontological' problem concerning the relationship between subject and object, a relationship which Marxism and feminism consider differently. Feminism, attuned to the subject and critical consciousness, aims to reconstitute the meaning of women's experience. Marxism, striving to establish its scientific credentials, posits an independent reality which has only 'objective', i.e. non-subjective, content.

There are a number of parallels between Marxism and theories of patriarchy that make this type of dual systems theory seem plausible. Both insist on a materialist account of history, both operate with the categories of class, and both attempt to investigate the origin of oppression. By extending and developing Marx's account of ideology it seemed possible to make some sense of women's 'false consciousness'. For this reason various dual systems theorists began to look to Althusserian Marxism and hoped to find in his theory of 'interpellation' an account of ideology which would be able to explain not only the exigencies but also the force of patriarchal ideology. But the problems encountered in attempting to marry the more phenomenologically attuned feminist method with the more 'scientific' economic Marxist method proved insurmountable. Mitchell herself tried to combine insights of structural linguistics with psychoanalysis, to flesh out an analysis of the development of subject identity. Her psychoanalytic analysis of patriarchy, the supposed transition from monocausal to polyvalent analyses, prefigures the move into postmodernism.

Identity theory: Move into postmodernism

Jameson uses the term 'postmodern' as a periodizing concept 'whose function is to correlate the emergence of formal features in culture with the emergence of a (new) type of social life and (new) social order [...] multinational capitalism' (Jameson, 1988, p. 3). Accordingly, there is a correlation between certain formal features of culture, including cultural texts, and the development of multinational capitalism. In a similar vein, I would say that there is an intricate and complicated relationship between the rise of Thatcherism, 'free market' fiscal policy, left disunity, the demise of feminism as a political force, the appearance of identity politics and theory focusing almost exclusively on the issue of identity, sexuality and 'the body'. Aside from this fascination with all things bodily, the other principal characteristic of postmodernist theory is the high value placed on fragmentation, diversity and difference. If there is a significant relationship between the conditions of theory and the theory itself then we might expect to find fragmentation and diversity as part of the modern experience, an experience heightened since 1970s (Harvey, 1989, p. 117).[7] Even a cursory account of the political context of identity theory provides some support to the idea that there exists a correlation between its formal features and the context of its production and reception.

Easthope describes the 1970s and 1980s in the UK as the time of 'British poststructuralism', when the British Left, most notably the *New Left Review*, moved on to a terrain that could accommodate psychoanalysis and theories concerning the cultural significance of various forms of representation (Easthope, 1988).[8] The broad project was to theorize 'the encounter of Marxism and psychoanalysis on the terrain of semiotics' (Stephen Heath, quoted in Easthope, 1988, p. 9). The convergence of textual and psychoanalytic theory with socio-historical analysis made cultural studies a natural habitat for feminist theory (Lovell, 1993). But, due to a suspicion that 'over-determinism' was an irretrievably essentialist notion, cultural studies replaced humanist and economistic readings of Marx with more 'marxian' theorists. Although just about everyone agreed that subject-identity is a consequence of antecedent linguistic and psycho-sexual processes, the priority assumed for psychoanalytic theory masked some real theoretical tensions. From a psychoanalytic perspective Marxists socialize structures that cause conflict and aggression and their explanations of commodity fetishism and ideology are profoundly one-dimensional. From a Marxist perspective psychoanalysis fetishizes subjectivity, naturalizes human motivation, and posits invariant and universal psychic structures.

Interestingly, and presciently some – such as Cora Kaplan – warned that unless semioticians and psychoanalytic theorists retained their materialist and *class* analyses they would end up producing no more than 'an anti-humanist avant-garde version of romance' (Kaplan, 1985, p. 148). Obviously there is a rich stream of psychoanalytic Marxism but, nevertheless, psychoanalytic theory ended up replacing Marxism as the dominant model of explanation and the Marxist critique of psychoanalysis has largely been lost. Indeed, it could be argued that this shift in attention to psychoanalytic and semiotic theory testified to a shift in the social structure itself; 'that the cult of subjectivity was a direct response to its eclipse' (Jacoby, 1973, p. 41).

At the same time, issues relating to sexuality were brought to the fore of the political agenda by feminist work in women's refuges, rape crisis centres, around pornography and culminated in the separatist and political lesbianism debates of the middle 1970s and 1980s. But the 1980s then saw a tremendous change in the political culture of the UK. It has been suggested that what distinguishes and shapes British feminism is its roots in the high levels of working class action in the 1960s and 1970s (Rowbotham, 1989). And during the 1980s, with a number of extremely important exceptions, including the Miner's Strike and Poll Tax and anti-Section 28 demonstrations, there was a general decline and a few significant defeats in trade union and labour activity.

But there had also been tensions within the women's movement that had been brewing for over a decade. Conflicts between radical and social-ist feminists, between middle class and working class feminists, between black feminists and white feminists and between heterosexual and lesbian feminists were played out in local organizations, at conferences and through various editorial boards. It is true that these conflicts forced feminists into recognizing their own location and acknowledging the universalizing ten-dencies within feminist thought. But following this the goals of feminism as a unified political movement became hard to justify. This recognition occurred as divisions concerning the appropriate place for feminist activity became more entrenched. Some, such as Sheila Rowbotham and Hilary Wainwright, attempted to transform labour politics from within, whilst oth-ers argued that a more open and democratic political movement was incom-patible with old style labour or workerist political groups. Vogel charts the withdrawal of Marxist women from socialist organizations and the women's movement (Vogel, 1983, p. 1). It was not just that the problematic intersec-tion of feminism and Marxism was shelved but that feminism itself lost its way; off the streets, from the Peace Camps and into the classroom.

'Municipal feminism', the filtering through of women and feminist theory into public institutions, including, but not exclusively, those of higher education, has been linked to academic feminism and to the de-radicalization of feminist theory (Lovenduski and Randall, 1993; for a discussion of municipal feminism in the US context see Hennessy, 2000, pp. 198–201). Corresponding to the waning of feminist activism noted above was the consolidation of academic feminism. Certainly tensions between feminist 'generations' have been exacerbated by the disciplining structures of the university system that pressurizes academics both to individuate themselves and to submit to fairly explicit institutional norms if they are to survive professionally. Conservative modernism, sweeping academia, rewards those who are integrated into managerial structures but also engenders a dialectic of aggressive individualism which tends to reward originality that must appear as newness and disavowal of the old.

All this may seem a little odd, given that from literary theory to epistemol-ogy, architecture to geography, biology to law, feminist academic theory has blossomed. But at the point when academic feminists were standardizing an academic canon, identity theory reigned supreme; non-UK generated poststructuralist-postmodernism exerted an hegemonic influence on the directions within feminism – an influence which presented strategic and theoretical problems. It has been argued that feminist discourses of difference pulled the rug from under feminism as politics. This is for three main reasons. Firstly, once the diversity of women is recognized and privileged over com-munity, any sort of collective and goal directed action becomes problematic, although not impossible, to conceive. However, secondly, theories tended to reject 'objectivist' or realist approaches to the world of experience. This meant that it became increasingly difficult to interrogate underlying and generative structures or mechanisms. So, as diversity was prioritized questions concerning mechanisms or causes of oppression were placed out of the frame. Thirdly – and not surprisingly given the experiences of feminist activists – the focus became feminism itself (Whelehan, 1995). Now we barely mention 'women's studies' and 'feminism' seems not only passé but also at times embarrassingly unsophisticated, replaced almost everywhere with 'gender and sexualities'.

Off the shelf

If postmodernism is a distorting mirror, reflecting something of the condition of its emergence, then what were the facts of its emergence? In the UK these include: the fragmentation of the labour market, appropriated and diversified by capital; an aggravated individualism of the 1980s; a splintered labour movement and a utopic – idealist – cognition of these conditions in 'philosophies of subjectivity and desire'. The theoretical assertion of difference was not inured from the conditions of its own emergence. The conflicting nature of its conditions has resulted in a conflicting set of theoretical commitments. 'The third wave', or feminist postmodernism, was prefigured by a recognition that feminist theory had to recognize not only one but multiple locations, not only one but polyvalent causes of oppression, had to acknowledge the universalizing racist tendencies of feminist thought and account for the fact that individuals are subsumed under universals. The recognition that feminist theory needed revision was a particular response to the experience of conflictual social conditions, but the theoretical commitments that emerged disguised continuities and made it actually less likely that the conflicts would be addressed in practice or that the relationship between theory and its own conditions could be assessed.

To address these conflicts and apprehend the correlation between the formal features of cultural theory and the conditions of production and reception, we need to return to the feminist canon and prise apart its inclusions, exclusions and genealogy. If we do not return to Barrett's original project, take it from the shelf and dust it down, then feminism will continue to sink into a version of cultural theory, 'an anti-humanist avant-garde version of romance'. In re-visionary mode, Judith Grant argues that Marxism is still useful to feminism but only if we begin with the humanism of the *1844 Manuscripts* and *German Ideology* rather than his economic theory. Grant believes that by resurrecting Marx's humanism, where 'the human' is an unevenly structured category, we have a starting point for a discussion of the 'infinite variability, mutability and difference among human beings' (Grant, 2003). It seems to me that for a number of reasons she is right to draw a line under some of the arguments concerning productive and unproductive labour, not least because individuals occupy (and have always occupied) more than one role at a time, and that there is no significant difference between the amount of time men and women now spend in work that is remunerated. But her revision of feminism and Marxism not only leaves unaddressed some of the very knotty problems of second-wave feminism, principally why gender relations were captured in a hierarchical fashion, but also isolates Marx's early 'humanism' from the value theory of labour.

With these insights, I think we can return to MacKinnon's earlier argument. Concentrating on the problem of sexual objectification, MacKinnon noted in her early essay that female sexuality cannot be lived or spoken or felt or even somatically sensed apart from through its own definition. Sexual objectification, holds MacKinnon, is not illusory but the reality that women live with. Reification, she says, is reality to the reified. If we re-glue reification to Marx's labour theory of value we can bring together this phenomenologically inspired feminism with critical social science. So we can say that ideological critique is central: it is a critique of constitutive consciousness itself. It is a short step to claim that the form of objectification uncovered by MacKinnon is another version of a more general alienated and reified cognitive orientation: a (causal) effect of a particular form of production. It has to be admitted that this line of argument runs the danger of submerging the feminist analysis of cultural and symbolic forms into a one-sided perspective of a single gender under the panoply of exploitation.

To resist this reduction we need to recover the distinction between knowing subject and a known object. A return to Barrett's project requires a return to a rather unfashionable dialectical method, one that retains subject and object, and only this can deliver to feminism critical tools to approach epistemological and psychological questions. By retaining the ontological integrity of subject and object, by recuperating the distinctions between exploitation, reification and objectification we can begin from the point of view of experience and explore the terrain 'that is the most damaged, most contaminated'. If there is an intimate relation between truth and method then this method will also need to de-naturalize appearance: a critique of purported generality, disinterestedness and universality.

From within contemporary feminist theory, problems have emerged that provoke this recuperative move. Third-wave feminists Heywood and Drake assess the global context of the third wave of feminism as transnational capital, downsizing, privatization, a shift to the service economy, general downward economic mobility and technoculture, all of which correspond to a new form of feminist anti-capital, local, anarchic activism. Yet this activism is always dispersed. In their attempt to navigate the few alternatives outside the production/consumption cycle of global commodification, third wavers critically engage with, and celebrate, consumer culture. Brooks, who claims that the intersection of postmodernism, popular culture and political economy coalesces around the issue of consumer culture, underlines this (Brooks, 1997, p. 155). According to Jennifer Baumgardner and Amy Richards third-wave feminists appropriate girls into a 'girlie culture'

(Baumgardner and Richards, 2006, p. 302). This often involves a celebration of popular modes of femininity – including Barbie dolls, makeup, fashion magazines, high heels – using them, they say, isn't short for 'we've been duped'. In other words, the argument about the commodification of the feminine aesthetic becomes an argument about whether or not 'playful celebration' is identical to reification and to address this we need to regroup economic analysis and recent sophisticated accounts of subjectivity.

It is important for third-wave feminists not only to have a handle on the ideological stakes of difference but also to address certain questions about the nature of developing global capital. Is there a general trend towards downward economic mobility or is there a global feminization of poverty? Is there necessarily a feminization of labour or is there a tendency towards homogeneity? Is the family a legal and ideological unit or/and is it a place of resistance? What is the connection between child poverty and family structures? What is the impact of multinationals in local economies? Is the labour market fragmented (according to race and gender) and is this incorporated into, perhaps created by, the efficient extraction of surplus? How do we understand the move into, and war fought over, the Middle East? Do questions of sexuality (such as transexuality and intersex) rise to the fore when gender relations are unsettled? Are gender relations unsettled because capitalism and patriarchy pull in different directions? How do we make visible, understand, respond to and fund our responses to child abuse, domestic violence, rape and international sex trade? Questions abandoned, rather than resolved, not only by some feminists but also by Marxists, social-ists and the New Left.

Conclusion

Notwithstanding Kristeva's protestations that 'generation' implies less a chronology than an attitude, the generational account actually maps social, intellectual and political history onto a linear model of historical progression. Rather than co-existing generations, it is linear generation which is woven through the wave metaphor. The wave metaphor does suggest that one wave is followed by another, supersedes and incorporates the previous wave and – despite some currents – that the movement is forwards. This sense of one wave sublating the previous wave, including it and moving onwards, echoes in the memory of feminists who would like to claim this time for their own and for feminists who are disposed to disavow their younger selves.

Mridula Chakraborty argues that the idea of a wave-based consciousness is itself an ideological construct of the Eurocentric subject that seeks to subsume and consume the challenges posed to it (Chakraborty, 2004, pp. 205–6). Here she underlines Chandra Mohanty's claim that when the singular identity of feminism was threatened by communities of resistance, dominant feminism had to insist that these racialized categories were neither politically contingent nor valid; rather that they were essentialist ways of imagining the female body (Mohanty, 2003). White privilege has remained intact while the arguments used to defuse the tension that difference produces have become much more sophisticated and insidious. We find echoes here from Nancy Hartsock who asked why, 'just at the moment in Western history when previously silenced populations had begun to speak for themselves, the concept of the subject and the possibility of discovering/creating a liberating truth became suspect?' (quoted by Di Stefano, 1990, pp. 75–6).

In her introduction to *The Unhappy Marriage of Marxism and Feminism*, Lydia Sargent wrote:

> [T]oday we have a movement. We have the beginnings of theory and practice. Never again will the 'woman question' be described as 'the problem with no name'. We have a name.
>
> (Sargent, 1986)

But by 1988 Denise Riley posed the troublesome question: am I that name? (Riley, 1988). Conceding that we have made few in-roads into the sex-based distribution of goods and roles – including the distribution of domestic (unpaid reproductive) labour – and noting the current fight women and girls have on their hands in Iran, Yemen, Iraq, Afghanistan and Turkey, perhaps it is time to return to the 'woman question' with a slightly different analytic frame of reference; let us break feminist waves. The present has brought to the fore questions that require us to negotiate our past in light of the future and to retrieve the counter-hegemonic critical (social) theory that has been produced throughout.

We have now entered a period after Marx when

> in a way we could not have done earlier, we can begin to understand Marx in new ways unencumbered by Marxist interpretations that have long dominated the discussions of both Marxists and non-Marxists.
>
> (Rockmore, 2002, p. xiii)

Göran Therborn describes Marxism as a triangulation, the poles of which can be identified as (1) an historical social science, focusing on the historical operations and processes of capitalism, (2) a philosophy of contradiction, or dialectics with epistemological and ethical ambition, and (3) a mode of politics which provides a compass or road map to the overthrow of the existing order (Therborn, 2007). If we can see feminism as a similar triangulation, a reinvigorated notion of dialectical materialism[9] (2) will help us to grasp the gendered dynamics of developed capitalism (1), and this will, in turn, inform, be informed by and support a refreshed politics (3). Further, giving due accord to third wave suspicions, we also need a move from out of the academy and a reconsideration of the role of the 'public intellectual'.

Notes

1. This is a revised version of a paper that was presented to the Marx and Philosophy Society on 4 December 2004 and published in a different form as Howie, 2007.
2. I worked out some of this historical account in Howie, 2002.
3. Firestone's and Millett's books both published in 1970, had a major influence on socialist feminism but had also themselves been influenced by socialist theory – Firestone for one saying: '[W]e have not thrown out the analyses of the socialists; on the contrary, radical feminism can enlarge their analysis, granting it an even deeper basis in objective conditions and thereby explaining many of its insolubles' (quoted in Vogel, 1983, p. 25).
4. *The Women Question* was originally a popular pamphlet written by E. Marx and E. Aveling (1886).
5. This came to a head in the domestic labour argument in the 1970s and 1980s concerning the origin of sex-based distribution of labour. An early formulation of the argument can be found in Benston, 1969, pp. 13–27. She argues that the cause of women's secondary status is unpaid domestic labour: the production of use-values without exchange-values. For an early presentation of the argument that the function of the family is to maintain and reproduce labour-power, see Morton, 1971.
6. It may be a mistake to strictly define Mitchell as a dual systems theorist, given that she identifies four separate structures: production, reproduction, sexuality and socialization.
7. There is an argument to be made here concerning continuity in the political and cultural conditions of production and reception in France post 1968, the context for much post-structuralism, and the conditions of its reception and dissemination in the UK as well as Australia and United States.
8. Easthope (1988, p. 21) names Perry Anderson and Tom Nairn in historical studies, Barry Hindess and Paul Hirst in sociology, The Birmingham Centre for Contemporary cultural Studies in cultural studies, Raymond Williams and Terry Eagleton in literary criticism, Norman Bryson and Griselda Pollack in art history and Alan Durant in musicology.
9. I am of course not alone in this. See e.g. critical realists such as Caroline New, as well as David Harvey, Sylvia Walby, Linda Alcoff and Teresa de Lauretis.

Bibliography

Barrett, Michèle (1988) *Women's Oppression Today: The Marxist-feminist Encounter* (London: Verso).
—— (1992) 'Words and Things: Materialism and Method in Contemporary Feminist Analysis', in *Destabilizing Theory: Contemporary Feminist Debates* (Cambridge: Polity Press).
Baumgardner, Jennifer and Richards, Amy (2006) 'Manifesta: Young Women, Feminism and the Future', in L. Heywood (ed) *The Women's Movement Today: An Encyclopedia of Third-Wave Feminism* (London: Greenwood Press).
Benston, Margaret (1969) 'The Political Economy of Women's Liberation', *Monthly Review*, 21 (4), 13–27.
Bordo, Susan (1990) 'Feminism, Postmodernism and Gender Scepticism', in L. Nicholson (ed.) *Feminism/Postmodernism* (London, Routledge).

Brooks, Ann (1997) *Postfeminisms: Feminism, Cultural Theory and Cultural Forms* (London: Routledge).

Chakraborty, Mridula (2004) 'Wa(i)ving it All Away: Producing Subject and Knowledge in Feminisms of Colour', in S. Gillis, G. Howie and R. Munford (eds) *Third Wave Feminism: A Critical Exploration* (Basingstoke: Palgrave Macmillan).

Di Stefano, Christine (1990) 'Dilemmas of Difference: Feminism, Modernity and Postmodernity', in L. Nicholson (ed.) *Feminism/Postmodernism* (London: Routledge).

Easthope, Anthony (1988) *British Post-structuralism: Since 1968* (London: Routledge).

Gillis, Stacy, Howie, Gillian, and Munford, Rebecca (eds) (2004) *Third Wave Feminism: A Critical Exploration* (Basingstoke: Palgrave Macmillan).

Gillis, Stacy and Munford, Rebecca (eds) (2003) 'Third Wave Feminism and Women's Studies', Special issue of *Journal of International Women's Studies*, 4 (2).

Grosz, Elizabeth (1990) 'A Note on Essentialism and Difference', in S. Gunew (ed.) *Feminist Knowledge: Critique and Construct* (London: Routledge).

Grant, Judith (2003) 'Gender and Marx's Radical Humanism in the Economic and Philosophical Manuscripts of 1844', *Rethinking Marxism*, 17 (1).

Hartmann, Heidi (1981) 'The Unhappy Marriage of Marxism and Feminism: Towards a More Progressive Union', in L. Sargent (ed.) *The Unhappy Marriage of Marxism and Feminism: A Debate on Class and Patriarchy* (London: Pluto Press).

Harvey, David (1989) *The Condition of Postmodernity* (Oxford: Basil Blackwell).

Hennessy, Roseanna (2000) *Profit and Pleasure: Sexual Identities in Late Capitalism* (London: Routledge).

Heywood, Leslie and Drake, Jennifer (2004) '"It's All About the Benjamins": Economic Determinants of Third Wave Feminism in the United States', in S. Gillis, G. Howie and R. Munford (eds) *Third Wave Feminism: A Critical Exploration* (Basingstoke and New York: Palgrave Macmillan).

Howie, Gillian (2002) 'Feminism, Materialism and British Universities', in J. Wolfreys (ed.) *The Edinburgh Encyclopaedia of Modern Criticism and Theory* (Edinburgh: Edinburgh University Press).

—— (2005) 'Natural Kinds and Essentialism in Feminist Theory', *Contemporary Political Theory*, 5, 238–58.

—— (2007) 'After Postmodernism: Feminism and Marxism Revisited', *Critical Matrix: The Princeton Journal of Women, Gender and Culture*, 16.

Jameson, Fredric (1998) *The Cultural Turn: Selected Writings on the Postmodern 1983–1998* (London: Verso).

Jacoby, Russell (1973) 'The Politics of Subjectivity', *New Left Review*, 79.

Kaplan, Cora (1985) 'Pandora's Box: Subjectivity, Class and Sexuality in Socialist Feminist Criticism', in G. Greene and C. Kahn (eds) *Making a Difference: Feminist Literary Criticism* (London: Routledge).

Kristeva, Julia (1982) 'Women's Time', in N. Keohane, M. Rosaldo and B. Gelpi (eds) *Feminist Theory: A Critique of Ideology* (Sussex: Harvester).

Lovell, Terry (1993) *British Feminist Thought: A Reader* (Oxford: Blackwell).

Lovenduski, Joni and Randall, Vicky (1993) *Contemporary Feminist Politics: Women and Power in Britain* (Oxford: Oxford University Press).

MacKinnon, Catherine A (1982) 'Feminism, Marxism, Method, and the State: An Agenda for Theory', in N. Keohane, M. Rosaldo and B. Gelpi (eds) *Feminist Theory: A Critique of Ideology* (Brighton: Harvester).

Mitchell, Juliet (1974) *Psychoanalysis and Feminism* (Middlesex: Penguin).

Mohanty, Chandra Talpady (2003) *Feminism without Borders: Decolonizing Theory, Practicing Solidarity* (Durham, N. C. and London: Duke University Press).

Morton, Peggy (1971) 'A Woman's Work is Never Done', in E. Altbach (ed.) *From Feminism to Liberation* (Cambridge: Schenkman).
Riley, Denise (1988) *Am I that Name? Feminism and the Category of Women in History* (Basingstoke: Macmillan).
Rockmore, Tom (2002) *Marx After Marxism: The Philosophy of Karl Marx* (Oxford: Wiley-Blackwell).
Rowbotham, Sheila (1989) *The Past is Before Us: Feminism in Action since the 1960s* (London: Pandora).
Sargent, Lydia (ed.) (1986) *The Unhappy Marriage of Marxism and Feminism: A Debate of Class and Patriarchy* (London: Pluto).
Shildrick, Margrit (2004) 'Sex and Gender', in S. Gillis, G. Howie and R. Munford (eds) *Third Wave Feminism: A Critical Exploration* (Basingstoke and New York: Palgrave Macmillan).
Spelman, Elizabeth (1990) *Inessential Women: Problems of Exclusion in Feminist Thought* (London: Women's Press).
Stone, Alison (2004) 'Essentialism and Anti-Essentialism in Feminist Philosophy', *Journal of Moral Philosophy*, 1(2), 135–53.
Therborn, Göran (2007) 'After Dialectics: Radical Social Theory in a Post-communist World', *New Left Review*, 43.
Vogel, Lise (1983) *Marxism and the Oppression of Women: Towards a Unitary Theory* (New Brunswick, N.J.: Rutgers University Press).
Whelehan, Imelda (1995) *Modern Feminist Thought: From the Second Wave to Post-feminism* (Edinburgh: Edinburgh University Press).
Wood, Ellen (1988) 'Capitalism and Human Emancipation', *New Left Review*, 167.

Index